Sports Law in the European Union

Sports Law in the European Union

Andrea Cattaneo
Richard Parrish

This book was originally published as a monograph in the International Encyclopaedia of Laws/Sports Law.

Founding Editor: Roger Blanpain
General Editor: Frank Hendrickx
Volume Editor: Michele Colucci

Wolters Kluwer

Published by:
Kluwer Law International B.V.
PO Box 316
2400 AH Alphen aan den Rijn
The Netherlands
E-mail: international-sales@wolterskluwer.com
Website: lrus.wolterskluwer.com

Sold and distributed in North, Central and South America by:
Wolters Kluwer Legal & Regulatory U.S.
7201 McKinney Circle
Frederick, MD 21704
United States of America
Email: customer.service@wolterskluwer.com

Sold and distributed in all other countries by:
Air Business Subscriptions
Rockwood House
Haywards Heath
West Sussex
RH16 3DH
United Kingdom
Email: international-customerservice@wolterskluwer.com

ISBN 978-94-035-2613-3

e-Book: ISBN 978-94-035-2614-0
web-PDF: ISBN 978-94-035-2615-7

The Authors

Dr Andrea Cattaneo lectures in EU Law at Edge Hill University. A graduate of the University of Milan, Andrea holds a PhD in EU Competition Law and Sport. He is author of a number of works on sports law, and he has worked on EU-funded projects exploring the regulation of football agents and the development of the EU's sports diplomacy strategy. He is a member of Edge Hill University's Centre for Sports Law Research.

Professor Richard Parrish is Jean Monnet Chair of EU Sports Law and Policy at Edge Hill University. He was a member of the European Commission's Group of Independent European Sports Experts and a member of its High-Level Group on Sport Diplomacy. He has authored many of the most influential EU-funded sports studies, and he acted as Special Advisor to the House of Lords Inquiry into 'Grassroots Sport and the European Union'. He is Director of Edge Hill University's Centre for Sports Law Research.

The Authors

Table of Contents

The Authors 3

List of Abbreviations 9

Preface 13

Chapter 1. The European Model of Sport & the European Union 15

§1. INTRODUCTION 15

§2. THE EUROPEAN MODEL OF SPORT 16
I. The European Model: Organisational Structure 19
II. The European Model: Competitive Structure 20
III. The European Model: Governing Body Philosophy 21
IV. The International Sports Federations' Source of Power 21

§3. EU SPORTS LAW 23
I. Sport and the Law 23
II. *Lex Sportiva* and Sports Law 25
III. The European Union 27
IV. EU Fundamental Freedoms and Sport 29
V. Restrictions and Justifications 32
VI. The Jurisdiction of the Court over Sporting Bodies 33
VII. Purely Sporting Rule and Economic Activity 36
VIII. The Inherency Argument 38
IX. From Free Movement to Competition Law 40
X. Sporting Objectives and Public Interest 42

§4. EU SPORTS POLICY 44
I. The Road to Article 165 TFEU 44
II. Article 165(1): The 'Specific Nature of Sport', 'Voluntary' Activity and Sport's 'Social and Educational Function' 47
III. Article 165(2): … 'developing the European dimension in sport, by promoting fairness and openness in sporting competitions and cooperation between bodies responsible for sports, and by protecting the physical and moral integrity of sportsmen and sportswomen, especially the youngest sportsmen and sportswomen' 49

IV. Article 165(3): … 'Foster Cooperation with Third Countries and International Organisations' 51
V. Article 165(4): … 'incentive measures, excluding any harmonisation of the laws and regulations of the Member States' and the adoption of 'recommendations' 52
VI. EU Sports Policy: Clarifying the Legal Environment 54

§5. Conclusions 57

Chapter 2. Organising Sport 60

§1. Introduction 60

§2. Authorisation Rules: FIA, MOTOE & ISU 61
I. Fédération Internationale de l'Automobile (FIA) 65
II. Motosykletistiki Omospondia Ellados NPID (MOTOE) 66
III. International Speed Skating Union (ISU) 67
IV. An Assessment of the EU's Scrutiny of Authorisation Rules 70

§3. Multiple Club Ownership 74

§4. Third-Party Ownership 79

§5. Club Location, Cross-Border Leagues and Breakaways 87

§6. Player Release 92

§7. Doping 95
I. The *Meca-Medina* Litigation 99

§8. Conclusion 101

Chapter 3. Playing Sport 104

§1. Introduction 104

§2. Players' Transfer System 105
I. The Football Transfer System 108
II. Training Compensation and Solidarity Payment 111
III. Transfer Windows 114
IV. Contractual Stability 118
V. International Transfers Involving Minors 122
VI. The Reform of the Transfer System 126

§3. Regulating Sports Agents 127
I. FIFA Regulation and *Piau* 128
II. The 2015 FIFA RWWI 130

III. Reforming the RWWI 132

§4. NATIONALITY-BASED RULES 135
I. Nationality Discrimination in Team Sports 136
II. Discrimination Against Non-EU Nationals 141
III. Nationality Discrimination in Individual Sports 143
IV. Nationality Discrimination in Amateur Sport 145

§5. THE INVOLVEMENT OF STAKEHOLDERS 148
I. From Collective Agreements to Social Dialogue 150
II. Social Dialogue in Professional Football 153

§6. CONCLUSION 156

Chapter 4. Funding Sport 159

§1. INTRODUCTION 159

§2. FINANCING SPORT 160

§3. FINANCIAL REGULATIONS 162
I. Assessing FFP 169

§4. STATE AID 171
I. Public Interest and Sports Facilities 174
II. State Aid to Professional Football Clubs 177

§5. SPORTS BROADCASTING RIGHTS 180
I. The Market for Sports Broadcasting Rights 182
II. Consumers, Citizens and Territorial Exclusivity 185

§6. MEDIA RIGHTS 189
I. Online Distribution 191
II. Digital Single Market 194

§7. ADVERTISING AND TICKETING 197
I. Advertising 199
II. Athletes' Endorsement 201
III. Tickets Sales Arrangement 204

§8. CONCLUSION 206

Conclusions: The EU, the European Model and the Pandemic 208

§1. THE CORONAVIRUS PANDEMIC AND THE EUROPEAN MODEL OF SPORT 211

Selected Bibliography 217

Table of Cases 229

Table of Legislation 235

Index 243

List of Abbreviations

General

ADAMS	Anti-Doping Administration and Management System (WADA)
ADR	Alternative Dispute Resolution
CAS	Court of Arbitration for Sport
CFCB	Club Financial Control Body (UEFA)
CFG	City Football Group
CFI	Court of First Instance (now General Court)
DG CONNECT	Directorate General for Communications Networks, Content and Technology
DG EAC	Directorate General for Education, Youth, Sport and Culture
DHB	Deutscher Handballbund (German Handball Federation)
DOSB	Deutscher Olympischer Sportbund (German Olympic Committee)
DRC	Dispute Resolution Chamber (FIFA)
EEA	European Economic Area
EBU	European Broadcasting Union
EC	Treaty Establishing the European Community
ECA	European Club Association
ECB	England and Wales Cricket Board
ECHR	European Convention on Human Rights
EFAA	European Football Agents Association
EFL	European Football League
EFTA	European Free Trade Association
EL	European Leagues
ELPA	Elliniki Leskhi Aftokinitou kai Periigiseon (Automobile and Touring Club of Greece)
ENIC	English National Investment Company

List of Abbreviations

EU	European Union
EURO	European Football Championship
FAPL	Football Association Premier League (England)
FFP	Financial Fair Play (UEFA)
FIA	Fédération Internationale de l'Automobile
FIBA	Fédération Internationale de Basketball Association
FIFA	Fédération Internationale de Football Association
FIFPro	Fédération Internationale des Associations de Footballeurs Professionnels
FIG	Fédération Internationale de Gymnastique
FIH	Fédération Internationale de Hockey
FIM	Fédération Internationale de Motocyclisme
FINA	Fédération Internationale de Natation
FOA	Formula One Administration Ltd
F1	Formula One
HPPD	EU-China High-Level People-to-People Dialogue
IOC	International Olympic Committee
ISF	International Sports Federation
ISL	International Swimming League
ISU	International Skating Union
MOTOE	Motosykletistiki Omospondia Ellados NPID (Greek Motorcycling Federation)
NCA	National Competition Authority
NSF	Norges Skiforbund (Norwegian Ski Federation)
Ofcom	Office of Communications (UK)
OTT	Over-the-Top Platforms
PAR	Players' Agent Regulation (FIFA)
PFSC	Professional Football Strategy Council (UEFA)
RSTP	Regulations on the Status and Transfer of Players (FIFA)
RWWI	Regulations on Working with Intermediaries (FIFA)
SFT	Swiss Federal Tribunal
TEU	Treaty on the European Union
TFEU	Treaty on the Functioning of the European Union
TPI	Third-Party Investment
TPO	Third-Party Ownership
UCI	Union Cycliste International
UEFA	Union of the European Football Associations
WADA	World Anti-Doping Agency
WPBSA	World Professional Billiards and Snooker Association

List of Abbreviations

Journals

CLR	Competition Law Review
CML Rev.	Common Market Law Review
ECLR	European Competition Law Review
EJSS	European Journal of Sport Science
EIPR	European Intellectual Property Review
ELJ	European Law Journal
EL Rev.	European Law Review
ESLJ	Entertainment and Sports Law Journal
ESMQ	European Sports Management Quarterly
EStAL	European State Aid Law Quarterly
Eur. J. Ind.	European Journal of Industrial Relations
Eur. J. Commun.	European Journal of Communication
Eur. Labour Law J.	European Labour Law Journal
German L.J.	German Law Journal
Hitotsubashi J. Arts Sci.	Hitotsubashi Journal of Arts and Sciences
ICON	International Journal of Constitutional Law
IJBM	International Journal of Business and Management
IJCLLIR	The International Journal of Comparative Labour Law and Industrial Relations
Int. Rev. Sociol. Sport	International Review for the Sociology of Sport
ISLJ	International Sports Law Journal
JCER	Journal of Contemporary European Research
JCMS	Journal of Common Market Studies
JECLP	Journal of European Competition Law & Practice
JEL	Journal of Economic Literature
J. Eur. Public Policy	Journal of European Public Policy
J. Eur. Integr.	Journal of European Integration
JIPLP	Journal of Intellectual Property Law & Practice
JPP	Journal of Public Policy
J. Sports Econ.	Journal of Sports Economics
Leg. Stud.	Legal Studies
Media Cult. Soc.	Media, Culture and Society
MJECL	Maastricht Journal of European and Comparative Law
Rev. Jur. Eco. Sport	Revue Juridique Et Economique Du Sport

List of Abbreviations

Scott. J. Political Econ.	Scottish Journal of Political Economy
Sport Mgt Rev.	Sport Management Review
Sport Soc.	Sport in Society

Preface

This monograph was conceived of during a car journey from Rijeka to Zagreb. The ever so persuasive editor of this series, Michele Colucci, was sitting in the back. Croatia was a new Member State of the EU and the UK had recently voted to leave. As we discussed the impact of Brexit on sport, the EU and the UK, we could not have imagined that another monumental event was looming. This monograph was completed in the UK during the coronavirus lockdown. The unprecedented closure of global sport and our inability to access sport for recreational purposes reminded us of just how important sport is, not only as economic activity but also as a source of fun and physical and mental well-being. This monograph is not an account of the impact of the coronavirus pandemic on sport, although we do discuss it in our conclusion. With this monograph, we want to add to a rich body of literature that has explored the relationship between sport and the EU. Our contribution to this literature is a monograph that navigates the EU's legal and political influence on the so-called European model of sport. This model is as old as the hills, but it has been weathered by many events, none bigger than the pandemic, and it has been landscaped through its interactions with the EU. We say landscaped to confront the assertion that the European model of sport has been assaulted by the EU. Our claim is that the EU has respected the autonomy and specificity of sport but that its patience has been tested by the adoption of some ill-thought-out sporting rules and practices that not only have interfered with the fundamentals of EU law but have also been detrimental to sport itself. Some EU interventions have improved sports governance – hence the landscaping. However, even though the EU regulates economic activity and it acquired new powers in the area of sport in 2009 with the adoption of Article 165 TFEU, the EU is not, and should not be, a sports regulator. Sport should be free to determine its own future, but this freedom is not limitless.

Andrea Cattaneo and Richard Parrish
May 2020

Chapter 1. The European Model of Sport & the European Union

§1. Introduction

1. Sport and the European Union are 'uneasy bedfellows'.[1] Sport is organised, albeit not universally, according to the principles of the so-called European model of sport. In sports falling under the umbrella of the International Olympic Committee (IOC), the Olympic Charter governs the organisation, actions and functioning of the Olympic movement and the relations between the bodies responsible for sport.[2] Commonly, each sport is controlled globally by one governing body with devolved powers at continental and national levels. Athletes and clubs have historically been relegated to the base of this organisational pyramid and subject to the exercise of near-monopoly power by the sports governing bodies. This is an international system of private regulation with the regulatory legitimacy of the governing bodies, including the 'supreme authority' of the IOC,[3] flowing from the voluntary participation of members who agree to be bound by rules and resolve disputes within the sporting 'family' and not through litigation.[4] These features are sheltered by self-imposed 'rights and obligations of autonomy'.[5]

2. The EU is organised differently. At its inception in 1957, the EU sought to establish a common market as a means of securing political objectives including reconciling former warring neighbours. Since then, the EU has worked towards securing an 'internal market' with the progressive erosion of measures, whether imposed by States or private parties, that interfere with the free movement of goods, persons, services and capital between Member States.[6] Of particular relevance is the EU's desire to eliminate, as far as possible, discrimination based on nationality and its attempts to endow EU citizens with rights of free movement.[7] Supplementing these provisions are rules on competition that govern the conduct of public and private entities that may harm the functioning of the internal market.[8] Taken together, these rules amount to a curtailment of the autonomy of States and private entities in exchange for wider economic and societal benefits, but for these to be secured

1. Stefaan Van den Bogaert & An Vermeersch, *Sport and the EC Treaty: A Tale of Uneasy Bedfellows?*, 31 EL Rev. 821 (2006).
2. International Olympic Movement, *Olympic Charter*, in force as from 26 Jun. 2019, https://stillmed.olympic.org/media/Document%20Library/OlympicOrg/General/EN-Olympic-Charter.pdf#_ga=2.18076863.729330968.1585815690-1864777391.1585815690 (accessed 2 Apr. 2020).
3. Fundamental Principles of Olympism no. 3, International Olympic Movement, *Olympic Charter*, in force as from 26 Jun. 2019.
4. For example, FIFA considers the global football community to be a 'family'. *See* Alan Tomlinson, *FIFA (Fédération Internationale de Football Association): The Men, The Myths and The Money* 54 (Routledge 2014).
5. Fundamental Principles of Olympism no. 5, International Olympic Movement, *Olympic Charter*, in force as from 26 Jun. 2019.
6. *See* Art. 3 Treaty on European Union (TEU) and Art. 26 Treaty on the Functioning of the European Union (TFEU).
7. Arts 18 and 21 TFEU.
8. *See* specifically Arts 101, 102 and 107 TFEU.

requires resisting the partitioning of the market along national lines. This philosophy sits uncomfortably with that of sport.

3. In this monograph, we assess these two organisational philosophies. We explain how, despite the EU not having a competence in sport until 2009, these cultures collided. We examine whether the clash of cultures can be reconciled and whether EU action in sport is injurious to sports' health and whether it is having a detrimental impact on the European model of sport. We do so through the lens of three key features of sporting activity: *organising sport*, *playing sport* and *funding sport*. Our argument is that the modern commercialisation of sport, the rise of organised stakeholder interests and the increasingly assertive role of the EU, is straining the European model of sport.

4. We accept that the EU should respect the autonomy of the sports movement and that sport has a specific character worthy of protection, but we argue that EU recognition of the autonomy and specificity of sport should be conditioned on substantive and procedural grounds. In substantive terms, sporting rules must, in a proportionate manner, pursue legitimate sporting objectives for them to pass assessment under EU law. Procedurally, sporting rules must be devised in a way that respects good governance, particularly in relation to the involvement of stakeholders.

5. Due to the somewhat nebulous and contested concept of the European model of sport and its evidential need to evolve in light of the developments discussed above, we are not convinced that the EU should accept the preservation of the European model, conceived of in monolithic terms, as a legitimate sporting objective. We are more sympathetic to claims that certain rules and practices that seek to preserve certain features of the European model of sport are worthy of protection, subject to the conditions stated above.

6. In this chapter, we commence with an assessment of the key features of the European model before turning to the stress points between these features and the requirements of EU law. In this regard, we review the sports-related jurisprudence of the Court of Justice before examining whether the EU has pieced together a sufficiently coherent policy on sport that reconciles the demands of sport, with those of the EU. In Chapters 2–4 we then assess the impact of Court jurisprudence and the decisional practice of the Commission in the three areas of sporting activity highlighted above: *organising sport*, *playing sport* and *funding sport*.

§2. The European Model of Sport

7. As the birthplace of modern organised sport, many European academics, politicians and sports administrators make loving reference to the existence of *the* (not a) European model of sport. Indeed, in its 1998 paper 'The European Model of Sport', the European Commission confidently declared that '[T]here is a European model of sport with its own characteristics' and '[T]his model has been exported to almost all other continents and countries, with the exception of North America.'[9] By heralding the exportability of the model, the Commission unwittingly, and perhaps unwisely, contributed to what some commentators observed as a 'political consensus' in Europe that the model existed and was worthy of protection.[10] In particular, international federations, suspicious of the potential impact of EU law on the European model, made pleas to public bodies, including the EU, to take steps to protect the European model and resist the pressures of Americanisation.[11]

8. These calls intensified following the European Court's judgment in *Bosman* in 1995.[12] The claim was that the judgment undermined the twin pillars supporting the European model, namely sporting autonomy and the specificity of sport. Without the ability, free from judicial oversight, to adopt rules to preserve the European model, international sports federations could not protect the special character of European sport such as ensuring the regularity and proper functioning of competitions, promoting fairness, solidarity and integrity at all levels of sport, ensuring competitive balance between participants and encouraging the development of young players.

9. In policy documents subsequent to its 1998 paper, the Commission toned down its language, no doubt informed by the greater experience it had acquired in sports policy and as it became clear that the idea of a European model was contested. By 2007, while recognising that 'certain values and traditions of European sport should be promoted', the Commission had conceded that '[I]n view of the diversity and complexities of European sport structures … it is unrealistic to try to define a unified model of organisation of sport in Europe.'[13] Rather than defining a European model, the Commission outlined three key features of sport: the societal role, the economic dimension, and the organisation of sport. These features have been repeated in subsequent Commission papers, particularly the 2011 Communication on Sport.[14]

10. The diversity and complexity to which the Commission refers is reference to two prominent features of modern sport. First, regarding diversity, the varying organisational approaches adopted by both sports bodies and national public authorities have made identifying a single model futile. For example, sports bodies

9. European Commission, *The European Model of Sport*, Consultation Document of DGX 5 (1998).
10. Anastasios Kaburakis, *The US and EU Systems of Sport Governance: Commercialized v. Socio-Cultural Model – Competition and Labor Law*, 3–4 ISLJ 109 (2008).
11. For a discussion *see* Stephen Weatherill, *Resisting the Pressures of Americanization: The Influence of European Community Law on the European Sport Model*, in *Law and Sport in Contemporary Society* 157–181 (Steve Greenfield & Guy Osborn eds, Frank Cass 2000).
12. Case C-415/93 *Union Royale Belge Sociétés de Football Association and others v. Bosman and others* [1995] ECR I-4921.
13. European Commission, *Commission staff working document. Impact assessment accompanying the White Paper on Sport*, SEC(2007) 935 final (2007).
14. European Commission, *Communication from the Commission to the European Parliament, the Council, the European Economic and Social Committee and the Committee of the Regions – Developing the European Dimension in Sport*, 11 COM(2011) 12 final (2011).

adopt varying legal forms,[15] varying governance styles,[16] and not all agree to be guided by the principles enshrined in various international sporting agreements such as the IOC's Olympic Charter, the World Anti-Doping Agency's Code and the Court of Arbitration for Sport's Statutes.[17] Sports are also subject to differing levels of public authority oversight. While some European countries adopt an interventionist approach to regulating sporting activities, others adopt a more arms-length approach.[18] To illustrate, in France, the Loi du Sport places the Ministry of Sport at the heart of sports regulation, whereas, in the UK, the State only legislates in sport to correct specific failures, such as those concerning safety and public order at sports grounds.[19]

11. Second, the rise of new commercial stakeholders has added complexity to the model. Commercial entities have found the so-called model impenetrable and have complained that they have been foreclosed from the sports market, while stakeholders within the model, particularly athletes and clubs, have voiced concern regarding the rigidity and undemocratic nature of the structure. As Halgreen has acknowledged, the European model is 'strongly self-serving' for the incumbent international federations.[20]

12. Nevertheless, international sports federations persisted with their campaign for the European model to be recognised and protected. They claimed their longevity had established a legitimate expectation that their autonomy was assured. To illustrate, the Fédération Internationale de Gymnastique (FIG) was established in 1881 in Belgium, the International Skating Union (ISU) in 1892 in the Netherlands, the Union Cycliste International (UCI) in 1900 in Switzerland, the Fédération Internationale de Football Association (FIFA) in 1904 in Paris and the Fédération Internationale de Natation (FINA) in 1908 in the UK. Since being established, these and other international federations have acquired the requisite expertise to regulate their own affairs, albeit within the IOC structure.

13. These claims of longevity have some merit, yet the role of an international sports federation at the turn of the twentieth century is very different from what it is today. Initially, an international federation performed three key functions. First, it regulated its sport by way of establishing standardised rules and equipment and by classifying competitors by category. Second, it organised and administered sporting

15. Adam Lewis & Jonathan Taylor, *Sport: Law and Practice* A3 (Bloomsbury 2014).
16. *See*, for example, Arnout Geeraert, *Sports Governance Observer 2018. An Assessment of Good Governance in Five International Sports Federations* (Play the Game/Danish Institute for Sports Studies 2018).
17. *See* Lloyd Freeburn, *Regulating International Sport: Power, Authority and Legitimacy* Ch.1 (Brill Nijhoff 2018).
18. For models of regulation *see* André-Nöel Chaker, *Study of National Sports Legislations in Europe* (Council of Europe 1999). *See* also Ian Henry, *European Models of Sport: Governance, Organisational Change and Sports Policy in the EU*, 50(1) Hitotsubashi J. Arts Sci. 41 (2009).
19. For further discussion *see* Chapters 8–10 of Mark James, *Sports Law* (Palgrave 2017).
20. Lars Halgreen, *European Sports Law – A Comparative Analysis of the European and American Models of Sport* (Forlaget Thompson 2004).

events. Third, federations took steps to promote and develop the sport at all levels from the elite to the grassroots and to protect the health, safety and welfare of athletes.

14. The modern international sports federation is now faced with many more pressures and these are altering its character. Federations now combine a regulatory function with a commercial role which includes the commercial exploitation of the sport, such as the sale of media rights and sponsorship linked to their increasingly significant 'impresario' event organiser role.[21] International federations have also had to respond to new governance challenges such as how to accommodate the rise of new and organised stakeholders, how to embrace technological change, and how to manage threats associated with commercialisation such as the fight against doping, match-fixing, financial regulation, alternative dispute resolution (ADR) and other integrity and welfare threats such as growing public concern regarding child protection. As Freeburn points out, these new functions involve 'significant intrusions' into the civil liberties and economic activities of participants and this activity is carried out by private bodies and not, as one would expect to see, the State.[22] This has led a number of commentators to identify these developments as a source of the 'juridification' of sport.[23]

I. The European Model: Organisational Structure

15. The organisational structure of the European model is commonly referred to as resembling a pyramid. At the pinnacle are the European federations, which are themselves often affiliated to global federations. Below them lie the national associations which generally hold a monopoly position in the sense that sport is organised by one federation per sport per country. Near the base of the pyramid are clubs and athletes with the grassroots forming the pyramid's base. Many sports, but not all, sit within the IOC's structure which encompasses international federations, the national Olympic committees, the organising committees for the Olympic Games, national associations, clubs, athletes and all other members including coaches, referees, judges, and other officials. One might, therefore, identify Olympic and non-Olympic pyramids.

16. This hierarchical structure is defended on the grounds of organisational efficiency in so far as it allows the federation, acting in the capacity of a natural monopoly, to establish standardised rules of the game, a uniform approach to integrity issues, a workable international match calendar and a high level of protection

21. Stefan Szymanski, *The Comparative Economics of Sport* 83 (Palgrave Macmillan 2010).
22. *See* Lloyd Freeburn, *Regulating International Sport: Power, Authority and Legitimacy* 16 (Brill Nijhoff 2018). Also, a point made by the General Court regarding FIFA's legitimacy to regulate private parties (agents): Case T-193/02, *Laurent Piau v. Commission of the European Communities* [2005] ECR II-209, para. 76.
23. *See* for instance Ken Foster, *Developments in Sporting Law*, in *The Changing Politics of Sport* 108 (Lincoln Allison ed., Manchester Univ. Press 1993), and Simon Gardiner, *Sports Law* 73 (Routledge 2012).

for the health, safety and welfare of athletes. In order to preserve these advantages, international federations require members to commit to the structure and so alternative structures are strongly discouraged.

17. In the modern era, this organisational rigidity gives rise to some concerns. For example, it is contested that the structure sufficiently promotes good governance. The allegation is that the organisational structure is opaque, lacking democratic controls, and that it fails to involve key stakeholders in decision-making. This lack of stakeholder empowerment, particularly in an era of commercialisation where clubs, athletes and commercial undertakings wish to maximise revenues from sport, gives rise to incentives to litigate. The central allegation is that international federations use regulatory powers as a mask to advance commercial interests and in doing so place undue restraints on the economic activity of key stakeholders. As Szymanski observes, 'governing bodies have become internal monoliths, claiming to regulate every aspect of their particular sport'.[24]

II. The European Model: Competitive Structure

18. The so-called pyramid also refers to the competitive structure of much of European sport. For example, the structure of the national league model means that participants move up and down the pyramid facilitated by the merit-based promotion and relegation system. This contrasts with the closed league model, such as that which commonly operates in the USA, in which franchises are issued based on the financial strength of the participant. The 'open' European system provides a link between the elite level and the grassroots, and being linked to a national league structure, it strongly promotes national identity and national team competitions which drive important revenues for international federations and national associations. These revenues help these bodies fulfil their solidarity function and their primary duty which is to nurture their respective sports at all levels. The philosophy underpinning the competitive pyramid therefore concerns promoting competition and vertical solidarity.

19. The suggestion that the European model is 'open' is contested. Evidence from a number of national leagues, particularly in football, suggests that de facto closed leagues operate with rotation of national champions and qualification for European competitions being limited to a small pool of teams. These competitive imbalances are reinforced by the national league structure, the maintenance of which requires clubs to commit to the structure. This means that clubs cannot take advantage of relocation opportunities in order to potentially become more competitive and profitable. This is to be contrasted with the situation for players, who, since the European Court's judgment in *Bosman*, can move cross-frontier within the territory of the EU. The national league structure also restricts opportunities for cross-border leagues, another potential solution to the problem of competitive imbalances in European sport. Restrictions adopted and enforced by international federations

24. Stefan Szymanski, *The Comparative Economics of Sport* 83 (Palgrave Macmillan 2010).

designed to maintain this structure give rise to competition law concerns. In addition to rules restricting cross-border movement of clubs and the formation of cross-border leagues, other questionable practices include the setting of the international match calendar and rules for the release of players for international matches, without sufficient stakeholder consultation.

III. The European Model: Governing Body Philosophy

20. It is claimed that the European approach to sports governance reflects the sociocultural philosophy of international federations and national sports governing bodies. Whereas in the USA, sports administrators have a profit-maximising mentality, in Europe the focus is on open competition and a strong commitment to develop the sport at all levels, primarily through redistributive mechanisms. Volunteering underpins this approach. In order to protect this philosophy and guard against commercial freeriding, sports governing bodies adopt rules to restrict the participation of rival event organisers who might not share the underlying philosophy. This philosophy does not reject commercialisation, but it subsumes it within a wider sociocultural context. When disputes between sports stakeholders do arise, sports bodies seek to resolve disputes through arbitration rather than litigation, thus further reinforcing the sealed nature of the sports ecosystem.[25]

21. Critics point out a number of flaws in these arguments. First, the much-heralded solidarity function is not working. Vertical solidarity between the elite and grassroots has failed to address a crisis of funding, participation and volunteering at amateur level. Horizontal solidarity has fared equally badly with chronic competitive imbalances identifiable across European sports. Second, the system is held together through restrictive practices. For example, rival event organisers require the permission of the governing body to stage an event. However, such authorisation rules can be abused if governing bodies cite the solidarity philosophy as a reason to refuse permission in order that they themselves can retain regulatory and commercial control of their respective sport. This mentality also stifles innovation as commercial operators can bring in new ideas that develop wider public and commercial interest in the sport. Finally, the type of ADR employed by sports bodies is inherently restrictive as it is not voluntary. Participants have no choice but to accept arbitration. ADR is, in effect, a mask for continued self-regulation.

IV. The International Sports Federations' Source of Power

22. Weatherill's examination of EU sports law highlights three sources of an international sports federations' power.[26] First, sports bodies derive authority from contractual relations with participants. These relations are, largely, ring-fenced from external judicial oversight as sports bodies invariably require participants to submit

---

25. *See* David McArdle, *Dispute Resolution in Sport. Athletes, Law and Arbitration* (Routledge 2015).
26. Stephen Weatherill, *Principles and Practice in EU Sports Law* Ch. 2 (Oxford Univ. Press 2017).

disputes to arbitration and not take cases before courts. At the pinnacle of this system of ADR sits the Court of Arbitration for Sport (CAS). These contractual requirements are evidenced expressly in writing or through some other relationship equivalent to a contract such as being a member of a club which itself is subject to international federation authority, participation in events run or regulated by the federation or a willingness of a participant to subject themselves to control of the sports body, such as with doping control.[27] Participants are, of course, free to decline to enter into these contracts, but the choice is stark – refusal to do so, combined with the monopoly power of the federation, means that participants are unable to engage in their respective sport. This form of 'compelled consent' in international sports arbitration is, according to one leading sports law QC, 'deeply concerning' but almost 'certainly necessary'.[28] It does, however, raise questions of what participants, particularly athletes, gain in return for this and what safeguards are in place to protect them.[29]

23. A second source of power is legislative. As Chaker observed, some sports bodies derive authority from the express consent of public authorities, such as is the case under the 'interventionist' sports model operating in France.[30] In another context, some international federations impose legislative requirements on States which wish to stage international sporting events such as the Olympic Games or FIFA World Cup.[31] Finally, the IOC succeeded in persuading the EU to amend its Treaty and insert a reference to the 'specific nature of sport'.[32]

24. Weatherill's third source of authority is judicial. Whereas the first two strategies for defending the European model of sport are pre-emptive, this strategy is reactive and as such one considered a last resort by the sports movement. Nevertheless, regulatory authority is assured if the sports body can persuade a court that the specificity of sport should be taken into account by the judge.[33] This strategy has met with mixed results for sport, but the literature generally points to a positive balance sheet in which courts have been somewhat receptive to sport's claims of specificity and generally deferential to the exercise of private regulatory authority.[34]

27. Mark James, *Sports Law* 29–32 (Palgrave 2017).
28. Nick De Marco, *Compelled Consent – Pechstein & the Dichotomy and Future of Sports Arbitration*, Blackstone Chambers Sports Law Bulletin, https://www.blackstonechambers.com/news/analysis-compelled_consent_/ 4 Jul. 2016 (accessed 25 Mar. 2020).
29. For a discussion *see* Antoine Duval, *Not in My Name! Claudia Pechstein and the Post-Consensual Foundations of the Court of Arbitration for Sport* (Max Planck Institute for Comparative Public Law & International Research, Research Paper No. 2017-01), https://papers.ssrn.com/sol3/papers.cfm?abstract_id=2920555 27 Feb. 2017 (accessed 8 Apr. 020).
30. André-Nöel Chaker, *Study of National Sports Legislations in Europe* (Council of Europe 1999).
31. *See*, for example, the expanding literature on Olympic Law: Alexandre Mestre, *The Law of the Olympic Games* (T.M.C. Asser Press 2009); Mark James & Guy Osborn, *The Olympics, Transnational Law and Legal Transplants: The International Olympic Committee, Ambush Marketing and Ticket Touting*, 36(1) Leg. Stud. 93 (2015); Ryan Gauthier, *The International Olympic Committee, Law, and Accountability* (Routledge 2017).
32. Art. 165 TFEU.
33. Stephen Weatherill, *Principles and Practice in EU Sports Law* 9 (Oxford Univ. Press 2017).
34. *See*, for example, Michael Beloff et al., *Sports Law* (Hart 2012); Jack Anderson, *Modern Sports Law* (Hart 2010); Adam Lewis & Jonathan Taylor, *Sport: Law and Practice* (Bloomsbury 2014).

§3. EU Sports Law

25. This judicial deference is observable at EU level, although certain conducts within the European model have not been tolerated and these prohibitions have been to the benefit of sports governance. The series of policy measures and decisional practice of the EU institutions have highlighted the need to protect certain characteristics of the preferred sociocultural vision of sport that is prevalent in Europe, as opposed to the hyper-commercialised nature commonly accepted as characterising the North American sports system.

26. The overview of the sports-related jurisprudence of the Court must be read in conjunction with the EU's development of its policy on sport. However, in order to have a comprehensive understanding of such an impact, it is first necessary to highlight the general framework in which EU law operates, and the way competences can be exercised in relation to sport. In this regard, account must be given of the way EU law applies to sport. This has developed from a system in which sporting rules were removed from the reach of EU law on account of the absence of economic activity or the sporting motives behind such rules, to a system in which sporting rules must be assessed in relation to the Treaty prohibitions. This highlights the trajectory of travel for sport in which the centripetal forces of European integration have attracted sport to the core of the EU Treaty and simultaneously created demands that this force should be resisted.

I. Sport and the Law

27. A discussion of the application of EU law and policy to sport cannot prescind from a definition of 'sport'. We all know what sport means when we participate in a game of football or tennis. It may be less clear whether we can refer to sport when we ice-skate at Christmas or cycle to work. In practical terms, there is very little difference between the type of activity undertaken. However, a fundamental aspect to consider in this regard is related to the competitive nature of the activity, as well as its physical component. Applying one criterion instead of the other would lead us to consider that a football game in the park must comply with certain authority, and is subject to a set of regulations, while an international chess competition would be excluded from any regulation and only exist in a vacuum.

28. A precise definition of the term employed is therefore necessary to understand which type of activity may be subject to the jurisdiction of sports governing bodies, and in which relation EU institutions can exercise their scrutiny. At European Union level, a commonly accepted definition of sport is lacking.[35] Often, the literature focuses on a specific aspect of sport, stressing its ability to constitute a vehicle through which an extensive range of objectives can be pursued: from the

35. Janwillem Soek, *Sport in National Sports Acts and Constitutions: Definition, Ratio Legis and Objectives*, 3–4 ISLJ 28–36 (2006).

promotion of health and well-being, to societal inclusion, to commercial aspects.[36] The social significance of sport and its potential role in forging European identity and bringing people together has been emphasised in the Amsterdam Treaty,[37] and mentioned by the Court of Justice in *Bosman*.[38] However, while sport exists as a mere leisure activity, it also constitutes a commercial and profit pursuing enterprise,[39] and any aspect related to sport may also be seen from an economic perspective.[40] The interdependence between the sporting activity, with its social and cultural importance, and the economic activity it generates, must be taken into account.[41] It is therefore difficult to sever the economic aspects from the sporting ones, as any rule adopted to regulate a sporting matter may be capable of exerting an economic impact.[42]

29. One definition of 'sport' comes from the European Sports Charter of the Council of Europe, which refers to sport as any form '[o]f physical activity which, through casual or organised participation, aim at expressing or improving physical fitness and mental well-being, forming social relationships or obtaining results in competition at all levels'.[43]

30. The EU Court of Justice has to some extent followed the approach of the Council of Europe, when it was asked to decide whether Bridge could qualify as 'sport' for tax exemption purposes, in the context of the VAT Directive.[44] The referring national court considered the physical nature of sport its pre-eminent characteristic, consequently preventing activities such as bridge and chess from being

---

36. The multifaceted nature of sport has been recognised also by the EU Commission. *See* Philip Kienapfel & Andreas Stein, *The Application of Articles 81 and 82 EC in the Sport Sector*, 3 Competition Policy Newsletter 6–14 (2007).
37. Treaty of Amsterdam amending the Treaty on European Union, the Treaties establishing the European Communities and certain related acts – Declarations adopted by the Conference – Declaration on sport, OJ C 340, 10 Nov. 1997.
38. Case C-415/93 *Union Royale Belge Sociétés de Football Association and others v. Bosman and others* [1995] ECR I-4921, para. 106.
39. In this regard, some authors draw a comparison with other sectors that present this dual side as well, such as cultural services in general and theatre, art, music, health care and education. *See* Aaron C.T. Smith & Bob Stewart, *The Special Features of Sport: A Critical Revisit*, 13(1) Sport Mgt Rev. 1–13 (2010).
40. As was recognised by the Court of Justice in *Bosman*, at para. 76 and Case C-519/04 P *David Meca-Medina and Igor Majcen v. Commission of the European Communities* [2006] ECR I-6991, at para. 26.
41. Robert C.R., Siekmann, *Is Sport 'Special' in EU Law and Policy?*, in *The Future of Sports law in the European Union – Beyond the EU Reform Treaty and the White Paper* 37–49 (Roger Blanpain ed., Kluwer Law International 2008).
42. Case C-415/93 *Union Royale Belge Sociétés de Football Association and others v. Bosman and others* [1995] ECR I-4921, para. 76, and Stephen Weatherill, *EU Sports Law: The Effect of the Lisbon Treaty*, Oxford Legal Studies Research Paper No. 3/2011 (2011).
43. *See* the definition of Sport given by the Council of Europe in the European Sports Charter (2001) and also European Commission, *The Development and Prospects for Community Action in the Field of Sport*, Commission Staff Working Paper (1998).
44. Case C-90/16 *The English Bridge Union Limited v. Commissioners for Her Majesty's Revenue & Customs* [2017] ECLI:EU:C:2017:814.

included in the category.[45] The Court of Justice held that the ordinary meaning of the notion of 'sport' must be characterised by a 'not negligible physical element'.[46] Failing this physical component, neither the competitive nature of the activity nor its ability to promote physical and mental health is a sufficient characteristic to identify 'sport'.[47]

31. While this position consolidates an approach that falls in line with the decision at national level and the definition of the Council of Europe, it must be noted that the judgment rendered by the CJEU is limited to the interpretation of the provisions of a specific Directive[48] and cannot be used as a general approach.

II. *Lex Sportiva* and Sports Law

32. Regardless of what the most appropriate definition might be, when someone thinks about sport, there are certain aspects that distinguish it from other sectors, and which may immediately confer upon it a degree of exemption from the application of ordinary law. The epitome of this concept is represented by contact disciplines, such as boxing, in which the main objective of the athlete is to 'render one's opponent unconscious'.[49] Outside the sporting arena, this could amount to a criminal offence, but when it takes place in a boxing ring, there is limited intervention of criminal law.[50] Similarly, labour law does not apply to athletes in the same way as it is applied to workers in other industries.[51] Furthermore, the commercial exploitation of sports rights may highlight again another different application of the law to sports-related matters. These kinds of considerations have led to a debate revolving around the general application of law to sport. Some scholars advocate the existence of 'sports law' as a discrete area of law connected to the specificities of sport. Others claim that sport, as with any other sector in society, is subject to the orthodox application of the law – the 'sport and the law' approach.[52]

33. One of the most prominent characteristics of the sport system is its ability to set rules and standards that apply across borders and disciplines, through the operation of dispute resolution systems and decision-making bodies at both national and

45. *The Queen (on the application of) English Bridge Union Limited v. The English Sports Council v. The Scottish Sports Council, The Sports Council for Wales, The Sports Council for Northern Ireland, The United Kingdom Sports Council, The Secretary of State for Culture, Media and Sport* [2015] EWHC 2875, para. 41.
46. Case C-90/16 *The English Bridge Union Limited v. Commissioners for Her Majesty's Revenue & Customs* [2017] ECLI:EU:C:2017:814, para. 22.
47. *Ibid.*, paras 24–25.
48. Council Directive 77/388/EEC of 17 May 1977 on the harmonization of the laws of the Member States relating to turnover taxes – Common system of value added tax: uniform basis of assessment, OJ L 145.
49. Jack Anderson, *The Legality of Boxing. A Punch Drunk Love?* 1 (Routledge Cavendish 2007).
50. Jack Anderson, *Modern Sports Law: A Textbook* 99 (Hart 2010).
51. Katarina Pijetlovic, *EU Sports Law and Breakaway Leagues in Football* 36 (T.M.C. Asser Press 2015).
52. Edward Grayson, *Sport and the Law* (Butterworths 1998).

international levels.[53] The body of principles and rules created and enforced by national and international sports federations and tribunals has effectively created an autonomous legal order which has been defined as *lex sportiva*.[54] The latter is in effect a private contractual legal order between the regulators within the sector – the sports governing bodies – and those subject to their jurisdiction such as athletes, coaches and any member of a sporting association. Such legal order comprises the range of statutes and regulation of sports governing bodies, as applied and interpreted by the dispute resolution system and the decision-making bodies.[55]

34. In this relation, the CAS has a fundamental role, as the 'Supreme Court of World Sport'.[56] The CAS is an arbitration tribunal established by the IOC in 1983, which has jurisdiction over disputes related to contracts that include arbitration clauses, or where a referral has been agreed by the parties, and – in appeal – against decisions of governing bodies in matters regarding anti-doping violations and disciplinary procedures, where the statutes of such governing bodies so provide.[57]

35. The concept of *lex sportiva* also comprises the notions of domestic sports law and global sports law, respectively referring to the area of influence that sporting bodies can exercise through rules and conduct at national and international level. In particular, the notion of global sports law has been theorised as the most apt to refer to the private contractual order established between international sporting federations and those subject to their jurisdiction, a form of transnational law applicable in the area of sport.[58]

36. The sport system has therefore created an autonomous legal order in which sports governing bodies are empowered to set rules and impose them on anyone subject to their jurisdiction. Such power, rather than been delegated by any public authority, derives from a set of contractual relationships. As such, it is fundamentally based on the voluntary consent of the subjects, who in theory have accepted the authority of a self-regulating institution that has created its own private legal order, with private dispute settlement procedures. However, ordinary legal principles and statutory provisions, coming from international, European and national law, may apply in this area as well. As opposed to the immunity claim represented by the existence of global sports law, the sporting sector and its governing bodies

---

53. Ken Foster, *Lex sportiva and Lex Ludica: The Court of Arbitration for Sport's Jurisprudence*, in *The Court of Arbitration for Sport 1984–2004* (Ian Blackshaw et al. eds, T.M.C. Asser Press 2006).
54. Jack Anderson, *Modern Sports Law: A Textbook* 20–23 (Hart 2010). Anderson contends that the term '*lex sportiva*' was first used by the Secretary General of CAS Matthieu Reeb.
55. Richard Parrish, *Lex Sportiva and EU Sports Law*, 37 EL Rev. 716–733 (2012).
56. Swiss Federal Tribunal, Judgment of 27 May 2003, *Lazutina & Danilova v. Comité International Olympique (IOC) & Fédération Internationale de Ski (FIS)*, at pp. 267 et seq.
57. *See* Mathieu Reeb, *The Role and Functions of the Court of Arbitration for Sport*, in *The Court of Arbitration for Sport 1984–2004* (Ian Blackshaw et al. eds, T.M.C. Asser Press 2006).
58. Ken Foster, *Is There a Global Sports Law*, in *Lex Sportiva: What Is Sports Law*? (Robert Siekmann & Janwillem Soek eds, T.M.C. Asser Press 2012), and Antoine Duval, *Lex Sportiva: A Playground for Transnational Law*, 19 ELJ 822–842 (2013).

are also subject to principles of international law, such as the fundamental safeguards existing in most western States.[59] Furthermore, national law applies as well, either through specific sport codes or simply through ordinary legislation and case law produced by national courts and tribunals.[60] Finally, and most importantly for the analysis that will follow, European Union law and policies may apply to sport. This may refer to the sports-related activity of the EU institutions, and in particular the case law of the Court of Justice and the decisional practice of the European Commission, as well as to any measures that, although not referred to sport in specific terms, may have an impact on related aspects.[61]

III. The European Union

37. The EU is an organisation in which a number of sovereign States have come together to pursue common objectives, through a set of international Treaties. While the EU was formally created by the Maastricht Treaty,[62] it is the resulting development of the original European Community, in turn created through the Treaty of Rome.[63] In its infancy, the primary political objective of the Community was the establishment of peaceful relationships between its members, through the stabilisation of a territory left devastated by the two World Wars. The founders of the European Community understood that the best way to attain this objective was by enhancing the integration between national economies and by exercising a form of control over the commercialisation of scarce resources.[64] The creation of the Common Market was not a specific goal to itself, but it constituted a means to achieve the objectives of promoting peace, the values of the EU and the well-being of its people.[65] To effectively attain these ambitious goals, provisions capable of eliminating any unreasonable and unjustified distortion of the market within the territories of the Member States were needed. Economic integration was therefore pursued through the protection of free movement of workers, goods, services and capital. Starting from the Single European Act,[66] these aims were also perfected with the constitution of the internal market, an area where direct and indirect barriers to trade

---

59. Such as the principle *pacta sunt servanda*, the principle of fairness and proportionality, to name but a few. Mark James, *Sports Law* 19 (Palgrave 2017).
60. André-Nöel Chaker, *Study of National Sports Legislations in Europe* (Council of Europe 1999).
61. Stephen Weatherill, *Is There Such Thing as EU Sports Law*, in *Lex Sportiva: What Is Sports Law?* (Robert Siekmann & Janwillem Soek eds, T.M.C. Asser Press 2012).
62. European Union, Treaty on European Union (Consolidated Version), Treaty of Maastricht [1992], OJ C 325/5; the most current versions of the Treaty have been enacted in Lisbon in 2007. *See* Treaty of Lisbon amending the Treaty on European Union and the Treaty establishing the European Community [2007] OJ C306/01. After the Treaty of Lisbon, the primary source of legislation within the European Union is thus the Consolidated version of the Treaty of the European Union, OJ C 326, [hereinafter 'TEU'] and the Consolidated version of the Treaty on the Functioning of the European Union, OJ C 326 [hereinafter 'TFEU'].
63. Treaty Establishing the European Economic Community [1957] 298 U.N.T.S. 11.
64. Paul Craig. & Grainne De Búrca, *EU Law: Text, Cases, and Materials* (Oxford Univ. Press 6th ed. 2015).
65. The Community not only has economic objectives but also pursues social goals. *See* Case C-341/05 *Laval un Partneri* [2007] ECR I-11767, paras 104–105.
66. Single European Act, 1987 OJ L 169/1.

between Member States had to be removed, and with the adoption of a common import and export policy related to commercial transactions occurring with third countries.[67] Furthermore, to guarantee the effectiveness of the system, a competition policy was needed to ensure that private operators could not divide the market alongside national barriers, and the intervention of the State in the economy could be limited in order to prevent further distortion of the competition.[68]

38. The origin of the EU, as an organisation created by sovereign States through the signing of international Treaties, directly relates to the setting of its objectives and the powers that can be exercised by its institutions. Member States that created the European Community, and those that have accessed it afterwards, have pooled some sovereignty and agreed to pursue common objectives.[69] In the context of this 'new legal order of international law',[70] the competences that the EU can exercise are therefore strictly limited to those areas that Member States have agreed to pool.[71] The principle of conferral, now set out in Article 5(2) of the Treaty on the European Union (TEU), guarantees to Member States that some particularly sensitive areas, such as immigration from third countries, are to be kept under their respective competence. The corollary to this principle is that the Union can take action only when a specific objective has been identified, and it has been determined that such an objective falls under one of the areas of competence granted to the institutions.

39. The powers that can be exercised by the EU institutions are further constrained by the principles of subsidiarity and proportionality which respectively establish that the Union shall take action only insofar as the objectives cannot be sufficiently achieved by Member States and such action should not go beyond what is necessary to achieve the objectives set by the Treaties.[72] In this context, the areas left to the exclusive competence of the Member States have been progressively eroded[73] by virtue of further amendments to the Treaties and in light of the interpretative activity of the Court of Justice.[74] Therefore, the European Union can exercise its competence in various forms, depending on the degree of harmonisation chosen in relation to the legislation of Member States. In the area of exclusive competence, only the Union can legislate and implement binding acts, which will have

---

67. Case 15/81 *Gaston Schul Douane Expediteur BV v. Inspecteur der Invoerrechten en Accijnzen, Roosendaal* [1982] ECR I-1409, para. 33.
68. Julio Baquero Cruz, *Between Competition and Free Movement: The Economic Constitutional Law of the European Community* (Hart 2002).
69. Klaus D. Borchardt, *The ABC of European Union Law* 10 (Publication Office of European Union 2010); Simon J. Bulmer, *The Governance of the European Union: A New Institutionalist Approach*, 13 JPP 351–380 (1993).
70. Case 26/62 *NV Algemene Transport- en Expeditie Onderneming van Gend en Loos v. Nederlandse Administratie der Belastingen* [1963] ECR 1.
71. This is confirmed in Art. 4 TEU, whereby the competences not conferred on the Union remain with the Member States.
72. Art. 5 TEU.
73. Jeremy Richardson, *European Union: Power and Policy-Making* (Routledge 3rd ed. 2006).
74. Stephen Weatherill, *The Limits of Legislative Harmonisation Ten Years after Tobacco Advertising: How the Court's Case Law Has Become a 'Drafting Guide'*, 12 German L.J. 827 (2011).

effects in all the Member States. In these areas, which includes the setting of competition rules within the internal market, Member States have ceded any autonomous legislative competence, and they cannot adopt any legally binding act, either legislative or not, unless specifically empowered by the Union. In a second area, competences are shared between the Union and Member States. Member States can take action only when the Union has not already exercised its own competence, or in the event it has decided to cease from exercising it. Finally, in a third set of areas, the Union can only adopt measures to support, coordinate or supplement the action of Member States. This type of competence is of particular relevance as it can be exercised in the area of education, culture, vocational training, youth and sport.

40. Supporting competences are the weakest form of competence, and in these areas the Union cannot legislate or carry out any form of harmonisation, effectively preventing any EU legislative measure based on them. However, insofar as the measure adopted is based on areas of exclusive or shared competence, such as the setting of the rules on the functioning of the internal market,[75] the Union can still adopt binding measures that affect and directly applies to the sporting sector.

41. The inclusion of sport under the area of competences of the European Union was formalised for the first time with the Treaty of Lisbon in 2009, with the introduction of Articles 6 and 165 Treaty on the Functioning of the European Union (TFEU). A comprehensive discussion of Article 165 and its impact on EU sports law and policy can be found later in this chapter.

IV. EU Fundamental Freedoms and Sport

42. While the competence of the EU to legislate directly in the field of sport is limited, this does not prevent EU law from engaging with conduct adopted by sporting bodies that may affect rights protected by EU law. Indeed, the law of the European Union is engaged whenever a conduct or an arrangement affects rights protected by the Treaties and secondary legislation, provided that its effects are produced within the territory of the Union. In that event, the Commission and the Court of Justice will have jurisdiction to assess the compliance of sporting regulations and conduct with the letter of the law. The provisions of the internal market are therefore the most effective way for EU institutions to exercise their influence over the conduct of private regulators.[76]

43. A number of provisions may therefore apply to conduct that is relevant under EU law. Articles 30–36 TFEU regulate the freedom of movement of goods between

---

75. For example, public health falls under this type of competence. The Court of Justice has allowed some form of harmonisation in this sector, justified under the need to regulate the internal market. The Court held that considerations related to public health were taken into account in this perspective as from Art. 114 TFEU. *See* Case C-376/98 *Germany v. Parliament and Council* [2000] ECR I-8419.

76. Mislav Mataija, *Private Regulation and the Internal Market: Sports, Legal Services, and Standard Setting in EU Economic Law* 188 (Oxford Univ. Press 2016).

Member States. Article 45 TFEU regulates the freedom of movement of EU workers within and across Member States. Article 48 TFEU protects the freedom of establishment and Article 56 TFEU the freedom to provide and receive services. Alongside rights granted to economically active individuals and legal persons, Article 21 TFEU recognises that nationals of Member States also enjoy free movement rights as EU citizens, regardless of whether they are engaged in economic activities.

44. The general principle underpinning these rules is the prohibition of discrimination on the grounds of nationality, established in Article 18 TFEU. Direct discrimination is prohibited, unless justified by reference to justifications of public policy, public security and public health expressly provided for in the Treaties.[77] Any conduct that is non-discriminatory, but nevertheless amounts to a restriction of free movement, has to be justified with reference to legitimate objectives relating to overriding public interests.[78] This open-ended justification was originally developed in the context of free movement of goods.[79] The body imposing the restriction can raise a range of public interest arguments, and exercise a significant level of discretion in setting the objectives to be pursued.[80] The Court, however, maintains some level of scrutiny over the legitimacy of such objectives and the proportionality of the restriction imposed in their pursuit.

45. Besides the four freedoms, the other relevant provisions are those that regulate competition on the market; namely, Articles 101 and 102 TFEU, respectively providing a discipline for restrictive agreements and abuse of dominant position, and Article 107 TFEU, regulating the granting of State aid. In detail, Article 101(1) TFEU prohibits any agreement between undertakings or other forms of arrangements made by an association of undertakings which have the object or the effect of preventing, restricting or distorting competition within the EU market. Agreements presenting prima facie restrictive characteristics may still be excused from the prohibition, when they pursue an aim that is recognised to improve competition within

77. These are some of the derogations expressly provided for in the Treaties. *See* Arts 45(3), 52 and 62 TFEU.
78. Indirectly discriminatory measures fall under the scope of application of EU law as well. Case C-55/94 *Gebhard v. Consiglio dell'Ordine degli Avvocati e Procuratori di Milano* [1995] ECR I-4165.
79. *Ibid.*, para. 37.
80. Niamh Shuibhne, *Exceptions to the Free Movement Rules*, in *European Union Law* 483 (Catherine Barnard & Steve Peers eds, Oxford Univ. Press 2017).

the market, or if they are necessary for the pursuit of public policy interests.[81] Alternatively, it must be demonstrated that the arrangement fulfils the conditions provided in Article 101(3) TFEU. The authority examining the conduct will therefore have to weigh up the restrictive effects produced with the pro-competitive effects that the arrangement creates.[82]

46. Article 102 TFEU prohibits an undertaking which holds a dominant position on a specific market from abusing its power. An undertaking will be subject to this provision when, due to its position of strength on the market,[83] it is able to prevent effective competition from rival undertakings and act to an appreciable extent independently of its competitors and consumers, thereby using its power to obtain advantages that would not be available in conditions of effective competition. [84] Under EU law, an undertaking in such a position has a responsibility to avoid behaviours which can influence the structure of the market where the level of competition is weakened, and that may hinder the competition still existing.[85]

47. Similar to Article 101 TFEU, conducts capable of infringing Article 102 TFEU might be objectively justified if represents a proportionate means[86] of pursuing legitimate commercial behaviours,[87] they seek efficiency objectives or they pursue public interests considerations.

48. Finally, Article 107 regulates the granting of economic subsidies by the State, or any public authority, in an attempt to establish a balance between some legitimate forms of public intervention on the market and the protection required to ensure that conditions of fair competition are respected.[88]

---

81. Art. 10 of Regulation 1/2003, granting the Commission the power to issue Decisions declaring Art. 101 not applicable to arrangements of this nature. *See* Council Regulation (EC) No 1/2003 of 16 Dec. 2002 on the implementation of the rules on competition laid down in Arts 81 and 82 of the Treaty OJ L 1.
82. The Commission is however specifically empowered to create block exemptions for agreements that fulfil the criteria of Art. 101(3) TFEU. *See* Regulation (EEC) No 2821/71 of the Council of 20 Dec. 1971 on application of Art. 85 (3) of the Treaty to categories of agreements, decisions and concerted practices, OJ L 285.
83. Case 85/76 *Hoffmann-La Roche & Co. AG v. Commission* [1979] ECR 00461, para. 41. Sport Associations usually have practical monopolies over their sport and therefore are likely to have a position of dominance over the organisation of sporting events in a specific territory. *See* Arnout Geeraert, *Limits to the Autonomy of Sport: EU Law*, in *Action for Good Governance in International Sports Organisations* 151–184 (Jens Alm ed. Play the Game/Danish Institute for Sports Studies 2013).
84. Case 27/76 *United Brands v. Commission* [1978] ECR 207, para. 65.
85. Case 322/81 *Nederlandshce Banden – Industrie Michelin* NV *v. Commission* [1983] ECR 3461, para. 57. However, it should be clear that even dominant undertakings have the right to take part fully in the competitive process. Tjarda Van der Vijver, *Article 102 TFEU: How to Claim the Application of Objective Justifications in the Case of Prima Facie Dominance Abuses?*, 129 JECLP (2012).
86. Case C-95/04 P *British Airways v. Commission* [2007] ECR I-2331, para. 86. Moreover, the restriction should not eliminate competition, as from Case C-209/10 *Post Danmark v. Konkurrencerådet* [2012] 4 CMLR 23, para. 42.
87. *See* Case C-209/10 *Post Danmark v. Konkurrencerådet* [2012] 4 CMLR 23, paras 21 and 22.
88. Jens-Daniel Braun, *Article 87 EC*, in *European Media Law* 207–244 (Oliver Castendyk et al. eds, Kluwer Law International 2008).

V. Restrictions and Justifications

49. Any restriction on the EU fundamental freedoms – and to the competition on the market – is unlawful unless justified. As a corollary, free movement and competition are not absolute values, but can be restricted, provided that restrictions are justified and proportionate.[89]

50. Under the rules protecting freedom of movement of workers and services, a restriction may be justified if it aims at protecting public order, public security or public health and it is proportionate to these objectives.[90] Public interests may be pursued as well, insofar as the restriction is proportionate and applied in a non-discriminatory way. Although relevant differences exist between free movement and competition law, the approach to restrictions in the two areas is not completely dissimilar. Indeed, restrictions that are inherent in the pursuit of legitimate objectives fall out of the scope of application of Article 101, and objective justifications can be used to exempt the conduct of dominant undertakings under Article 102. Finally, legitimate objectives can be pursued by Member States when they finance private undertakings through State aid measures.

51. A common theme is therefore that, in the absence of an express justification provided by the Treaties, the body imposing restrictive rules must demonstrate that the objective pursued through its conduct is legitimate and that the restriction does not fall under the prohibitions set by EU law. As this consideration is relevant for both competition law and freedom of movement provisions, academics have postulated that this creates a convergence between the two areas.[91] In particular, this convergence has been identified in the application of a rule of reason test, whereby conduct examined under competition law is assessed on the basis of the legitimate objective it pursues and the necessity and proportionality of the restriction caused,[92] following an approach strikingly similar to the test applied under free movement provisions.

52. A convergence of the two areas is coherent with the idea that free movement and competition law provisions are complementary in protecting the functioning of the internal market.[93] However, the argument for a complete convergence has been weakened by the position held by the CJEU, which in *Meca-Medina* expressly

---

89. Toni Marzal, *From Hercules to Pareto: Of Bathos, Proportionality, and EU Law*, 15(3) ICON 621–64 (2017).
90. Directive 2004/38/EC, Arts 27–33. *See* Directive 2004/38/EC of the European Parliament and of the Council of 29 Apr. 2004 on the right of citizens of the Union and their family members to move and reside freely within the territory of the Member States amending Regulation (EEC) No 1612/68 and repealing Directives 64/221/EEC, 68/360/EEC, 72/194/EEC, 73/148/EEC, 75/34/EEC, 75/35/EEC, 90/364/EEC, 90/365/EEC and 93/96/EEC, OJ L 158.
91. Kamiel Mortelmans, *Towards Convergence in the Application of the Rules on Free Movement and on Competition*, 38 CML Rev. 613–649 (2001).
92. Case C-1/12 *Ordem dos Técnicos Oficiais de Contas (OTOC) v. Autoridade da Concorrência* [2013] EU:C:2013:127, paras 94–96.
93. The role of competition law in this regard was recognised by the CJEU in *Eco Swiss*. *See* Case C-126/97, *Eco Swiss China Time Ltd v. Benetton International NV* [1999] ECR I-03055, para. 36.

affirmed the need to assess the restriction under separate and different requirements, stating that a conduct may escape the application of one set of rules, but still constitute a restriction under the other.[94]

53. The legitimacy of the objective pursued is therefore a fundamental aspect of the assessment of any conduct, and governing bodies have progressively understood its importance in the context of drafting their rules and regulations. In this regard, claims related to the need to protect the fundamentally unique characteristics of sport as an activity and a sector have been used as arguments to justify conduct and arrangements which in other areas could be construed as restrictions of freedoms protected under EU law. Sports governing bodies have attempted to claim a complete immunity from the application of the law which, under the pressure of case law and decisional practice from the EU institutions, had to morph into a form of autonomy, conditional on respecting the principles of good governance.[95]

54. The following section will provide an account of this development, whereby from the claim of complete immunity from EU law, governing bodies have moved to engage with the EU in order to retain as much of their regulatory autonomy as possible.[96]

VI. The Jurisdiction of the Court over Sporting Bodies

55. As mentioned above, EU law is engaged when a conduct produces effects within the territory of the EU, even when the conduct is put in place in the sporting sector. This principle was established in response to an argument put forward by the UCI in *Walrave.*[97] The UCI submitted that the private nature of sporting entities and sports governing bodies prevented the application of EU law to their conduct.[98] In a system based on a set of private relationships, in which governing bodies exercise regulatory powers over the participants, under the voluntary consent of those wishing to enter into the system, the UCI was arguing that the Court of Justice lacked jurisdiction to decide on the case.

56. In the context of the present discussion, this consideration is relevant as the provisions protecting the four freedoms under EU law – free movement of goods, free movement of labour, free movement of services and freedom of establishment – predominantly apply to Member States, or authorities acting on their behalf. This

94. Case C-519/04 P *David Meca-Medina and Igor Majcen v. Commission of the European Communities* [2006] ECR I-6991, para. 31.
95. Stephen Weatherill, *Principles and Practice in EU Sports Law* 157–175 (Oxford Univ. Press 2017).
96. Borja García & Stephen Weatherill, *Engaging with the EU in Order to Minimise Its Impact: Sport and the Negotiation of the Treaty of Lisbon*, 19(2) J. Eur. Public Policy 241 (2012).
97. Case 36/74 *Walrave & Koch v. Association Union cycliste internationale* [1974] ECR 1405.
98. *Ibid.*, para. 15.

is normally referred to as the vertical direct effect of EU law, that allows individuals – or private parties in general – to bring a case against a Member State for failure to comply with EU law.[99] In this regard, the issue raised in *Walrave* and subsequently in *Bosman*[100] was whether the relevant Treaty articles could carry horizontal direct effect as well: this would have made them capable of being invoked by a private party such as an athlete, against another private party such as an international federation.

57. In *Walrave*, the Court held that the rules on free movement were applicable to the conduct of any entity, regardless of its status, aiming at collectively regulating gainful employment and services.[101] This definition comprises governing bodies which, acting as private regulators of the sporting sector, are able to control the activities of individual employees, workers or service providers.[102] A claim of immunity based on the status of the governing body, which ultimately failed in *Walrave* and *Bosman*, would not have been successful in assessments under competition law either. Indeed, the rules of competition law apply to individual undertakings; any natural and legal person involved in an economic activity, defined by the offering of goods and services on the market, is subject to those rules.[103]

58. A further claim of jurisdictional limit was also raised in relation to the territorial scope of the power that can be exercised by EU institutions, and in particular the Court of Justice.[104] In this regard, it must be remembered that the vast majority of international federations have their seats in Switzerland, and therefore outside the territory of the EU. The question was therefore whether Treaty articles could affect and invalidate statutes and regulations of international associations sitting outside the jurisdictional reach of EU law. In response, the Court held in *Walrave* that the ambit of application of EU law extends to any legal relationship that can be located within the territory of the Union, by reason of the place where it is entered into, or where it takes effect.[105] This principle, defined as the extraterritorial jurisdiction of the EU and its institutions, is not new or sports-specific, and other

99. Paul Craig & Grainne De Búrca, *EU Law: Text, Cases, and Materials* 192 (Oxford Univ. Press 6th ed. 2015).
100. Case C-415/93 *Union Royale Belge Sociétés de Football Association and others v. Bosman and others* [1995] ECR I-4921, para. 84.
101. Case 36/74 *Walrave & Koch v. Association Union cycliste internationale* [1974] ECR 1405, para. 17.
102. Richard Parrish, *Case C-36/74 Walrave and Koch [1974] ECR 1405*, in *Leading Cases in Sports Law* 45–64 (Jack Anderson ed., T.M.C. Asser Press 2013). Parrish noted that the CJEU jurisprudence has evolved in areas not concerning sport, expanding the horizontal effect of Treaty articles to comprise also the activity of individual employers and private persons. *See* Case 43/75 *Gabrielle Defrenne v. Société anonyme belge de navigation aérienne Sabena* [1976] ECR 455, para. 39, and Case C-281/98 *Roman Angonese v. Cassa di Risparmio di Bolzano SpA*. [2000] ECR I-4139, para. 36.
103. *See* Case C-41/90 *Klaus Höfner and Fritz Elser v. Macrotron GmbH* [1991] ECR I-1979, para. 21.
104. Richard Parrish, *Case C-36/74 Walrave and Koch [1974] ECR 1405*, in *Leading Cases in Sports Law* 55 (Jack Anderson ed., T.M.C. Asser Press 2013).
105. Case 36/74 *Walrave & Koch v. Association Union cycliste internationale* [1974] ECR 1405, para. 28.

examples of its application can be seen in the numerous decisions of the European Commission in cases against media and technology companies based in the United States.[106]

59. The extent of the jurisdiction that EU institutions can exercise is instrumental to the role of the EU as a global regulator. By imposing compliance with its standards and rules to those who are active in its territory, the EU is capable of affecting the conduct of international organisations on a global scale. While traditionally located outside the territory of the EU, when sports governing bodies exercise their power through rules and decisions that impact the EU internal market, they fall under the scope of the regulatory demand of the EU institutions.[107] This is in fact a common occurrence, as the EU internal market tends to correspond to a significant part of the territory regulated by the sports governing bodies. This is what effectively occurred with the FIFA transfer system in the post-*Bosman* era, challenged at EU level, but leading to a global reform, and what may be a future occurrence with legislation such as the EU General Data Protection Regulation.[108]

60. In this regard, even a hard form of Brexit will not automatically shield the UK sports system from the application of EU law. The ability of EU law to capture any conduct that affects its internal market allows it to exercise scrutiny over the activity of regulatory bodies that are seated outside its territory, from Switzerland to the United Kingdom.

61. The argument related to the jurisdictional limits of EU law, however, may still be capable of having significant effects in relation to the recognition and enforcement of judgments of the Court of Justice outside the EU jurisdiction. Indeed, as Switzerland is not a Member State of the EU, the Lugano II Convention[109] on the jurisdiction and the recognition and enforcement of judgments in civil and commercial matters apply. According to Article 33 of the Convention, the recognition and enforcement of judgments in another signatory state is possible only after an application has been submitted by an interested party. Therefore, while the Court of Justice could apply EU law to international sports organisations seated in Switzerland, it can only do so if the complaint has come from an interested party. As seen below, this is the main reason for the rejection of a complaint filed by a football players' agent against the Union of the European Football Associations (UEFA) Financial Fair Play (FFP) Rules. The case, having been referred by a

106. *See*, for example, Case COMP/37792 Microsoft, and the judgment of the General Court upholding the decision of the Commission Case T-201/04 *Microsoft Corp. v. Commission of the European Communities* [2007] ECR II-03601.

107. Arnout Geeraert & Edith Drieskens, *Normative Market Europe: the EU as a Force for Good in International Sports Governance?*, 39(1) J. Eur. Integr. 79–94, 87 (2017).

108. Regulation (EU) 2016/679 of the European Parliament and of the Council of 27 Apr. 2016 on the protection of natural persons with regard to the processing of personal data and on the free movement of such data, and repealing Directive 95/46/EC (General Data Protection Regulation), OJ L 119.

109. Convention on the jurisdiction and the recognition and enforcement of judgments in civil and commercial matters L339, 21 Dec. 2007 (Lugano II Convention).

national court to the Court of Justice, was rejected as the individual filing the complaint could not demonstrate a direct interest in the issue.[110]

VII. Purely Sporting Rule and Economic Activity

62. Having established the scope of the jurisdiction of EU institutions, we can now move to examine the first series of cases where the application of EU law to sport was discussed. In common with the discussion above, in these cases governing bodies argued for a total inapplicability of EU law to sport, in light of the differences existing between a sporting activity and an economic activity, and the lack of competence of the EU to act in the field of sport.

63. In *Walrave*,[111] two Dutch professional pacemakers argued that the rule of the UCI requiring pacemakers to be of the same nationality of the cyclist in medium distance races was restricting the freedom of movement of workers and services.[112] In the absence of an express competence on sport, the Court of Justice was tasked with establishing whether EU law could apply to the case and whether the provisions of the Treaty protecting fundamental freedoms, traditionally applicable only against public bodies, could also be used to challenge the conduct of private bodies.

64. On the first issue, the Court held that sport was subject to EU law insofar as it constituted an economic activity[113] within the meaning of what is now Article 3 TEU.[114] In particular, when such activity had the character of gainful employment or remunerated service, the law had to be applied to it in an orthodox manner. The principle established by the Court, however, left considerable discretion to the sporting world: the approach developed in *Walrave* did not disregard the possibility that the rule could have an economic impact, but focussed instead on whether the rule had as its motive an economic objective.[115] Therefore, rules devised as 'purely sporting' could be exempt from the application of EU law.[116]

65. This approach was later confirmed in *Donà v. Mantero*,[117] where the Court had to assess the legality under EU law of rules adopted by a sporting organisation

110. The Court of Justice has rejected this complaint as inadmissible. *See* Court of Justice of the European Union, Order of the Court – 16 Jul. 2015, Case C-299/15 *Daniele Striani and Others v. Union européenne des Sociétés de Football Association (UEFA) and Union Royale Belge des Sociétés de Football – Association (URBSFA)* [2015] EU:C:2015:519.
111. Case 36/74 *Walrave & Koch v. Association Union cycliste internationale* [1974] ECR 1405.
112. Richard Parrish, *Case C-36/74 Walrave and Koch [1974] ECR 1405*, in *Leading Cases in Sports Law* 47 (Jack Anderson ed., T.M.C. Asser Press 2013).
113. Case 36/74 *Walrave & Koch v. Association Union cycliste internationale* [1974] ECR 1405, para. 4.
114. At the time of the judgment, Art. 2 of the EEC Treaty.
115. Richard Parrish & Samuli Miettinen, *The Sporting Exception in European Union Law* (T.M.C. Asser Press 2009).
116. Case 36/74 *Walrave & Koch v. Association Union cycliste internationale* [1974] ECR 1405, para. 8.
117. Case 13/76 *Donà v. Mantero* [1976] ECR 1333.

limiting the right of professional or semi-professional football players to take part in matches solely on nationality grounds.[118] In the case, the combination of rules of the Italian Football Federation establishing that only football players affiliated to the Italian federation could take part in matches, and allowing affiliation only to players having the Italian nationality, was held to be incompatible with EU law. Rules regulating the conduct of professional and semi-professional sports players were to be considered economic in nature and could not be deemed to be of sporting interest only.[119] However, such rules could still be exempt if justified by reasons that were not economic in nature.[120]

66. It took twenty years for these issues to be raised again. In *Bosman*, in one of the most famous judgments delivered by the Court of Justice, the legality of the FIFA players' registration system was called into question.[121] The system allowed football clubs to retain the registration of their players even after the expiry of their contract. Unless a transfer fee was paid by a new club willing to engage the player, the player himself would have been out of contract with the original club, but still prevented from offering his services to any other club. Furthermore, the 3+2 rule allowed national associations to limit the number of foreign nationals that could be fielded by clubs to three players, with further two players who played in the territory of the relevant national association for an interrupted period of 5 years.

67. In defence of the transfer rules, it was claimed that only major sports leagues could be regarded as undertakings, as the economic activity of sports clubs had to be considered negligible; as such, the regulation was not economic in nature and was therefore falling outside the scope of EU law. The Court dismissed this reasoning[122] and held that the players' registration system constituted a restriction of the freedom of movement of workers.[123] In particular, while the Court recognised the legitimate objectives pursued through the transfer system, namely protecting the competitive balance between clubs and ensuring the development of young players, it held that the restriction caused was disproportionate to them.[124]

118. *Ibid.*, para. 19, and Jack Anderson, *Leading Cases in Sports Law* 51 (T.M.C. Asser Press 2013).
119. Case 13/76 *Donà v. Mantero* [1976] ECR 1333, para. 12.
120. *Ibid.*, para. 18 and Arnout Geeraert, *The Role of the EU in Better Governance in International Sports Organisations*, in *Action for Good Governance in International Sports Organisations* 25–37 (Jens Alm ed., Play the Game/Danish Institute for Sports Studies 2013).
121. Case C-415/93 *Union Royale Belge Sociétés de Football Association and others v. Bosman and others* [1995] ECR I-4921.
122. *Ibid.*, paras 70–72.
123. One of the questions asked to the Court was related to the compatibility of such a rule with EU competition law. However, having held that the rule was infringing freedom of movement provisions, the Court stated that it was not necessary to assess its compliance with competition law as well. *See ibid.*, para. 138.
124. Case C-415/93 *Union Royale Belge Sociétés de Football Association and others v. Bosman and others* [1995] ECR I-4921, para. 107. *See* also Stephen Weatherill, *Resisting the Pressures of Americanization: The Influence of European Community Law on the European Sport Model*, in *Law and Sport in Contemporary Society* 157–181 (Steve Greenfield & Guy Osborn eds, Frank Cass 2000).

68. The judgment will be discussed to a greater extent elsewhere in this monograph. However, in the context of this chapter, it must be stressed how *Bosman* represented a significant change from the approach seen in *Walrave* and *Donà*. Recognising the difficulty of severing the economic aspects from merely sporting ones,[125] and acknowledging that the vast majority of sporting rules do exert economic effects, the CJEU abandoned the deference to the 'sporting nature' of rules adopted by governing bodies. Therefore, the economic activity that sport generates undoubtedly falls under the scope of application of EU law.[126]

69. Furthermore, the Court affirmed the idea that governing bodies are entitled to identify objectives to pursue in their regulatory practice, and in which regard restrictions may be needed. Effectively, this constitutes the recognition of a margin of discretion that can be exercised by private entities which, in carrying out their regulatory autonomy, can invoke justifications of public interests.[127] However, such discretion is limited, in that governing bodies are forced to consider the proportionality of the measure they adopt and therefore to balance the effects of their conduct with the interests of other stakeholders.[128]

VIII. The Inherency Argument

70. Having abandoned the 'purely sporting rule' exception for an approach that weighs up the objectives pursued and the restrictions caused, the Court of Justice further developed its approach in *Deliège*.[129] In the case, a Belgian judoka challenged the selection criteria applied by the national governing body, which prevented her from competing at international championships. Deliège argued that the selection policy of the international federation restricted her rights to provide services. In response, the Ligue Francophone de Judo stated that the amateur status of the athlete prevented her from successfully arguing that the conduct of the association was restricting her economic rights.[130]

71. The Court sided with the athlete, holding that the mere fact that a governing body identifies its members as amateurs does not deprive the activity of the athlete from its economic character.[131] Even when the athlete is not remunerated by the event organiser, as in the circumstances of the case, the services offered are normally remunerated and they are likely to generate economic activity, through the

125. *Ibid.*, para. 76.
126. Stephen Weatherill, *EU Sports Law: The Effect of the Lisbon Treaty*, Oxford Legal Studies Research Paper No. 3/2011 (2011).
127. Mislav Mataija, *Private Regulation and the Internal Market: Sports, Legal Services, and Standard Setting in EU Economic Law* 179 (Oxford Univ. Press 2016).
128. Antoine Duval, & Ben Van Rompuy (eds), *The Legacy of Bosman, Revisiting the Relationship Between EU Law and Sport* 8 (T.M.C. Asser Press 2016).
129. Joined Cases C-51/96 and C-191/97 *Deliège v. Ligue francophone de Judo et disciplines Associeés Asb* [2000] ECR I-2549.
130. *Ibid.*, para. 45.
131. *Ibid.*, para. 46.

selling of tickets, merchandising and property rights. Athletes themselves could extract high levels of income from their participation, by entering into endorsements and other commercial agreements. Therefore, participating in competitions at international level had to be regarded as a form of provision of services, regardless of the economic value attached to the performance of the individual athletes, their professional or non-professional status and even their direct remuneration.[132]

72. However, notwithstanding the ability of such rules to restrict the number of participants in the competition, the Court held that selection rules for competing at international championships had to be considered inherent and necessary to the organisation of sport.[133] Restrictions of these rights were consented if proportionate to legitimate objectives, even when they were capable of producing a detrimental effect on athletes.[134] Deferring to the expertise of governing bodies, the Court considered that certain selection rules are necessarily involved in the organisation of international high-level sporting events and as such they do not constitute a restriction under EU law.[135]

73. In *Deliège*, the Court broke new ground by considering the inherency of the restriction to the organisation of the sporting event, adopting an approach that was later translated into competition law cases as well.[136] In doing so, the conduct was considered not to be a restriction of free movement. Furthermore, the Court avoided employing any strict proportionality test, preferring to rely on the assessment made by the governing body.

74. The Court departed from the inherent rules approach in *Lehtonen*.[137] In this case, the Court held that the setting of a transfer deadline for players, albeit restricting the freedom of movement of workers and their chances of employment, could meet the objective of ensuring the regularity of competition.[138] The Court therefore applied an orthodox approach, assessing the existence of a restriction, the justification for it, and its proportionality.

---

132. Richard Parrish & Samuli Miettinen, *The Sporting Exception in European Union Law* (T.M.C. Asser Press 2009).
133. Joined Cases C-51/96 and C-191/97 *Deliège v. Ligue francophone de Judo et disciplines Associeés Asb* [2000] ECR I-2549, para. 64.
134. Stephen Weatherill, *EU Sports Law: The Effect of the Lisbon Treaty*, Oxford Legal Studies Research Paper No. 3/2011 (2011).
135. Joined Cases C-51/96 and C-191/97 *Deliège v. Ligue francophone de Judo et disciplines Associeés Asb* [2000] ECR I-2549, para. 68.
136. Case C-309/99 *J.C.J. Wouters, J.W. Savelbergh, Price Waterhouse Belastingadviseurs BV v. Algemene Raad van de Nederlandse Orde van Advocaten* [2002] ECR I-1577 and Case C-519/04 P *David Meca-Medina and Igor Majcen v. Commission of the European Communities* [2006] ECR I-6991.
137. *See* Case C-176/96 *Lehtonen and Castors Canada Dry Namur-Braine ASBL v. Fédération royale belge des sociétés de basket-ball (FRBSB)* [2000] ECR I-02681.
138. *Ibid.*, paras 50–53.

75. Without mentioning the inherency of such conduct to the objective pursued, the Court relied on justifications related to the specific needs of the sporting system to assess the legitimacy of the restriction.[139]

76. Similarly, in *Bernard*, the Court relied on an orthodox objective justification approach to assess the conduct of sporting bodies.[140] In the case, discussed to a greater extent in Chapter 3, the Court identified a restriction of free movement in the rule of the French Football Federation requiring young players to sign their first professional contract with the club that had trained them, with compensation due in the event of lack of compliance. Subsequently, the Court accepted the legitimacy of the objective pursued, namely the need to encourage the recruitment and training of young players. Finally, the Court embarked in a strict proportionality test, noting that the rule imposing compensation was disproportionately restricting the freedom of movement of the players.[141]

IX. From Free Movement to Competition Law

77. The inherent approach, applied first in *Deliège*, has since assumed the position of the new orthodoxy of EU sports law. This was confirmed in the seminal *Meca-Medina* judgment, in which the Court of Justice applied the inherent rules approach to the competition law provisions of the Treaty.[142]

78. In *Meca-Medina*, an integrity rule adopted by the International Swimming Federation prohibiting the use of doping was considered inherent to the organisation of sport, therefore not falling within the prohibitions established under Article 101(1) TFEU.[143] The case involved two swimmers, David Meca-Medina and Igor Majcen, both of whom failed an anti-doping test in 1999 in Brazil. They were subsequently suspended by FINA for four years.[144] The swimmers first lodged a complaint with the European Commission contending that the fixing of the level of the prohibited substance was arbitrary and had to be construed as a concerted practice between the IOC, FINA and the accredited network of laboratories carrying out the analysis.[145] As this practice had the effect of restricting the market to participate in international sporting events, the athletes argued that the conduct was in breach of Article 81(1) EC (now Article 101(1) TFEU).

---

139. However, the restriction was still considered to be disproportionate in relation to the objectives pursued. *See ibid.*, paras 56–58, and Adam Lewis & Jonathan Taylor, *Sport: Law and Practice* (Bloomsbury 2014).
140. Case C-325/08 *Olympique Lyonnais SASP v. Olivier Bernard and Newcastle UFC* [2010] ECR I-02177.
141. This case is also relevant as in this instance the Court cited for the first time Art. 165 TFEU, stating that the specific characteristics of sport and its social and educational function must be taken into account within the analysis of sporting rules. *Ibid.*, para. 40.
142. *See* Case C-519/04 P *David Meca-Medina and Igor Majcen v. Commission of the European Communities* [2006] ECR I-6991, paras 28–30.
143. *Ibid.*, para. 42.
144. After a first appeal to CAS, the sanction was reduced to a two-year ban. *See ibid.*, paras 8–13.
145. *Ibid.*, para. 16.

79. The Commission held that the rules in question had to be considered necessary for the organisation of the sporting competition and that they did not have as their object the restriction of competition on the market.[146] Instead, the restrictions were inherent in the pursuit of protecting the fairness of the competition, the health of the athletes, and the ethical values of sport.[147] In this regard, the Commission referred to a set of criteria developed in *Wouters* establishing that a restriction that is inherent in the pursuit of legitimate objectives does not fall under what was Article 81(1) EC, so long as it remains proportionate.[148]

80. Following an unexpected detour taken by the Court of First Instance (CFI; now General Court), the Court of Justice mostly upheld the Commission's decision on appeal. It first excluded any form of possible exception based on the sporting nature of the rule challenged, by holding that the mere fact that a rule is sporting in nature does not have the effect of removing the person engaging in the sporting activity from the scope of application of EU law.[149] In effect, this amounted to a rejection of the division between economic and sporting aspects of the activity. This constituted a recognition that the two spheres necessarily overlap, where a conduct of sporting nature can still exert economic effects that have to be analysed under EU law.[150]

81. The Court subsequently pointed out that when assessing a restrictive conduct, account must be taken of the overall context in which the conduct itself has taken place, its objective(s), whether or not the rule and its restrictive effects are inherent in the pursuit of it, and whether they are proportionate.[151] In the case, the Court considered the existence of a legitimate aim, being the protection of health and of the fairness of the competition, and held that the rule was necessary and proportionate to achieve such objective.[152]

82. Effectively, the adoption of these criteria prevents any abstract assessment and the possibility of drafting a list of conduct immediately compatible or incompatible with EU law. This case-by-case approach effectively brings competition law assessments in line with free movement. More importantly, it provides a framework to discuss the autonomy of sport. Rather than as a way to dispute the application of

146. Case COMP/38158 – Meca-Medina and Majcen/IOC, para. 41.
147. *Ibid.*, paras 42–45.
148. *See* Case C-309/99 *J.C.J. Wouters, J.W. Savelbergh, Price Waterhouse Belastingadviseurs BV v. Algemene Raad van de Nederlandse Orde van Advocaten* [2002] ECR I-1577. The Commission also referred to a case it previously decided, Case COMP/37 806: ENIC/UEFA.
149. Case C-519/04 P *David Meca-Medina and Igor Majcen v. Commission of the European Communities* [2006] ECR I-6991, para. 27.
150. Stephen Weatherill, *Case C-519/04 P Meca-Medina [2006] ECR I-6991*, in *Leading Cases in Sports Law* 137–151 (Jack Anderson ed., T.M.C. Asser Press 2013).
151. Case C-519/04 P *David Meca-Medina and Igor Majcen v. Commission of the European Communities* [2006] ECR I-6991, para. 42, citing Case C-309/99 *J.C.J. Wouters, J.W. Savelbergh, Price Waterhouse Belastingadviseurs BV v. Algemene Raad van de Nederlandse Orde van Advocaten* [2002] ECR I-1577, para. 96.
152. Case C-519/04 P *David Meca-Medina and Igor Majcen v. Commission of the European Communities* [2006] ECR I-6991, para. 43.

EU law, the autonomy of sport is considered in the assessment of the justifications used and the objectives pursued by governing bodies.

83. The expertise of the governing bodies enables them, much like other self-regulating collective actors in other sectors, to use their margin of appreciation in setting objectives and pursue them within the limits of EU law.[153] However, as claims of complete autonomy are prevented, regulatory autonomy is conditioned on respecting the principle of proportionality. In this regard, governing bodies are required to balance the interests they have chosen to pursue, with the restriction they impose on concurring interests.[154] This is a broad level of discretion and only where governing bodies fail to undertake this exercise do the EU institutions and the enforcement agencies maintain the possibility to subject the rules to significant scrutiny. However, the scrutiny is translated from a substantive assessment of the rules, to a procedural one, where the role of the Court is to ensure that the governing bodies exercise their competence in adopting measures that are efficient, considering the objectives pursued and the other interests involved.[155]

X. Sporting Objectives and Public Interest

84. In exercising their regulatory authority, sports bodies have a margin of discretion to set objectives that must be pursued in a proportionate manner. Such objectives may at times overlap with general interests or be perceived as such in the context of sociocultural values attached to sport. However, a sports body's perception of public interest does not always necessarily accord with that of a public authority. Sporting autonomy therefore has its limits, and this is why the EU has sought to define the public interest in sport, notably encapsulated in Article 165 TFEU and its sports policy papers discussed below.

85. In *Wouters* and *Meca-Medina*, the Court of Justice had to assess the legality of restrictive rules laid down by private bodies, respectively the Dutch Bar Association and the International Swimming Federation. These bodies were in fact pursuing public interests, being the protection of the integrity of the legal service and sound administration of justice[156] and the protection of the health and safety of athletes.[157] One would therefore assume that the restrictions were imposed by collective private parties that were designated or implicitly delegated to regulate a specific

153. Stephen Weatherill, *EU Sports Law: The Effect of the Lisbon Treaty*, Oxford Legal Studies Research Paper No. 3/2011 (2011).
154. Mislav Mataija, *Private Regulation and the Internal Market: Sports, Legal Services, and Standard Setting in EU Economic Law* 161 (Oxford Univ. Press 2016).
155. Toni Marzal, *From Hercules to Pareto: Of Bathos, Proportionality, and EU Law*, 15(3) ICON 621–64 (2017).
156. Case C-309/99 *J.C.J. Wouters, J.W. Savelbergh, Price Waterhouse Belastingadviseurs BV v. Algemene Raad van de Nederlandse Orde van Advocaten* [2002] ECR I-1577, para. 97.
157. Case C-519/04 P *David Meca-Medina and Igor Majcen v. Commission of the European Communities* [2006] ECR I-6991, paras 42–45.

sector.[158] However, the majority of sports governing bodies do not derive their power from public laws, but from a set of contractual relationships. Nevertheless, their role is to protect the public interest in areas where there is no responsible public authority, or where there is a legislative vacuum.[159]

86. As primary legislation is unlikely to establish a framework where public interest values are specifically identified and supported, it may be up to the regulator itself to identify, interpret and possibly achieve the desirable objectives.[160] The EU institutions have recognised the expertise of the governing bodies and their ability to set their own objectives for the benefit of sport.[161] In this context, the expertise of governing bodies can be channelled into pursuing legitimate public objectives as well.

87. However, there are also significant economic interests underlying the pursuit of objectives of general interests. Governing bodies need to protect the fans' perception of the integrity of the competition as ultimately they are the final consumers of the sports product.[162] It is therefore possible to see a private economic interest overlapping with the protection of the original nature of sport and its ethical principles. There is thus the need to prevent and control any possible conflict of interests, where a regulatory rule may in effect hide an abusive conduct aiming at impairing the activities of competitors.

88. Integrity objectives in the sporting sector are pursued through measures tackling match-fixing and anti-doping, for example, but could also potentially refer to measures aiming to protect competitive balance within a league. Rules upholding these principles range from safety rules to rules concerning the practical organisation of the competition and the events, to rules related to the contractual relationships between sportspersons and clubs and disciplinary matters.

89. In this regard, the Court's approach in *MOTOE* is of particular interest[163] In the case, the Greek Motorcycling Federation was vested with public powers alongside its regulatory and commercial rights. Objectives of public interests that were delegated to it included the need to guarantee the safety of participants and spectators. The latter, alongside the need for the integrity of the competition, are of utmost importance for any governing bodies, and they are considered legitimate

158. In some countries, sports governing bodies derive their powers from national legislation. *See* Robert Siekmann & Janwillem Soek, *Models of Sport Governance in the European Union: The Relationship Between State and Sport Authorities*, 3–4 ISLJ 93–102 (2010).
159. A similar point was raised by the CJEU in *Piau*. *See* Case T-193/02 *Laurent Piau v. Commission of the European Communities* [2005] ECR II-209, para. 77.
160. Mike Feintuck, *'The Public Interest' in Regulation* 164 (Oxford Univ. Press 2004).
161. Joined Cases C-51/96 and C-191/97 *Deliège v. Ligue francophone de Judo et disciplines Associeés Asb* [2000] ECR I-2549, para. 68.
162. *See* Commission Decision, Case COMP/37 806: ENIC/ UEFA, para. 20.
163. Case C-49/07 *Motosykletistiki Omospondia Ellados NPID (MOTOE) v. Elliniko Dimosio* [2008] ECR I-04863.

objectives that could justify a restrictive conduct under EU law. However, as undertakings exercising economic activity, sports bodies that are endowed with regulatory powers are also in a position of dominance and they have to be prevented from abusing their regulatory function to advance their own economic interests under Article 102 TFEU.[164] This aspect was also touched upon by the CFI in *Piau* in which it was held that the task of regulating the economic activity of private individuals or entities is part of the competence of public authorities and not private bodies.[165] Even when a delegation of public power may be identified, when the regulator is also carrying out an economic activity, the exercise of such a power has to be subject to control.[166]

90. The role of sports governing bodies has a fundamental relevance in relation to the legality of both integrity and regulatory rules that they enact. Their margin of appreciation, recognised and respected by the EU institutions, is conditioned on respecting the notion of good governance. In this regard, the impact of EU law is not to dictate the way the sports system is to develop,[167] but rather to ensure that its development does not disproportionately disrupt the sociocultural values now entrenched in Article 165. The commercial aspirations of governing bodies can be legitimately pursued, insofar as they are not concealed under regulatory pretences, or they give way to discriminatory measures contrary to EU law.

§4. EU Sports Policy

I. The Road to Article 165 TFEU

91. The contours of EU sports law described above reveal a somewhat inconsistent jurisprudential journey of discovery. The Court commenced by removing non-economic and purely sporting rules from the scope of the Treaty. Its approach evolved into one that asserted that sporting rules giving rise to restrictive effects require justification or that certain conduct does not amount to a restriction of free movement or competition law if the restrictive effects are inherent in the pursuit of legitimate sporting objectives. Both approaches are subject to proportionality control. While the approach has varied, the trajectory of travel has been consistent – sporting rules are no longer effectively exempt from scrutiny under the Treaty; they must be assessed in light of the Treaty requirements. Accompanying this jurisprudential journey, the EU institutions have attempted to piece together a policy on

164. Samuli Miettinen, *Policing the Boundaries Between Regulation and Commercial Exploitation: Lessons from the MOTOE Case*, 3(4) ISLJ 11–18 (2008).
165. Case T-193/02 *Laurent Piau v. Commission of the European Communities* [2005] ECR II-209, paras 77–78.
166. Case C-49/07 *Motosykletistiki Omospondia Ellados NPID (MOTOE) v. Elliniko Dimosio* [2008] ECR I-04863.
167. Joined Cases C-51/96 and C-191/97 *Deliège v. Ligue francophone de Judo et disciplines Associeés Asb* [2000] ECR I-2549, Opinion of Advocate General Cosmas, para. 87.

sport in an effort to communicate the EU's approach to the sports movement while at the same time sensitising the EU's judicial and decisional bodies on the specificity of the sector.

92. This policy is a relatively new area of activity. There is no evidence that in the mid-1950s, the founders of the European Economic Community contemplated developing a policy on sport. This omission became 'one of the biggest headaches' for the EU.[168] By the 1970s and 1980s, the EU began to formulate a position on sport as other Treaty competences became applied to the sector.[169] A very large headache was avoided in *Walrave* as the Court employed its purely sporting rules formula to avoid the awkward issue of how Treaty prohibitions on nationality discrimination could be reconciled with national eligibility rules in sport.

93. The mere fact that this had been discussed in Luxembourg generated political debate in Brussels and Strasbourg on the role of sport in the European integration process. In the 1980s, this discussion amounted to a series of ad hoc and largely unsuccessful ventures into this new area of activity. In 1984, the Adonnino Committee attempted to use sport as a means of promoting European integration in the aftermath of the stagnation that set in during the period of intergovernmentalism in the 1970s.[170] The EU dabbled at sponsoring a number of sporting events such as the European Sailing Regatta, some cycling tours and a tennis tournament in Belgium, all questionable activity, given the EU's lack of competence in sport.[171] In 1991, the Commission published a Communication on the European Community and Sport[172] which highlighted the impact the completion of the internal market was having on sport, a theme repeated in 1995 in the Commission's Coopers and Lybrand study.[173]

94. By the 1990s, it was becoming more widely debated that in the absence of Treaty recognition for sport, the sector could suffer the unintended consequences of activity elsewhere in the Treaty. The idea of inserting an article on sport in the Treaty was first mooted at the time of the Maastricht Treaty negotiations in the early 1990s. Soon after, the *Bosman* judgment confirmed the sports movement's worst fears and resulted in the IOC leading a more sustained campaign to convince the Member States of the EU to constitutionally recognise the autonomy and specificity

168. Stefan Szymanski, *The Comparative Economics of Sport* 79 (Palgrave Macmillan 2010).
169. Case 36/74 *Walrave v. Union Cycliste Internationale* [1974] ECR 1405, Case 13/76 *Donà v. Mantero* [1976] ECR 1333 & Case 222/86 *UNECTEF v. Heylens* [1987] ECR 4097.
170. *A People's Europe, Reports from the ad hoc Committee*, COM(1984) 446 Final.
171. Walter Tokarski et al., *Two Players One Goal? Sport in the European Union* 62–63 (Meyer and Meyer 2004).
172. European Commission, *The European Community and Sport*, SEC(91) 1438, 31 Jul.1991 (1991).
173. As highlighted in European Commission, *The Impact of European Union Activities on Sport*, Study by Coopers and Lybrand for DG X of the European Commission (1995).

of sport within the Treaty. For the sports movement, *Bosman* demonstrated the need for some reference to the specific nature of sport as a counterbalance to the 'economic bias inherent in the Treaty'.[174]

95. Further opportunity was presented in 1997 during the negotiations that led to the adoption of the Amsterdam Treaty. However, once again, the Heads of State and Government declined the invitation to endow the EU with a sports competence, but it did release a non-legally binding political declaration annexed to the Treaty that read, '[t]he conference emphasises the social significance of sport, in particular its role in forging identity and bringing people together. The conference therefore calls on the bodies of the European Union to listen to sports associations when important questions affecting sport are at issue. In this connection, special consideration should be given to the particular characteristics of amateur sport'.[175]

96. Although a disappointment for sport, the Amsterdam Declaration was cited by the Court in *Deliège*, *Lehtonen* and most notably *TopFit*.[176] It also gave birth to a number of policy initiatives, notably the Vienna European Council Conclusions (1998), the Commission working paper, 'The Development and Prospects for Community Activity in the Field of Sport' (1998), the Commission consultation document, 'The European Model of Sport' (1998), and the resulting paper, 'The Helsinki Report on Sport' (1999).[177] All gave rise to non-binding statements indicating general support for the European model of sport while at the same time acknowledging that sport had to adjust to a new economic and legal climate.[178] The significance of these measures lays in the momentum that was now building around the IOC's campaign for Treaty recognition.

97. The intergovernmental conference preparing for what would become the December 2000 Nice Treaty came close to adopting sport as a competence, but once again, the sports movement was left with non-binding political statements. In a long statement on sport, the Nice Declaration stated that '[e]ven though not having any direct powers in this area, the Community must, in its action under the various

174. Borja García & Stephen Weatherill, *Engaging with the EU in Order to Minimise Its Impact: Sport and the Negotiation of the Treaty of Lisbon*, 19(2) J. Eur. Public Policy 241 (2012).
175. Treaty of Amsterdam amending the Treaty on European Union, the Treaties establishing the European Communities and certain related acts – Declarations adopted by the Conference – Declaration on sport, OJ C 340, 10 Nov. 1997.
176. Joined Cases C-51/96 and C-191/97 *Deliège v. Ligue francophone de Judo et disciplines Associeés Asb* [2000] ECR I-2549, Case C-176/96 *Lehtonen and Castors Canada Dry Namur-Braine ASBL v. Fédération royale belge des sociétés de basket-ball (FRBSB)* [2000] ECR I-02681, and Case C-22/18, *TopFit e.V. and Daniele Biffi v. Deutscher Leichtathletikverband e.V.* [2019] EU:C:2019:497.
177. These initiatives are discussed in Richard Parrish & Samuli Miettinen, *The Sporting Exception in European Union Law* 43–47 (T.M.C. Asser Press 2008).
178. For an analysis of the Helsinki Report *see* Stephen Weatherill, *Principles and Practice in EU Sports Law* 131–135 (Oxford Univ. Press 2017).

Treaty provisions, take account of the social, educational and cultural functions inherent in sport and making it special … '.[179]

98. In 2003, the Convention on the Future of Europe recommended that sport be included within the proposed Treaty establishing a Constitution, but that project floundered in public referenda in France and the Netherlands in 2005 although the sports article survived and was reborn as Articles 6 and 165 of the 2009 Lisbon Treaty. Article 6 establishes sport as a competence in which the EU can carry out actions to 'support, co-ordinate or supplement the actions of the Member States'. The substance of the competence was presented in Article 165 which provides for:

1. The Union shall contribute to the promotion of European sporting issues, while taking account of the specific nature of sport, its structures based on voluntary activity and its social and educational function.
2. Union action shall be aimed at: developing the European dimension in sport, by promoting fairness and openness in sporting competitions and cooperation between bodies responsible for sports, and by protecting the physical and moral integrity of sportsmen and sportswomen, especially the youngest sportsmen and sportswomen.
3. The Union and the Member States shall foster cooperation with third countries and the competent international organisations in the field of education and sport, in particular the Council of Europe.
4. In order to contribute to the achievement of the objectives referred to in this Article – the European Parliament and the Council, acting in accordance with the ordinary legislative procedure, after consulting the Economic and Social Committee and the Committee of the Regions, shall adopt incentive measures, excluding any harmonisation of the laws and regulations of the Member States – the Council, on a proposal from the Commission, shall adopt recommendations.

II. Article 165(1): The 'Specific Nature of Sport', 'Voluntary' Activity and Sport's 'Social and Educational Function'

99. Reference in the first paragraph of Article 165 to the 'specific nature of sport' was the breakthrough the sports movement had campaigned for and was championed by them as amounting to the 'cornerstone of a new EU policy in the field of sport'.[180] Their expectation was, and still is, that this statement amounts to a horizontal obligation which should be applied to the exercise of other EU powers

179. European Council, Nice, 7–10 Dec. 2000, Conclusions of the Presidency. Annex IV, *Declaration on the specific characteristics of sport and its social function in Europe, of which account should be taken in implementing common policies* (2000).

180. International Olympic Committee, *Common position of the Olympic and Sports Movement on the implementation of the new Treaty on the Functioning of the European Union (TFEU) on sport (Lisbon Treaty)*, 2 Jan. 2010, https://www.idrettsforbundet.no/contentassets/ed8107d55ad049dfa26b610dbbaac62c/common_position_of_the_olympic_and_sports_movement.pdf (accessed 29 Mar. 2020).

such as free movement and competition law when sporting disputes are presented before the Court and Commission. The horizontal question has been debated in the academic press, by domestic public authorities and in EU studies.[181] The key issue centres on whether reference to 'taking account of the specific nature of sport' is analogous with other areas of the Treaty in which horizontal obligations are presented more forcefully. For example, Article 11 TFEU provides that '[e]nvironmental protection requirements *must* be integrated into the definition and implementation of the Union's policies and activities' and Article 12 states that '[c]onsumer protection requirements *shall* be taken into account in defining and implementing other Union policies and activities'. The Article 165(1) reference only appears to only bind those actions connected to the 'promotion of European sporting issues'.

100. Ultimately, it is for the Court to decide the strength and relevance of Article 165. In *Bernard* and *Murphy*, fleeting reference was made to Article 165.[182] In *Bernard,* Article 165 was cited in support of the position the Court had already arrived at regarding training compensation schemes in football,[183] and in *Murphy*, the Court did likewise to note that Article 165 supports the view that sporting events have a unique and original character which can transform them into subject matter that is worthy of legal protection.[184] A more significant contribution came in *TopFit* where the Court gave the strength of Article 165 a significant boost by reading it into the Treaty's non-discrimination and citizenship provisions.[185]

101. Article 165(1) also cites the significance of voluntary structures and the social and educational functions of sport. These elements, which have a pronounced grassroots sports dimension, have been the focus of a number of Commission policy interventions including the 2007 White Paper on Sport, a paper published with the entry into force of Article 165 in mind, and the 2011 Communication on Sport which laid out the Commission's post-Article 165 strategy.[186] In *ISU*, the 'volunteer model of sport' was cited by the ISU as part of the justification

181. *See*, for example, Stephen Weatherill, *Fairness, Openness and the Specific Nature of Sport: Does the Lisbon Treaty Change EU Sports Law*, 3–4 ISLJ 11–17 (2010); House of Lords, European Union Committee, 16th Report of Session 2010-11, *Grassroots Sport and the European Union*, The Stationary Office Limited, HL Paper 130 (2011) & Richard Parrish et al., *The Lisbon Treaty and EU Sports Policy*, Report for the European Parliament Committee on Culture and Education, European Parliament (2010).
182. Case C-325/08 *Olympique Lyonnais v. Olivier Bernard and Newcastle UFC* [2010] I-2177 and Joined Cases C-403/08 and C-429/08 *FA Premier League and others v. QC Leisure and others, Karen Murphy v. Media Protection Services Ltd* [2011] ECR I-9083.
183. Case C-325/08 *Olympique Lyonnais SASP v. Olivier Bernard and Newcastle UFC* [2010] ECR I-02177, para. 40.
184. Joined Cases C-403/08 and C-429/08 *FA Premier League and others v. QC Leisure and others, Karen Murphy v. Media Protection Services Ltd* [2011] ECR I-9083, paras 100–101.
185. Case C-22/18, *TopFit e.V. and Daniele Biffi v. Deutscher Leichtathletikverband e.V.* [2019] EU:C:2019:497.
186. European Commission, *White Paper on Sport*, COM(2007), 391 final (2007) & European Commission, *Communication from the Commission to the European Parliament, the Council, the European Economic and Social Committee and the Committee of the Regions – Developing the European Dimension in Sport*, 11 COM(2011) 12 final (2011).

for the use of its authorisation rules.[187] Although the Commission found against the ISU, it did 'not exclude that the protection of the volunteer model of sport, as mentioned in Article 165 of the Treaty, may be considered as a legitimate objective of general interest'.[188] However, the ISU failed to justify why prohibiting the participation of athletes in events organised by third-party organisers was necessary to protect the volunteer model of sport and proportionate.[189] This finding does not cast doubt on the horizontal reach of Article 165 or the importance of volunteering to European sport.[190]

102. Volunteering in sport is connected to 'the social and educational functions of sport'. The White Paper and the Communication on Sport stress the positive effects of sport on, *inter alia*, social inclusion, education and training and public health. For example, the White Paper considered that '[s]port makes an important contribution to economic and social cohesion and more integrated societies' and that '[a]ll residents should have access to sport'.[191] It argued that 'membership of sports clubs and participation in competitions are relevant factors to promote the integration of residents into the society of the host country' and that Member States and sports organisations should 'address discrimination based on nationality in all sports'.[192] These pleas were eventually given status in *TopFit* where the Court took the significant constitutional step of finding that amateur sport does not sit outside the scope of the fundamental principles of free movement.[193] The first paragraph of Article 165 therefore has judicial bite.

III. Article 165(2): … 'developing the European dimension in sport, by promoting fairness and openness in sporting competitions and cooperation between bodies responsible for sports, and by protecting the physical and moral integrity of sportsmen and sportswomen, especially the youngest sportsmen and sportswomen'

103. Reference to the 'European dimension in sport' is a reminder, outlined in Article 6 TFEU, that Article 165 only grants the EU a supporting competence in the field of sport as opposed to those competences that are shared between the EU and its Member States or those that fall within the exclusive preserve of the EU.[194] The European dimension must be evident for the EU to take the type of action outlined in the fourth paragraph of Article 165.

---

187. Case AT.40208 – International Skating Union's Eligibility Rules, para. 216. The case is discussed in the chapter 'Organising Sport'.
188. *Ibid.*, para. 223.
189. *Ibid.*, para. 249.
190. As highlighted in GHK, *Volunteering in the European Union*, Study for the Directorate General for Education and Culture (2010) https://ec.europa.eu/citizenship/pdf/doc1018_en.pdf (accessed 27 Mar. 2020).
191. European Commission, *White Paper on Sport*, COM(2007), 391 final (2007), s. 2.5.
192. *Ibid.*, s. 4.2.
193. Case C-22/18 *TopFit e.V. and Daniele Biffi v. Deutscher Leichtathletikverband e.V.* [2019] EU:C:2019:497.
194. *See* Arts 2–6 TFEU.

104. For the sports movement, reference in the second paragraph of Article 165 to 'fairness and openness in sporting competitions' can only be read one way – it concerns the essence of sporting rules 'whether they concern grassroots sports or elite sports, whether they concern club competitions or national teams, individual or team sports, whether they concern local sports competitions or international sports competitions'.[195] The argument is that the language employed in Article 165 strengthens the claims of sporting autonomy and the specific application of EU law to the sector. However, fairness and openness are terms that pose some troubling questions for sport, for without further definition and judicial interpretation, both words can also be employed by those seeking to attack sporting rules.[196] For example, anti-doping rules pursue the objective of fair competition, but they might be applied unfairly to athletes. Equally, openness could be interpreted as giving support to the merit-based system of promotion and relegation that characterises the European model of sport, or it could be cited in support of a claim brought by a non-national who has been excluded from a national competition[197] or a club wanting to break free of the shackles of the national segmentation model and relocate to another Member State.

105. 'Promoting co-operation between the bodies responsible for sports' has been a feature of the EU's post-Lisbon sports policy. The two principal pillars of this policy have been 'structured' and 'social' dialogue. Structured dialogue 'is a regular dialogue between the EU and its Member States, the representatives of international, particularly European, sport movement and other relevant sport stakeholders, such as organisations representing athletes or coaches, with the aim of mutual cooperation and successful definition and implementation of sports policies'.[198] The annual EU Sport Forum, inaugurated in 1991, is the most visible expression of this dialogue. The Forum is organised by the European Commission, and it brings together hundreds of attendees from the world of sport and public administration.[199] Although not a decision-making body, the Forum fosters mutual understanding between the EU and sport and it promotes dialogue within the sports movement more generally. Supplementing this multilateral dialogue are bilateral discussions between the EU and sports bodies, often held in the margin of official EU meetings, and these have resulted in a number of joint statements and agreements including the 2018 agreement between the European Commission and UEFA adopting the

195. International Olympic Committee, *Common position of the Olympic and Sports Movement on the implementation of the new Treaty on the Functioning of the European Union (TFEU) on sport (Lisbon Treaty)*, 2 Jan. 2010, https://www.idrettsforbundet.no/contentassets/ed8107d55ad049dfa26b610dbbaac62c/common_position_of_the_olympic_and_sports_movement.pdf (accessed 29 Mar. 2020).

196. Stephen Weatherill, *Fairness, Openness and the Specific Nature of Sport: Does the Lisbon Treaty Change EU Sports Law*, 3–4 ISLJ 11–17 (2010).

197. As it was in Case C-22/18, *TopFit e.V. and Daniele Biffi v. Deutscher Leichtathletikverband e.V.* [2019] EU:C:2019:497, para. 63.

198. Resolution of the Council and of the representatives of the Governments of the Member States, meeting within the Council, on further developing the EU Structured Dialogue on sport, para. 9 (2017).

199. The 2020 EU Sport Forum scheduled for Zagreb in March was postponed due to the COVID-19 outbreak.

Arrangement for Cooperation between the European Commission and UEFA.[200] By contrast, 'social dialogue', discussed in more detail in Chapter 3, refers to discussions and potentially joint actions facilitated by the Commission but involving organisations representing the two sides of the industry, namely employers and workers.[201]

106. The inclusion of reference to the protection of the 'physical and moral integrity' of athletes reflects the EU's focus on the fight against doping and the protection of young athletes, both dealt with elsewhere in this monograph.

IV. Article 165(3): ... 'Foster Cooperation with Third Countries and International Organisations'

107. The EU has a range of diplomatic tools, such as its economic size, through which it can seek to achieve its foreign policy objectives, and since the Maastricht Treaty, it has also sought to endow itself with a traditional diplomatic persona akin to those seen in national capitals.[202] While the Lisbon Treaty was equipping the EU with a diplomatic service, the European External Action Service, the third paragraph of Article 165 established the groundwork for sport to play its role in this new diplomacy with third States.

108. For the worlds of sport and diplomacy to come together required more than just a legal basis. In 2015, it received a political impetus when the European Commissioner responsible for Education and Culture, Tibor Navracsics, established two High-Level Groups, one on Sport Diplomacy and the other on Grassroots Sport. Both groups reported their findings in 2016.[203] The Sport Diplomacy group advanced recommendations in the areas of EU external relations, the promotion of EU values in the context of major sporting events and the development of an organisational culture of sport diplomacy.[204]

---

200. European Commission, *Annex to the Commission Decision adopting the Arrangement for Cooperation between the European Commission and the Union of the European Football Associations (UEFA)*, COM(2018) 876 final, https://www.uefa.com/MultimediaFiles/Download/EuroExperience/uefaorg/EuropeanUnion/02/53/98/34/2539834_DOWNLOAD.pdf (accessed 8 Apr. 2020).

201. *See*, for example, *Agreement regarding the minimum requirements for standard player contracts in the professional football sector in the European Union and the rest of the UEFA territory*, https://ec.europa.eu/social/main.jsp?catId=521&langId=en&agreementId=5241 19 Apr. 2012 (accessed 22 Apr. 2020).

202. For discussion *see* Joachim Koops & Gjovalin Macaj (eds), *The European Union as a Diplomatic Actor* (Palgrave Macmillan 2015).

203. European Commission, *High Level Group on Sport Diplomacy*, http://ec.europa.eu/assets/eac/sport/policy/cooperation/documents/290616-hlg-sd-final-report_en.pdf June 2016 (accessed 8 Apr. 2020) & European Commission, *High Level Group on Grassroots Sport*, http://ec.europa.eu/assets/eac/sport/policy/cooperation/documents/290616-hlg-gs-final-report_en.pdf June 2016 (accessed 8 Apr. 2020).

204. There is a growing field of research in the area of sport diplomacy, or, as Murray refers to it, sports diplomacy. *See* among others Stuart Murray, *Sports Diplomacy: Origins, Theory and Practice* (Routledge 2018) and Simon Rofe (ed.), *Sport and Diplomacy: Games Within Games* (Manchester Univ. Press 2018).

109. The nascent EU sport diplomacy received Council endorsement in November 2016 with the release of the Council Conclusions on Sport Diplomacy under the auspices of the Slovak Presidency.[205] The conclusions recommended, among other things: raising awareness of sport diplomacy in the EU; encouraging cooperation between the EU, public authorities and the sports movement; using sport to promote positive sporting and European values; using sport diplomacy to advance economic objectives; maintaining sport diplomacy on the EU's political agenda; exploring the possibility of using Sport Ambassadors; promoting evidence base research and activities; using sport within the framework of Accession, Association, Cooperation and European Neighbourhood agreements; and funding sport diplomacy projects, including engaging third countries in the European Week of Sport. The 2017–2020 EU Work Plan for Sport identified sport diplomacy as a priority theme.[206] Paragraph 8 acknowledged, 'the need to cooperate with third countries, in particular candidate countries and potential candidates to the EU, to promote European values through sport diplomacy, and with the competent international organisations in the field of sport, including the Council of Europe, WADA and the World Health Organization'.

110. In terms of concrete achievements, EU sport diplomacy is in its infancy. In November 2017, sport was integrated into the EU-China High-Level People-to-People Dialogue (HPPD)[207] and the Commission made adjustments to the 2018 Erasmus+ funding criteria and the European Week of Sport programme in order to facilitate the participation from third countries.[208] In 2018, the European Commission and UEFA adopted the Arrangement for Cooperation.[209]

V. Article 165(4): ... 'incentive measures, excluding any harmonisation of the laws and regulations of the Member States' and the adoption of 'recommendations'

111. Article 165 grants the EU a supporting competence in sports policy. This means that Member States retain the primary competence over their respective sport

205. Council of the European Union, *Council Conclusions on Sport Diplomacy*, 14279/16, http://data.consilium.europa.eu/doc/document/ST-14279-2016-INIT/en/pdf 23 Nov. 2016 (accessed 8 Apr. 2020).

206. Council of the European Union, *Work Plan for Sport (1 July 2017–31 December 2020)*, 9639/17, http://data.consilium.europa.eu/doc/document/ST-9639-2017-INIT/en/pdf 24 May 2017 (accessed 8 Apr. 2020).

207. *See* European Commission, *EU and China strength cooperation on education, culture, youth, gender equality and sport*, IP/17/4548, http://europa.eu/rapid/press-release_IP-17-4548_en.htm 15 Nov. 2017 (accessed 8 Apr. 2020).

208. For the European Week of Sport *see*: European Commission, Press Release: *European Week of Sport, 23–30 September* (2018). http://europa.eu/rapid/press-release_AGENDA-18-5910_en.htm (accessed 8 Apr. 2020).

209. European Commission, *Annex to the Commission Decision adopting the Arrangement for Cooperation between the European Commission and the Union of the European Football Associations (UEFA)*, COM(2018) 876 final, https://www.uefa.com/MultimediaFiles/Download/EuroExperience/uefaorg/EuropeanUnion/02/53/98/34/2539834_DOWNLOAD.pdf (accessed 8 Apr. 2020).

policies, with the EU institutions only being able to support national actions where there is a European dimension. In this regard, Article 165(4) foresees the use of two instruments – Incentive Measures and Recommendations.

112. Incentive Measures are designed to support and complement the actions of EU Member States. The key tool here is the Sport Chapter in the EU's Erasmus+ Programme, a Chapter seeking to support European partnerships on grassroots sport in order to pursue the EU's sports-related objectives as set down in its Work Plans for Sport.[210] The Sport Chapter owes its existence to the adoption of Article 165 which established the requisite legal basis for budgetary appropriations in this area.[211] Before this, spending on sports projects would have been susceptible to legal challenge. In *UK v. Commission*, the UK successfully applied for annulment of certain grants for European projects seeking to overcome social exclusion on the basis that the Commission lacked the necessary legal base.[212] In light of this judgment, sports-related projects were either abandoned or tethered to policy areas that did have Treaty footing. For example, 2004 was designated the European Year of Education Through Sport, as even though sport was not, at that time, a competence of the EU, education policy was.[213] Incentive Measures are adopted by the Council and the European Parliament in accordance with the ordinary legislative procedure.

113. Recommendations allow the EU institutions to outline their thinking on a particular issue without that giving rise to any legal obligations on whom it is addressed. For example, in the field of sport, in 2013 the Commission proposed a Council Recommendation, subsequently adopted by the Member States, on promoting health-enhancing physical activity across sectors.[214] Article 165(4) provides that Recommendations be adopted by the Council on a proposal from a Commission.

114. Article 165(4) specifically rules out the harmonisation of national laws and regulations relevant to sport. This places serious limitations on the ability of the EU to act in the field of sport as it rules out the adoption of sports-related Directives and Regulations that connect to Article 165 as the legal basis for action. For example, the 2007 White Paper on Sport envisaged possible legislative action in only two areas, public disorder at sporting events and the regulation of sports agents.[215] To date, EU action in this area has not resulted in any legislative action and Article 165 cannot be used as the legal base for such measures. However, other Treaty provisions could be envisaged as the required legal base, such as Article 114

---

210. Resolution of the Council and of the Representatives of the Governments of the Member States, meeting within the Council, on a European Union Work Plan for Sport for 2011–2014, 2011/C 162/01; 2014–2017, 2014/C 183/03 & 2017–2020, 9639/17.
211. Regulation (EU) No 1288/2013 of the European Parliament and of the Council of 11 Dec. 2013 establishing 'Erasmus+': the Union programme for education, training, youth and sport and repealing Decisions No 1719/2006/EC, No 1720/2006/EC and No 1298/2008/EC, OJ L 347, pp. 50–73.
212. Case C-106/96 *United Kingdom v. Commission* [1998] ECR I-2729.
213. Decision No 291/2003/EC of the European Parliament and of the Council of 6 February 2003 establishing the European Year of Education through Sport 2004, OJ L 043, 1–5.
214. Proposal for a Council Recommendation on promoting health-enhancing physical activity across sectors, COM(2013)0603 final – 2013/0291 (NLE).
215. European Commission, *White Paper on Sport*, COM(2007), 391 final (2007), ss 2.6 & 4.4.

TFEU which concerns the adoption of legal measures necessary for the establishment and functioning of the internal market.

115. In institutional terms, Article 165 places the Commission at the heart of EU sports policy. Formal responsibility for it lies with the Directorate General for Education, Youth, Sport and Culture (DG EAC) with the specialist Sport Unit sitting within it. The softness of DG EAC's powers in the field of sport inevitably means that the activities of other DGs and EU institutions often have a more significant impact on sport, particularly the legal environment it operates within. DG Competition's role in enforcing the EU's competition laws has resulted in a number of key sports Decisions, and the jurisprudence of the Court has, undoubtedly, given the greatest steer to EU sports policy. An example of the work of another DG impacting on sport is the digital single market and media activity of the Directorate General for Communications Networks, Content and Technology (DG CONNECT) which has had significant implications for sports media rights.

116. Article 165(4) restricts the European Parliament's role in sport to giving its approval for Incentive Measures, although not Recommendations. In addition to this, the Parliament has adopted opinions, reports and resolutions on sport, asked questions of the Commission, commissioned its own sports-related studies and organised hearings on sporting issues. Since the entry into force of Article 165, sports ministers now meet formally in the Council as part of the Education, Culture, Youth and Sport Council. Given that Article 165(4) prohibits harmonising measures, the Council's legislative role is very limited although its approval is required for both Incentive Measures and Recommendations. The Council frequently expresses its political position on sports-related issues through Council Conclusions, for example on EU Sport Diplomacy in 2016[216] and Council Resolutions which set out a future plan, as seen with the adoption of successive Work Plans for Sport.[217]

VI. EU Sports Policy: Clarifying the Legal Environment

117. Since *Bosman*, the EU has faced repeated calls from the sports movement to provide guidelines on the application of EU law to sport. The sports movement craved such guidelines in order, minimally, to secure a greater level of legal certainty than that provided by the interventions of the Court of Justice and DG Competition but maximally, sport wanted a fundamental rethink on the status of sport in EU law with a view to safeguarding its autonomy.

216. Conclusions of the Council of the European Union, Sport Diplomacy (Council of Europe, Doc. 14279/16).

217. *See*, for example, Resolution of the Council and of the Representatives of the Governments of the Member States, meeting within the Council, on a European Union Work Plan for Sport for 2017–2020, 9639/17.

118. Guidelines have not been forthcoming. In 1998, the Commission published a working paper, 'The Development and Prospects for Community Activity in the Field of Sport' that argued that despite the educational, health, social, cultural and recreational significance of sport, it still amounts to considerable economic activity, and as such, no deviation from the approach taken by the Court in *Bosman* was recommended.[218] In coming to that conclusion, the Commission acknowledged the difficulty in clarifying how EU law 'can be applied to the economic aspects of sport while taking account of its uniqueness and character'.[219] No doubt, it was also mindful of the rebuke it received by the Court in *Bosman* for its role in approving the 3+2 quota that was ultimately condemned by the Court.[220]

119. In the following year, the Commission published the Helsinki Report on Sport which included a chapter on 'clarifying the legal environment of sport'.[221] In it, the Commission again declined to offer formal guidelines, and instead favoured a 'new approach' involving a better definition of the legal environment which will preserve 'the traditional values of sport, while at the same time assimilating a changing economic and legal environment'.[222] In this regard, the Commission gave 'without prejudice' examples of practices which do not fall under the EU's competition rules, those that are in principle prohibited by them and those practices likely to be exempt from the competition rules.[223] These examples did not, however, amount to guidelines as they merely restated the existing jurisprudence of the Court and decisional practice of the Commission. European Commissioner for Competition, Mario Monti, rather overstated the significance of this approach by saying that '[t]his guideline for applying the competition rules to sport will make it possible to create a framework that provides the world of sport with the legal certainty which it quite legitimately seeks'.[224] However, he also accepted that exemption requests under the EU competition law would have to be made on 'a case-by-case basis'.[225]

120. A further call for the issuance of guidelines on the application of EU law to sport was made in the 2006 Arnaut Report, a report initiated by the UK Presidency of the EU, the mandate of which was agreed at a meeting in Leipzig in December 2005 between the sports ministers of the UK, France, Germany, Italy and

---

218. European Commission, *The Development and Prospects for Community Action in the Field of Sport*, Commission Staff Working Paper (1998).
219. *Ibid.*, p. 7.
220. Case C-415/93 *Union Royale Belge Sociétés de Football Association and others v. Bosman and others* [1995] ECR I-4921, para. 136.
221. European Commission, *Report from the Commission to the European Council with a view to safeguarding current sports structures and maintaining the social function of sport within the Community framework – the Helsinki Report on Sport*, COM(1999) 644 (1999).
222. *Ibid.*, p. 7.
223. *Ibid.*, p. 8.
224. European Commission Press Release, *Limits to application of Treaty competition rules to sport: Commission gives clear signal*, IP/99/965 9/12/99.
225. *Ibid.*

Spain and members of the European Commission and relevant football authorities.[226] It argued that the Commission should use its powers under Article 211 EC, since repealed and replaced in substance by Article 17(1) TEU, to issue guidelines on the application of both competition and free movement laws.[227] The report then proceeded to make a case for such guidelines to offer sport a very wide margin of appreciation under EU law.[228]

121. For Weatherill, the Arnaut Report was 'legally unsound' as it relied on *Walrave's* construction of purely sporting rules and not on the *Meca-Medina* judgment that had been handed down shortly before the publication of the Report.[229] *Meca-Medina* rendered the prospect of the EU issuing guidelines more remote as the Court highlighted the importance of a case-by-case contextual assessment of whether the restrictive effects of sporting rules were inherent and proportionate in the pursuit of legitimate sporting objectives.[230]

122. In the White Paper on Sport, the Commission was left with no other option than to endorse this approach. In doing so it claimed that the 'necessity of a proportionality test implies the need to take into account the individual features of each case. It does not allow for the formulation of general guidelines on the application of competition law to the sport sector'.[231] In the accompanying Staff Working Document, the Commission was more forthright in stating that the '*Meca-Medina* judgment strongly confirms that it is not possible to pre-determine an exhaustive list of sporting rules which breach Article 81 and/or 82 EC (now 101 and 102 TFEU) (or those which do not)' and that a 'general exemption of sporting rules or of activities of sports associations is therefore neither possible nor warranted'.[232] This approach attracted criticism from the European Parliament. It stated in its Resolution on the White Paper that the Commission should have 'due respect for the specificity of sports, by not taking a case-by-case approach and to provide more legal certainty by creating clear guidelines on the applicability of European law to sports in Europe'.[233]

123. The adoption of Article 165 presented the sports movement with another opportunity to seek clarification on the relationship between sport and EU, particularly in light of its reference to the 'specific nature of sport'. Shortly after Article

226. José Arnaut, *Independent European Sport Review*, http://eose.org/wp-content/uploads/2014/03/independant_european_sports_review1.pdf, October 2006 (accessed 29 Mar. 2020).
227. *Ibid.*, p.103.
228. For discussion *see* Samuli Miettinen, *The 'Independent European Sport Review': A Critical Overview*, 3(4) ISLJ 57–62 (2006) and Borja García, *The Independent European Sport Review: Half Full or Half Empty?* 4(3) ESLJ (2007).
229. Stephen Weatherill, *Principles and Practice in EU Sports Law* 121 (Oxford Univ. Press 2017).
230. Case C-519/04 P *David Meca-Medina and Igor Majcen v. Commission of the European Communities* [2006] ECR I-6991.
231. European Commission, *White Paper on Sport*, COM(2007) 391 final (2007), s. 4.1.
232. European Commission, *Commission staff working document. Impact assessment accompanying the White Paper on Sport*, SEC(2007) 935 final (2007), s. 2.1.7.
233. European Parliament Resolution of 8 May 2008 on the White Paper on Sport (2007/2261(INI)), para. 4.

165 entered into force, the Olympic and sports movement issued a common position on its implementation in which it requested that the EU adopt, after consultation 'a recommendation on the EU's competence in the field of sport, which should provide concrete guidance on how to better take into account the specific nature of sport and confirm the autonomy of sports organisations'.[234]

124. Soon after, the Commission published the Communication on Sport and once again, absent from it were guidelines on the application of EU law to sport. Nevertheless, the Commission did set out what it considered to be good practice in sports' search to achieve more favourable treatment by the EU institutions. In the White Paper, the Commission regarded good governance in sport as the gateway to securing the self-regulation of sport.[235] The Communication was more forceful in stating that '[g]ood governance in sport is a *condition* for the autonomy and self-regulation of sport organisations' and that 'there are inter-linked principles that underpin sport governance at European level, such as autonomy within the limits of the law, democracy, transparency and accountability in decision-making, and inclusiveness in the representation of interested stakeholders'.[236]

§5. CONCLUSIONS

125. This chapter has highlighted what can, on the face of it, be considered irreconcilable differences between the organisation of sport and the requirements of EU law. However, the review of the sports-related jurisprudence of the Court of Justice reveals a willingness to recognise the specific nature of sport. Furthermore, the increasingly coherent policy on sport developed by the EU since the adoption of Article 165 TFEU shows, albeit conditional, support for the autonomy of sport.[237] The grounds for such conditional autonomy are substantive and procedural. In substantive terms, sporting rules must pursue, in a proportionate manner, legitimate sporting objectives. Requests for blanket immunity from the reach of EU law or the issuance of guidelines on its application are unrealistic. These substantive requirements are little more than a restatement of the Court's sports-related jurisprudence. Procedurally, the Commission has asserted that sporting rules should be framed with

---

234. International Olympic Committee, *Common position of the Olympic and Sports Movement on the implementation of the new Treaty on the Functioning of the European Union (TFEU) on sport (Lisbon Treaty)*, 2 Jan. 2010, https://www.idrettsforbundet.no/contentassets/ed8107d55ad049dfa26b610dbbaac62c/common_position_of_the_olympic_and_sports_movement.pdf (accessed 29 Mar. 2020).

235. European Commission, *White Paper on Sport*, COM(2007) 391 final (2007), s. 4.

236. European Commission, *Communication from the Commission to the European Parliament, the Council, the European Economic and Social Committee and the Committee of the Regions – Developing the European Dimension in Sport*, 11 COM(2011) 12 final (2011), s. 4.1.

237. On the concept of 'supervised autonomy', *see* Ken Foster, *Can Sport Be Regulated by Europe?: An Analysis of Alternative Models*, in *Professional Sport in the EU: Regulation and Re-regulation* 57–60 (Andrew Caiger & Simon Gardiner eds, T.M.C. Asser Press 2000) and for 'conditional autonomy', *see* Stephen Weatherill, *Principles and Practice in EU Sports Law* 157–175 (Oxford Univ. Press 2017).

good governance in mind, including the involvement of stakeholders in decision-making. In that regard, the Commission has repeatedly suggested social dialogue as a potentially fruitful avenue for engaging stakeholders. In the remainder of the monograph, we attempt to further support these arguments by assessing the impact of EU sports law and policy on three core activities of modern international sport – organising sport, playing sport and funding sport:

Organising Sport: Initially, sports governing bodies were regulatory entities, establishing standardised rules, formats and equipment, organising and administering events, recording achievement and developing and promoting the sport at all levels. The modern sports governing body has evolved into a commercial creature, an exploiter of sports' commercial potential, a collective regulator of labour standards and, above all, the financial beneficiary of lucrative sporting events. At the same time, it has attempted to maintain its grip on its traditional functions and it is here that some third-party event organisers, athletes, broadcasters, sponsors, ancillary undertakings and regulators have called foul play. In this regard, the chapter examines the application of EU law to authorisation rules, club ownership rules, the regulation of third-party ownership (TPO), rules on club location, cross-border leagues and breakaways, player release rules and anti-doping rules.
Playing Sport: How professional and amateur athletes engage with sport is strongly influenced, even determined, by the prevailing structure of the European model of sport. Within this structure, sport is organised along national lines with nationality discrimination being a common feature of the sporting landscape. At the same time, sports bodies exercise a decisive influence over how employment relationships are formed. This regulatory power exercised by governing bodies derives from their pre-eminent, and some would say, monopolistic position within the European model's pyramid. This structure has traditionally relegated those that participate in sport to the base of the pyramid, and this is becoming an increasing source of dissatisfaction and litigation. The chapter explores these issues through an analysis of the application of EU law to rules regulating the activities of athletes, such as transfer and nationality-based rules. Furthermore, the chapter also discusses rules regulating players' representatives, such as agents, and the necessity of involving a broad range of stakeholders in the governance of sport.
Funding Sport: The final substantive chapter examines the influence of the EU on how sport is funded. The commercialisation and commodification of sport has increased the pressure on sports organisations and sports clubs to consider their economic objectives and strategies, in order to maintain the competitiveness and attractiveness of their product on an increasingly global market. In turn, governing bodies have enacted rules to regulate the collecting and sharing of the revenues and the expenditure on the transfer market. The activity of private regulators conditioning a particular relevant market has raised numerous concerns under competition law. The chapter will therefore examine the application of EU law on rules related to the collective selling of media rights, as well as the impact of the Digital Single

Market strategy in this field, rules regulating the expenditure on the players' transfer market such as FFP, and the intervention of Member States on the market under the EU's State aid provisions.

Chapter 2. Organising Sport

§1. Introduction

126. For a number of years, the EU has structured its sports policy through three lenses: the *societal* role of sport, its *economic* function and how sport is *organised* in Europe.[238] The organisational question has become inextricably linked to the debate on the merits, or otherwise, of preserving the European model of sport and retaining its fabled pyramid structure, discussed more fully in Chapter 1. This structure grants sports governing bodies considerable regulatory authority, as the governance norm is that each sport is regulated by one authority per country, usually with a continental and global authority sitting above these national structures. This furnishes European sport with a distinctly national character with sport organised along national lines and characterised by the existence of national leagues, national competitions and competitions between national teams. In 1998, the European Commission highlighted a looming challenge for this structure. It stated, '[i]n light of the rapid growth of sport in Europe, this system could face radical transformation. Therefore, it is important for sport to start to consider the shape of its organisation for the years to come. If it fails to do so, European sport risks being crushed under the pressure of economic interests … '.[239]

127. In the years since that statement, sports bodies, specifically those aligned to the Olympic movement, have doggedly sought to protect the pyramid and most have adopted organisational rules designed to protect and promote this organisational structure. However, commercial developments in sport, the rise of organised stakeholders and perceived governance failures have placed a strain on this model, and the EU is increasingly being asked to supervise the governance choices made by sports bodies. This chapter examines the EU's influence in six such areas. First, it explores the use of authorisation rules in sport which are used to regulate the circumstances in which third-party event organisers, unaligned to the governing body, can stage their own sporting events. Second, it examines rules regulating multiple club ownership. Third, the chapter provides a legal analysis of how TPO/TPI has been regulated in football. Fourth, the EU's impact on club location, the formation of cross-border leagues and the legality of breakaway structures is examined. Fifth, the chapter examines the question of mandatory release of players for national teams. Finally, an examination of some legal issues in the regulation of doping in sport is provided. A final organisational rule, that of arbitration clauses in sport, is a discussion that runs through much of the above.

---

238. *See*, for example, European Commission, *White Paper on Sport*, COM(2007) 391 final (2007), and European Commission, *Communication from the Commission to the European Parliament, the Council, the European Economic and Social Committee and the Committee of the Regions – Developing the European Dimension in Sport*, 11 COM(2011) 12 final (2011).

239. European Commission, *The Development and Prospects for Community Action in the Field of Sport, Commission Staff Working Paper*, 7 (1998).

128. The chapter argues that the EU's assessment of these rules has been driven by an organisational deficiency in the European model. The model has evolved in such a way that sports bodies are empowered to exercise a considerable influence over both stakeholders and third parties, yet the temptation to exploit this power is overwhelming and conflicts of interest and protectionist practices taint their operation. We argue that the EU has not undermined the legitimate organisational basis of European sport, but it has been a force for good in sports governance. The chapter acknowledges that in relation to sports organisational rules, the jurisprudence of the Court and the decisional practice of the European Commission has not always been consistent. Nevertheless, since the European Court's judgment in *Meca-Medina*, the EU's approach has a coherent logic and when read alongside an ever-maturing EU sports policy strengthened by the existence of Article 165 TFEU, a consistent approach can now be discerned.

129. This approach has been referred to as 'supervised' or 'conditional' autonomy and it rests on the acceptance by the sports movement that sporting rules must be adopted within a substantive and procedural context.[240] In substantive terms, sport's organisational rules must be based on the pursuit of legitimate sporting objectives and must remain limited in the pursuit of them. In procedural terms, sporting rules should be adopted in conformity with principles of good governance, which includes adequate stakeholder representation in the framing of such rules.[241] This approach should reduce the risks of damaging conflicts of interests infecting sports governance, an issue that is a key source of dispute in sport. The chapter concludes by arguing that the EU's assessment of sport's organisational rules has improved sports governance and that the arbitral organs of the sports movement, specifically the CAS, are well advised to apply the EU's approach when rights derived from EU law are at issue before them.

§2. Authorisation Rules: FIA, MOTOE & ISU

130. Authorisation rules are a central means through which sports bodies, specifically international sports federations (ISFs), maintain the organisational structure of the European model. Although different sports employ varying language in their respective regulations, the objective of each rule is clear – that members of the governing body, specifically athletes and clubs, must not participate in any event that has not been authorised by the governing body.[242] Should this rule be flouted,

240. On the concept of 'supervised autonomy' *see* Ken Foster, *Can Sport Be Regulated by Europe?: An Analysis of Alternative Models*, in *Professional Sport in the EU: Regulation and Re-regulation* 57–60 (Andrew Caiger & Simon Gardiner eds, T.M.C. Asser Press 2000) and for 'conditional autonomy' *see* Stephen Weatherill, *Principles and Practice in EU Sports Law* 157–175 (Oxford Univ. Press 2017).

241. On the EU and the quest for good governance in sport *see* Borja García & Mads de Wolf, *European Law and the Governance of Sport*, in *Research Handbook on EU Sports Law and Policy* 79–97 (Jack Anderson, Richard Parrish, & Borja García eds, Edward Elgar 2018).

242. To illustrate, below is a small selection of rules that are or have been in place governing unsanctioned events:

the offending party can expect to receive a sanction, in some cases amounting to very lengthy bans, from participation in 'official' events which could include potentially lucrative and prestigious events such as national, European and world championships and Olympic Games.

131. Sports governing bodies defend the use of authorisation rules with reference to a number of 'sporting' justifications. The first is a broad conceptual claim – authorisation rules fit into a pattern of sports governance designed to preserve the autonomy and specificity of sport. Sporting autonomy is similar to the concept of sovereignty in international governmental relations. The argument is that a sports governing body is a form of government and it has the right to insist that its sovereignty is respected.[243] According to the sports movement, this is sufficient to insulate them from those seeking to attack this system.

132. Second, authorisation rules are a means of protecting against the rise multiple governing bodies which runs counter the principle of one federation per sport, a fundamental organisational feature of the European model.[244] It is claimed, without much support, that the public favours the one federation per sport model because having multiple governing bodies is confusing in terms of the identification of

---

Swimming: FINA General Rules, 2014 edition, GR 4.1: 'No affiliated Member shall have any kind of relationship with a non-affiliated or suspended body.' GR 4.5: 'Any individual or group violating this Rule shall be suspended by the affiliated Member for a minimum period of one year, up to a maximum period of two years.'
Hockey: FIH Regulations on Sanctioned & Unsanctioned Events, 2013 edition: Art. 2.1: 'It is prohibited for any National Association, and for any organisation or individual (including Athletes, technical officials, umpires, coaching or management staff) under the jurisdiction of a National Association, to participate in any manner in an Unsanctioned Event.' Art. 2.2: 'Any Athlete or other individual who participates in any capacity in an Unsanctioned Event is automatically ineligible for twelve months thereafter to participate in any capacity in any International Event.'
Cycling: UCI Regulations, 2019 edition: s. 3, 1.2.019: 'No licence holder may participate in an event that has not been included on a national, continental or world calendar or that has not been recognised by a national federation, a continental confederation or the UCI.' S3, 1.2.022: breaches of the above 'shall render the licence holder liable to one month's suspension and a fine of CHF 50 to 100'.

243. This argument was raised by a CAS panel in *AEK Athens v. UEFA*, CAS 98/200 in which CAS stated that '… there is an evident analogy between sports-governing bodies and governmental bodies with respect to their role and functions as regulatory, administrative and sanctioning entities, and that similar principles should govern their actions'. Cited in Adam Lewis & Jonathan Taylor, *Sport: Law and Practice* 71 (Bloomsbury 2014).
244. For example, Art. 11 of the FIFA Statutes, 2018 edition states: 'Any association which is responsible for organising and supervising football in all of its forms in its country may become a member association. Consequently, it is recommended that all member associations involve all relevant stakeholders in football in their own structure. Subject to par. 5 and par. 6 below, only one association shall be recognised as a member association in each country.'

national and international champions. For example, there are four major sanctioning bodies in professional boxing with each awarding a world title. This results in 'too many belts, too many champions'.[245]

133. Third, authorisation rules ensure a consistent application of the rules of the sport and this preserves the integrity of the sport. Permitting third-party events without a governing body control mechanism could result in third-party event organisers amending rules, thus calling into question comparability of results and undermining the public's confidence in the sport. Authorisation rules are a means through which a sport can maintain ethical standards, such as ensuring uniform doping control or upholding prohibitions on certain practices, such as tobacco, alcohol and gambling advertising. They are necessary to ensure that participants are accountable for compliance with rules.

134. Fourth, authorisation rules are a means of protecting the health and safety of athletes. A federation needs to be able to verify that athlete welfare is sufficiently taken into account when third-party event organisers intend staging an event. Some sports are inherently dangerous, not only to athletes but also to spectators and any animals that are used within the sport. Athletes and animals are also susceptible to overwork unless their participation is regulated by a central authority.

135. Fifth, authorisation rules protect the proper organisation and functioning of sport because, without them, a damaging system of competition between rival events would ensue. This would be to the detriment of effective planning in, for example, the setting of the international calendar and the avoidance of fixture clashes. Rival event organisers may have little concern for a balanced, integrated and coordinated match calendar, and without authorisation rules, the governing body would not be able to establish scheduling priorities. This would call into question the future of certain competitions which could threaten national representative competitions, which are important for driving the revenues of governing bodies so that they can fulfil their redistributive function. At a practical level, athletes, animals, coaches, match officials and spectators cannot be in two places at once.

136. Sixth, it is claimed that authorisation rules safeguard against freeriding by commercial entities. The primary function of a sports governing body is to act as guardian of its sport and drive the sport's popularity, participation levels and general development. This necessitates a strong commitment to the grassroots, which is underpinned by volunteers. The commercially profitable element of a governing body's function, such as the staging of national and international tournaments, helps subsidise this grassroots commitment. A concern is that commercial entities wanting to stage rival events might have no such grassroots commitment and simply

245. Former professional boxer Floyd Mayweather quoted in The Guardian, *What If Boxing Had One Champion for Every Weight Division?*, https://www.theguardian.com/sport/queensberry-rules-boxing-blog/2013/oct/15/boxing-one-champion-every-weight 15 Oct. 2013 (accessed 19 Jan. 2020).

want to hive off the profitable elements of sport, thus severing the link between the elite and grassroots levels and calling into question the sustainability and viability of the sport.

137. The counterarguments to the veracity of these sporting justifications are grouped around two broad headings: conflicts of interest and proportionality. On the issue of conflicts of interest, the argument is that sports governing bodies use their monopolistic regulatory power to advance their own commercial interests. In other words, the sporting justifications are a mask for market foreclosure and continued dominance in the sporting marketplace that is becoming increasingly commercialised and profitable. Many sports governing bodies are not only regulatory entities but also event organisers who use authorisation rules to eliminate competition with their own events and in doing so stifle innovation in sport.[246] This is not only to the detriment of consumers, who are denied choice, but also to third-party event organisers who wish to enter the market and athletes, many of whom would like to exercise choice in where they ply their trade. In many sports, even elite-level athletes struggle to make a living out of their sport, and participation in commercially oriented third-party events would be financially attractive to athletes who are, effectively, workers. The anticompetitive effects of these rules are reinforced by the undemocratic manner in which authorisation rules and the related disciplinary regime of sports governing bodies are promulgated and imposed on stakeholders, and through the system of dispute resolution which compels stakeholders to submit disputes arising from the authorisation rules to sports arbitration. There are also concerns that authorisation is often denied even though no legitimate sporting objective is at stake.

138. The second objection concerns the proportionality of authorisation rules and the system of disciplinary sanctioning that accompanies them. Critics argue that even if the sporting justifications discussed above are considered legitimate, the availability of less restrictive alternatives renders these rules incompatible with EU competition law. For example, on the question of commercial freeriding, it can be envisaged that a system of mandatory solidarity payments can be agreed so that third-party event organisers contribute to the development of the sport at all levels. The system of disciplinary sanctioning for participation in unauthorised events also raises concerns. Sanctioning regimes vary across sports, but athletes can face very severe punishments, including lengthy bans, for unauthorised participation. Given the proximity of authorisation rules to the pursuit of commercial, as opposed to purely sporting, objectives, it is questionable that very lengthy bans imposed on athletes for participation in unauthorised events will be considered compatible with public policy within and across the territory of the EU.

139. Given the inherently monopolistic structure of sports governance within the European model and the increasingly commercialised and internationalised sporting environment, it is unsurprising that the EU has issued three important decisions on

246. On the innovation point, *see* Tom Verdonk, *Rivalry among Sports Associations: The Compatibility of Sports Associations' Exclusivity Clauses with EU Competition Law*, 38(2) ECLR 86 (2017).

the question of authorisation rules, two by the European Commission and one by the Grand Chamber of the European Court.

I. Fédération Internationale de l'Automobile (FIA)

140. In June 2000, the European Commission issued a Statement of Objections citing a number of anticompetitive practices in motor sport. The main allegation was that its governing body, the Fédération Internationale de l'Automobile (FIA), had a conflict of interest in that it was using its regulatory powers to block the organisation of races which competed with its own events and through which it generated revenue. Furthermore, the FIA was abusing its dominant position under, now, Article 102 TFEU by claiming the TV rights to motor sport series it authorised. The Commission also alleged further market foreclosure as the promoters' contracts prevented circuits used for Formula One (F1) from being used for races which could compete with F1 for a period of ten years; the teams were prevented from racing in any other series comparable to F1 and agreements with broadcasters placed a financial penalty on them if they showed motor sports that competed with F1 series.

141. Modifications to their arrangements offered by the FIA and Formula One Administration Ltd (FOA) were sufficient for the Commission to consider that the anticompetitive elements of the arrangements had been removed. Of particular relevance was the obligation to establish a complete separation of the commercial and regulatory functions in relation to the FIA Formula One World Championship and the FIA World Rally Championship where new agreements were proposed which placed the commercial exploitation of these championships at arm's length.[247] Other relevant commitments included improving transparency of decision-making and appeals procedures, guaranteeing access to motor sport to any person meeting relevant safety and fairness criteria, guaranteeing access to the international sporting calendar and ensuring that no restriction is placed on access to external independent appeals. These obligations satisfied the Commission that the FIA rules could not be enforced so as to prevent or impede a competition or the participation of a competitor, except for reasons inherently linked to FIA's regulatory role of maintaining safety standards.

247. COMP 35.163, Notification of FIA Regulations, COMP 36.638, Notification by FIA/FOA of agreements relating to the FIA Formula One World Championships, COMP 36.776, GTR/FIA, Notice published 13 Jun. 2001 OJ C 169, para. 5.

II. Motosykletistiki Omospondia Ellados NPID (MOTOE)

142. The first occasion in which the Court of Justice addressed the issue of authorisation rules in sport was in *MOTOE*, a Grand Chamber decision.[248] This gave the European Court the opportunity to endorse the 'separation of powers' solution found in *FIA*. It declined to do so.

143. In Greece, under the relevant law, motorcycle events were only permitted to take place after authorisation was secured. The law stated that authorisation shall be given 'for all competitions involving ... motorcycles or mopeds, by the Minister for Public Order or the authorities empowered by him, following the consent of the legal person which officially represents in Greece the ... Fédération Internationale de Motocyclisme (International Motorcycling Federation) [('the FIM')]'.[249]

144. MOTOE organised motorcycling competitions in Greece. As required by the Greek law, it submitted an application to the Greek minister to stage one such event. The application was passed to the representative of the FIM, the Elliniki Leskhi Aftokinitou kai Periigiseon (ELPA), the Automobile and Touring Club of Greece, for consideration. The application was not granted and a dispute ensued. As part of its plea within the Greek courts, MOTOE cited potential infringements of EU competition law, particularly that as ELPA itself organised motorcycling events, it, and by extension the Greek state, was abusing its dominant position to protect its own commercial interests from commercial competition from MOTOE.

145. Following a preliminary reference from the national court, the European Court first established that ELPA was an undertaking pursuant to EU law due to its active participation in the market for organising and commercially exploiting motorcycling events. The Court then determined that ELPA occupied a position of dominance within that market. This was due to the special position accorded to it by Greek law for authorising events. The abusive element of this dominant position was set out in paragraph 51 of the judgment in which the Court stated that a 'system of undistorted competition, such as that provided for by the Treaty, can be guaranteed only if equality of opportunity is secured as between the various economic operators'. This equality of opportunity was eroded as ELPA not only had the unfettered legal means to prevent other service providers from entering the Greek market but also had the economic interest to do so.

146. As Advocate General Kokott stated in her Opinion, 'rules on consent such as those in question here lead to a conflict of interest'.[250] Weatherill describes this as amounting to the concept of 'inevitable abuse' in which the manner in which

248. Case C-49/07 *Motosykletistiki Omospondia Ellados NPID (MOTOE) v. Elliniko Dimosio* [2008] ECR I-04863.
249. Section 49 Greek Road Traffic Code, Law No. 2696/1999.
250. Case C-49/07 *Motosykletistiki Omospondia Ellados NPID (MOTOE) v. Elliniko Dimosio* [2008] ECR I-04863, Opinion of Advocate General Kokott, para. 98.

dominance was constructed will inevitably result in abusive conduct.[251] He cites a number of authorities pre and post *MOTOE* to highlight how this approach is by no means unique to sports cases.[252]

147. The fact that ELPA's conduct related to a situation internal to Greece did not preclude the application of EU competition law as the conduct 'may have the effect of reinforcing the partitioning of markets on a national basis'.[253] This statement is reasonable given that at the time of the litigation, sport within the EU had already experienced a growing commercialisation and internationalisation, a point acknowledged by Kokott in her Opinion.[254]

148. Accordingly, the Court held that EU competition law precludes a national rule which confers on a legal person which organises motorcycling events and enters, in that connection, into sponsorship, advertising and insurance contracts, the power to give consent to applications for authorisation to organise such competitions, without that power being made subject to restrictions, obligations and review.

III. International Speed Skating Union (ISU)

149. In June 2014, two speed skaters, Mark Tuitert and Niels Kerstholt, complained to the European Commission about ISU Eligibility Rules deterring them from participating in unsanctioned skating events.[255] The skaters wanted to participate in an event organised by Icederby International, an event that offered the skaters good financial opportunities, thanks to prize money which was far in advance of what a speed skater could normally earn. For example, the Dutch Olympic Committee offered the best speed skaters a monthly stipend of between EUR 738 and EUR 2271[256] and prize money at ISU events amounted to a maximum of only USD 15,000 for a World Cup Champion.[257] According to the Icederby's website, its model was to combine 'the speed and power of Long Track Speed Skating and the excitement and thrills of Short Track Speed Skating. Now the Long Track Skaters and Short Track Skaters meet in the middle by skating Icederby races on a 220-meter oval'. Not only were Icederby changing the rules of the sport but they were also proposing a relaxation on the prohibition of betting on the sport.[258]

---

251. Stephen Weatherill, *Principles and Practice in EU Sports Law* 253 (Oxford Univ. Press 2017).
252. *Ibid.*, 253–254.
253. Case C-49/07, *Motosykletistiki Omospondia Ellados NPID (MOTOE) v. Elliniko Dimosio* [2008] ECR I-04863, para. 42.
254. *Ibid.*, Opinion of Advocate General Kokott, para. 66.
255. Here, Eligibility Rules and Authorisation Rules are terms used interchangeably.
256. Case AT.40208 – International Skating Union's Eligibility Rules, para. 39.
257. *Ibid.*, para. 40.
258. For discussion *see* Alex Haffner, *Why the International Skating Union Was Found in Breach of EU Competition Law*, LawInSport, www.LawinSport.com 17 Jan. 2018 (accessed 12 Jul. 2019).

150. The contested ISU rules, stated in the Constitution and General Regulations, provided that only 'eligible' persons can participate in ISU events.[259] Eligibility is defined as a person who elects to take part in international competitions which are sanctioned by the ISU. Individuals become ineligible if they participate in an international competition that is not sanctioned by the ISU. The sanction for violating this provision ranges from a warning, a period of ineligibility of up to five or ten years, or a life ban, although as the ISU stated, it had never actually issued a life ban.[260] As the eligibility rules also apply to other categories of participants, including officials, referees, judges and stewards, it appears that a banned skater would also be debarred from, for instance, coaching after retirement.

151. Naturally, these eligibility rules had the effect of severely deterring athletes taking part in an unsanctioned event, for if they did, they risked ineligibility from participation in the major international speed skating events such as the Winter Olympic Games and the World Championship.

152. The Commission initiated proceedings in October 2015 and issued a Statement of Objections to the ISU in September 2017.[261] In the Commission's view, the eligibility rules restricted the commercial freedom of athletes and prevented new organisers of international speed skating events from entering the market because they are unable to attract top athletes who are fearful of having severe sanctions, including a life ban, imposed upon them. The Commission took this view despite the ISU making a number of amendments in 2016 to its eligibility rules. The ISU defended this system with reference to a number of sporting justifications including the protection of integrity, health and safety and the good functioning of sport.[262]

153. In the formal decision in December 2017, the Commission found that the eligibility rules breached Article 101 TFEU. Three restrictive effects were found.[263] First, the ISU's rules created barriers to finding skaters for third parties wishing to start organising and commercially exploiting international speed skating events in competition with ISU and its members as skaters will not risk becoming ineligible and forego the possibility of competing in international events, including the Olympics, the ISU World Cup and the ISU Championships. Second, the rules limited the skaters' commercial freedom to participate in events that are not authorised by the ISU. Finally, the ISU's Appeals Arbitration rules which grant exclusive jurisdiction to the CAS reinforce the anticompetitive effects of the ISU's authorisation rules. Under the rules, athletes have no choice but to accept arbitration and EU law protections are not sufficiently aired.

259. Rule 102, International Skating Union, Constitution and General Regulations, 2016 edition.
260. ISU Statement – EU Commission Decision, https://www.isu.org/news-inside-isu/145-news/11810-isu-statement-european-commission-decision?templateParam=15 8 Dec. 2017 (accessed 9 Apr. 2020).
261. European Commission, *Antitrust: Commission sends Statement of Objections to International Skating Union on its eligibility rules*, Press Release, IP/16/3201, 27 Sep. 2016.
262. Case AT.40208 – International Skating Union's Eligibility Rules, para. 213.
263. *Ibid.*, paras 3–6.

154. As the ISU Eligibility Rules form part of ISU's Constitution and General Regulations and were adopted by the ISU members which are the individual national skating federations, the Commission found that the rule constituted a decision by an association of undertakings within the meaning of Article 101(1) TFEU.[264] The Commission required the ISU to cease its conduct by abolishing or modify its eligibility rules 'so that they are based only on legitimate objectives, explicitly excluding the ISU's own economic interests, and that they are inherent and proportionate to achieve those objectives'.[265] The Commission did not impose a fine on the ISU, a decision that critics argue 'signals that the sports sector is getting special treatment'.[266] In February 2018 the ISU appealed the Commission Decision to the General Court.[267]

155. A similar case is pending in Basketball, a dispute between FIBA and EuroLeague that has rumbled for years. FIBA, the International Basketball Federation, was once, through its European Division, the sole organiser of basketball club competitions in Europe. Since 2006, EuroLeague, a commercial entity, has run these competitions with FIBA focussing on organising national team games. A dispute has since arisen concerning the organisational role of each party, with each accusing the other of anticompetitive practices, particularly since FIBA attempted to wrestle back control over club competitions and EuroLeague responded by threatening leagues with the exclusion of its league champions from EuroLeague unless other clubs in the league would commit to participate in its competitions. The dispute has been subject to litigation in Germany and both parties have lodged complaints with the European Commission.[268]

156. Swimming has also been the subject of organisational disputes. FINA, the world governing body of swimming, and other aquatic sports have been in dispute with the International Swimming League (ISL), a commercial entity, over the organisation of swimming events.[269] The ISL wanted to establish a swimming competition, but for its business model to work, it needed access to the best swimmers, who were generally very willing to participate given the higher financial rewards on

---

264. *Ibid.*, paras 146–153.
265. European Commission, *Antitrust: International Skating Union's restrictive penalties on athletes breach EU competition rules*, Press Release, IP/17/5184 8 Dec. 2017.
266. Ben Van Rompuy, *EU Commission adopts first-ever antitrust prohibition decision on regulatory aspects of sport*, Regulating for Globalisation, http://regulatingforglobalization.com/2018/02/12/eu-commission-adopts-first-ever-antitrust-prohibition-decision-regulatory-aspects-sport/?print=pdf 12 Feb. 2018 (accessed 9 Apr. 2020).
267. Case T-93/18 *International Skating Union v. Commission.*
268. For the background *see* Alexander Engelhard & Luka Milanovic, *An Overview of the Dispute Between FIBA & EuroLeague – Is There and End in Sight*, LawInSport https://www.lawinsport.com/topics/item/an-overview-of-the-dispute-between-fiba-euroleague-is-there-an-end-in-sight 25 Feb. 2018 (accessed 12 Jul. 2019).
269. For discussion *see* Katarina Pijetlovic, *FINA's Decision to Allow Market Access to Rival Competitions – A Turn of the Tide in Professional Swimming*, LawInSport https://www.lawinsport.com/topics/item/fina-s-decision-to-allow-market-access-to-rival-competitions-a-turn-of-the-tide-in-professional-swimming 26 Mar. 2019 (accessed 12 Jul. 2019).

offer. However, through its authorisation rules for third-party events, these swimmers were effectively controlled by FINA and FINA was not willing to approve the ISL format. The dispute was the subject of litigation in the US by a number of swimmers.[270] The class action cited 'clear antitrust violations arising from FINA's complete control, by unlawful means, over the promotion and organization of international swimming competitions and its efforts to ensure that FINA, and only FINA, can determine what swimming athletes will be paid for their efforts'.[271] In January 2019, FINA relented by allowing swimmers 'to participate in competitions or events staged by independent organisers' although all results or records of swimmers achieved in events not authorised by FINA will not be recognised but, other than that, swimmers would not face sanction.[272]

IV. An Assessment of the EU's Scrutiny of Authorisation Rules

157. The ISU's response to the Commission's investigation and negative decision was somewhat reminiscent of football's response to *Bosman* over twenty years earlier. Following the Commission's Statement of Objections, the ISU accused the Commission of misunderstanding sports governance. It stated that '[a]ny allegation that the ISU's rules are somehow anti-competitive appears to be based on a misplaced understanding of the governance structure of sport and the Olympic movement'.[273] It continued, '[t]he decision fails to consider the specific nature of sport by putting commercial interests ahead of the principles of integrity, health and safety that protect fair play in sport'[274] and that '[a] neoliberal and deregulated approach to sport could destroy the Olympic values underpinning sport'.[275]

158. Thomas Bach, IOC President, stated that the case was 'a major risk for the European model of sport'[276] and he asked the Commission 'to safeguard the volunteer engagement and to protect the European Model of Sport, rather than destroying it by applying the same rules as it does for industries, like car manufacturing or

270. Case 3:18-cv-07393 *Shields and others v. FINA*, 12 Jul. 2018, Class Action Complaint for Violations of the Sherman Act and the Common Law.

271. *Ibid.*, para. 1.

272. FINA, *FINA meets with NFs on Athlete participation in international competitions*, https://www.fina.org/print/50461 (accessed 8 Apr. 2020).

273. ISU, *ISU believes that the European Commission's antitrust allegations are unfounded*, https://www.isu.org/news/65-isu-news/11268-ec-antitrust-allegations-are-unfounded?templateParam=15 27 Sep. 2016 (accessed 8 Apr. 2020).

274. ISU, *ISU Statement – EU Commission Decision*, https://www.isu.org/news-inside-isu/145-news/11810-isu-statement-european-commission-decision?templateParam=15 8 Dec. 2017 (accessed 8 Apr. 2020).

275. ISU, *ISU believes that the European Commission's antitrust allegations are unfounded*, https://www.isu.org/docman-documents-links/isu-files/documents-communications/press-releases/2016/2076-press-release-ec-antitrust2/file 27 Sep. 2016 (accessed 8 Apr. 2020).

276. Quoted in Ben Van Rompuy, *EU Commission adopts first-ever antitrust prohibition decision on regulatory aspects of sport,* Regulating for Globalisation, http://regulatingforglobalization.com/2018/02/12/eu-commission-adopts-first-ever-antitrust-prohibition-decision-regulatory-aspects-sport/?print=pdf 12 Feb. 2018 (accessed 9 Apr. 2020).

steel production. Otherwise investments of sport organisations, such as in the education of young athletes, referees or in women and sport, are at stake'.[277]

159. The concern of international sports federations is that these decisions make it easier for rival event organisers to establish competitions, thus undermining their traditional organisational function. This threatens their solidarity function as independent event organisers would be able to freeride off their efforts and hive off the profitable elements of the sport. However, a closer inspection of *FIA*, *MOTOE* and *ISU* does not support the concern that the EU's treatment of authorisation rules is a threat to the European model.

160. The three cases are not authority for the proposition that sports governing bodies are required by EU law to separate their regulatory and commercial functions. This was the solution found in *FIA*, but this governance amendment was offered by the parties, and it was not imposed on them by the Commission. Becoming a pure regulator might, or not, be attractive for a sports governing body to consider, for such a step would probably remove them from EU law oversight which concerns itself with the regulation of economic activity carried out by undertakings.[278] At the very least, instances of abuse would be hard to find given the inherent conflict of interest involved in regulating and commercially exploiting sport had been removed.

161. In the English snooker case of *Hendry v. WPBSA*, *FIA* was raised by one of the parties to support the claim that the combination of both the regulatory power over, and commercial exploitation of, the sport was objectionable.[279] The Court found that the fact that the World Professional Billiards and Snooker Association (WPBSA) is the regulator 'does not itself amount to a barrier to entry, which must depend on how the regulatory power has been exercised'.[280] Consequently, WPBSA was not required to choose whether it was to be a sports regulator or a commercial exploiter of the sport.[281]

162. The view of the English Court was subsequently endorsed by the European Court in *MOTOE* in which the Court imposed no such condition to separate regulatory and commercial functions. The Court simply insisted that conflicts of interest in sports governance should be avoided and that the power to give consent to applications for authorisation to organise third-party competitions should be limited and that power should be made subject to restrictions, obligations and review.

---

277. European Olympic Committees, *IOC President Thomas Bach calls for protection of European Sport Model at European Evening of Sports, Press Release*, http://www.euoffice.eurolympic.org/blog/press-release-ioc-president-thomas-bach-calls-protection-european-sport-model-european-evening 22 Jun. 2017 (accessed 8 Apr. 2020).
278. A point made by Stephen Weatherill, *Principles and Practice in EU Sports Law* 257–258 (Oxford Univ. Press 2017).
279. *Hendry v. WPBSA* [2001] All ER (D) 71, para. 31.
280. *Ibid.*, para. 96.
281. *Ibid.*, para. 163.

163. *ISU* has added further clarity to the limits of sports governance. Rather than unleashing, as the ISU claimed, a 'neoliberal and deregulated approach to sport', the Decision grants significant freedom for a sports governing body to continue to build authorisation rules into their respective constitutions. The challenge for sport is to ensure that these authorisation rules pursue legitimate sporting, as opposed to commercial, objectives. They should not be applied to rival events that pose no risk to legitimate sporting objectives. They must be based on objective, transparent and non-discriminatory criteria. They cannot be used to restrict competition, foreclose markets and advance federation's own commercial interests, and sanctions imposed on parties for breaching these rules must be proportionate. The assessment as to whether a sports governing body is leveraging regulatory power to achieve commercial objectives can only be made on a case-by-case basis. This proposition underlines the continued importance of the Court's approach outlined in *Meca-Medina.*

164. In *ISU*, the Commission also made a notable contribution to the discussion on the validity of arbitration clauses in sport. Mandatory arbitration clauses lie at the cornerstone of the so-called *lex sportiva*, yet in *ISU*, the Commission cast considerable doubt on the efficacy of the system. At paragraphs 5 and 6 of its Decision, the Commission expressed three concerns. First, it stated that judicial recourse against CAS arbitral awards is possible, but only before the Swiss Federal Tribunal (SFT) and on a very limited number of grounds, which do not include a violation of EU competition rules. Second, it considered that athletes had no choice but to accept the Appeals Arbitration rules and the exclusive competence of the CAS. Finally, the Commission argued that in relation to authorisation rules, the hurdles that these rules impose on athletes in obtaining effective judicial protection reinforce the restrictive effects of such rules since EU law is not applied to such disputes.[282]

165. The Commission's first criticism is factually correct in that appealing a CAS decision in the Swiss Courts is allowable only on limited grounds, not including a violation of EU law,[283] and challenge is rarely successful.[284] However, that in itself is not a sufficient argument to undermine the system of arbitration in sport, and indeed there are compelling reasons why judicial scrutiny of arbitral awards should be discouraged. But, if relitigation is preferred, the SFT can intervene should CAS refuse to hear all arguments raised by the parties, of which compatibility with EU law could be one.[285] Furthermore, other judicial opportunities exist for an aggrieved party subject to a CAS decision. Once issued and left untouched by the Swiss Courts, a CAS award is final, binding and enforceable in the national courts of countries who are signatories to the New York Convention on the Recognition and Enforcement of Foreign Arbitral Awards. A national court can refuse to recognise an arbitral award on a number of limited grounds, including incompatibility

282. Case AT.40208 – International Skating Union's Eligibility Rules, paras 5–6.
283. *See* Arts 190–191 Swiss Federal Act on Private International Law.
284. For successful challenges before the SFT *see* 4P_172/2006, 22 Mar. 2007 (*Guillermo Cañas v. ATP Tour*) and 4A_558/2011, 27 Mar. 2012 (*Matuzalem*).
285. In 4P_172/2006, 22 Mar. 2007 (*Guillermo Cañas v. ATP Tour*), the Swiss Court upheld Cañas' appeal on the grounds that CAS had not considered legal arguments raised by the tennis player.

with the public policy of the country concerned. Following the judgment of the Court of Justice in *Eco Swiss*, EU competition law is to be regarded as a matter of public policy within the meaning of the New York Convention.[286] The reach of EU law is not so curtailed as the Commission asserts. Furthermore, it should be recalled that some of the leading cases of EU sports law, such as *ENIC* and *Meca-Medina*, both discussed below, stemmed from dissatisfaction with CAS awards.[287]

166. The Commission's second objection, the question of forced arbitration, has dogged the CAS for years and was central to the *Pechstein* litigation. Claudia Pechstein, a German professional speed skater, received a ban for a doping offence. She sought to challenge her suspension in a number of venues including CAS, the SFT, the German Courts and ultimately in the European Court of Human Rights, there citing a breach of Article 6 of the European Convention on Human Rights (Right to a Fair Trial).[288] Her claim was that CAS lacked independence from the sports movement and that she was denied a public hearing.[289] Her challenge was mostly dismissed. The Court of Human Rights considered CAS to have sufficient independence from the sports movement, although two of the seven judges dissented on this question. On the specific question of forced arbitration, the Court acknowledged that consent was not freely given, based as it is on a take-it-or-leave-it basis, but this is a necessary characteristic of sports arbitration. Nevertheless, because of this, rights under the Convention cannot be waived and the failure to offer Pechstein a public hearing breached her Article 6 rights.[290] Illustrating the increasing influence of the European Court of Human Rights, in January 2020 it handed down its judgment in *Riza v. Turkey*.[291] Here, Turkey was found to have violated Article 6 of the Convention as the arbitral system in Turkish football was deficient in that it lacked independence from the Turkish Football Federation. Although the Court of Human Rights is not a European Union court and it does not judge on the basis of EU law, its decisions are highly regarded. In particular, the question of the independence and impartiality of the dispute resolution system is also relevant

286. Case C-126/97 *Eco Swiss China Time Ltd v. Benetton International NV* [1999] ECR I-03055. For comment *see* Assimakis Komninos, *Eco Swiss China Time Ltd v Benetton International NV (C126/97)*, 37(2) CML Rev. 459 (2000).
287. Case COMP/37 806: ENIC/UEFA and Case C-519/04 P *David Meca-Medina and Igor Majcen v. Commission of the European Communities* [2006] ECR I-6991.
288. *Mutu & Pechstein v. Switzerland*, nos 40575/10 et 67474/10, 2 Oct. 2018.
289. For discussion *see* Nick De Marco, *The Right to a Fair Hearing in Sports' Cases: Lessons from the ECtHR's Decision in Mutu & Pechstein*, LawInSport, https://www.lawinsport.com/topics/item/the-right-to-a-fair-hearing-in-sports-cases-lessons-from-the-ecthr-s-decision-in-mutu-pechstein 15 Oct. 2018 (accessed 18 Jan. 2020).
290. *See* Antoine Duval, *The 'Victory' of the Court of Arbitration for Sport at the European Court of Human Rights: the End of the Beginning for the CAS*, Asser International Sports Law Blog, https://www.asser.nl/SportsLaw/Blog/post/the-victory-of-the-court-of-arbitration-for-sport-at-the-european-court-of-human-rights-the-end-of-the-beginning-for-the-cas 10 Oct. 2018 (accessed 17 Jan. 2020).
291. *Ali Riza and Others v. Turkey*, 30226/10, 28 Jan. 2020. For commentary *see* Despina Mavromati, *Riza v Turkey: European Court of Human Rights Gives Further Guidance on Establishing Independent Arbitral Tribunals*, LawInSport, https://www.lawinsport.com/topics/item/riza-v-turkey-european-court-of-human-rights-gives-further-guidance-on-establishing-independent-arbitral-tribunals#_ftn1 5 May 2020 (accessed 12 Apr. 2020).

in the context of EU competition law. A system of forced arbitration tainted with undue influence of the panel could represent an abuse of dominant position by the governing bodies.[292]

167. On the Commission's third criticism, regarding the curtailment of the reach of EU law into potentially anticompetitive agreements, it is true that there has been 'a degree of inconsistency in the attitude of CAS panels to the application of EU law'.[293] Nevertheless, as is discussed throughout this chapter and elsewhere in this monograph, the CAS has applied EU law to a number of cases, although it should do so more systematically.[294]

§3. Multiple Club Ownership

168. The motivations for an individual, undertaking or club to hold a financial interest in more than one sports club are varied. In the world of football, multiple club ownership can be financially profitable if the clubs are well run and operate in competitions with lucrative broadcasting contracts. Entities can use the wide appeal of football to develop marketing and sponsorship opportunities, and clubs can be used and rebranded as the face of related business activities the owner wishes to promote or as a means of pushing the brand of the club itself in emerging markets. For the owner, owning more than one club can also promote the sharing of best practice, cost efficiencies and a range of related sporting objectives such as improved scouting networks, reduced player acquisition costs, maximised transfer fees on player sales and the wider provision of playing opportunities for players within the club 'family'. A well-established club whose owner has a stake in another club can use that second club to recruit playing talent at a low cost, possibly taking advantage of less strict immigration and naturalisation requirements, and then develop the player in the culture and style of the lead club. The lead club then has access to a first-team ready player whose transfer value is likely to have increased well above the costs actually incurred in developing the player at the feeder club.

169. Multiple club ownership is an increasingly common feature of the football landscape. For example, the City Football Group (CFG) holds majority investments in Manchester City, New York City and Melbourne City and minority shareholdings in Yokohama F Marinos, Club Atletico Torque, Girona FC, Sichuan Jiuniu and Mumbai City FC. CFG is owned by Abu Dhabi United Group, an undertaking owned by Sheikh Mansour bin Zayed Al Nahyan. Alongside CFG, Red Bull is perhaps the most prominent case of multiple club ownership. Red Bull, an Austrian energy drink company, has as a means of generating brand awareness, built a sporting portfolio across a range of sports including ice hockey, eSports, extreme sports,

---

292. Antoine Duval & Ben Van Rompuy, *The Compatibility of Forced CAS Arbitration with EU Competition Law: Pechstein Reloaded*, available at SSRN: http://ssrn.com/abstract=2621983 (2015).
293. Stephen Weatherill, *Principles and Practice in EU Sports Law* 15 (Oxford Univ. Press 2017).
294. Antoine Duval, *The Court of Arbitration for Sport and EU Law: Chronicle of an Encounter*, 22(2) MJECL (2015).

motor racing and football. Its football portfolio began with the acquisition of Austrian club SV Wüstenrot Salzburg and its transformation into RB Salzburg. Red Bull then acquired a Major League Soccer team in the US, naming it New York Red Bulls and a team in Brazil (now known as Red Bull Bragantino). In 2009, it acquired German club SSV Markranstädt and rebranded it as RB Leipzig.

170. The 'pioneer' of this business model in football was the English National Investment Company (ENIC).[295] In the late 1990s, ENIC built an investment portfolio in a number of European football clubs: AEK Athens, Slavia Prague, Vicenza Calcio SpA, FC Basel, Glasgow Rangers FC and Tottenham Hotspur. This business model attracted the attention of Europe's continental federation, UEFA. Although club ownership was regulated at a national association level, UEFA's interest is connected to the organisational structure of the European model of sport which has a pronounced national character, evidenced by the existence of national leagues. Teams that perform well in these national leagues can qualify for UEFA's two club competitions, the Champions League and the Europa League. In order to ensure the credibility and therefore the viability of these competitions, UEFA has, since 1998, deemed it necessary to regulate club ownership.

171. Two or more clubs participating in UEFA club competitions cannot be controlled, directly or indirectly, by the same undertaking or person.[296] If two or more clubs fail to meet this criterion, when otherwise eligible to participate in UEFA competitions, only one of them can be admitted to that competition. The rule was adopted in order to preserve the integrity of sporting competitions and avoid conflicts of interest that may arise from more than one club being controlled by the same owner. For example, a scenario could arise or be perceived, whereby the commonly owned clubs could conspire to obtain results that were mutually beneficial to them, at the expense of other teams. The rule was introduced following a situation in the 1997/98 season when three clubs owned by ENIC reached the quarter-finals of the UEFA Cup Winners' Cup, a competition since abolished. Even though the teams did not meet, the case caused concern for UEFA.

172. In the 1998/99 season, AEK Athens and Slavia Prague qualified for the UEFA Cup, since renamed the Europa League. ENIC held a controlling stake in both clubs. As per the 1998 rule, UEFA informed AEK that it was not admitted to the UEFA Cup as per the criteria in force at the time.

173. AEK and Slavia Prague submitted the case to CAS.[297] In its award of August 1999, CAS rejected the petitions to have the UEFA rule set aside by finding merit in the objective of the rule which it considered 'an essential feature for the organization of a professional football competition and is not more extensive than

---

295. Tomás Grell, *Multi-Club Ownership in European Football – Part 1: General Introduction and the ENIC Saga*, Asser International Sports Law Blog, https://www.asser.nl/SportsLaw/Blog/post/multi-club-ownership-in-european-football-part-i-general-introduction-and-the-enic-saga-by-tomas-grell 24 Oct. 2017 (accessed 9 Jan. 2020).
296. *See*, for example, Art. 5 of the Regulations of the UEFA Champions League 2018-21 Cycle.
297. Case CAS 98/200, *AEK Athens and Slavia Prague v. UEFA*.

necessary to serve the fundamental goal of preventing conflicts of interest which would be publicly perceived as affecting the authenticity, and thus the uncertainty, of results in UEFA competitions'.[298] Despite confirming the validity of UEFA's rule, the CAS panel did stay its implementation in order to allow clubs time to adapt their operations to the new rule.[299]

174. In February 2000, ENIC lodged a complaint with the European Commission citing potential infringements of the rule with EU competition law. Its argument was that the rule prevents, restricts and distorts competition by: (1) preventing and restricting investment in European clubs; (2) changing the nature, intensity and patterns of competition between commonly controlled clubs and those having other ownership structures; (3) enhancing the economic imbalance between football clubs leading to increasing market dominance of a few clubs over the majority of smaller- and medium-sized clubs with the result of decreasing uncertainty in the outcome of the matches. Added to this, it cited the impact on clubs excluded from UEFA competitions which will lose a competitive edge on the transfer market and will be deprived of reputation and substantial revenues needed to retain and attract top-class players. Finally, ENIC claimed that the loss of opportunity to participate in UEFA competitions would have an economic impact on gate revenues and on sponsorship, merchandising and media rights arrangements.[300]

175. ENIC rejected UEFA's connection between multiple club ownership and a heightened risk of match-fixing and claimed that UEFA's dominant purpose for adopting the rule was to preserve its 'monopoly control over European football competitions'.[301] In making this allegation, ENIC claimed that the rule amounted not only to a restrictive practice under what is now Article 101 TFEU, but UEFA was also abusing its dominant position under Article 102 (Article 82 EC at the time of the Decision).

176. The Commission concluded its examination in July 2002 with the formal rejection of ENIC's complaint. In doing so, the Commission wisely declined to classify the rule as falling within *Walrave's* 'purely sporting' formula. Severing the considerable economic activity at issue – the ownership of clubs – from the sporting rule would have been a somewhat contrived exercise, and the Commission acknowledged that questions as to a competitions' integrity would impact on its marketability. Neither did the Commission attempt to assess the rule under the Article 101(3) exemption criteria.

177. Instead, the Commission found that the contested rule fell outside the scope of Article 101 (ex 81 EC). The *object* of the contested rule was not to distort competition, rather it aimed 'to ensure the uncertainty of the outcome and to guarantee

298. *Ibid.*, para. 136.
299. For a discussion *see* Ivan Cherpillod, *CAS 98/200 AEK Athens and Slavia Prague v UEFA*, in *CAS and Football: Landmark Cases* 11 (Alexander Wild ed., T.M.C. Asser Press 2011).
300. Case COMP/37 806: ENIC/UEFA, para. 14.
301. *Ibid.*, para. 15.

that the consumer has the perception that the games played represent honest sporting competition between the participants, as consumers may suspect that teams with a common owner will not genuinely compete'.[302]

178. As to the *effect* of the rule, the Commission stated that the possible effect on clubs and potential investors was inherent to the very existence of credible pan-European football competitions. The Commission found that '[w]ithout the UEFA rule, the proper functioning of the market where the clubs develop their economic activities would be under threat, since the public's perception that the underlying sporting competition is fair and honest is an essential precondition to keep its interest and marketability'.[303] Furthermore, the measure did not go beyond what was necessary to ensure the legitimate aim of protecting the uncertainty of the results and maintaining the integrity of the competition.

179. This decision is notable for its reliance on *Wouters*, a case concerning a Dutch rule prohibiting the creation of multidisciplinary partnerships between barristers and accountants.[304] Here, the Court of Justice stated that not all agreements between undertakings which restrict competition falls within the prohibition now laid down in Article 101 of the Treaty and that a contextual assessment must be made of whether the consequential effects restrictive of competition are inherent in the pursuit of legitimate objectives.[305]

180. It must be recalled that just prior to *ENIC*, this 'inherent rule' approach had found expression in *Deliège*, a case concerning the application of EU free movement to sport.[306] Even though *Deliège* was a sports case, *Wouters* was a competition case and that, no doubt, swayed the Commission's thinking on its reliance. For the Commission in *ENIC*, the consequential effects restrictive of competition felt by ENIC were inherent in the pursuit of UEFA's legitimate sporting objectives and as such were incapable of being defined as restrictions of competition. In that connection, a subtle difference with *Wouters* can be discerned. In *Wouters*, a necessary restriction of competition was identified, whereas in *ENIC* and *Deliège*, no restriction was identified. Regardless, the outcome is the same.

181. In its submission, UEFA argued that it has the responsibility to take appropriate measures to protect the integrity of competition without having 'a legal duty to divine the least restrictive alternative to protect integrity of competition'.[307] If that were not the case, according to UEFA, the European Commission would end up as the de facto regulator of sport. While acknowledging that the rule must comply with the principle of proportionality, UEFA considered that 'this does not mean

302. *Ibid.*, para. 28.
303. *Ibid.*, para. 32.
304. Case C-309/99 *J.C.J. Wouters, J.W. Savelbergh, Price Waterhouse Belastingadviseurs BV v. Algemene Raad van de Nederlandse Orde van Advocaten* [2002] ECR I-1577.
305. *Ibid.*, para. 97.
306. Joined Cases C-51/96 and C-191/97 *Deliège v. Ligue francophone de Judo et disciplines Associeés Asb* [2000] ECR I-2549.
307. Case COMP/37 806: ENIC/UEFA, para. 21.

that the rule would be necessarily illegal in the sole event that somebody conceives a less restrictive alternative to achieve the same objective'.[308] The Commission granted UEFA a wide margin of appreciation under proportionality control by dismissing some less restrictive alternatives and placing heavy emphasis not on the actual prospect of match-fixing, but the public's perception of it which if negative could cause serious damage to the integrity and viability of the competition.

182. The Commission also dismissed ENIC's argument that UEFA was abusing its position of dominance in the market for the organisation of European competitions, a position strengthened by the organisational structure of the European model of sport. Here, the Commission's analysis is less comprehensive than its assessment under Article 101. The Commission contended that even if UEFA is considered to enjoy a dominant position, there is no evidence of it abusing this position and there is no evidence that the contested rule was applied in a discriminatory manner to clubs liable to take part in its competitions.[309] ENIC decided not to appeal the Commission's Decision.

183. To date, the only other decided multiple club ownership case came in 2017, when the UEFA General Secretary referred to the UEFA Club Financial Control Body (CFCB) the case of Red Bull's influence over Leipzig and Salzburg. The case was heard by the CFCB Adjudicatory Chamber.[310] The case arose out of both clubs' qualification for the 2017/18 UEFA Champions League and a concern that the clubs did not comply with UEFA's multiple club ownership rule given that Red Bull exercised an alleged 'decisive influence' in both clubs.[311]

184. The Adjudicatory Chamber noted that Salzburg had made a number of changes in an attempt to address the possibility of Red Bull's decisive influence including removing certain individuals who were linked to Red Bull, terminating loan and cooperation agreements between the two entities, amending statutes and sponsorship agreements and rebranding the visual identity of its kit. In light of these disengagement initiatives, the Chamber found that the relationship between the club and Red Bull 'resembles only a standard sponsorship relationship' with no decisive influence evident.[312] Despite both clubs forging 'close co-operation' involving player transfers and a cooperation agreement, the Chamber also found no evidence of one club exercising a decisive influence over the other.[313] Having come to that conclusion, there was no need to assess the relationship between Red Bull and

308. *Ibid.*
309. *Ibid.*, para. 45.
310. Case AC-01/2017, *Rasenballsport Leipzig GMBH & FC Red Bull Salzburg GMBH*, UEFA Club Financial Control Body, Adjudicatory Chamber, 16 Jun. 2017.
311. *Ibid.*, para. 11. The decisive influence test was introduced after *ENIC* and it is set out in the UEFA regulations. For the 2019 edition, *see* UEFA, Regulations of the Champions League, Art. 5 – Integrity of the Competition.
312. Case AC-01/2017, *Rasenballsport Leipzig GMBH & FC Red Bull Salzburg GMBH*, para. 55.
313. Tomás Grell, *Multi-Club Ownership in European Football – Part II: The Concept of Decisive Influence in the Red Bull Case,* Asser International Sports Law Blog, https://www.asser.nl/SportsLaw/Blog/post/multi-club-ownership-in-european-football-part-ii-the-concept-of-decisive-influence-in-the-red-bull-case-by-tomas-grell 25 Oct. 17 (accessed 9 Jan. 2020).

Leipzig and accordingly both clubs could enter the UEFA Champions League. RB Leipzig and Red Bull Salzburg eventually met in the UEFA Europa League in 2018/19 season.

185. *ENIC* and *Red Bull* are the only source of guidance in this area, but multiple club ownership continues to be a source of debate in European football. Given the Commission's reliance on *Wouters*, a case that found expression again in the seminal *Meca-Medina* case, if a further challenge was forthcoming, the same methodological approach would no doubt be repeated. Given the prevalence of multiple club ownership in European football, and the ever-increasing financial importance of qualification to UEFA club competitions, the prospect of further challenge cannot be discounted. This prospect is probably heightened by the different regulatory regimes that operate at national association level, and the system devised by UEFA. For example, in some national associations, multiple club ownership is defined with reference to a low percentage of the shareholders voting rights, whereas the UEFA regulation prohibits multiple ownership where the entity holds a 'majority of the shareholders' voting rights'.[314] As some national associations adopt a more restrictive approach, a complaint could conceivably arise in a national court, competition authority or through national arbitration. UEFA's catch-all 'decisive influence' regulation may also be open to question from those who wish to test its precision. Ultimately, for the football authorities to secure the greatest level of legal certainty in this area, a harmonisation of national and UEFA measures should be considered.

§4. Third-Party Ownership

186. TPO refers to an agreement between a football club and a third party in which, in exchange for financial investment, the third party acquires an economic interest in a player. The third party receives a financial return on that investment by receiving a percentage of the transfer fee when the player is ultimately sold to another club. The term 'third party' implies a party other than the player being transferred, the two clubs transferring the player or any previous club with which the player has been registered.[315] Commonly, it refers to companies, investment funds, agencies, individual agents or private individuals.

---

314. For example, in the English Premier League, the threshold is 10%. *See* A.1.171 Premier League Handbook, 2018/19 season. For discussion *see* Daniel Geey, *Multiple Football Club Ownership: Disparities Between Rules*, https://www.danielgeey.com/post/multiple-football-club-ownership-disparities-between-rules/ (accessed 10 Jan 2020).

315. *See* 'Definitions', FIFA Regulations on the Status and Transfer of Players. An amendment in 2019 clarified that a player is not considered a third party, meaning that players can have a right to compensation related to their future transfer. For a discussion *see* Nick De Marco, *TPO in Football: What It Is, How It Is Developing, and What It Should Be*, Blackstone Chambers Sports Law Bulletin, https://www.sportslawbulletin.org/tpo-football-what-it-how-it-developing-and-what-it-should-be/ 6 Jan. 2020 (accessed 14 Jan. 2020).

187. Although a range of TPO models exists, the two most common are Financing and Investment TPO.[316] Financing TPO refers to an agreement whereby a third party, for a fee, acquires a financial interest in the economic rights of a player at a club. At the point at which the player is sold, the third party is entitled to a percentage of the transfer fee. Investment TPO facilitates a club acquiring a player. Under this model, a third party provides funds to a club which then uses this to purchase a player. The third party is entitled to a percentage of the transfer fee once that player is sold. Critics of the use of the term TPO point out that as a third party does not actually own the players' registration (federative) rights, rather just their economic (transfer fee) rights, a more accurate description is Third-Party Investment (TPI).

188. Some clubs favour TPO agreements because by sharing costs with third parties, it gives them access to players that would otherwise be out of their financial reach. This makes them more competitive and can go some way to address some of the financial, and hence sporting, imbalances that operate between leagues in Europe due to substantial differences in the value of broadcasting contracts. For example, historically, TPO has operated in Portugal where in 2017/18 the value of the broadcasting contract for top division football was EUR 225 million. By contrast, in the English Premier League which operated a prohibition on TPO, the equivalent contract was EUR 3210 million.[317] Without TPO, Portuguese clubs simply could not compete with the buying power of their English competitors. Investment TPO also allows clubs to secure short-term financing while retaining the playing talent in question. Financial difficulties for a club need not necessarily result in fire sales and the resultant diminution of sporting competitiveness. Of course, TPO comes at a cost to the club – they forego a percentage of the future transfer value of the player, and the autonomy of club decision-making can be potentially compromised if the third party can decide when the player is sold.

189. The attraction of TPO for the third party is obvious. TPO is a relatively low-risk means of securing substantial profit. TPO is a form of talent speculation but the risk to the third party is low. As some clubs struggle to secure finance at reasonable rates from financial institutions, third-party investors offer an alternative, but this places them at an advantage – they can draft contacts in such a way that they are guaranteed minimum returns on their investments. TPO is not entirely risk-free for an investor. Third parties are exposed should a club become insolvent, and there is a risk that a club could refuse to honour its agreement with a third party if the club cites incompatibility with national/EU laws or football regulations.[318]

---

316. For discussion on the TPO models *see* KMPG, *Project TPO*, https://www.ecaeurope.com/media/1682/tpo-report.pdf 8 Aug. 2013 (accessed 12 Jan. 2020).
317. Deloitte, *World in Motion: Annual Review of Football Finance 2019*, 9 (2019).
318. *See* CAS 2014/O/3781 & 3782, *Sporting Clube de Portugal Futebol SAD v. Doyen Sports Investment Limited*, Award of 21 Dec. 2015.

190. The prevalence of TPO in recent years has attracted the interest of the football regulators, FIFA, UEFA and the national associations.[319] The main concern with this practice is that it draws clubs into an unhealthy financial reliance on third parties and potentially compromises the autonomy of club decision-making, thus calling into question the integrity of the sport. The issue of financial reliance is illustrated by the example of FC Porto, who at one time owned 100% of the total economic transfer rights of only seven out of a squad of twenty-nine.[320] Club decision-making is said to be compromised if, in order to maximise returns, a third-party investor exerts undue influence over a club with the objective of effecting his sale when that player's transfer fee is calculated to be at its highest. This may conflict with the club's sporting strategy. This also calls into question the objective of contract stability that underpins the FIFA Regulations on the Status and Transfer of Players (RSTP)[321] and, potentially, the UEFA Regulations on FFP. The argument here is that clubs that enter into TPO agreements do not have to account for 100% of player transfers, unlike clubs in leagues where TPO is prohibited. TPO clubs therefore gain an advantage in terms of FFP compliance.

191. Some object to TPO on moral grounds. First, it is claimed that TPO results in too much money leaving football. This argument may have merit if connected to issues of fulfilling financial solidarity functions in football, but as a purely financial consideration, it is unlikely to be considered a legitimate sporting objective by a court.[322] Second, others believe that the suggestion that human beings can be part-owned, like racehorses, is distasteful and ethically and morally questionable. Some have even suggested that TPO is akin to slavery. Lindholm argues that these analogies are 'entirely misplaced' as TPO does not equate with ownership of a player and the same criticism could be labelled at the transfer system generally whereby players are traded for money between clubs.[323]

192. For some time, FIFA has regulated third-party *influence*. Article 18bis RSTP provides that '[n]o club shall enter into a contract which enables the counter club/counter clubs, and vice versa, or any third party to acquire the ability to influence in employment and transfer-related matters its independence, its policies or the

319. For a review of developments and cases *see* Nick De Marco, Ariel Reck & Pedro Fida, *Third Party Investment*, in *Football and the Law* 183 (Nick De Marco QC ed., Bloomsbury 2018).

320. KEA European Affairs & CDES, *The Economic and Legal Aspects of Transfer of Players*, at https://ec.europa.eu/assets/eac/sport/library/documents/cons-study-transfers-final-rpt.pdf January 2013 (accessed 13 Jan. 2020).

321. *See* s. IV of the FIFA RSTP.

322. *See* Johan Lindholm, *Can I Please Have a Slice of Ronaldo? The Legality of FIFA's Ban on Third Party Ownership Under European Union Law*, 15 ISLJ 137–148 (2016).

323. The former Premier League Chief Executive compared it to 'indentured slavery', former UEFA President referred to it as 'a type of slavery' and FIFPro stated that it is a type of 'modern-day slavery'. All cited in Johan Lindholm, *Can I Please Have a Slice of Ronaldo? The Legality of FIFA's Ban on Third Party Ownership under European Union Law*, 15 ISLJ 137–148 (2016). The slavery analogy is also rejected by Nick De Marco, Ariel Reck & Pedro Fida, *Third Party Investment*, in *Football and the Law* 211 (Nick De Marco QC ed., Bloomsbury 2018) in which the authors provide a comprehensive assessment of the advantages and disadvantages of TPO.

performance of its teams'.[324] This provision, in its original form, was intended to protect the autonomy of club decision and it did not foresee the rise of the TPO model.

193. In May 2015, FIFA introduced a new provision designed to capture TPO scenarios. Article 18ter RSTP ('Third Party Ownership of Players' Economic Rights) provides that '[n]o club or player shall enter into an agreement with a third party whereby a third party is being entitled to participate, either in full or in part, in compensation payable in relation to the future transfer of a player from one club to another, or is being assigned any rights in relation to a future transfer or transfer compensation'. FIFA's objectives for this new provision were set out in CAS proceedings after a club sought to challenge them. FIFA stated that the objective is 'the preservation of the stability of player contracts, to guarantee the independence and autonomy of clubs and players in terms of recruitment and transfers, safeguarding integrity in football and fair and equitable nature of competitions, prevention of conflicts of interest and maintaining transparency in transactions related to transfers of players'.[325]

194. With FIFA's amendment, TPO is now prohibited worldwide. Prior to this, only the national associations of England, France and Poland had enacted TPO prohibitions, although UEFA had called for such a ban 'as a matter of principle' in 2012.[326] The ban in England stemmed from fallout from the Tevez and Mascherano affair in 2007. Both players were TPO players who were transferred to West Ham United in the English Premier League. At the time, the practice was only regulated by Article 18bis RSTP and a similar provision in the Premier League Regulations, but West Ham was in breach of this by concealing the true relationship between the players and the third party. West Ham received a fine but avoided a points deduction that would have relegated them.[327] This sanction resulted in the relegation of Sheffield United who sought to challenge the leniency of the sanction.[328] In light of the problems the case caused for the English football authorities, in 2008 the Football Association, Premier League and Football League agreed to introduce an outright prohibition on TPO in England, the view being that 'if any form of TPI was permitted, then third party influence was inevitable'.[329]

195. With TPO prohibited globally, a number of parties have sought to test the ban against the requirements of EU law. One prominent case concerned Belgian football club RFC Seraing who had entered into TPO agreements with Maltese 'third-party', Doyen Sports Investment Limited. In light of its TPO prohibition,

324. Art. 18 bis, FIFA RSTP, 2019 edition.
325. Authors' translation from CAS 2016/A/4490 *RFC Seraing v. FIFA*.
326. UEFA, *UEFA Welcomes Brussels Court of Appeal Ruling on Third-Party Ownership*, https://www.uefa.com/insideuefa/protecting-the-game/integrity/news/newsid=2637091.html 14 Dec. 2019 (accessed 13 Jan. 2020).
327. *FAPL v. West Ham United*, FAPL Disciplinary Committee, 27 Apr. 2007.
328. *Sheffield United FC v. West Ham United FC*, FA Rule K Arbitration, 2009.
329. Nick De Marco, Ariel Reck & Pedro Fida, *Third Party Investment*, in *Football and the Law* 199 (Nick De Marco QC ed., Bloomsbury 2018).

FIFA initiated an investigation and its Disciplinary Commission imposed a fine and a transfer ban of four registration periods on RFC Seraing, a sanction confirmed by the FIFA Appeal Committee. Seraing sought interim relief in the Belgian Courts to prevent FIFA from implementing the ban and they appealed FIFA's sanction to CAS. Although Seraing is the chief complainant, it was considered the vehicle through which Doyen sought to challenge FIFA's TPO ban.[330]

196. At first instance, the Brussels Regional Court found no breach of EU law.[331] On appeal, in 2018, the Brussels Court of Appeal took two significant decisions.[332] First, it declined Seraing's invitation to refer the case to the Court of Justice of the European Union thus, at this stage at least, denying the opportunity for the legality of the TPO ban to be ultimately tested against the requirements of EU law. Second, it rejected the arguments presented by FIFA and UEFA that the Brussels Court was not competent to hear the case due to a valid arbitration clause being in place. FIFA Statutes require parties to submit disputes to arbitration, ultimately CAS, rather than courts. However, the Court found that the clause in question was too vague and lacked a defined legal relationship, in that it did not sufficiently specify the nature of the disputes that can be arbitrated. In other words, FIFA intended the arbitration clause to capture all disputes, including those involving clubs, whereas the Court considered this too broad for validity under Belgium law and the New York Convention.

197. The significance of this decision is twofold. First, it requires FIFA, and other relevant sports bodies, to sharpen arbitration clauses so as to define more clearly the types of disputes that are subject to arbitration, but it does not fundamentally undermine the principle that these bodies can draft and rely on such clauses. The impact on CAS and the *lex sportiva* should not, therefore, be 'exaggerated'.[333] Second, the decision prolonged Seraing's case as a finding in the reverse would have ended their claim. Unfortunately for Seraing, when the Court returned to the case the following year, it dismissed Seraing's substantive challenge to FIFA's TPO ban thus ending the litigation in Belgium.[334]

---

330. This is the view expressed by Antoine Duval, *RFC Seraing at the Court of Arbitration for Sport: How FIFA's TPO Ban Survived (Again) EU Law Scrutiny*, Asser International Sports Law Blog, https://www.asser.nl/SportsLaw/Blog/post/rfc-seraing-at-the-court-of-arbitration-for-sport-how-fifa-s-tpo-ban-survived-again-eu-law-scrutiny 26 Apr. 2017 (accessed 13 Jan. 2020). For additional background to the litigation *see* Charlotte Peiffer, RFC *Seraing & Doyen Sports v FIFA: Changing the Rules of the Game in International Sports Arbitration?* N. Y. Univ. J. Int. Law Politics, 1359, http://nyujilp.org/wp-content/uploads/2019/09/NYI410.pdf 29/07/19 (accessed 14 Jan. 2020).
331. Regional Court of Brussels, Judgment of 24 Jul. 2015.
332. Brussels Court of Appeal, Judgment of 18 Aug. 2018.
333. For discussion *see* Antoine Duval, *Seraing v FIFA: Why Rumours of CAS's Death Have been Greatly Exaggerated*, Asser International Sports Law Blog, https://www.asser.nl/SportsLaw/Blog/post/seraing-vs-fifa-why-the-rumours-of-cas-s-death-have-been-greatly-exaggerated 10 Sep. 18 (accessed 14 Jan. 2020).
334. Brussels Court of Appeal, Judgment of 12 Dec. 2019. *See* also FIFA, *FIFA Welcomes Brussels Court of Appeal Ruling on FIFA's TPO and TPI Rules*, https://www.fifa.com/about-fifa/who-we-are/news/fifa-welcomes-brussels-court-of-appeal-ruling-on-fifa-s-tpo-and-tpi-rules 13 Dec. 2019 (accessed 14 Jan. 2020).

198. With regards Seraing's appeal to CAS against the FIFA sanction, the case is notable for being one of the few occasions in which the appellants' request for EU law to apply was accepted and wholeheartedly embraced by the CAS, even though it missed the opportunity to reference the impact of Article 165 TFEU.[335] This is a welcome development and one that, if employed more widely, will further protect, rather than undermine the emerging *lex sportiva* by underscoring the credibility of its decision-making.[336]

199. Seraing claimed that Articles 18bis and 18ter infringe EU free movement and competition laws. In the case, the CAS panel first considered the relationship between 18bis and 18ter and EU provisions on the free movement of capital (Article 63 TFEU). To date, the Court of Justice has yet to decide a case on sport and free movement of capital and the question of whether the provision can be relied on by private parties, such as an investor, was also 'unchartered territory' for the Court of Justice.[337] Lindholm argues that it would be 'quite certain' that an individual would be able to invoke Article 63 against FIFA based on the Court's treatment of sports bodies in *Walrave*.[338] In other words, the objectives of EU law could be defeated if private entities could erect obstacles to free movement. The CAS panel skipped this assessment and noted that the FIFA provisions establish a restriction under Article 63 TFEU but that FIFA was pursuing legitimate objectives, summarised above. In doing so, CAS rejected the argument that FIFA's real objectives were to guarantee that financial flows generated by player transfers remain within football clubs. Seraing provided no evidence of this assertion.

200. With regard to the application of Article 45 TFEU governing the free movement of workers, Seraing argued that FIFA's ban limits the opportunities available to some EU players to secure cross-border employment as TPO arrangements provide opportunities for clubs to recruit players who would normally be out of reach for the club. Seraing's somewhat contrived claim under Article 56 TFEU (free movement of services) was that the ban would restrict a club's financing opportunities resulting in a deflationary effect on player costs and a limitation on the fees players' agent are able to claim. CAS considered that the effect of FIFA's TPO ban on player mobility is uncertain and that the free movement of services and agent fees question was hypothetical. In any event, even if restrictions under Articles 45

335. CAS 2016/A/4490 – *RFC Seraing v. FIFA*.

336. Those that have argued for CAS applying EU law more systematically to cases include Antoine Duval, *The Court of Arbitration for Sport and EU Law: Chronicle of an Encounter*, 22(2) MJECL (2015) and Richard Parrish, *Article 17 of the FIFA Regulations on the Status and Transfer of Players: Compatibility with EU Law*, 22(2) MJECL (2015). In European Parliament Report on the European Dimension in Sport, 21 Nov. 2011, 2011/2087 (INI), the rapporteur recommended the establishment of a European Chamber of CAS.

337. Antoine Duval, *RFC Seraing at the Court of Arbitration for Sport: How FIFA's TPO Ban Survived (Again) EU Law Scrutiny*, Asser International Sports Law Blog, https://www.asser.nl/SportsLaw/Blog/post/rfc-seraing-at-the-court-of-arbitration-for-sport-how-fifa-s-tpo-ban-survived-again-eu-law-scrutiny 26 Apr. 2017 (accessed 13 Jan. 2020).

338. Johan Lindholm, *Can I Please Have a Slice of Ronaldo? The Legality of FIFA's Ban on Third Party Ownership under European Union Law*, 15 ISLJ 137–148 (2016).

and 56 TEFU could be identified, the panel considered that FIFA justified the existence of the restriction with reference to the pursuit of the legitimate sporting objectives discussed above.

201. CAS also examined the claim that the FIFA TPO ban was incompatible with EU competition law. Seraing's claim was that the TPO ban restricted player recruitment and would lead to competitive imbalances in European football as second-order clubs would lose one means of competing with first-order teams. The competitive balance argument was acknowledged in a study for the European Commission in which the authors stated that the TPO ban 'might actually worsen the current unbalances of the system, because of the difficulties for smaller clubs to receive external forms of investments'.[339] Following closely the approach of the European Court and European Commission, CAS found that FIFA's decision to prohibit TPO was a decision of an association of undertakings and that trade between Member States was affected. However, it rejected the substance of Seraing's claim. In doing so, it noted that the burden of proof fell on Seraing and that it had supplied no evidence of restrictive effects being present. In any event, CAS found that Articles 18bis and 18ter did not intend to restrict, prevent or distort competition but rather regulate the player transfer market in order to pursue legitimate sporting objectives. The reasoning of CAS was, therefore, in line with that of the Court of Justice in *Wouters* and *Meca-Medina* in that not all restrictions of competition fall within the prohibitions established in Article 101 TFEU and that a contextual assessment of the rule must be made. The Article 102 TFEU claim concerning an abuse of a dominant position was also rejected with reference to FIFA's pursuit of legitimate objectives.[340]

202. Much of the above analysis, focussing as it did on the legitimacy of sporting objectives, was somewhat of an open goal for CAS. As Duval reminds us, no sports case in front of the Court of Justice has been lost on the grounds that the contested rule lacked a legitimate sporting objective and indeed in the case, Seraing did not contest the legitimacy of FIFA's claimed objectives.[341] Arguably, the real contribution of the CAS decision in this case was its scrutiny of the question of proportionality under its Article 63 TFEU analysis. Aficionados of EU sports law are aware that since the Court's judgment in *Meca-Medina*, the question of the proportionality of sporting rules has achieved heightened significance. Here CAS made a number of observations.

---

339. KEA European Affairs and ECORYS, *An Update on Change Drivers and Economic and Legal Implications of Transfers of Players: Final Report to the DG Education, Youth, Culture and Sport of the European Commission*, 56 (2018).
340. For the sake of completeness, it should be noted that the CAS also rejected arguments in relation to the application of the European Convention of Human Rights, the EU Fundamental Rights Charter and Swiss Law.
341. Antoine Duval, *RFC Seraing at the Court of Arbitration for Sport: How FIFA's TPO Ban Survived (Again) EU Law Scrutiny*, Asser International Sports Law Blog, https://www.asser.nl/SportsLaw/Blog/post/rfc-seraing-at-the-court-of-arbitration-for-sport-how-fifa-s-tpo-ban-survived-again-eu-law-scrutiny 26 Apr. 2017 (accessed 13 Jan. 2020).

203. First, the restrictive effects of the TPO ban are limited as only TPO investments and not all investments by third parties are prohibited. Second, CAS acknowledged that Article 18ter was introduced after a significant phase of independent study and consultation. This observation was disputed by La Liga, who claimed that the two independent studies commissioned by FIFA did not support the prohibition on TPO, the FIFA Working Party on TPO only held one meeting prior to the ban and FIFA did not consult governments, authorities or the EU prior to the ban.[342] Third, a number of years had elapsed between the adoption of the more limited Article 18bis and the outright ban introduced by Article 18ter RSTP and this period was sufficient for FIFA to conclude that 18bis was insufficient to achieve the objectives pursued. Fourth, CAS agreed with FIFA that only an outright ban on TPO agreements is capable of achieving the stated objectives as a complete lack of transparency in TPO arrangements and an absence of any means of football authorities exercising any control over investors renders less restrictive means of regulation ineffective. The reverse argument was not aired – that an outright ban is likely to push the practice underground, thus compounding the transparency deficit.[343] Finally, CAS pointed to existing TPO bans in France, England and Poland and argued that FIFA was legitimately seeking to harmonise standards.[344]

204. In light of the above, CAS confirmed the FIFA sanction on Seraing but reduced the transfer ban from four registration periods to three. Seraing appealed the CAS decision to the SFT on the grounds, *inter alia*, that CAS was not a true arbitral tribunal due to its lack of independence from FIFA and its reliance on it for cases, and that by endorsing FIFA's ban, CAS had acted in violation of substantive public policy.[345] The SFT effectively closed off Seraing's litigation in Switzerland by finding that CAS is an independent arbitral tribunal having sufficient independence from FIFA, despite the volume of business FIFA put its way.[346]

205. In parallel to the above, in 2015 the European Commission received a number of complaints from, among others, RFC Seraing, Doyen and the Spanish and Portuguese leagues.[347] Countering this move, UEFA and FIFPro launched their own

342. Oskar van Maren et al, *Debating FIFA's TPO Ban*, Asser International Sports Law Blog Symposium, 3–4 ISLJ 233 (2015).
343. As outlined in KEA European Affairs and ECORYS, *An Update on Change Drivers and Economic and Legal Implications of Transfers of Players: Final Report to the DG Education, Youth, Culture and Sport of the European Commission*, 41 (2018).
344. For a discussion on less restrictive alternatives and TPO generally *see* Johan Lindholm, *Can I Please Have a Slice of Ronaldo? The Legality of FIFA's Ban on Third Party Ownership Under European Union Law*, 15 ISLJ 137 (2016).
345. For discussion *see* Despina Mavromati, *The Validity of FIFA's Arbitration Clause and the Independence of the CAS: A Detailed Review of the RFC Seraing Cases*, LawInSport https://www.lawinsport.com/topics/item/the-validity-of-fifa-s-arbitration-clause-and-the-independence-of-the-cas-a-detailed-review-of-the-rfc-seraing-cases 4 Oct. 2018 (accessed 13 Jan. 2020).
346. Judgment of the Swiss Federal Tribunal, Case 4A_260/2017, *Seraing v. FIFA*, 20 Feb. 2018.
347. *See*, for example, La Liga, *Las ligas española y portuguesa denuncian ante la Comisión Europea la prohibición de los TPO de la FIFA*, https://www.laliga.com/noticias/las-ligas-espanola-y-portuguesa-denuncian-ante-la-comision-europea-la-prohibicion-de-los-tpo-de-la-fifa 9 Feb. 2015 (accessed 13 Jan. 2020).

complaint with the Commission, questioning the legality of TPO.[348] In 2017, the European Commission informed the complainants that it did not intend initiating formal proceedings and that 'potential conflicts of interests between clubs, players, and investors resulting from third-party ownership of players justify the proportionality of the absolute ban'.[349] With this, and the decisions of the Brussels Court of Appeal, CAS and the SFT, FIFA's legitimacy to regulate TPO by way of an outright ban appears to be secure. Only a referral from a national court to the European Court could undermine this confidence, although the reasoning of CAS is, in the authors' view, likely to find favour in Luxembourg.

§5. Club Location, Cross-Border Leagues and Breakaways

206. In *Bosman*, the Court of Justice helped liberalise the European player market by permitting players to move cross-border without undue restriction. Overseas players are now a common sight within national football leagues across Europe. Far less common is the sight of a club playing in one national league but being located in the territory of another country. Perhaps the best-known examples are the presence of Welsh clubs Cardiff City, Swansea City, Newport County and Wrexham in the English leagues. But little-known Berwick Rangers, an English team, play in Scotland and Derry City, a team located in Northern Ireland, play in the Republic of Ireland. These examples can be explained as historical peculiarities, and those not familiar with football governance in Europe might not even consider these as examples of cross-border movement at all. After all, these clubs are located in one country, the UK, even though for FIFA and UEFA purposes, the UK is composed of four national football associations.

207. The European landscape is littered with historical examples with the only major current case being AS Monaco, from the city-state country of Monaco, who play in France. A not entirely complete list of other examples includes San Marino Calcio who play in Italy, FC Andorra who play in Spain, Liechtenstein club FC Vaduz play in the Swiss leagues, Spanish team Union Esportiva de Bossost play in France and German club FC Büsingen play in Switzerland. The incentives of being located in one country while playing in another are heightened if the home league is relatively small and underdeveloped commercially, whereas the host league offers better sporting and financial opportunities.

208. A number of teams have explored the option of cross-border moves. Wimbledon FC, at the time an English Premier League team, proposed a move to Dublin while retaining its share in the Premier League. Faced with low attendances at its South London home, Wimbledon expected to attract much higher gates and

348. UEFA, *UEFA and FIFPro Launch Complaint Against Third-Party Ownership*, https://www.uefa.com/insideuefa/stakeholders/players-unions/news/newsid=2230203.html?redirectFromOrg=true 1 Apr. 2015 (accessed 13 Jan. 2020).

349. Branislav Hock & Suren Gomtsian, *Private Order Building: The State in the Role of the Civil Society and the Case of FIFA*, 17 ISLJ 197 (2018).

hence higher revenues when playing its 'home' matches in Dublin. The move never happened, and Wimbledon eventually relocated to Milton Keynes, an English town some 75 km from London. The move, and the clubs rebranding as Milton Keynes Dons FC, was criticised as soulless US-style 'franchising'.[350] Scottish league side Clydebank also explored the possibility of relocating to Dublin and like Wimbledon wished to continue playing in their home (Scottish) league.[351] It is frequently reported that Scottish clubs Celtic and Rangers are interested in joining the English league[352] and that a number of top Dutch clubs want to join the German Bundesliga.

209. Another model, often proposed, is for the creation of cross-border leagues, either organised within the current governing body structure or outside – so-called breakaway structures. Cross-border leagues are a feature of some sports. For example, an all-Ireland competition has operated in Rugby Union since 1990, and in Rugby League, English and French clubs participate in the Super League competition, which since 2017 also includes a team from Canada. In football, such leagues do not exist but are frequently discussed. Cross-border leagues mooted include an all-Ireland league,[353] a Dutch/Belgian league,[354] an Atlantic League composed of clubs from Scotland, the Netherlands, Belgium, Denmark, Norway and Sweden,[355] a Czech-Slovak league, a Balkan league and a 'Habsburg League' in Central and Eastern Europe.[356]

210. Some commentators have argued that sporting competition within and between the European leagues will always be unbalanced unless the product market is liberalised in the same way that the European labour market was following *Bosman*.[357] Allowing new cross-border leagues to develop is one means of granting large clubs in small national markets the ability to compete more equally with clubs

350. Guardian, *Wimbledon Become MK Dons FC*, https://www.theguardian.com/football/2004/jun/21/newsstory.mkdons 21 Jun. 2004 (accessed 14 Jan. 2020).
351. Alistair Duff, *Scottish Update: A Brief Synopsis of Newsworthy Matters Concerning Football, Rugby & Others from 1997 to Date*, 6(3) Sport & the L.J. (1997).
352. The Scotsman, *Celtic and Rangers Joining the English Premier League Would 'Save Scottish Football', Claims Steven Gerrard*, https://www.scotsman.com/sport/football/celtic/celtic-and-rangers-joining-the-english-premier-league-would-save-scottish-football-claims-steven-gerrard-1-5072488 9 Jan. 2020 (accessed 14 Jan. 2020).
353. Reuters, *Irish Clubs Set to Meet to Discuss a New Cross-Border League*, https://uk.reuters.com/article/uk-soccer-ireland-league/irish-clubs-set-to-meet-to-discuss-a-new-cross-border-league-idUKKBN1WX23R 18 Oct. 2019 (accessed 14 Jan. 2020).
354. i News, *Dutch and Belgian Football Associations in Talks to Create Cross-Border Superleague*, https://inews.co.uk/news/dutch-belgian-football-superleague-cross-border-uefa-proposal-506046 19 Oct. 2019 (accessed 14 Jan. 2020).
355. BBC, *Atlantic League: 'A Bad Idea, But Absolutely Necessary'*, https://www.bbc.co.uk/sport/football/37727876 21 Oct. 2016 (accessed 14 Jan. 2020).
356. Reuters, *FIFA May Be Open to 'Cross-Border' Leagues – Infantino*, https://www.reuters.com/article/uk-soccer-fifa-leagues/fifa-may-be-open-to-cross-border-leagues-infantino-idUKKBN1YO1E6 20 Dec.2019 (accessed 14 Jan. 2020).
357. Stefan Késenne, *The Bosman Case and European Football*, in *Handbook on the Economics of Sport* 632–641 (Wladimir Andreff & Stefan Szymanski eds, Edward Elgar 2006) and Stefan Késenne, *The Peculiar International Economics of Professional Football in Europe*, 54(3) Scott. J. Political. Econ. 388–399 (2007).

in larger national markets. In football, these arguments are beginning to find traction with FIFA, a traditionally staunch proponent of the national football governance structure, signalling a softening of its attitude.[358] This view might reflect a growing realisation that the best way of protecting the national structure of the European model of sport is to embrace change as a means of heading off a growing breakaway threat.

211. The threat of a breakaway league in European football has been mooted for many years.[359] In 1998, Italian marketing firm Media Partners International Limited complained to the European Commission that UEFA's approval policy for alternative competitions amounted to an abuse of a dominant market position under EU competition law. In February 1999, Media Partners then notified the Commission of their intention to establish a new European Football League (EFL), independent of UEFA, comprising two main pan-European football competitions, the Super League and the ProCup involving a total of 132 clubs from across the UEFA-affiliated associations.[360] A total of 18 founder clubs committed themselves to participate in the EFL exclusively for a three-year period, thereby establishing an effective closed league, although provision was made for new entrants based on national league performance. Participants would assign all intellectual property rights, including media rights, to the EFL.

212. Ultimately, the Media Partners proposal was not implemented as the top European clubs accepted UEFA's proposal to reform the European Cup and establish the Champions League in 1991/92. The European Cup ran on the basis of only national league title winners qualifying with other clubs entering the less prestigious, but arguably more competitive, UEFA Cup. As both competitions were organised on a knockout basis, clubs risked their participation being restricted to two games. Wanting more guaranteed fixtures and hence income, the clubs accepted a reformed competition under UEFA control in which clubs, other than just the national champion, could qualify and take part in a league structure. These competitions are now known as the Champions League and the Europa League. While UEFA's actions headed off the immediate threat of a breakaway, the creation of the Champions League has resulted in a renewed interest in alternative football structures, for two reasons. First, teams that routinely qualify for the financially lucrative Champions League also play in domestic leagues and compete with teams who do not have access to that revenue. Competitive balance in European leagues has suffered as a result, and the creation of cross-border leagues, discussed above, is seen as one possible solution to this. Second, the success of the reformed UEFA club competitions highlighted to leading clubs the financial potential of this type of format, particularly if income distribution was restricted to the founder members only.

358. Reuters, *FIFA May Be Open to 'Cross-Border' Leagues – Infantino*, https://www.reuters.com/article/uk-soccer-fifa-leagues/fifa-may-be-open-to-cross-border-leagues-infantino-idUKKBN1YO1E6 20 Dec. 2019 (accessed 14 Jan. 2020).

359. Breakaways have been mooted in other sports. *See*, for example, Lloyd Freeburn, *A Breakaway League in Professional Cycling: Issues for the Governance and Organisation of the Sport*, 13(3/4) ISLJ 193 (2013).

360. Case No. IV/37.400 – Project Gandalf, OJ C 70, 13 Mar. 1999.

In 2018, *De Spiegel* released leaked documents claiming that elite European football clubs were seeking to establish a new Super League.[361] It was reported that, once again, UEFA agreed to amend the Champions League qualification and financial distributions in order to avoid this development.[362]

213. There has, to date, been little scrutiny of club location issues in European sport. In *Mouscron*, the Commission was asked to consider the temporary relocation of a club from Belgian to France. Belgian football club Excelsior Mouscron made a request to UEFA to stage the home leg of a 1997/98 UEFA Cup tie against French side F.C. Metz in a nearby stadium in Lille, France. Mouscron's request was due to the limited capacity of its stadium and the opportunity to play the match in a larger one. UEFA blocked the move referring to the home and away structure of its competitions which required clubs to play their home matches on the ground of the home club or on another ground in the same or another city within the territory of its national association. The French Communauté Urbaine de Lille lodged a complaint challenging UEFA's home and away rule, on the grounds that it amounted to an abuse of its dominant market position.

214. In an unpublished Decision, the Commission rejected the complaint on *de minimis* grounds; in other words, there was insufficient EU interest to intervene.[363] In the press release accompanying the Decision, the Commission stated that the rule constituted a sporting rule that did not fall within the scope of EU competition law.[364] Commenting on the case in the 2007 White Paper on Sport, the Commission stated that the 'the organisation of football on a national territorial basis was not called into question by Community law' as the rule was 'indispensable for the organisation of national and international competitions in view of ensuring equality of chances between clubs' and that it did not go beyond what was necessary[365] In the Communication on Sport, the Commission discussed the relevance of Article 165 TFEU and stated the specific nature of sport 'encompasses all the characteristics that make sport special, such as for instance the interdependence between competing adversaries or the pyramid structure of open competitions'.[366]

215. From the above, and considering the guidance provided by *Meca-Medina*, the so-called home and away rule under challenge in *Mouscron* appears secure

361. Spiegel International, *Documents Show Secret Plans for Elite League of Top Clubs*, https://www.spiegel.de/international/world/football-documents-show-secret-plans-for-elite-league-of-top-clubs-a-1236447.html 2 Nov. 2018 (accessed 17 Jan. 2020).
362. The Guardian, *Der Spiegel's Email Leaks More Evidence that Elite Will Never Be Satisfied*, https://www.theguardian.com/football/2018/nov/03/der-spiegel-email-leaks-european-super-league-show-elite-will-never-be-satisfied 3 Nov. 2018 (accessed 17 Jan. 2020).
363. Unpublished Commission Decision of 9 Dec. 1999, Case 36851, C.U. de Lille/UEFA (Mouscron).
364. European Commission, *Limits to application of Treaty competition rules to sport: Commission gives clear signal*, DN: IP/99/965, 9 Dec. 1999.
365. European Commission, *Commission staff working document. Impact assessment accompanying the White Paper on Sport*, SEC(2007) 935 final (2007), s. 2.2.1.2.
366. European Commission, *Communication from the Commission to the European Parliament, the Council, the European Economic and Social Committee and the Committee of the Regions – Developing the European Dimension in Sport*, 11 COM(2011) 12 final (2011).

under EU law.[367] The rule is designed to secure equality of chances under an organisational model structured along national leagues lines. In this light, the rule could be considered inherent in the pursuit of that objective. However, this analysis could be questioned if FIFA and UEFA were to sanction the formation of cross-border leagues in Europe. This would alter the national character of the pyramid and call into question the organisational necessity of requiring a team to play its home matches in its home state when the league in which it operates is organised on cross-border lines.

216. More intriguing is the question of how EU law would consider the breakaway scenario.[368] Much of the discussion entered into above concerning *ISU* and authorisation rules in sport are applicable to this question so there is no need to repeat it. The starting point is that there is nothing objectionable per se in EU law preventing a sports body adopting authorisation rules or, indeed, a third-party event organiser from ignoring them and establishing its own competition. The rule in question stems from Article 49 of the UEFA Statutes which provides that 'UEFA shall have the sole jurisdiction to organise or abolish international competitions in Europe in which Member Associations and/or their clubs participate ... International matches, competitions or tournaments which are not organised by UEFA but are played on UEFA's territory shall require the prior approval of FIFA and/or UEFA and/or the relevant Member Associations in accordance with FIFA Regulations Governing International matches and any additional implementing rules adopted by the UEFA Executive Committee.'[369] Should a club participate in any competition in breach of the above, sanctions will be imposed. The issue for UEFA is connecting this rule to the proportionate pursuit of legitimate sporting objectives, as per *ISU*, and ensuring that conflicts of interest do not contaminate the rule.

217. Should a breakaway league be established, EU law would, no doubt, be asked to intervene. Least objectionable under EU law would be a breakaway league based on open, transparent and non-discriminatory access conditions, such as a merit-based open system of promotion and relegation.[370] A closed or semi-closed league, similar to the one proposed in the Media Partners proposal, could raise market foreclosure concerns and it risks contradicting the Treaty's concern for 'fairness

367. This is the view of Stephen Weatherill, *Principles and Practice in EU Sports Law* 268–269 (Oxford Univ. Press 2017).
368. Perhaps the only monograph-length enquiry into this is supplied by Katarina Pijetlovic, *EU Sports Law and Breakaway Leagues in Football* (T.M.C. Asser Press 2015). An early discussion of it was provided by Jens Van den Brink, *E.C. Competition Law and the Regulation of Football: Part 1*, 21(8) ECL Rev. 359 (2000).
369. Art. 49, UEFA Statutes, 2018 edition.
370. Richard Parrish & Samuli Miettinen, *The Sporting Exception in European Union Law* 214 (T.M.C. Asser Press 2008).

and openness in sporting competitions'.[371] As is discussed elsewhere in this monograph, since *TopFit*, the wording of Article 165 can no longer be dismissed as hollow words.[372]

§6. Player Release

218. The organisational principle of 'one federation per sport per country' places national team sport at the heart of the European model. As is explained above, the ability of sports governing bodies to adopt authorisation rules allows them to control the sporting calendar. This means an international federation can create space to schedule certain priority competitions, particularly those involving national representative teams. National team sports not only are very popular among Europe's public but also drive very important revenues for the governing bodies. For example, FIFA's 2018 Financial Report highlighted how its revenue reached USD 6,421 million, of which USD 5,357 million or 83% was delivered by the 2018 FIFA World Cup in Russia.[373] This revenue allows FIFA to pay for its administration and make financial payments to its member associations to support the development of the game. At national association level, national team sport is a crucial source of income, and for some sports, such as cricket, national team sports revenues are the 'lifeblood of the sport'.[374]

219. In order to ensure the survival of national team competitions, and hence the revenues derived from them, sports bodies have adopted player release rules. The FIFA provisions, expressed in the FIFA RSTP, provides that '[c]lubs are obliged to release their registered players to the representative teams of the country for which the player is eligible to play on the basis of his nationality if they are called up by the association concerned. Any agreement between a player and a club to the contrary is prohibited'.[375] This provision is mandatory for all international windows listed in the international match calendar, a calendar set by FIFA after consultation with stakeholders.[376]

220. The regulations make no provision for the releasing clubs to receive compensation for the loss of its player. The Association calling up a player is expected to bear the costs of travel actually incurred by the player as a result of the call-up.

---

371. Art. 165(2) TFEU. For an interesting discussion on a closed league in eSports *see* Thomas Terraz, *Can a Closed League in e-Sports Survive EU Competition Law Scrutiny?* Asser International Sports Law Blog, https://www.asser.nl/SportsLaw/Blog/?tag=/EU-Law 8 Aug. 2019 (accessed 17 Jan. 2020).
372. Case C-22/18 *TopFit e.V. and Daniele Biffi v. Deutscher Leichtathletikverband e.V.* [2019] EU:C:2019:497.
373. FIFA, *Financial Report 2018*, https://resources.fifa.com/image/upload/xzshsoe2ayttyquuxhq0.pdf (accessed 17 Jul. 2019).
374. Adam Lewis & Jonathan Taylor, *Sport: Law and Practice* A2.18 (Bloomsbury 2014).
375. Annex 1, Art. 1, FIFA RSTP, 2018 edition.
376. FIFA also operates player release rules for the women's game and for futsal.

The club for which the player concerned is registered is responsible for his insurance cover against illness and accident during the entire period of his release. This cover must also extend to any injuries sustained by the player during the international match for which he was released.[377] The Regulations require every player who has received a call-up to 'respond affirmatively' save for if he is verifiably injured or ill.[378] If called up, the player cannot play for his club team during the duration of the call-up. Violations of these player release provisions can result in disciplinary measures being applied by the FIFA Disciplinary Committee based on the FIFA disciplinary Code.

221. The legality of player release rules has yet to be tested under EU law, but in *L'Affaire Oulmers*, known as *Chareroi*, the Court of Justice came close to doing so. In this case, a Charleroi player, Abdelmajid Oulmers, was selected by Morocco to play in a friendly match against Burkina Faso in 2004. He returned from international duty with a serious ankle injury and without him the fortunes of the Belgian First Division club slumped. In missing out on Champions League qualification, Charleroi suffered, what they considered to be, financial harm related to the player's injury. Litigation commenced and the G14 grouping of leading clubs, equally annoyed with the player release system, joined the complaint, one that ultimately reached the Court of Justice.[379]

222. The G14's gripe was that FIFA was employing a regulatory function, namely the efficient organisation of international football, as a mask for the pursuit of their and their affiliate members' own commercial objectives. The complaint was not only that the clubs objected to the substance of the rule but they also lamented the process of agreeing to it, a process that excluded their voice. Their litigious motivation was clear. International tournaments such as the FIFA World Cup or the UEFA European Football Championship's (EURO) are financially very lucrative for the event organiser, but unviable without the ability of national teams to gain access to the employees (players) of the clubs. Access to decision-making gives the clubs the ability to influence the distribution of the revenues. As with much modern sports litigation, *Charleroi* concerned power and money.

223. The referring court in *Charleroi* asked the Court of Justice to consider whether the provisions of FIFA's statutes and regulations providing for the obligatory release of players to national federations without compensation and the unilateral and binding determination of the coordinated international match calendar constituted unlawful restrictions of competition, abuses of a dominant position or obstacles to the exercise of the fundamental freedoms.[380] The case was settled prior to the Court supplying an answer to this question.

---

377. Annex 1, Art. 2, FIFA RSTP, 2018 edition.
378. Annex 1, Arts 3 and 4, FIFA RSTP, 2018 edition.
379. Case C-243/06 *SA Sporting du Pays de Charleroi, G-14 Groupment des Clubs de Football Européens v. Fédération Internationale de Football Association (FIFA)* reference for a preliminary ruling from the Tribunal de Commerce de Charleroi lodged on 30 May 2006.
380. *Ibid.*

224. One can only speculate as to the reason for settlement, but FIFA was caught between the proverbial rock and hard place. A victory for FIFA would have soured relations with a key stakeholder and risked bringing back to the surface questions of clubs leaving the traditional football governance structure. A defeat for FIFA would have been politically and financially damaging.[381] The calculation to settle was no doubt informed by a somewhat different legal environment following *Meca-Medina*. After this case, FIFA faced a methodological challenge to persuade the Court, not of the merits of *a* player release system, but those of *its* system.

225. Assuming the pre-eminent question concerned the interpretation of EU competition law, FIFA would have had good grounds to argue that the player release system and the fixing of the international match calendar are inherent in the operation of international football. Without some system of mandatory player release which grants national associations access to players, international football could not survive. This would have consequentially damaging effects on the sport as a whole as it deprives national associations of an important revenue source, thereby calling in question the associations' ability to fulfil their solidarity function.

226. But FIFA's problem lay not in the merits of its assertion that a mandatory player release rule is indispensable for the survival of international football. Its problem was justifying the proportionality of the rule. The concessions made by FIFA in the settlement agreement suggest that they harboured doubts, for in order to satisfy the *Meca-Medina* methodology, they would also need to demonstrate that the system was limited to what was necessary to secure this legitimate sporting objective. The failure to offer clubs financial compensation or a say in the framing of the rules weighed against FIFA. The settlement rectified these issues – a compensation fund for clubs was established and clubs were given a greater voice in international football governance, particularly within FIFA and UEFA structures. In exchange, the litigation was ended and the G14 disbanded, reforming as the European Club Association (ECA), an organisation with over 240 member clubs as opposed to the 18 that made up the G14.[382]

227. Due to its early settlement, *Charleroi* has not gone down as an EU sports law classic, but aficionados of the state of the art rarely ignore it. The litigation was one of the first to highlight growing dissatisfaction with prevailing governance standards in modern sport. It revealed a willingness on the part of organised stakeholders to strategically challenge sports governance through litigation, and the settlement helped change the shape of the European model of sport. Although 'the

381. Weatherill argues that FIFA would have lost the case, whereas Pijetlovic cites grounds for a FIFA victory. *See* Katarina Pijetlovic, *EU Sports Law and Breakaway Leagues in Football* 62–68 (T.M.C. Asser Press 2015) & Stephen Weatherill, *Principles and Practice in EU Sports Law* 266–268 (Oxford Univ. Press 2017).

382. Although as Geeraert argues, the ECA is still an agent of the elite clubs. *See* Arnout Geeraert, *The EU in International Sports Governance: A Principal Agent Perspective on EU Control of FIFA and UEFA* 67–68 (Palgrave Macmillan 2016).

pyramid survived',[383] its middle fattened in order to incorporate the newly empowered stakeholders who took their place in international football governance alongside federations as active participants rather than mere passive recipients of regulations.[384] In doing so, *Charleroi* has also changed the contours of EU sports law by helping to improve sports governance and thus reduce the incentives for litigation. The legality of UEFA's FFP and Locally Trained Player regulations benefited from wider discussion among stakeholders.

§7. DOPING

228. A fundamental principle underpinning the European model of sport is that sporting competition should be fair. In that light, the regulation of doping has become a central function of sports governing bodies. Following the 1998 Festina doping scandal in professional cycling, the IOC convened the World Conference on Doping in Sport which ultimately resulted in the creation of the World Anti-Doping Agency (WADA).[385] Initially funded by sport, WADA is now a hybrid body funded by both the sports movement and governments. Through the World Anti-Doping Code, WADA's mission is to set harmonised doping standards throughout the sports movement.[386]

229. Save for one notable exception, *Meca-Medina* discussed below, the EU's involvement in doping has been limited.[387] Some anti-doping initiatives were adopted at Member State level, such as national legislation adopted by Italy, France and Belgium in the 1950s and 1960s[388] and the EU's organisational neighbour, the Council of Europe, adopted the Anti-Doping Convention in 1989.[389] Mindful of its limited competence in the area of sport, it seemed that the EU was happy for the Member States and the Council of Europe to lead on the issue and as such, EU action was 'sporadically expressed'.[390]

---

383. Katarina Pijetlovic, *EU Sports Law and Breakaway Leagues in Football* 66 (T.M.C. Asser Press 2015).
384. For a discussion on the changing shape of the 'pyramid', *see* Borja García, *UEFA and the European Union: From Confrontation to Co-operation*, 3(3) JCER 202 (2007).
385. For background *see*, Jack Anderson, *Modern Sports Law* Ch.4 (Hart 2010).
386. The list of sport organisations to have signed the Code is comprehensive. *See* https://www.wada-ama.org/en/what-we-do/the-code/code-signatories (accessed 16 Jul. 2019).
387. For a record of early EU activity *see*: Robert Siekmann & Janwillem Soek, *The European Union and Sport: Legal and Policy Documents*, 643–648 T.M.C. Asser Press (2005). *See* also: An Vermeersch, *The European Union and the Fight Against Doping in Sport: On the Field or on the Sidelines?* 4(1) ESLJ (2006); Magdalena Kedzior, *Effects of the EU Anti-Doping Laws and Politics for the International and Domestic Sports Law in Member States*, 7(1/2) ISLJ 111–114 (2007); Jack Anderson, *The EU's Role on Doping in Sport*, in *Research Handbook on EU Sports Law and Policy* 79–97 (Jack Anderson, Richard Parrish & Borja García eds, Edward Elgar 2018).
388. An Vermeersch, *The European Union and the Fight Against Doping in Sport: On the Field or on the Sidelines?*, 4(1) ESLJ 3 (2006).
389. Council of Europe Convention No.135, *Anti-Doping Convention*, Strasbourg, 16, XI, 1989.
390. Jack Anderson, *The EU's Role on Doping in Sport*, in *Research Handbook on EU Sports Law and Policy* 84 (Jack Anderson, Richard Parrish & Borja García eds, Edward Elgar 2018).

230. In the late 1980s, the European Parliament first highlighted the dangers of doping in sport.[391] In 1990, the EU adopted the Council Resolution on Community action to combat the use of drugs, including the abuse of medicinal products, particularly in sport, followed by the 1992 Council Resolution on doping in sport, made by the EU Health Ministers, which resulted in a European anti-doping campaign.[392] The impact of this campaign on EU policy in doping appeared to be limited, as the 1997 Amsterdam Declaration on Sport, referred to as the 'breakthrough' moment for sport's relationship with the Treaty, did not even mention doping.[393]

231. The first post-Amsterdam discussion on doping came in 1998 with the publication of the European Commission working paper, 'The Development and Prospects for Community Action in the Field of Sport' in which the Commission briefly discussed doping within the context of 'problems and challenges for European sport' including the 'ineffectiveness of anti-doping measures'.[394] Shortly after this paper, the Commission published a Consultation Document, 'The European Model of Sport' in which the Commission acknowledged its limited competence to act in the area of doping. However, in the document the Commission did highlight how it possessed powers in related areas, such as justice and home affairs, health and employment that could be used should the actions of the sports movement and national governments be ineffective.[395] Also in 1998, the Austrian Presidency of the European Union meeting during the Vienna European Council expressed its 'concern at the extent and seriousness of doping in sports' and emphasised 'the need for mobilisation at European Union level' and for Member States and the Commission 'to examine possible measures to intensify the fight against this danger'.[396]

232. Following the Austrian Presidency, doping became more routinely discussed at EU level. In 1999, the Commission published the 'Helsinki Report on Sport' which included a section on 'joining forces to combat doping'.[397] The Report advocated a partnership between the sports movement and public authorities to combat doping although it did state that this partnership would come to nothing unless both parties 'tackle the root cause of the rise of doping'.[398] Earlier in the

391. An Vermeersch, *The European Union and the Fight Against Doping in Sport: On the Field or on the Sidelines?*, 4(1) ESLJ 4 (2006).
392. Resolution of the Council and of the representatives of the Governments of the Member States, meeting within the Council of 3 Dec. 1990 concerning an action programme on nutrition and health, 3 Dec. 1990, OJ C 329, and Resolution of the Council and of the representatives of the Governments of the Member States, meeting within the Council on a code of conduct against doping in sport, 8 Feb. 1992, OJ C 44.
393. Richard Parrish, *Sports Law and Policy in the European Union* 173 (Manchester Univ. Press 2003).
394. European Commission, *The Developments and Prospects for Community Action in the Field of Sport*, Commission Staff Working Paper, 8 (1998).
395. European Commission, *The European Model of Sport*, Consultation Document of DGX 5 (1998), s. 14.
396. Presidency Conclusions, Title XII (Sport), Vienna European Council, 11–12/12/1998.
397. European Commission, *Report from the Commission to the European Council with a view to safeguarding current sports structures and maintaining the social function of sport within the Community framework – the Helsinki Report on Sport*, COM(1999) 644 (1999), s. 3.2.
398. *Ibid.*, at 5.

Report, the Commission suggested that the commercialisation of sport, the overloading of sporting calendars and the pressure to win could be such root causes.[399] Also in 1999, the Commission published the 'Community Support Plan to Combat Doping in Sport' in which it recommended greater research, a contribution to preparing for the creation of WADA and the mobilisation of EU instruments and competences relevant to doping.[400] Although 'enthusiastically welcomed' by some EU institutions, the Plan 'did not lead to a structured Community anti-doping policy'.[401]

233. In December 2000, the Member States adopted the Nice Declaration on Sport during the Nice European Council meeting. A fleeting reference to doping suggested a cooling of interest on the issue, although, at the same time, the Council also released specific conclusions on combatting doping.[402] The Conclusions reiterated concern about doping in sport but suggested that arrangements should be made for the Member States and the EU to play a role in WADA, particularly on its Foundation Board, and that the EU should consider part-funding the activities of WADA. With these statements, it seemed that, notwithstanding its limited Treaty-based powers in this area,[403] the EU would play a significant role in world anti-doping policy. Those hopes were dashed. The EU's participation in WADA became so problematic that European Commissioner Reding ultimately withdrew from the WADA Board and ruled out any EU funding for the body.[404] The problem was the inability of both parties to agree the conditions under which a contribution was made. Legally, due to strict EU budgetary rules, the EU could not commit to WADA procedures that could increase its contribution without the EU's approval. Politically, the EU was wary of making a financial contribution which was not in proportion to its influence within WADA.[405]

234. EU sports policy was given considerable impetus with the adoption of the White Paper on Sport in 2007.[406] As counted by Anderson, the word 'doping' was mentioned fifteen times.[407] The Commission suggested that the EU could facilitate efforts to develop partnerships between Member State law enforcement agencies, WADA-accredited laboratories and INTERPOL to exchange information about new

---

399. *Ibid.*, at 4.
400. European Commission, *Communication from the Commission to the Council, European Parliament, the Economic and Social Committee and the Committee of the Regions – Community support plan to combat doping in sport*, COM/99/0643 (1999).
401. An Vermeersch, *The European Union and the Fight Against Doping in Sport: On the Field or on the Sidelines?*, 4(1) ESLJ 4 (2006).
402. Conclusions of the Council and the Representatives of the Governments of the Member States, meeting within the Council of 4 Dec. 2000 on combatting doping, 2000/C 356/01, 12 Dec. 2000.
403. Art. 129 EC (Public Health), now Art. 152 TFEU.
404. European Commission, *Community funding of the operating budget of the World Antidoping Agency has been ruled out*, IP/01/1727, http://europa.eu/rapid/press-release_IP-01-1727_en.htm 12 Dec. 2001 (accessed 17 Jul. 2019).
405. European Commission, *Funding of the World Anti-Doping Agency*, IP/01/983, http://europa.eu/rapid/press-release_IP-01-983_en.htm 11 Jul. 2001 (accessed 17 Jul. 2019).
406. European Commission, *White Paper on Sport*, COM(2007), 391 final (2007).
407. Jack Anderson, *The EU's Role on Doping in Sport*, in *Research Handbook on EU Sports Law and Policy* 87 (Jack Anderson, Richard Parrish & Borja García eds, Edward Elgar 2018).

doping substances and practices. It also recommended that trade in illicit doping substances be treated in the same manner as trade in illicit drugs throughout the EU. Reflecting its limited competence in this area, the Commission requested the sports movement to take action in this area and that the EU build partnerships with other national and international bodies with an interest in the subject, such as Member States, the Council of Europe, WADA and UNESCO.

235. The White Paper was adopted in preparation for the EU acquiring a new competence in sport by way of the inclusion of Article 165 TFEU. This new competence came into force in 2009 and launched a new phase of EU sports policy. Although the word doping was not mentioned in Article 165, its place within EU sports policy was implied. The first paragraph of Article 165 referred to the EU's contribution to 'European sporting issues', of which doping was undoubtedly one. The second paragraph made mention of 'promoting fairness' in sporting competitions and 'protecting the physical and moral integrity of sportsmen and sportswomen'. The third paragraph called on the EU to foster cooperation with the competent international organisation in the field of sport, of which WADA and the Council of Europe (which has in place an anti-doping convention) are two. However, the fourth paragraph revealed the EU's limited competence in this area, Article 165 being a third-tier competence that only permits the EU to support the actions of Member States. This is limited to the adoption of Incentive Measures and Recommendations, and it specifically rules out the harmonisation of national laws and regulations of the Member States.[408]

236. As a follow up to the adoption of Article 165, in 2011, the Commission published its paper, 'The European Dimension of Sport' – also known as the Communication on Sport.[409] In preparation for its adoption, the Commission consulted Member States and an independent expert group, and both cited the need to establish doping as one of the priority themes of EU sports policy. In a new turn, the Commission conceived of the doping issue as affecting not only professional sport but also recreational sport such as that practised in fitness centres.[410] The Commission highlighted that primary responsibility for anti-doping measures lies with the sports movement, including through new forms of cooperation such as social dialogue between representatives of sports employers and athletes.[411]

408. For a review of Member State laws on anti-doping, *see* European Commission, *Study on Doping Prevention: A Map of Legal, Regulatory and Prevention Practice Provisions in EU 28* (2015).

409. European Commission, *Communication from the Commission to the European Parliament, the Council, the European Economic and Social Committee and the Committee of the Regions – Developing the European Dimension in Sport*, 11 COM(2011) 12 final (2011).

410. For a discussion on doping in recreational sport, *see* Jack Anderson, *The EU's Role on Doping in Sport*, in *Research Handbook on EU Sports Law and Policy* 95 (Jack Anderson, Richard Parrish & Borja García eds, Edward Elgar 2018).

411. On the social dialogue point *see* European Commission, *White Paper on Sport*, COM(2007) 391 final (2007), s. 4.6.

237. The Commission suggested that the EU is able to play a supporting role, but it also warned of the need for anti-doping measures to comply with EU law, particularly fundamental rights and principles such as respect for private and family life, the protection of personal data, the right to a fair trial and the presumption of innocence.[412] Of particular concern were data privacy issues connected with WADA's use of its anti-doping administration and management system (ADAMS). This system is used to facilitate the operation of its whereabouts policy which requires athletes to notify WADA of their location so as to facilitate anti-doping testing.[413] The sharing of this personal data raised concerns as to its compatibility with Article 8 of the EU Charter of Fundamental Rights and Directive 95/46/EC (Data Protection).

238. The Communication on Sport made three commitments in the area of anti-doping. First, it proposed a draft mandate for negotiations on EU accession to the Anti-Doping Convention of the Council of Europe. Second, it committed the Commission to examine the most appropriate way to reinforce measures against trade in doping substances by organised networks, including if possible through criminal law. Finally, it proposed to support transnational anti-doping networks, including networks focusing on preventive measures targeting amateur sport, sport for all and fitness.[414]

239. Since the adoption of the Communication on Sport, anti-doping has been identified as one of the EU's priority themes in all three EU Work Plans for Sport, 2011–2014, 2014–2017 and 2017–2020.[415] Each Work Plan has been supported by Expert Groups on anti-doping.

I. The *Meca-Medina* Litigation

240. As is explained above, EU action in the area of anti-doping has been limited, with one notable exception, and that is its scrutiny of the compatibility of anti-doping rules in sport with EU competition law. This came to a head in the seminal decision of the Court in *Meca-Medina*.[416] The case involved two swimmers seeking to challenge an anti-doping sanction imposed on them by FINA, the International

---

412. European Commission, *Communication from the Commission to the European Parliament, the Council, the European Economic and Social Committee and the Committee of the Regions – Developing the European Dimension in Sport*, 11 COM(2011) 12 final (2011), s. 2.1.
413. *See* Council of the European Union, *EU contribution to the revision of the World Anti-Doping Code*, 6846/12, https://register.consilium.europa.eu/doc/srv?l=EN&f=ST%206846%202012%20 INIT 23 Feb. 2012 (accessed 17 Jul. 2019).
414. European Commission, *Communication from the Commission to the European Parliament, the Council, the European Economic and Social Committee and the Committee of the Regions – Developing the European Dimension in Sport*, 11 COM(2011) 12 final (2011), s. 2.5.
415. Resolution of the Council and of the Representatives of the Governments of the Member States, meeting within the Council, on a European Union Work Plan for Sport for 2011–2014, 2011/C 162/01; 2014–2017, 2014/C 183/03 & 2017–2020, 9639/17.
416. Case C-519/04 P *David Meca-Medina and Igor Majcen v. Commission of the European Communities* [2006] ECR I-6991.

Swimming Federation. The contours of this case, which involved an appeal to CAS, a complaint to the European Commission, an appeal to the CFI (now General Court) and a final appeal to the Court of Justice, are described elsewhere in this monograph.[417] The judgment of the Court of Justice is significant as, for the first time, it provides a framework for assessing the compatibility of certain sporting rules, such as anti-doping rules, with EU law.

241. The swimmers' initial complaint to the Commission was that the anti-doping rule in question was a concerted practice between the IOC and the twenty-seven laboratories accredited by it, and the prescribed limit was scientifically unfounded and could result in the exclusion of innocent or merely negligent athletes. They also attacked the strict liability principle which operated in sports doping cases and argued that dispute resolution in sport, such as that provided by the CAS, was insufficiently independent of the IOC.

242. In August 2002, the Commission rejected the complaint by finding that the contested rules fell outside the scope of the Treaty.[418] On appeal, the General Court also dismissed the swimmers' claim, this time by leaning on the reasoning in *Walrave* to find that anti-doping rules concerned an exclusively '... non-economic aspect of that sporting action, which constitutes its very essence'.[419]

243. On further, and final, appeal, the CJEU attracted the anger of the sports movement by finding that 'it is apparent that the mere fact that a rule is purely sporting in nature does not have the effect of removing from the scope of the Treaty the person engaging in the activity governed by that rule or the body which has laid it down'.[420] For the sports movement, the comfortable terrain of post-*Walrave* EU sports law in which 'non-economic rules' and 'rules of purely sporting interest' found shelter from the application of EU law had been fatally disturbed. The view of the sports movement was very much in line with that of the CFI that there can be no better example of a non-economic and purely sporting rule than anti-doping rules.

244. The change of approach adopted by the Court of Justice was insufficient for the swimmers to win their case, for in determining whether the contested anti-doping rule fell within the scope of Article 101 TFEU (ex Article 81 EC), the Court found that 'account must first of all be taken of the overall context in which the decision of the association of undertakings was taken or produces its effects and, more specifically, of its objectives. It has then to be considered whether the consequential effects restrictive of competition are inherent in the pursuit of those objectives ... and are proportionate to them'.[421] The Court considered anti-doping sanctions

---

417. And also elsewhere in the literature. *See*, for example, Stephen Weatherill, *Anti-doping Revisited – The Demise of the Rule of Purely Sporting Interest*, 27 ECLR 645–657 (2006).
418. Decision in Case COMP 38.158 *Meca-Medina and Majcen*, 1 Aug. 2002.
419. Case T-313/02 *Meca-Medina and Majcen v. Commission* [2004] ECR II-3291 para. 45.
420. Case C-519/04 P *David Meca-Medina and Igor Majcen v. Commission of the European Communities* [2006] ECR I-6991, para. 27.
421. *Ibid.*, para. 45.

legitimate in order 'to combat doping in order for competitive sport to be conducted fairly' and 'to safeguard equal chances for athletes, athletes' health, the integrity and objectivity of competitive sport and ethical values in sport'.[422]

245. The Court, however, conditioned the above on the anti-doping rule being proportionate to the legitimate sporting aims being pursued. Here again, the Court's logic drew criticism from the sports movement. For example, UEFA complained that subjecting sporting rules, such as anti-doping rules, to proportionality control under EU law invites litigation, undermines legal certainty and challenges the autonomy of sport.[423] For the sports movement, respecting the autonomy and specificity of sport means the sports movement, and not judicial bodies, are best placed to make such judgments on, for example, the level of a prohibited substance found in an athletes body and the extent of the sanction that should accompany that finding.

246. Meca-Medina matters, not only in the context of assessing anti-doping rules but also for the assessment of all sporting rules under EU law, be they considered under the competition or free movement provisions of the Treaty. Anti-doping rules can no longer be swept out of reach of the Treaty on the grounds that they pursue noble objectives, such as ensuring fair competition and athlete welfare. The scrutiny is now contextual, recognising the economic effects anti-doping sanctions actually have on those affected. That is not to say that anti-doping rules are likely to be found incompatible with the Treaty as the lines of defence are still wide. The question now rests on their restrictive effects being inherent in the pursuit of the legitimate objectives and proportionate.

§8. Conclusion

247. The European model of sport is organisationally both efficient and deficient. Its structure allows governing bodies to efficiently adopt uniform approaches to rules, participant welfare and integrity matters, it allows governing bodies to execute their solidarity functions and it protects them against naked profiteering from third parties uninterested in the history, traditions and grassroots of sport. However, this hierarchical structure gives rise to potential conflicts of interest, many of which are so organisationally entrenched that the impulse for abuse is almost irresistible. The overwhelming temptation is that sports governing bodies use their monopolistic regulatory power to advance their own commercial interests. In short, conflicts of interest taint the European model. This is reinforced by questionable dispute resolution practices that see aggrieved parties unable to seek redress as these conflicts permeate arbitral arrangements.

422. *Ibid.*, para. 43.
423. *See* Gianni Infantino, *Meca-Medina: A Step Backwards for the European Sports Model and Specificity of Sport*, https://www.uefa.com/MultimediaFiles/Download/uefa/KeyTopics/480401_DOWNLOAD.pdf 2 Oct. 2006 (accessed 16 Jul. 2019).

248. In this context, it is understandable why the EU has been asked to intervene. However, if the European model of sport is under threat, its assailant is not the EU. After a jurisprudential journey of discovery, not all which was entirely consistent, the EU's framework for applying EU law to sport's organisational rules is becoming clearer. When read in conjunction with a maturing EU sports policy based on Article 165 TFEU, the sports movement can now rely on an approach and, if necessary, amend its behaviour accordingly. The approach is best defined as 'conditional autonomy'. The autonomy of the sports movement to adopt organisational rules designed to protect the European model of sport is conditioned on substantive and procedural grounds. In terms of substance, rules should be based on the pursuit of legitimate sporting objectives and should be proportionately framed and pursued. Procedurally, rules should conform with principles of good governance and include a commitment to include the participation of stakeholders.

249. The Court and the Commission have acquired a quarter of a century's experience of assessing the compatibility of sports organisational rules with EU law, and while far from all issues have received attention, the approach is now relatively settled. Sporting rules are compatible with EU law if they pursue a legitimate objective and if the restrictions that they create are inherent and proportionate to reaching that objective. This assessment is capable of repetition by national courts, national competition authorities (NCAs) and arbitral bodies, a point specifically highlighted by the Commission in *ISU*.[424] The Press Release accompanying the ISU decision stated, '[m]any disputes about sporting rules raise primarily issues related to governance of the sport, i.e. relations between different stakeholders belonging or being closely connected to the structure headed by sports federations. Such disputes can usually be best handled by national courts rather than by the European Commission. The same goes for disputes resulting from the application of sporting rules to individuals, e.g. athletes being sanctioned for breach of relevant anti-doping or match-fixing regulations, which can be handled by relevant arbitration bodies or national courts'.

250. These statements suggest that the future contours of European sports law, at least in terms of sports organisational rules, are likely to be shaped within national courts or at CAS. But in this regard, *ISU* contains a contradiction as the Commission cast considerable doubt on the efficacy of arbitral proceedings in sport, particularly in terms of protecting the rights of EU citizens and undertakings.[425] CAS' EU law analysis in *ENIC* and *Seraing*, and its assessment of other sporting rules discussed elsewhere in this monograph, highlights the flaw in the Commission's argument. Here, the Commission might have gone too far, but equally CAS has not gone far enough in routinely using EU law as the analytical basis for assessing disputes that clearly engage EU-derived rights.

424. European Commission, *Antitrust: International Skating Union's restrictive penalties on athletes breach EU competition rules*, Press Release, IP/17/5184, 8 Dec. 2017.

425. Case AT.40208 – International Skating Union's Eligibility Rules, paras 5–6.

251. Evidence presented throughout this chapter suggests that the EU's scrutiny of sport's organisational rules has improved sports governance. But the EU is not and should not be a de facto sports regulator, a concern raised by UEFA in *ENIC*. It is for sport to define its own organisational rules and structure, subject to compliance with EU law. While it is true that the EU has told sport what it cannot do to defend the European model, it must not instruct it on what it should do.

Chapter 3. Playing Sport

§1. Introduction

252. The regulatory power of sports governing bodies extends to rules establishing eligibility for participation in sport. In this context, the traditional hierarchical structure of the European model of sport grants sports bodies a significant degree of control over the sporting labour market. Athletes are the main protagonists of sporting events, the reason that fans, advertisers and broadcasters are attracted to them. They are also the main factor of production for the industry and the source of supply of labour for clubs. The power exercised by sports governing bodies over athletes often encourages them to seek labour market interventions in order to secure a number of objectives. In sporting terms, labour market regulation can promote balanced competition and encourage youth development. In terms of sports governance, intervention can help a governing body retain regulatory control over its sport. Financially, labour regulation can reduce costs, particularly as the cost of training, recruiting and paying athletes is, in many sports, the most significant expense felt by those engaging professional athlete services. These incentives to regulate the labour market often translate into wage restraints and other labour market restrictions. Here lies a source of legal conflict as athletes seek a normalisation of labour rights with 'traditional' workers.

253. Practising sport is not, however, just an expression of economic activity. Most sport in Europe is practised by amateurs as a basic human activity. Practising sport promotes health, well-being, social inclusion and it satisfies our competitive instincts. As discussed in Chapter 1, EU law is primarily concerned with the regulation of economic activity. It is not concerned with sport practised in casual settings, such as a kick-about by friends in a park or a game of tennis in a leisure centre. It does, however, have an interest in how organised amateur sport conducts its affairs, particularly as the EU has recognised the social importance of sport to EU citizens. In this regard, and as discussed in Chapter 1, the European model of sport places heavy emphasis on the organisation of sport along national lines in which each sport is regulated by one governing body, per sport, per country. Protecting this structure, at both professional and amateur levels, are rules governing participation, and these are often linked to nationality. Prohibiting discrimination based on nationality is a long-standing principle of EU law and one that, in recent years, has come to play a role even in amateur sport.

254. From the above, it should be apparent that while the influence of the EU is likely to be felt most intensely in professional sport, the operation of amateur sport is not immune. This chapter explores these issues. It does so by examining the impact of the EU in three key areas pertaining to the practice of sport by professional and amateur athletes: the operation of the transfer system (specifically in football); the work and regulation of sports agents; and the application of nationality-based rules in sport. In this regard, this chapter examines the impact of EU intervention in this area on the contours of the European model of sport. We also assess the extent to which the EU has conditioned the autonomy of sports bodies to promulgate athlete-related restraints on the implementation of good governance in sport. The chapter ends with a discussion of the EU's role in promoting dialogue between stakeholders and consultation within sport.

§2. Players' Transfer System

255. The football transfer system emerged in England in the 1890s.[426] Without a system in which players were tied to their club via a registration system, the football authorities were concerned that competition would become so unbalanced that it would threaten the viability of the sport. So a retain-and-transfer system was developed which allowed a club to retain a player's registration even after expiry of the contract. Players not retained were placed on a transfer list and were not free to sign for a new club, except to those willing to pay a transfer fee. This system resulted in the club having a 'virtual monopoly over the players' services'.[427] A few years later in 1900, further restrictions were imposed on players with the introduction of the maximum wage which limited a player's salary to no more than GBP 4 a week.

256. The unionisation of players in England contributed to a campaign for greater contractual and financial freedom for players. Even though by 1910 the players had scored a legal victory concerning their employment status,[428] attempts at challenging the transfer system failed.[429] It took until the 1960s for the maximum wage to be abolished and for retain-and-transfer system to be successfully challenged in *Eastham*, and even here, only the 'retain' element was found in restraint of trade.[430] A series of reforms after *Eastham* loosened the controls clubs exercised over players, but the basic principle of the transfer system remained – the registration of a player could be bought and sold and so a 'transfer market' existed.

257. Across Europe, different transfer systems and markets emerged, inspired by the English model.[431] Some, such as in Belgium, contained *Eastham* style restraints that became subject to legal challenge.[432] Ultimately, FIFA brought some uniformity through its regulation of cross-border transfers provided by in its RSTP, although this regime permitted national associations to adopt national regulations governing purely domestic transfers. The existence of these transfer markets

426. John Harding, *Behind the Glory: 100 Years of the PFA* (Breedon Books 2009).
427. Dennis Thomas, *The Retain and Transfer System*, in *Handbook on the Economics of Sport* 630 (Wladimir Andreff & Stefan Szymanski eds, Edward Elgar 2006).
428. *Walker v. Crystal Palace Football Club* [1910] 1 KB 87.
429. *Kingaby v. Aston Villa FC*, The Times 27 and 28 Mar. 1912.
430. *Eastham v. Newcastle United Football Club Ltd and others* [1964] Ch. 413, 430.
431. Pierre Lanfranchi & Matthew Taylor, *Moving with the Ball: The Migration of Professional Footballers* 216 (Berg 2001).
432. Case C-415/93 *Union Royale Belge Sociétés de Football Association and others v. Bosman and others* [1995] ECR I-4921. *See* Roger Blanpain, *The Legal Status of Sportsmen and Sportswomen under International, European and Belgian and Regional Law* (Kluwer Law International 2003).

attracted the attention of those seeking access to it. Football agency emerged as a profession and TPO developed as a business practice. Attempts made by the football authorities at restricting the access of these individuals to this market has been subject to litigation, discussed below (agents) and in Chapter 2 (TPO).

258. Modern transfer rules reflect the unique business model of many sports clubs, which concerns the recruitment and transfer of players.[433] They are an expression of the autonomy of the relevant associations, and the epitome of the self-regulatory power held by international and national sports organisations.[434] Regardless of the specific content of such rules, and the subjects to whom they are addressed, the transfer system in European sport cannot be considered as the result of negotiations between management and labour. Employment relationships in sport have been modelled by a united cross-border front of employers, at a time in which collective representation of players was not developed.[435]

259. The existence of restrictions on the movement of players represents a unique feature of the sport system. In any other industry, employees are free to move from one employer to another, to terminate unilaterally their contract with certainty over the consequences they are going to face, as dictated by their contract or general employment law.[436] Conversely, the transfer rules in sport impose forms of contractual stability between clubs and players, and hence between employers and employees, that cannot be observed elsewhere.

260. The basic principle of the transfer system that the registration of the player can be sold not only places restrictions on the freedom of players but also affects the recruitment opportunities of clubs. Furthermore, transfer windows prevent clubs from registering new players after a certain point of the season, allowing players to move from one club to another only during a limited time, usually less than four months every given year, and only with the consent of their current employer.[437] Termination of employment contracts by either party is allowed only in the presence of a 'just cause', with disciplinary sanctions imposed as a deterrent.[438] In football, the existence of a 'sporting just cause' is assessed by the FIFA Dispute

433. Raffaele Poli, Loïc Ravenel & Roger Besson, *Transfer Values and Probabilities: The CIES Football Observatory Approach* (CIES Football Observatory 2016).
434. KEA/CDES, *Study on the Economic and Legal Aspects of Transfers of Players,* European Commission, 33 (2013).
435. *See Eastham v. Newcastle United Football Club* [1964] Ch 413, 430. On labour relations in sport generally *see* Leanne O'Leary, *Employment and Labour Relations Law in the Premier League, NBA and International Rugby Union* 21 (T.M.C. Asser Press 2017).
436. Simon Gardiner & Roger Welch, *The Contractual Dynamics of Team Stability Versus Player Mobility: Who Rules 'The Beautiful Game'?*, 5(1) ESLJ 1–14 (2007).
437. Geoff Pearson, *Sporting Justifications under EU Free Movement and Competition Law: The Case of the Football 'Transfer System'*, 21(2) ELJ 220–238 (2015).
438. KEA/CDES, *Study on the Economic and Legal Aspects of Transfers of Players,* European Commission, 20 (2013).

Resolution Chamber (DRC).[439] This set of regulations is further strengthened through the rules designed to enforce compliance, entrenched in the pyramidal structure of the European model of sport and its tie to the system of *lex sportiva.*

261. The combined effect of these rules is to reduce the mobility of players and the ability of clubs to compete in the market for the best players, as only elite clubs will be able to afford high transfer fees. This means that clubs see their access to their only source of supply restricted, but the system ultimately produces effects on the exploitation market as well. As economically weaker clubs struggle to rely on the market to enhance the quality of their sporting performance, the final product might become less attractive to consumers.[440]

262. The restrictions that these rules can cause to the fundamental freedoms of athletes and undertakings – clubs, athletes, or commercial operators – have been assessed on a number of occasions under free movement provisions and competition law.[441] In this regard, governing bodies have been successful in identifying legitimate objectives that could justify restrictive conduct, such as the need to protect solidarity within the system, the redistribution of resources among clubs to enhance competitive balance, and the training and development of young athletes.[442] The restrictions, however, need to be proportionate to such objectives and inherent in their pursuit.[443]

263. The upholding of these characteristics, which may be legitimately considered as one of the fundamental elements of the specificity of sport, represents a clear example of the regulatory autonomy of sports governing bodies against the strict

439. The DRC is one of the FIFA's judicial body, which has jurisdiction to hear disputes between clubs and players over contractual stability and employment-related disputes, as well as disputes between clubs over training compensation and solidarity payments. *See* Arts 22–24 FIFA RSTP.

440. Christine Stix-Hackl & Alexander Egger, *Sports and Competition Law: A Never-Ending Story?*, 23(2) ECLR 81–91 (2002).

441. For cases dealing with restrictions of free movement, *see*, among others Case C-176/96 *Lehtonen and Castors Canada Dry Namur-Braine ASBL v. Fédération royale belge des sociétés de basketball (FRBSB)* [2000] ECR I-02681, and Case C-415/93 *Union Royale Belge Sociétés de Football Association and others v. Bosman and others* [1995] ECR I-4921. Competition law has been used to a lesser extent. In *Bosman*, the CJEU refused to assess the compatibility of the football transfer system with EU competition law, as it had already held that the system was infringing freedom of movement of workers and freedom to provide services. *See* Case C-415/93 *Union Royale Belge Sociétés de Football Association and others v. Bosman and others* [1995] ECR I-4921, para. 138. Similarly, in *Lehtonen* the Court did not consider the question, holding that it did not receive enough information from the national court to decide on the issue. *See* Case C-176/96 *Lehtonen and Castors Canada Dry Namur-Braine ASBL* v. *Fédération royale belge des sociétés de basketball (FRBSB)* [2000] ECR I-02681, para. 107.

442. Case C-415/93 *Union Royale Belge Sociétés de Football Association and others v. Bosman and others* [1995] ECR I-4921, para. 106, and Case C-325/08 *Olympique Lyonnais SASP v. Olivier Bernard and Newcastle UFC* [2010] ECR I-02177, para. 39. *See* also KEA/CDES, *Study on the Economic and Legal Aspects of Transfers of Players*, European Commission, 7 (2013).

443. Joined Cases C-51/96 and C-191/97 *Deliège v. Ligue francophone de Judo et disciplines Associeés Asb* [2000] ECR I-2549, para. 64 and Case C-519/04 P *David Meca-Medina and Igor Majcen v. Commission of the European Communities* [2006] ECR I-6991, para. 42.

application of EU law. On the other hand, the intervention of the EU has helped shape some elements of these regulations, steering the conduct of governing bodies towards principles of good governance.

I. The Football Transfer System

264. The rules regulating the relationship between athletes and sports clubs represent a departure from the general principles of contract and employment law. Governing bodies have implemented various rules that differ as to the obligations of the parties and the extent of the restrictions posed. While these rules can be seen as an expression of the governing bodies' autonomy, it must be noted that, at the time of writing, the rules regulating the transfer system in football are broadly the outcome of a process that was significantly affected by the intervention of EU institutions. Through judgments of the CJEU and measures adopted by the Commission, the institutions have used the tools of free movement and competition law to push amendments aiming to incorporate good governance principles.

265. As seen in Chapter 1, the first case discussing rules regulating the transfer of players was *Donà v. Mantero*.[444] The Court of Justice held that nationality discrimination on the registration of players was an illegitimate restriction of the free movement of workers. The leading case in the area, however, is of course *Bosman*. Here, the Court of Justice assessed the FIFA players' registration system, which allowed clubs to retain the registration of their players even after the expiry of their employment contract, unless a transfer fee was paid by the engaging club. The Court maintained that the transfer system was an inadequate means to achieve its legitimate objective, namely protecting the competitive balance between clubs, as it restricted the freedom of movement of players in a disproportionate way.[445] However, the decision of the Court considered only restrictions imposed on out-of-contract players; the legality of transfer fees for players under contract still remains to be assessed.[446] Furthermore, while considering the rules under scrutiny unlawful, the Court did recognise the legitimacy of the objectives pursued through the system, thereby demonstrating that a proportionate restriction could have been upheld.[447]

---

444. Case 13/76 *Donà v. Mantero* [1976] ECR 1333.

445. Case C-415/93 *Union Royale Belge Sociétés de Football Association and others v. Bosman and others* [1995] ECR I-4921, para. 106. For a discussion on this point, *see* Stephen Weatherill, *Resisting the Pressures of Americanization: The Influence of European Community Law on the European Sport Model*, in *Law and Sport in Contemporary Society* 157–181 (Steve Greenfield & Guy Osborn eds, Frank Cass 2000).

446. Geoff Pearson, *Sporting Justifications under EU Free Movement and Competition Law: The Case of the Football 'Transfer System'*, 21(2) Eur. L.J. 220–238 (2015). On the other hand, it could be argued that the Commission has accepted a fee-based transfer system for players under contract through the 2001 Agreement. *See* Adam Berry, *Challenging Football Transfer Windows: A Disproportionate Response to a Legitimate Aim*, 20 Sport & L.J. 1 (2012).

447. Stephen Weatherill, *Principles and Practice in EU Sports Law* 206 (Oxford Univ. Press 2017).

266. Through the deference demonstrated to the pursuit of legitimate objectives, but the firmness used in assessing the proportionality of the restriction, *Bosman* convinced sports governing bodies to change their traditional approach. Rather than denying any possible area where law would apply to sporting regulations, governing bodies commenced a form of dialogue with the EU institutions, in an attempt to maintain ownership and control over the regulation of the labour market and avoid the imposition of sanctions.[448]

267. In football, this relationship led to the 2001 Informal Agreement on the International Transfer System, concluded between the European Commission and FIFA and UEFA.[449] This non-legally binding settlement was the result of the pressure exercised by the Commission on the European and international governing bodies to amend the system and avoid any further legal action. The agreement was therefore the solution to a process that started in 1998, when the Commission opened an investigation against FIFA, arguing that the football transfer system, or what survived of it after *Bosman*, presented a number of features that were constituting unlawful restrictions under what is now Article 101 TFEU.[450]

268. First, unilateral termination of the contract was prohibited: even after players had broken their contract with a club, and paid damages for the breach, they were still not allowed to register with another club in another country. Second, although the transfer fee could be agreed freely by the parties involved, the sum paid did not have to be in any way related to the costs borne for the training or the development of the player. This could lead to excessively high fees being demanded to allow the movement of players. Finally, national associations were obliged to implement the same system within their domestic transfer regime, and clubs and players were prevented from taking disputes related to transfers to civil courts.[451] The arrangement could thus be considered as a decision of an association of undertakings that distorted the competition on the market for signing players.

269. The investigation led to a dialogue between the European Commission and the governing bodies, which were later joined by FIFPro. The process, which has been defined as an example of a horizontal model of regulation where networks of

---

448. Borja García & Stephen Weatherill, *Engaging with the EU in Order to Minimise Its Impact: Sport and the Negotiation of the Treaty of Lisbon*, 19(2) J. Eur. Public Policy (2012), and Arnout Geeraert & Edith Drieskens *Normative Market Europe: The EU as a Force for Good in International Sports Governance?*, 39(1) J. Eur. Integr. 79–94, 87 (2017).
449. European Commission, Press Release IP/01/314, *Outcome of discussions between the Commission and FIFA/UEFA on FIFA Regulations on international football transfers*, Brussels, 5 Mar. 2001. For a complete overview of the agreement and the process that led to its conclusion, *see* Borja García, *The 2001 Informal Agreement on the International Transfer System*, I-2011 European Sports Law and Policy Bulletin 17–29 (2011).
450. *See* the summary provided by the DG Competition in Lenita Linstrom-Rossi, Sandra De Waele & Dovile Vaigauskaite, *Application of EC Antitrust Rules in the Sport Sector: An Update*, Competition Policy Newsletter 3 (2005).
451. Richard Parrish, *Sports Law and Policy in the European Union* 141 (Manchester Univ. Press 2003).

stakeholders collaborate to define the rules,[452] led to the adoption of the new FIFA rules on International Transfers.[453] Satisfied by FIFA's amendments made to the transfer system, the Commission closed its investigation. However, it did not expressly exempt the arrangement under Article 101(3) TFEU (ex Article 81(3) EC) and it made no determination on the inherency of the measure; the investigation was merely halted.[454] According to the Press Release issued by the Commission, the amended rules struck a balance between the freedom of players and clubs and the need to protect the integrity of sport, the stability of contracts, and the stability of championships.[455]

270. The reformed transfer system confirmed the abolition of transfer fees for players moving to a club in a different Member State at the expiration of their contract. The Regulations replaced the old transfer fees, declared illegal in *Bosman*, with a training compensation scheme. In effect, FIFA followed the recommendation made by Advocate General Lenz in *Bosman*, where he considered that transfer rules in football were disproportionate to the objective of ensuring competitive balance between clubs, while training compensations were more likely to achieve such an aim.[456] Furthermore, as the Court had recognised the training of young players as a legitimate objective,[457] FIFA decided to link that specific aim to the payment of a fee. This has to be paid to the club that lost the player at the end of the contract and has to be calculated in relation to the real costs incurred for his training. Additionally, in order to protect contractual stability, the system created one transfer period per season, with a mid-season window, and imposed a limit of one transfer per player per season. Sanctions were provided against unilateral breaches of contract, whether carried out by the players or the clubs.

271. The reformed system and its subsequent updates are now collated into the FIFA RSTP.[458] The Regulations govern international transfers only, although rules adopted at domestic level tend to replicate the international regulations at national

---

452. Antoine Duval, *The FIFA Regulations on the Status and Transfer of Players: Transnational Law-Making in the Shadow of Bosman*, in *The Legacy of Bosman, Revisiting the Relationship between EU law and Sport* 91 (Antoine Duval & Ben Van Rompuy eds, T.M.C. Asser Press 2016).
453. FIFA Regulations for the Status and Transfer of Players, July 2001. The latest version can be found here https://resources.fifa.com/image/upload/regulations-on-the-status-and-transfer-of-players-june-2019.pdf?cloudid=ao68trzk4bbaezlipx9u (accessed 6 May 2020).
454. Adam Lewis & Jonathan Taylor, *Sport: Law and Practice* 1177 (Bloomsbury Professional 2014).
455. *See* European Commission, *Commission Closes Investigations into FIFA Regulations on International Football Transfers*, IP/02/824, 5 Jun. 2002. By this time, however, FIFPro had withdrawn from the negotiation and was not part of the final agreement.
456. Case C-415/93 *Union des Associations Européennes de Football (UEFA) and others v. Jean-Marc Bosman* [1995] ECR I-04921, Opinion of Advocate General Lenz, para. 239.
457. Case C-415/93 *Union Royale Belge Sociétés de Football Association and others v. Bosman and others* [1995] ECR I-4921, para. 106. However, the Court held in that instance that the specific form taken by the transfer system was neither capable of encouraging the recruitment and training of young players nor constituted an adequate means to finance such activities. *See ibid.*, para. 109.
458. FIFA RSTP. The 2019 Version is available at https://resources.fifa.com/image/upload/regulations-on-the-status-and-transfer-of-players-june-2019.pdf?cloudid=ao68trzk4bbaezlipx9u (accessed 18 Mar. 2020).

level. The provisions of the RSTP analysed in the following sections concern training compensation and solidarity mechanism (Articles 20 & 21), player registration and transfer windows (Articles 4–12), the maintenance of contract stability between professionals and clubs (Articles 13–18), and the international transfers involving minors (Article 19 and 19bis). Other aspects of the RSTP are addressed in Chapter 2 of this monograph: third-party influence and ownership of players' economic rights (Article 18bis and 18ter), the jurisdiction of FIFA and dispute resolution (Articles 22–25) and the release of players to association teams (Annexe 1).

II. Training Compensation and Solidarity Payment

272. One argument used by FIFA to justify the need for rules regulating the transfer of players is the need to protect the economic and sporting equilibrium between clubs.[459] This, alongside the need to encourage youth development, was accepted as a legitimate objective by the Court in *Bosman*, although ultimately deemed to be pursued in a disproportionate manner.

273. The need to provide incentives to the funding of youth development is one of the main characteristics of the sports labour market, and in particular of the European model of sport, where the system needs to guarantee effective ways to nurture its own talents. As opposed to the College system in place in North America, sports clubs in Europe tend to invest to develop their own academies in order to produce talent, which may then be used in the squad, or sold on the market.[460] Therefore, youth development is an objective of clubs and sports associations in general, and it is important to assess the value recognised to this training process, and how it can be protected. However, the need to train employees is not a unique characteristic of the sporting industry. It is common to many other industries and to many employers, certainly so if they aim to enhance the benefits received from their employees while they operate in the company or in the sector.[461]

274. The objective of recruiting and training young players was also discussed in *Bernard*, in the context of a case involving a form of training compensation imposed by the French Football Federation.[462] The definition of training compensation refers to payments made to clubs that have been involved in the training of the players during their formation period. In this case, the Court assessed the legality of a measure introduced by the French Football Federation, which imposed on young footballers the obligation to sign their first professional contract with the club

459. Case C-415/93 *Union Royale Belge Sociétés de Football Association and others v. Bosman and others* [1995] ECR I-4921, para. 105.

460. For example, expenses incurred as investments on youth development are not considered under the break-even requirement imposed as part of the UEFA Financial Fair Play Regulations.

461. Stephen Weatherill, *Resisting the Pressures of Americanization: The Influence of European Community Law on the European Sport Model*, in *Law and Sport in Contemporary Society* 157–181 (Steve Greenfield & Guy Osborn eds, Frank Cass 2000).

462. Case C-325/08 *Olympique Lyonnais SASP v. Olivier Bernard and Newcastle UFC* [2010] ECR I-02177.

that trained them. In the event the player was to refuse to sign this contract, the player was obliged to correspond a sum to the club as damage. The rule effectively granted football clubs an option to sign the players coming out of their own academies, which was aimed at rewarding the investment already undertaken in training them.[463]

275. In this regard, the Court was asked to decide whether such a measure, which restricted the contractual freedom of young players, was to be considered a breach of free movement provisions, and whether the governing body could refer to the pursuit of any legitimate objective to justify such a restriction. The Court found that, even though such a rule fell short of effectively preventing players from signing their first professional contract with clubs other than the one which trained them, it had the practical effect of rendering the exercise of free movement less attractive.[464] In its analysis, the Court stated that account had to be taken of the specific characteristics of sport in general, and football in particular, and of their social and educational function.[465] Following the Opinion of the Advocate General Sharpston, the specific characteristics of sport should be considered in the context of assessing the justifications for the restriction caused, in the same way as it would be done in other sectors with reference to the specific characteristics applicable in those circumstances. These considerations were therefore used within the assessment of the proportionality of the restriction, and its ability to achieve the legitimate objectives.[466]

276. The relevance of this aspect should not be underestimated. The Court, while interpreting the wording of Article 165 TFEU in line with its own case law, extended the relevance of the specific characteristics of sports: from a reference to the legitimacy of objectives pursued by the system in relation to its specific characteristics to the proportionality of the restriction assessed, which should include reference to the social and educational function of sport.[467]

277. The Court therefore reiterated the legitimacy of the objective of recruiting and training young players and acknowledged that in order to effectively pursue it, an incentive in the form of reward for the clubs for their investments in those activities is necessary. The latter was considered essential to guarantee the viability of the system, in light of the social and educational function of sport. While the promotion of solidarity mechanisms and training of young players constitute one fundamental

463. Stephen Weatherill, *Principles and Practice in EU Sports Law* 216 (Oxford Univ. Press 2017).
464. Case C-325/08 *Olympique Lyonnais SASP v. Olivier Bernard and Newcastle UFC* [2010] ECR I-02177, para. 36.
465. *Ibid.*, para. 40, citing the Opinion of Advocate General Sharpston, paras 30 and 47. Sharpston clarified that such characteristics should not be considered in assessing whether the restriction exists, but only when examining the possible justification for such a restriction.
466. Richard Parrish, *Lex Sportiva and EU Sports Law*, 37 EL Rev. 716–733 (2012).
467. Katarina Pijetlovic, *EU Sports Law and Breakaway Leagues in Football* 128 (T.M.C. Asser Press 2015).

justification for a system regulating the transfer of players,[468] in *Bernard* the CJEU held the assessed solidarity scheme to be disproportionate, as the damage that could be paid by the player did not have any connection with the investment made by the club. Instead, the Court suggested that a proportionate system would take into due account the costs effectively borne by the clubs in training both future professional players and those who will never play professionally.[469]

278. The FIFA RSTP reflect the need to create a system that could reward the effort undertaken by clubs in training young players and ensure a degree of solidarity between the clubs at different levels of the football pyramid. The rules therefore introduced provisions on training compensation[470] and solidarity payments.[471] Training compensation is a sum calculated on the basis of training costs, paid to any club that has trained the players when they sign their first professional contract and every time they transfer to a new club, until the end of the season in which they turn 23.[472] Conversely, solidarity payments are due each time players are transferred during the course of their contract, to the clubs which contributed to the education and training of such players between their 12th and 23rd birthday, and calculated as a percentage of the transfer fee.[473]

279. The objectives of these regulations are similar to those underlining the rules in *Bernard*, but the FIFA RSTP differ in that they impose an obligation on prospective new clubs, rather than on the players themselves. However, questions remain as the practical effect may be to disincentivise clubs from signing young players, for which they will have to correspond solidarity and training compensation. In turn, this would constitute an obstacle to the mobility of those players. In assessing the proportionality of the restrictions, a relevant consideration is the suitability of such regulations to achieve the desired objectives.

---

468. Jakub Laskowski, *Solidarity Compensation Framework in Football Revisited*, 18 ISLJ 150–184 (2019).
469. Case C-325/08 *Olympique Lyonnais SASP v. Olivier Bernard and Newcastle UFC* [2010] ECR I-02177, para. 45. This principle was later discussed in the 2011 Commission Staff Working Document, where the Commission stated that the training cost must be calculated on the basis of the number of players who need to be trained in order to produce a professional football player. *See* European Commission, *Commission staff working document 'Sport and Free Movement' Accompanying document to the Communication from the Commission to the European Parliament, the Council, the European Economic and Social Committee and the Committee of the Regions – Developing the European Dimension in Sport*, SEC(2011) 66 final (2011) https://eur-lex.europa.eu/legal-content/EN/TXT/?uri=CELEX%3A52011SC0066 (accessed 18 Mar. 2020).
470. Art. 20, FIFA RSTP.
471. Art. 21, FIFA RSTP.
472. Annexe 4, FIFA RSTP.
473. Annex 5, FIFA RSTP. For a discussion on solidarity payments and training compensation, *see* Jakub Laskowski, *Solidarity Compensation Framework in Football Revisited*, 18 ISLJ 150–184 (2019). *See also* Sports Law and Policy Centre, *The Bernard Case. Sports and Training Compensation*, I-2010 European Sports Law and Policy Bulletin (2010).

280. A rule aimed at compensating clubs for costs incurred in training athletes can mitigate the loss of a player and incentivise investments in youth development.[474] However, solidarity payments were not due when the transfer was between clubs affiliated to the same national association, or when the transfer did not involve the payment of any fee. The limited impact of the rules and the lack of enforcement is demonstrated by the evidence provided by FIFA, according to which the amounts paid by clubs as solidarity and training compensation at global level are relatively small.[475]

281. The lack of transparency in the transfer market and the lack of enforcement of the rules led to calls for a reform of the system. As part of the reforms introduced by FIFA since 2018, the solidarity payment and training compensation will be administered through the creation of a clearing house. In FIFA's plans, the clearing house will process all transfer fees and distribute training compensation and solidarity payments where needed. This would effectively provide certainty as to when clubs can claim these sums, and their amount. Furthermore, FIFA has announced that solidarity contributions will apply to domestic transfers as well, provided that they have an international dimension.[476] However, at the moment of writing, no details have been provided as to the practical application of such a system. The effectiveness of the measure, as mentioned before, will constitute a relevant criterion in assessing the proportionality of any restriction.

III. Transfer Windows

282. Another characteristic of any sporting transfer system is the existence of transfer windows. In football, players can move from one club to another, and be registered by the latter, only during two fixed periods: during the summer break and during a short period in winter.[477] As part of the 2001 Agreement between FIFA and the European Commission, FIFA made transfer windows compulsory starting from the 2002/2003 season.[478] Furthermore, the same regulations establish that a player

474. Richard Parrish, *Article 17 of the FIFA Regulations on the Status and Transfer of Players: Compatibility with EU Law*, 22(2) MJECL 256–282 (2015).
475. FIFA Football Stakeholder Committee, *Task Force Transfer System, White Paper – Transfer System Reform* 48 (2018). *See* also KEA, *An update on change drivers and economic and legal implications of transfers of players*, European Commission (2018) stating at p. 8: 'the lack of transparency on the transfer market has direct impacts on the enforcement of the training compensation and solidarity mechanisms, which remains a challenge and shows no signs of improvement over the years'.
476. FIFA Council makes key decisions for the future of football development, https://www.fifa.com/about-fifa/news/y=2018/m=10/news=fifa-council-makes-key-decisions-for-the-future-of-football-development.html (accessed 15 Apr. 2020).
477. Art. 6(1) and (2) FIFA RSTP. In basketball, instead there is a transfer deadline, after which players cannot be registered by teams. *See* KEA/CDES, *Study on the Economic and Legal Aspects of Transfers of Players,* 67 European Commission (2013).
478. Borja García, *The 2001 Informal Agreement on the International Transfer System*, I-2011 European Sports Law and Policy Bulletin 17–29 (2011).

may be registered with a maximum of three clubs during one season, but play official matches only for two of these clubs.[479] Finally, for knockout European competitions there are even more stringent rules: a player cannot be fielded to take part in the competition for more than one club in the course of the same season.[480]

283. Transfer windows have been assessed by the Court of Justice in *Lehtonen*, although only under the free movement provisions.[481] In that case, Mr Lehtonen, a Finnish basketball player who had played in his home country during the first part of the 1995/1996 season, was transferred to the Belgian club Castors Braine for the final stage of the Belgian Championship. As the transfer occurred after the closure of the transfer window imposed by the Belgian Federation for the transfer of foreign players, the player could not be registered with Castors Braine and was therefore excluded from taking part in the competition. The rules effectively prevented the worker from undertaking his professional activity, for which he entered into an employment contract with the Belgian club, and as such the Court of Justice recognised that they constituted an obstacle to the freedom of movement of the worker. However, the Court considered that non-economic grounds, such as the need of ensuring the regularity of the competition, and the proper functioning of the championship as a whole, could constitute a legitimate objective for the sporting system.[482]

284. While the Court adopted an approach, which now may seem outdated, that was distinguishing between the economic and non-economic nature of the rule in object,[483] its assessment still focused on the legitimacy of the objective pursued, and the proportionality of the restriction caused. In this regard, the Court held that, provided that the restriction to the freedom of movement is proportionate, the need to ensure the regularity of the competition could justify the existence of transfer windows. However, in the particular circumstances of the case, the Court considered that the rule was disproportionate, as it imposed a discriminatory burden on foreign players, which were subject to a deadline not applicable to national players.[484] The approach of the Court on the legitimacy of transfer windows was later extended by

479. *See* Art. 5(3) FIFA RSTP.
480. Art. 43.06, Regulations of the UEFA Champions League, Edition 2019/20.
481. Case C-176/96 *Lehtonen and Castors Canada Dry Namur-Braine ASBL v. Fédération royale belge des sociétés de basket-ball (FRBSB)* [2000] ECR I-02681.
482. *Ibid.*, paras 52–54.
483. This approach, and the distinction used, was later disregarded by the Court of Justice in *Meca-Medina. See* Case C-519/04 P *David Meca-Medina and Igor Majcen v. Commission of the European Communities* [2006] ECR I-6991, para. 27 and Stephen Weatherill, *Case C-519/04 P Meca-Medina [2006] ECR I-6991*, in *Leading Cases in Sports Law* 141 (Jack Anderson ed., T.M.C. Asser Press 2013).
484. Case C-176/96 *Lehtonen and Castors Canada Dry Namur-Braine ASBL v. Fédération royale belge des sociétés de basket-ball (FRBSB)* [2000] ECR I-02681, para. 58.

the Commission beyond free movement provisions, maintaining that the regulation of transfer periods is likely to constitute a sporting rule that would not infringe competition law either.[485]

285. The main aim of transfer windows, or registration periods, is to avoid disruptions of the competition.[486] In their absence, a club could sign the best players on the market the day before the decisive final matches of the competition and significantly increase its chances of success. Hence, transfer windows pursue the aim of protecting seasonal stability and competitive balance, but also the integrity of the competition and its perception by fans.[487] In this regard, it may be argued that rules of this kind protect the interests of all the stakeholders in sport, including fans, broadcasters, teams and governing bodies.[488]

286. On the other hand, transfer windows may run against the goal of competitive balance. The time restriction imposed on the activity of clubs constricts the market and inflates prices, thereby favouring clubs that can afford to spend high sums in a short span.[489] Moreover, as players are the main asset of smaller clubs, limiting their ability to sell them may have a significant impact on their finances, thereby further increasing competitive imbalance. This may be considered yet another inherent characteristic of sport: while in any other business a cash-flow problem could be resolved by selling some of the assets, in sport, clubs are allowed to rely on this option only during a limited period of time.

287. If transfer windows would be assessed under competition law, the Court would most likely employ the approach made famous in *Meca-Medina*. In this context, any alleged restrictive effect caused by a registration period may be considered inherent in the organisation of a sporting competition, including the protection of integrity of the competition and its perception by fans. This is the most convincing argument available to governing bodies, as transfer windows are unlikely to create economic efficiency, as they do not improve the promotion or distribution of 'goods' and may in fact render the market for players' services more expensive.

---

485. European Commission, *Commission staff working document. Impact assessment accompanying the White Paper on Sport*, SEC(2007) 935 final (2007) s. 2.21.6 and *see* Adam Lewis & Jonathan Taylor, *Sport: Law and Practice* 1515 (Bloomsbury Professional 2014). However, in its Communication on Developing European Dimension in Sport, the Commission also pointed out that the transfer of players may raise concerns about the legality of the system and the transparency of financial flows. *See* European Commission, *Communication from the Commission to the European Parliament, the Council, the European Economic and Social Committee and the Committee of the Regions – Developing the European Dimension in Sport*, 11 COM(2011) 12 final (2011), s. 4.4.

486. Adam Lewis & Jonathan Taylor, *Sport: Law and Practice* 1173 (Bloomsbury Professional 2014).

487. The objective of protecting the perception of fans was accepted by the Commission in *ENIC. See* Case COMP/37 806: ENIC/UEFA, para. 32.

488. Adam Berry, *Challenging Football Transfer Windows: A Disproportionate Response to a Legitimate Aim*, 20 Sport & L.J. 1 (2012).

489. Geoff Pearson, *Sporting Justifications under EU Free Movement and Competition Law: The Case of the Football 'Transfer System'*, 21(2) ELJ 220–238 (2015).

288. If the legitimacy of the objectives, and the inherency of the restrictive effects are to be accepted, the next question to be addressed concerns the proportionality. In this sense, it should be assessed whether any distortion caused is proportionate to the objective pursued, and whether less restrictive means could meet the same goals. In particular, an example of a less restrictive arrangement would see the prohibition of transfers only in the latter part of the season, when a late transfer could have very significant effects on the regularity of the competition. In the event that this type of measure would be considered sufficient to achieve the objectives stated, the legality of any restriction going beyond this ideal threshold should be questioned.

289. In this regard, one could question whether the task of assessing the proportionality of any restrictive effect would be for the Court to undertake, thereby substituting its judgment for any assessment made by the governing body. The Court would then be required to have significant knowledge of the area discussed that would allow it to identify possible alternatives and assess their suitability in the pursuit of a legitimate objective. Alternatively, the Court would rely on the expertise of governing bodies in adopting the contested rule and evaluating its proportionality.[490]

290. In *Bosman*, the CJEU dismissed the claim of the governing bodies, suggesting that less restrictive means to achieve the legitimate objectives were available.[491] In *Lehtonen*, the Court held that the imposition of stricter deadlines for the transfer of players from other Member States was disproportionate, without considering alternatives.[492] In *Bernard*, the Court took account of the social and educational function of sport in the context of assessing the proportionality of the restriction.[493] However, this reference was missing in *Murphy*,[494] where the stricter proportionality test was employed to assess a conduct exclusively considered in its commercial nature.[495]

291. Effectively, this is a matter related to the intensity of the proportionality test employed by the Court to review the regulatory authority of governing bodies.[496] In this regard, the Court assesses whether governing bodies have operated within the

490. Joined Cases C-51/96 and C-191/97 *Deliège v. Ligue francophone de Judo et disciplines Associeés Asb* [2000] ECR I-2549, para. 68 and Case C-519/04 P *David Meca-Medina and Igor Majcen v. Commission of the European Communities* [2006] ECR I-6991, paras 49 et seq.
491. Case C-415/93 *Union Royale Belge Sociétés de Football Association and others v. Bosman and others* [1995] ECR I-4921, para. 110.
492. Case C-176/96 *Lehtonen and Castors Canada Dry Namur-Braine ASBL v. Fédération royale belge des sociétés de basket-ball (FRBSB)* [2000] ECR I-02681, para. 58. Similarly, in Case C-325/08 *Olympique Lyonnais SASP v. Olivier Bernard and Newcastle UFC* [2010] ECR I-02177, para. 48.
493. *Ibid.*, para. 40.
494. Joined Cases C-403/08 and C-429/08 *FA Premier League and others v. QC Leisure and others, Karen Murphy v. Media Protection Services Ltd* [2011] ECR I-9083.
495. Katarina Pijetlovic, *EU Sports Law and Breakaway Leagues in Football* 128 (T.M.C. Asser Press 2015).
496. Tor-Inge Harbo, *The Function of the Proportionality Principle in EU Law*, 16(2) ELJ 158–185 (2010).

limits of a margin of discretion that is granted to them in light of their expertise.[497] Governing bodies are therefore free to identify objectives to be pursued, and restrictions needed to achieve them, but the Court may modulate the intensity of its review on the basis of the nature of such objectives, and the consideration given to interests that may be conflicting with those pursued.

IV. Contractual Stability

292. An issue significantly affected by the decision of the CJEU in *Bosman* is that of contractual stability in football. As previously mentioned, the transfer-related aspect of the judgment only addressed the player's status once the contract had ended. As a consequence, clubs amended their behaviour and sought to renew contracts of their players in order to avoid losing them without any compensation at the end of their contract.[498]

293. While the restriction on out-of-contract players was therefore removed after *Bosman*, other rules stemming from the FIFA RSTP curtailed the freedom of players and clubs with the objective of protecting the stability of contracts. These can be found in Articles 13–18 of the FIFA RSTP and are underpinned by the principle that contracts can only be terminated by mutual agreement of the parties or upon their expiry.[499] Therefore, contracts cannot be terminated unilaterally, unless in presence of a just cause, or a sporting just cause.[500]

294. To strengthen these principles, Article 17 establishes that, in the event of termination without just cause, the party in breach must pay compensation. When the party in breach is the player, he and the new club will be jointly and severally liable for the payment of compensation. Parties can stipulate in the contract or otherwise the amount due as compensation for the breach.[501] However, when such a determination is missing, the compensation should be '[c]alculated with due consideration for the law of the country concerned, the specificity of sport, and any other objective criteria'.[502] Objective criteria can include, among other elements, the remuneration of the player, under both the existing and the new contract, the time remaining on the existing contract, and the fees paid by the former club. It is apparent how this set of criteria could give rise to evaluations differing as to the amount

497. Mislav Mataija, *Private Regulation and the Internal Market: Sports, Legal Services, and Standard Setting in EU Economic Law* 93 (Oxford Univ. Press 2016).
498. Stephen Weatherill, *Principles and Practice in EU Sports Law* 223 (Oxford Univ. Press 2017).
499. Art. 13, FIFA RSTP.
500. 'Sporting just cause' refers to the occurrence in which a player has, in the course of the season, appeared in fewer than 10% of the official matches in which his club has been involved. *See* Art. 15 FIFA RSTP.
501. This would amount to a buy-out clause, not to be confused with a release clause, which amounts to an undertaking by the club to release the player when it receives an offer over a certain amount. Nick De Marco, *Football and the Law* 102 (Bloomsbury Professional 2018).
502. Art. 17 (1), FIFA RSTP.

of compensation due. In case this determination leads to a dispute, the Regulations establish the jurisdiction of the FIFA DRC, with appeals heard by CAS.[503]

295. The calculation of the compensation due under Article 17 has proved controversial and has been the subject of a number of conflicting CAS awards.[504] In *Webster*, CAS held that the damages for unilateral termination without just cause should be calculated on the basis of the outstanding remuneration due to the player until the expiry of the contract.[505] This approach, defined as compensating the 'residual value' of the contract, was certainly an interpretation favourable to the interests of the players,[506] while disregarding the loss of the club, often exceeding the wages left to be paid.[507] Shortly after that in *Matuzalem*, CAS adopted a different approach, applying the principle of 'positive interest', which aims at putting the party that has suffered the breach of contract in the position it would have been if the contract would have been performed properly. Thereby, the calculation of the compensation could include the costs of replacing the player who left the club, and hence his transfer value.[508] CAS therefore upheld the principle of contractual stability, increasing the deterrent effect of Article 17 to its fullest potential. Its effect is to discourage players from terminating the contract, as well as deter potential future clubs from signing them, considering that they would be jointly liable for the payment of the compensation.[509]

296. However, the uncertainty created by the methodological difference between the decisions in *Webster* and *Matuzalem* led to a number of other disputes. In *De Sanctis*, CAS attempted to find a suitable middle ground between the two approaches outlined above. The Court made reference to the entire set of criteria presented in Article 17, none of which should be decisive in calculating the compensation due. In this context it considered that under 'the specificity of sport', other objectives not directly addressed by Article 17 should be taken into account.[510] Effectively, this allowed CAS to consider aspects such as the importance of the player for the club and its fan base and its role in the team, in assessing the value due as compensation.

297. When crafted in 2001, Article 17 sought to balance the interests of players with that of clubs and since then the CAS has attempted to navigate this balance. This balance was tested in *Mutu* where the CAS rejected the claim to hold jointly liable the player and the club that hired him, once Chelsea terminated the contract

503. Art. 24, FIFA RSTP.
504. For a comprehensive discussion of the cases decided by CAS on the matter, *see* Alexander Wild, *CAS and Football: Landmark Cases* (T.M.C. Asser Press 2012).
505. CAS 2007/A/1298/1299/1300 – *Heart of Midlothian v/ Webster & Wigan Athletic FC.*
506. Stephen Weatherill, *Principles and Practice in EU Sports Law* 231 (Oxford Univ. Press 2017).
507. Juan de Dios Crespo Pérez et al., *Contractual Stability: Breach of Contract*, in *CAS and Football: Landmark Cases* 37–105 (Alexander Wild ed., T.M.C. Asser Press 2012).
508. CAS 2008/A/159 – *FC Shakhtar Donetsk (Ukraine) v/ Mr. Matuzalem Francelino da Silva (Brazil) & Real Zaragoza SAD (Spain) & FIFA.*
509. Richard Parrish, *Article 17 of the FIFA Regulations on the Status and Transfer of Players: Compatibility with EU Law*, 22(2) MJECL 256–282 (2015).
510. CAS 2010/A/2145-2147 – *Udinese Calcio S.p.a. v. Morgan De Sanctis & Sevilla FC Sad*, para. 96.

after he was banned for using a prohibited substance.[511] The rationale of such a decision was that an opposite award would have made it significantly more difficult for players in similar circumstances to resume their careers and find employment.

298. In an amendment adopted in 2018, further additions were made to Article 17. Next to the criteria to be used to calculate the compensation due when the contract has been terminated without just cause, the 2018 version introduced new elements to be considered. In particular, a mitigated compensation is introduced, where the value of the new contract signed by the player and referring to the time covered by the previous contract is deducted from the calculation of the compensation due.

299. In assessing the balance between the rights and interests of the parties, it should be considered that, to further protect the principle of contractual stability, the FIFA RSTP also introduced a so-called protected period.[512] This corresponds to the first three years from the entry into force of the contract between a player and a club, or two years if the player is older than 28, during which sporting sanctions will be imposed on the athlete in the event of a unilateral breach of contract on his side.[513] During the protected period, which starts again and is extended every time the contract is renewed, the player who terminates the contract without just cause is subject to both the payment of compensation and the imposition of sporting sanctions. Once this period has expired, the player will be able to terminate the contract with no sanctions, provided that compensation is paid to his current club. The strength of this provision is further increased by the presumption that the club signing a professional player that has breached his previous contract without just cause has induced the breach. The new club, alongside being jointly and severally liable, can then be subject to sporting sanctions if the breach has occurred during the protected period.[514]

300. The introduction of Article 17 allowed the system to respond to the liberalisation of the market for players' services that occurred with *Bosman*. As players can move freely at the end of their contract, clubs tend now to extend contracts more regularly, thereby renewing the protected period as well. While this situation increased the leverage power that players may have during the negotiation of the new contract, partially explaining the increase in players' wages from the pre-*Bosman* era, the main consequence is that clubs will retain a significant level of control over their players.[515] Effectively, the system reintroduced transfer fees in cases

511. CAS 2013/3365 – *Juventus Football Club S.p.A. v. Chelsea Football Club Ltd.*
512. Definition n. 7, FIFA RSTP.
513. The sanction may range from four to six months' suspension from playing in official matches. *See* Art. 17(3), FIFA RSTP.
514. Art. 17(4), FIFA RSTP. The club breaching a contract or that has induced the breach during the protected period is banned from registering any new players, either nationally or internationally, for two entire and consecutive registration periods.
515. Richard Parrish, *Article 17 of the FIFA Regulations on the Status and Transfer of Players: Compatibility with EU Law*, 22(2) MJECL 256–282 (2015).

of unilateral breach of contract.[516] The existence of sporting sanctions, imposed both on the players terminating the contract and the new clubs, is a very powerful incentive against unilateral termination. The effects of such a system are further strengthened by the uncertainty over the amount of compensation due, demonstrated by the brief analysis of the CAS jurisprudence discussed above.[517]

301. It is apparent how these rules can cause significant restrictions on the market. However, rules imposing contractual stability in team sports can address the need for stabilising relations between clubs and athletes. This protects the stability of the competition by ensuring that teams will not sign decisive players at a critical point of the season.[518]

302. Since its adoption, the FIFA RSTP has been subject to reform, progressively attempting to improve the balance between the rights and obligations of clubs and players. One important addition is included in Article 12bis. This provision establishes that sanctions may be imposed on clubs that have overdue payables towards players or other clubs.[519] The rationale behind this provision is to create a system of enforcement for the financial obligations that clubs incurred in their activity with players and other clubs.[520] This obligation covers any sum overdue for more than thirty days without a contractual basis. Overdue payables have also been included as an express circumstance allowing parties to terminate the contract with just cause. Players in particular are allowed to terminate the contract in the event the club has failed to pay their salary for two consecutive months. If the termination occurs due to overdue payables, the player is also entitled to an additional three months' salary that could be increased to six months' salary in case of egregious circumstances, but that cannot exceed the value of the contract.[521] Players are also explicitly allowed to terminate the contract with just cause in the event the clubs have put in place conduct attempting to force them to accept reductions in salary or termination of the contract.[522]

303. These amendments aim to provide greater certainty of the rights of the players and an enforcement route. They reflect the contribution FIFPro and the other stakeholders have made in their consultative role as part of the FIFA Stakeholders Committee. Importantly for the current assessment, they demonstrate FIFA's awareness of different interests of the stakeholders and an attempt to find a suitable balance between them.

---

516. Geoff Pearson, *Sporting Justifications under EU Free Movement and Competition Law: The Case of the Football 'Transfer System'*, 21(2) ELJ 220–238 (2015).
517. Stephen Weatherill, *Principles and Practice in EU Sports Law* 228 (Oxford Univ. Press 2017).
518. Adam Lewis & Jonathan Taylor, *Sport: Law and Practice* 578 (Bloomsbury Professional 2014).
519. Art. 12 bis (4), FIFA RSTP. Sanctions, which may be applied cumulatively, range from a warning, a reprimand, a fine and a ban from registering any new players, either nationally or internationally, for one or two entire and consecutive registration periods.
520. Frans de Weger, *The Jurisprudence of the FIFA Dispute Resolution Chamber* 22 (T.M.C. Asser Press 2016).
521. Art. 14 bis, FIFA RSTP.
522. The same right applies to the club, in the event the player has employed similar conduct.

V. International Transfers Involving Minors

304. The FIFA RSTP also regulates the international transfer of minors, generally defined as players that are younger than 18.[523] The provisions of EU law protecting the free movement of workers, and citizens, apply to minors as well as adults. Minors who are citizens of a Member State can therefore exercise their citizenship rights stemming from Article 21 TFEU and the Charter of Fundamental Rights.[524] These provisions prohibit private entities that exercise 'certain power over individuals' from adopting discriminatory measures even against non-economically active individuals.[525]

305. Furthermore, the definition of 'worker' under EU law does not make reference to the age of the individual who, for a certain period of time and under the direction of another person, provides services in return for remuneration.[526] This interpretation has been confirmed in EU legislation, through the Charter of the Fundamental Social Rights of Workers[527] and the Directive on the Protection of Young People at work.[528] The Directive mandates Member States to ensure that '[Y]oung people are protected against economic exploitation and against any work likely to harm their safety, health or physical, mental, moral or social development or to jeopardize their education.'[529] The Directive also requires Member States to prohibit the work of children under 15, but provides for a derogation that can be applied to children employed for the purposes of cultural, artistic, sports or advertising activities. In this regard, Member States can authorise the employment of children as young as 13 in individual cases.[530] It is therefore clear that a minor can be classed as a worker for the purposes of free movement provisions. Any restriction in this regard must be assessed in relation to the objective pursued and its proportionality.

306. Finally, minors (and adults under the age of 21) who are direct descendants of a Union citizen can also draw protection from the free movement rights exercised by their parents. Under Directive 2004/38, the direct descendant of a Union citizen that has moved to another Member State has rights to departure, entry and return, as well as equal treatment.[531]

---

523. Definition 11, FIFA RSTP.
524. Art. 34, Charter of Fundamental Rights of the European Union.
525. Case C-22/18 *TopFit e.V. and Daniele Biffi v. Deutscher Leichtathletikverband e.V.* [2019] EU:C:2019:497, para. 34.
526. Case 66/85 *Lawrie Blum v. Land Baden-Württemberg* [1986] ECR 2135, paras 17 and 21.
527. Community Charter of the Fundamental Social Rights of workers. At point 20 the Charter provides that the minimum working or employment age is not lower than the minimum age at which compulsory full-time schooling as imposed by national law ends or fifteen years in any event.
528. Council Directive 94/33/EC of 22 Jun. 1994 on the Protection of Young People at Work, OJ L 216/12.
529. *Ibid.*, Art. 1(3).
530. *Ibid.*, Art. 5.
531. Art. 24, Directive 2004/38/EC of the European Parliament and of the Council of 29 Apr. 2004 on the right of citizens of the Union and their family members to move and reside freely within the territory of the Member States, OJ L 158.

307. Rules restricting minors from being registered with a football club in another State may therefore also constitute a hindrance to the free movement of their parents, dissuading them from exercising their rights under EU law in the fear the child will be prevented from registering with the new club.[532]

308. The task of FIFA in this area is therefore particularly delicate, as it needs to balance legitimate yet possibly conflicting objectives. On the one hand, it needs to encourage the training and development of young players, but, on the other, it seeks the protection of a particularly vulnerable category, exposed to a range of threats.[533] The significance of this area is highlighted by the fact that the EU institutions have expressed their concerns about aspects related to transfers involving minors in a number of instances.[534] In particular, the Commission has stressed the concern related to the exploitation of children from third countries, and its incompatibility with the EU values and sporting values. This was also highlighted in a study on the transfer market undertaken on behalf of the Commission, according to which the aim of the rules regulating the transfer of minors was to '[P]revent that young and promising future football players fall victim of unscrupulous traffics generated by the promises of future financial gains.'[535] Furthermore, Article 165(2) TFEU places significant emphasis on these issues, as it specifically states that the action of the EU in sport should aim at 'protecting the physical and moral integrity of sportsmen and sportswomen, especially the youngest sportsmen and sportswomen'.

309. Article 19 of the FIFA RSTP establishes that minors may not be subject to international transfers. However, the rule provides for a series of exceptions, of which the market makes great use.[536] Underpinning this approach is the recognition that, in some specific circumstances, an international transfer may be in the best interest of the minor. The transfer of a minor is therefore permitted when the parents move to the country of the new club for reasons other than football or when the

---

532. For a discussion on this topic, *see* Kester Mekenkamp, *FIFA's Provision on the Protection of Minors – Part 3: The Compatibility of Article 19 with EU Law*, Asser International Sports Law Blog, https://www.asser.nl/SportsLaw/Blog/post/fifa-s-provision-on-the-protection-of-minors-part-3-the-compatibility-of-article-19-with-eu-law-by-kester-mekenkamp 3 Jan.2017 (accessed 30 Apr. 2020).
533. *See*, for example, the Resolution of the UN General Assembly underlining that minors face threats such as '[v]iolence, doping, early specialization, over-training and exploitative forms of commercialization, as well as […] premature severance of family bonds and the loss of sporting, social and cultural ties'. UN Resolution 58/5, 17 Nov. 2003, Sport as a means to promote education, health, development and peace, available at http://research.un.org/en/docs/ga/quick/regular/58 (accessed 20 Apr. 2020).
534. *See* European Council, Nice, 7–10 Dec. 2000, Conclusions of the Presidency. Annex IV, *Declaration on the specific characteristics of sport and its social function in Europe, of which account should be taken in implementing common policies* (2000), para. 13, and European Commission, *White Paper on Sport*, COM(2007), 391 final (2007), s 4.5.
535. KEA/CDES, *Study on the Economic and Legal Aspects of Transfers of Players*, European Commission, 54 (2013).
536. *See* FIFA, Global Transfer Market Report 2019, stating that more than 4,500 minor applications were decided in 2019. Available https://resources.fifa.com/image/upload/global-transfer-market-report-2019-men.pdf?cloudid=x2wrqjstwjoailnncnod (accessed 20 Apr. 2020).

player and the clubs are located within 50 kilometres from the border that separates the two countries, therefore at a maximum distance of 100 kilometres between each other. Furthermore, a specific exception applies within the territory of the EU (and European Economic Area (EEA)), where international transfers are allowed if the player is older than 16.[537] This exception has been used to a significant extent to boost youth academies of European clubs, particularly those from England where the loss of the exception due to Brexit will be keenly felt. To outweigh the obligation imposed by the home-grown player rule, clubs have been able to recruit players as young as 16 from other EU countries, field them in their academies and then claim them as home-grown.[538]

310. The EU/EEA exception is significant in its scope. First, the rule does not make reference to the nationality of the player, thereby covering also transfers of non-EU nationals, provided that the transfer occurs within the EU/EEA territory. Second, the provision covers any EU/EEA national, regardless of whether the transfer involves a club from a national association outside the territory of the EU/EEA. Indeed, under the interpretation of this rule given by CAS, players who may have dual nationality, one of which is of an EU Member State, can benefit from the exception.[539] Third, extending the scope of application of this rule even further, the principle established in *Kolpak* means that minors who are nationals of a State that has an association agreement with the EU would be covered by this exception, once they are in the territory of the EU.[540]

311. It must be noticed how, to balance the economic considerations that permeate the use of this last exception, further requirements have to be satisfied: the new club has to provide the player with adequate football education, academic or vocational education as well as living standards.[541] In the last iteration of Article 19, further exceptions are provided: players who are students can move for academic reasons for a temporary period in another country and register with an amateur club there and players who flee their country of origin for humanitarian reasons may register with a club in the new country.

312. The application of the exception to individual circumstances has to be approved by a subcommittee of the FIFA Players' Status Committee. Such an assessment is also rendered necessary by the fact that the list of exceptions provided for in Article 19(2) is not exhaustive. Other circumstances where the transfer of a minor will be permitted have been developed through the decisions of the FIFA PSC and by CAS. They include the event in which the player moves to the country

537. Art. 19 (2), FIFA RSTP.

538. For a discussion of home-grown player rule, *see* Chapter 3.

539. *See* CAS 2012/A/2862 *FC Girondins de Bordeaux*.

540. Case C-438/00 *Deutscher Handballbund v. Kolpak* [2003] ECR I-4135. In CAS 2008/A/1485, *Midtjylland v. FIFA*, the CAS considered the principle not applicable, because the players in the case did not have an employment contract with the club, Midtjylland. As such, they were not considered workers, but students.

541. The new club must provide evidence to the national association of the player that such requirements are satisfied.

of the new club to study, and not to play football; and when the player has lived continuously for at least five years in the country of the new club, before being registered with it.[542] In the event a club is found to have breached Article 19, the FIFA Disciplinary Committee can impose sanctions against the club and the association to which it is affiliated.[543]

313. Finally, Article 19bis includes a number of provisions, mainly directed at national associations and youth academies, to increase the transparency and accountability of the system. Clubs operating an academy in any capacity are obliged to report all the minors attending the academy to the relevant national association. In turn, national associations are obliged to monitor and enforce such obligations on the clubs of their territory.[544]

314. The limits imposed on the transfer of minors in the EU potentially constitute a restriction on their freedom of movement. Following an orthodox approach, the legitimacy of the objective pursued by FIFA should be assessed. In this regard, it must be considered how FIFA is, in this area, required to pursue objectives of public interest, such as the protection of minors. This objective is connected, but arguably not exactly corresponding, to the legitimate objective of encouraging the training of young players, discussed in *Bernard*. Nevertheless, the protection of minors has been considered a legitimate objective in other instances, where the Court assessed free movement of goods restrictions in a case not related to sport.[545] On the basis of the case law of the Court of Justice, and the wording of the White Paper and Directive 94/33, it is safe to assume that the protection of minors constitutes a legitimate objective that may justify restrictions to free movement.

315. A relevant consideration is the authority that the governing body exercises in identifying and pursuing the interests and well-being of young footballers.[546] In particular, FIFA restricts the freedom of movement of young workers under the assumption that international transfers will be detrimental to the system and the interests of the minors. However, circumstances can be envisaged where an international transfer can be highly beneficial for the minor. For instance if the minor moves to a country that offers better opportunities, regardless of how the future sporting career progresses. It would appear that the task of FIFA could go beyond its powers, but the Commission itself has identified the protection of minors as a concern that must be addressed by governing bodies in regulating the transfer of players. The protection of minors in football is therefore delegated to governing bodies and it includes the regulation of aspects related to their transfer.

542. For a discussion of these exceptions, *see* Nick De Marco, *Football and the Law* 172 (Bloomsbury Professional 2018).
543. Art. 19(4), FIFA RSTP.
544. CAS 2014/A/3813 – *Real Federación Española de Fútbol (RFEF) v. Fédération Internationale de Football Association (FIFA)*.
545. Case C-244/06 *Dynamic Medien Vertriebs GmbH v. Avides Media AG* [2008] ECR I-505.
546. Serhat Yilmaz et al., *Children's Rights and the Regulations on the Transfer of Young Players in Football*, 55(1) Int. Rev. Soc. Sport 115–124 (2018).

316. In relation to the proportionality of the restriction, particular attention should be given to its suitability to achieve the legitimate objective pursued. The liberalisation of the market, the increase in transfer fees and their impact on the financing of clubs, and the imposition of home-grown players rules have had the effect of creating a market for young footballers. When clubs recruit from abroad, they aim to sign players as young as possible.[547] This is further demonstrated by the number of applications for transfers involving minors made to the subcommittee of the FIFA Players' Status Committee and the number of decisions appealed to CAS. An assessment of the proportionality of the restriction should carefully consider the relevance of this argument. In particular, the number of exceptions granted may in itself constitute an obstacle to the effectiveness of the rule in achieving its own objectives.

317. It may, however, be too simplistic to reduce the objective of the rule to the protection of minors. In its assessment of Article 19, CAS has outlined that the real objective of the rule is to strike a balance between legitimate yet conflicting interests. In this, the rule is a proportionate means to balance the requirement to train young players and the need to protect them, especially when they relocate in a country other than their own.[548]

318. This approach is particularly interesting, as CAS has effectively adopted a reasoning that follows the analysis of the Court of Justice in case such as *Bernard*. CAS, as guardian of the autonomy of sport, has embarked in an assessment of the proportionality of the measure that recognised a margin of appreciation of FIFA in the pursuit of a range of objectives. The focus of the proportionality test is therefore on the suitability of the exercise undertaken by the governing body in balancing these interests. When appropriate consideration is given to these interests, it may be argued that FIFA has satisfied the requirement of proportionality.

VI. The Reform of the Transfer System

319. The modern transfer regulations have been amended since being adopted in 2001, but the substance has remained untouched.[549] Many elements that characterised the transfer system in the pre-*Bosman* era are still present.[550] As opposed to the transfer fees due for players after the expiry of their contract, the system now features compensation payments and protected periods, but the effect is similar.

---

547. Eleanor Drywood, *'When We Buy a Young Boy … ': Migrant Footballers, Children's Rights and the Case for EU Intervention*, in *The EU as a Children's Rights Actor*, 191–221, 200 (Ingi Iusmen & Helen Stalford eds, Barbara Budrich 2016).
548. CAS 2014/A/3792 – *Futbol Club Barcelona v. FIFA*, para. 9.34.
549. For an overview of the rules, principles and legal issues related to the regulation of transfers in football, *see* Michele Colucci & Ornella Bellia (eds), *Transfers of Football Players, A Practical Approach to Implementing FIFA Rules*, Sports Law and Policy Centre (2020).
550. That is, provisions protecting contractual stability and transfer fees. The only exception is the introduction of the new training compensation.

320. In their assessment, Stix-Hackl and Egger considered that the 2001 amendments did not sufficiently address the concerns.[551] It should then be considered whether the subsequent amendments have in any way affected this assessment, and if the transfer system persists in breach of EU law. This is especially relevant when Article 165 TFEU is taken into account. The promotion of openness and fairness can hardly be considered compatible with a transfer system that restricts the ability of players to move and of clubs to sign them. The system could also be subject to criticism in relation to the proportionality of the restriction and their effectiveness to pursue legitimate objectives. If the principle of contractual stability must be understood as requiring contracts to run until their natural termination, the conduct of clubs constantly renewing contracts or deciding to transfer players as an alternative, demonstrates a failure to achieve such an objective.

321. At the time of writing, the system is being reformed by FIFA.[552] The reform, due to enter into force in 2022, has identified a number of objectives that can be legitimately pursued, including protecting the integrity of football; incentivising and promoting the training of young professional players and ensuring solidarity within the system; ensuring uncertainty of outcome in competitions, and promoting competitive balance; ensuring the regularity and proper functioning of sporting competition; and improving the general transparency of the system. To this effect, FIFA has addressed a number of areas discussed in this monograph: training compensation, transfer of young players, transfer windows, home-grown players, and the regulation of agents.

322. The general principles informing the reform package have been agreed by the FIFA Football Stakeholders Committee, a body created to include in the decision-making process representatives from clubs, leagues and players as well as member associations, confederations and the FIFA administration. The package includes the establishment of a clearing house that working alongside the Transfer Matching System should process all transfer fees and ensure solidarity and training compensation would be effectively paid where due; the introduction of limitations on the number of international loans of players aged 22 and older for each team, with a transitional period phasing in the system; the reintroduction of licensing requirements for agents alongside the setting of restrictions on agents commission and representation activity.

§3. Regulating Sports Agents

323. An activity closely connected to the operation of the transfer system is the work of sports agents. The prevalence of agency work is most well developed in

551. Christine Stix-Hackl & Alexander Egger, *Sports and Competition Law: A Never-Ending Story?*, 23(2) ECLR 81–91 (2002).
552. FIFA, *Football Stakeholders Agree Further Steps in the Reform of the Transfer System*, https://www.fifa.com/who-we-are/news/football-stakeholders-agree-further-steps-in-the-reform-of-the-transfer-system, 27 Feb. 2020 (accessed 25 Mar. 2020).

the football sector, although agents operate quite extensively in other sports, such as basketball, rugby and athletics.[553] Traditionally, agents have been viewed with a degree of suspicion by the sports authorities, largely due to reports of bad practice and the earnings they make out of sport.[554] This has contributed to agents being perceived as a third-party operating outside the European model's 'family'. In this way, the regulation of agents has traditionally proceeded on the same basis as the regulation of other third-party entities in sport, such as third-party investors in players and the regulation of undertakings wanting to assume control of more than one club. This raises important legal issues under EU law. Are agents stakeholders within the sports sector and subject to the internal regulation of the sports authorities, or are they normal economic actors operating outside the European model's structure and as such able to avail themselves of the same legal protections as other economic actors? In essence, this question asks whether the regulation of agents should fall within the concept of the specificity of sport.

I. FIFA Regulation and *Piau*

324. In football, FIFA has regulated agents since the early 1990s.[555] The 1994 Players' Agent Regulations (PAR) required an individual wanting to provide agent services to be in possession of a licence issued by the competent national association. Clubs and players were under an obligation only to engage the services of such licensed agents during transfer or contract negotiations. To be in receipt of a licence, the individual was required to undertake an interview to ascertain the candidate's knowledge, particularly of sport and the law. The candidate was also required to satisfy certain conditions, such as having no criminal record and depositing a bank guarantee of 200,000 Swiss Francs (CHF).

325. The 1994 regulations were challenged, notably in 1998 by the French agent Laurent Piau who complained that they were in conflict with EU competition law and EU laws on freedom to provide services. Specifically, Piau complained that the licensing conditions unfairly restricted access to the market, the regulations were likely to give rise to discrimination between citizens of the Member States and they did not include any legal remedies against decisions or applicable sanctions.

326. In 1999, the European Commission issued a Statement of Objections resulting in FIFA making some amendments to the regulations. The new 2001 FIFA PARs retained the licencing requirement but instead of undergoing an interview, the applicant, who was required to have an 'impeccable reputation', was required to take a

553. As identified in KEA, CDES, EOSE, *Study on Sports Agents in the European Union*, a Study commissioned by the European Commission (2009).

554. For a useful overview of the work of agents *see* Giambattista Rossi et al., *Sports Agents and Labour Markets* (Routledge 2016).

555. For an account of the history of agent regulation in football *see* Richard Parrish et al.., *Promoting and Supporting Good Governance in the European Football Agents Industry* (2019), European Commission Representation in Croatia, https://www.edgehill.ac.uk/law/files/2020/02/On-line-book-final.pdf 28–36, October 2019 (accessed 2 Mar. 2020).

written multiple-choice examination testing the candidate's knowledge of sport and the law. The agent was also required to take out a professional liability insurance policy or, failing that, deposit a bank guarantee. As before, the relationship between the agent and the player was governed by a written contract for a maximum period of two years, which could be renewed. The contract had to stipulate the agent's remuneration, which was calculated on the basis of the player's basic gross salary and, if the parties could not reach an agreement, was fixed at 5% of the salary.

327. On the basis of the amended regulations, the Commission closed its investigation[556] but soon after, Piau lodged an appeal before the European CFI, since renamed the General Court. Piau claimed that by rejecting his complaint, the Commission had gone beyond the powers conferred upon it by the Treaty by implicitly delegating to FIFA a power to regulate an activity of providing services. On this point, the Court stated that FIFA's legitimacy to regulate agents was 'open to question'.[557] FIFA's self-proclaimed statutory purpose is to promote football and the 2001 PAR, which the Court had established do not have a sports-related object, regulate an economic activity that is peripheral to the sporting activity in question and touch on fundamental freedoms. Regulating a profession, such as the activity of agents, would normally fall to a public authority and not a private entity such as FIFA and the Court found that this situation 'cannot from the outset be regarded as compatible with Community law, in particular with regard to respect for civil and economic liberties'.[558]

328. Despite these reservations, the Court accepted FIFA's rule-making authority in this area due to 'the almost complete absence of national rules' on agents regulation[559] and because 'collectively, players' agents do not, at present, constitute a profession with its own internal organisation'.[560]

329. The Court found no restriction of competition. The most restrictive elements of the 1994 regulations had been removed in the 2001 version. The Court found that the examination offered satisfactory guarantees of objectivity and transparency, the professional liability insurance obligation and the code of professional conduct did not impose disproportionate obligations on players' agents and the remuneration provisions of the regulations referred to an objective, transparent criterion (the player's basic gross salary) with the 5% cap merely a subsidiary mechanism for the settlement of disputes. Neither did the Court agree with Piau's remaining objections. The content of the standard contract, and its limited duration, was found not to restrict competition, but in fact stimulate it. The sanctions system could not be considered manifestly excessive for a system of professional sanctions. Finally, the Court disagreed with Piau's assessment of the regulations that

556. *See* European Commission, Press Release IP/02/585, Commission closes investigations into FIFA rules on players' agents, 18 Apr. 2002.
557. Case T-193/02 *Laurent Piau v. Commission of the European Communities* [2005] ECR II-209, para. 76.
558. *Ibid.*, para. 77.
559. *Ibid.*, para. 78.
560. *Ibid.*, para. 102.

denied him access to ordinary courts in case of a dispute. The Court pointed out that interested parties can access ordinary courts, in particular in order to assert their rights under national or EU law, and actions for annulment can also be brought before the Swiss Federal Court against decisions by the CAS.

330. The Court concluded that the Commission committed no error in finding that the compulsory nature of the licence might be justified and that the amended regulations could be eligible for an exemption under what is now Article 101 TFEU. In this regard, the Court considered that the licence system did not result in competition being eliminated, as the system resulted in a qualitative selection process, rather than a quantitative restriction on access to that occupation. This was necessary in order to raise professional standards for the occupation of a players' agent, particularly as players' careers were short and they needed protection. Although the Court disagreed with the Commission's assessment that FIFA did not hold a dominant position in the market of services of players' agents, the Court went on to find no abuse of market dominance. The position of dominance was established as FIFA operates as an emanation of the clubs and in that role holds a collectively dominant position on the market for players' agents' services. However, no abuse of dominance could be established as the system resulted in a qualitative selection process, rather than a quantitative restriction on access to that occupation. On further appeal, and dispensed with by Order of the Court, the European Court of Justice upheld the judgment of the CFI.[561]

II. The 2015 FIFA RWWI

331. Shortly after the conclusion of the case, FIFA announced its intention to reform the system of agent regulation. FIFA identified an inefficient licensing of players' agents, resulting in the conclusion of many international transfers without the use of licensed agents. Marco Villiger, FIFA Director of Legal Affairs stated at the EU Conference on Sports Agents in 2011 that 'only 25–30% of transfers are managed by official FIFA licensed agents'.[562] FIFA was also concerned that even transfers concluded with the use of licensed agents were often not transparent and thereby not verifiable and they considered there to be confusion regarding the differences between club representatives and players' agents and their respective financial obligations.[563] In 2015, in what was considered a revolutionary step, FIFA replaced the PAR with the Regulations on Working with Intermediaries (RWWI).

561. Case C-171/05 P *Laurent Piau v. Commission of the European Communities*, Order of the Court (Third Chamber) of 23 Feb. 2006, ECR 2006 I-37.
562. Marco Villiger speaking at the EU Conference on Sports Agents, Brussels, https://ec.europa.eu/assets/eac/sport/library/studies/final-report-eu-conference-sports-agents.pdf 9–10 Nov. 2011 (accessed 9 Apr. 2020).
563. FIFA, Working with Intermediaries – reform of the players' agents system, https://www.fifa.com/news/working-with-intermediaries-reform-of-fifa-s-players-agents-system-2583543 (accessed 20 May 2020).

332. The 2015 RWWI shifted the regulatory focus from the agent themselves to the activity they facilitate – the transfer or contract negotiation. Reflecting this, the RWWI dispensed with the word 'agent' and instead referred to 'intermediaries' with an intermediary being both a natural or legal person. Under the RWWI, intermediaries no longer require a licence and so the examination requirement was dispensed with. Intermediaries are required to certify that they have no conflicts of interest, unless declared, and that they have an impeccable reputation. The regulations require that each time intermediaries are involved in a transaction, they must be registered with the national association to which the club is affiliated. National associations are required to maintain the register.

333. Although no mandatory fee cap was established, FIFA recommended that national associations adopt a remuneration cap of 3% on the services provided by intermediaries. Intermediaries are prohibited from being remunerated in terms of employment contracts and/or transfer agreements if the player concerned is a minor. Breaches of the RWWI are enforced by national associations and any sanctions imposed may be extended by the FIFA Disciplinary Committee. The RWWI are effectively minimum standards requiring national associations to adopt national intermediary regulations. Crucially, these national measures can go beyond the specified minimum standards, and this contributed to a lack of regulatory consistency and uniformity across the thirty-one national associations operating within the territory of the EU.[564]

334. The 2015 regulations amounted to delicensing and deregulation and this attracted considerable criticism. For example, at a 2017 meeting of the EU Sectoral Social Dialogue Committee for Professional Football, attended by UEFA, FIFPro Division Europe, the ECA and the EPFL, a number of concerns were raised including a lack of stakeholder consultation with the adoption of the 2015 regime; a lack of transparency in financial transactions involving intermediaries; an increase in the number of individuals or companies acting as intermediaries which pushed demand for ever younger players; a diminution of the quality of the services provided to clubs and players by intermediaries; inflation of fees paid to intermediaries, who, it was felt, were disproportionately well remunerated for their services; continuation of conflicts of interest; a lack of consistency in the implementation of the rules from one territory to another which resulted in some national 'markets' being more attractive than others for intermediaries/agents; an unnecessary and ineffective increase in the administrative burden on all parties; an absence of effective sanctions; and a growing problem of rule circumvention.[565]

---

564. For discussion *see* Richard Parrish et al., *Promoting and Supporting Good Governance in the European Football Agents Industry*, European Commission Representation in Croatia (2019), https://www.edgehill.ac.uk/law/files/2020/02/On-line-book-final.pdf October 2019 (accessed 2 Mar. 2020).

565. EU Sectoral Social Dialogue Committee for Professional Football: Resolution on Intermediaries/Agents, 17 Nov. 2017.

335. On the basis of the above, the resulting resolution of the Committee called for reform which should include: 'a harmonised, uniform European approach' incorporating a reasonable, proportionate cap on fees for intermediaries/agents; enhanced transparency, disclosures and accountability; appropriate and dissuasive sanctions in case of non-compliance; stronger provisions to protect minors in their relations with intermediaries/agents; and an efficient monitoring and enforcement framework.[566]

III. Reforming the RWWI

336. In the same month as the Social Dialogue Committee Resolution, FIFA and FIFPro concluded a six-year cooperation agreement which formed part of the settlement to FIFPro's legal challenge regarding the operation of the transfer system.[567] As described elsewhere in this chapter, FIFPro had lodged a complaint with the European Commission in September 2015 alleging incompatibilities between the FIFA transfer system and EU law. As part of the settlement seeing the withdrawal of the complaint, FIFA established a Transfer System Task Force with a view to conduct a review of the transfer system, including the role played by intermediaries within it. The Task Force operated as a subcommittee to FIFA's newly established Football Stakeholders Committee.

337. Football agents were invited to participate as part of consultative workshops held in Zurich in April and May 2018 although they were not formally part of the Task Force itself.[568] The Task Force deliberated throughout 2018 and 2019, and in September 2019 a final package of reforms was sent to and approved by the Football Stakeholders Committee.[569] These reforms were subsequently approved by the FIFA Council meeting at the end of October 2019.[570] The principles are, at the time of writing, being transposed into formal regulations and are expected to be in force no sooner than the 2021 season.

338. Aspects of the reform package unlikely to result in significant conflict between the agents and FIFA include the reintroduction of a mandatory licensing system for agents, which will include further education measures and a requirement for continuing professional development; the payment of agents' commissions via a new FIFA Clearing House; and the establishment of a new FIFA dispute resolution

566. *Ibid.*
567. FIFA, *FIFA and FIFPro sign landmark agreement and announce measures to enhance professional football*, https://www.fifa.com/about-fifa/who-we-are/news/fifa-and-fifpro-sign-landmark-agreement-and-announce-measures-to-enhan-2918747 6 Nov. 2017 (accessed 9 Apr. 2020).
568. FIFA, *FIFA holds talks with agents on possible revision of football intermediaries system*, https://www.fifa.com/about-fifa/news/y=2018/m=4/news=fifa-holds-talks-with-agents-on-possible-revision-of-football-intermediaries-sys.html 20 Apr. 2018 (accessed 9 Apr. 2020).
569. FIFA, *FIFA and football stakeholders recommend cap on agents' commissions and limit on loans*, https://www.fifa.com/about-fifa/who-we-are/news/fifa-and-football-stakeholders-recommend-cap-on-agents-commissions-and-limit-on- 25 Sep. 2019 (accessed 9 Apr. 2020).
570. FIFA, *FIFA Council unanimously appoints China PR as hosts of new Club World Cup in 2021*, https://www.fifa.com/about-fifa/who-we-are/news/fifa-council-unanimously-appoints-china-pr-as-hosts-of-new-club-world-cup-in-202 24 Oct. 2019 (accessed 9 Apr. 2020).

system to solve disputes between agents, players and clubs. Following *Piau*, a transparent, non-discriminatory and proportionate licensing system should not adversely engage EU law if the sporting objective of it is to improve professional standards rather than to set quantitative limits on access to the profession.

339. The contentious elements of the reforms concern proposals to restrict agent remuneration and limit the practice of dual representation, the practice of an agent representing more than one party in the same transaction. Under the RWWI, a fee cap of 3% was recommended, but largely ignored. The new proposal is for a mandatory cap being introduced amounting to 10% of the transfer fee for agents of releasing clubs, 3% of the player's remuneration for player agents and 3% of the player's remuneration for agents of engaging clubs. Under a dual representation scenario involving the player and engaging club, a cap on the commission at 6% of the player's salary will be set, which amounts to 3% from each party. Under this proposal, only one dual representation scenario is envisaged meaning that other forms of multiple representation, such as the practice of an agent representing all three parties in a transaction, are prohibited.

340. By early 2020, agent bodies, the most prominent being the European Football Agents Association (EFAA), had decided that remuneration and representation restrictions would be challenged.[571] Legal action could be commenced in national courts and a referral sought to the Court of Justice of the EU, or the regulations could be the subject of a complaint before the European Commission. Despite the subject matter, *Piau* is not the most authoritative judgment from which to receive guidance as the formula in *Meca-Medina* is more likely to be followed.

341. The *Meca-Medina* approach, assessed in detail elsewhere in this monograph, places emphasis on a contextual assessment of whether the effects restrictive of competition (or indeed free movement) are inherent in the proportionate pursuit of legitimate sporting objectives. As seemingly economic objectives, arguments concerned with limiting the 'power' of agents and restricting the amount of money 'leaving football' are unlikely to be accepted as legitimate by the Court or Commission.[572] To repeat the reasoning of the Court in *Piau*, FIFA regulation of agent activity does 'not have a sport-related object' and it regulates economic activity that is 'peripheral to the sporting activity in question' and touches on fundamental freedoms.[573]

342. The legitimacy of FIFA to impose a mandatory fee cap on such agent activity would be strengthened if agents were not considered a third-party, peripheral to

---

571. BBC, *Agents threaten FIFA with legal challenge over transfer payment cap plans*, https://www.bbc.co.uk/sport/football/51211078 2 Mar. 2020 (accessed 9 Apr. 2020).
572. *See*, for example, The Daily Telegraph, *Backlash grows over 'immoral fees' after claim Paul Pogba's agent made £41m from transfers*, https://www.telegraph.co.uk/football/2017/05/10/backlash-grows-immoral-fees-claim-paul-pogbas-agent-made-41m/ 10 May 2017 (accessed 9 Apr. 2020).
573. Case T-193/02 *Laurent Piau v. Commission of the European Communities* [2005] ECR II-209, para. 76.

the sporting activity, but rather a stakeholder central to it. A study on agent regulation published in 2019 claimed wide support within the football industry for the proposition that agents are a necessary part of the football industry and should be recognised as stakeholders.[574] It must be recalled that under the principles established by the EU institutions, the sport system is entitled to self-governance, insofar as the principles of good governance are respected.[575] One such principle is stakeholder consultation and representation.

343. For FIFA, the safest territory for justifying a fee cap lies in the safe harbour of *Meca-Medina*. In other words, justifications must be connected to the proportionate pursuit of legitimate sporting objectives. In this regard, an argument that can soften the edges of purely economic justifications relates to a cap being necessary to ensure consistency with the training compensation and solidarity objectives of the transfer system.[576] For example, in 2017, whereas club spending on agents' commissions reached USD 446 million, solidarity payments totalled only USD 64 million and training compensation USD 20.3 million. While agent fees have risen considerably since 2013, solidarity and training compensation sums have been stable.[577] The problem with this argument is that the solidarity and training compensation regimes are not connected with the activity of agents and agents cannot be held responsible for poor collection and redistribution rates for solidarity payments.

344. A stronger argument centres on the objective of protecting players. A cap limits the amount a player has to pay an agent and it might align remuneration more closely with the value of the services provided by agents.[578] EU law will seek to protect the weaker party in any relationship where there is scope for damaging exploitation.[579] Players are generally young, not always particularly well educated due to the nature of their training development and their careers are quite short. This argument presupposes that agents are a source of abuse in the system, whereas many agents rebalance the inequality of arms a player has with a club. In this regard, it is difficult to argue that clubs, as consumers of agent services, amount to a weaker party and require regulatory protection. Clubs have access to in-house or external

---

574. Richard Parrish et al., *Promoting and Supporting Good Governance in the European Football Agents Industry*, European Commission Representation in Croatia 116 (2019), https://www.edgehill.ac.uk/law/files/2020/02/On-line-book-final.pdf October 2019 (accessed 2 Mar. 2020).
575. European Commission, *White Paper on Sport*, COM(2007) 391 final (2007), s. 4.
576. As laid out in the FIFA RSTP, 2019 Edition, Arts 20–21.
577. FIFA Football Stakeholder Committee, *Task Force Transfer System, White Paper – Transfer System Reform* 48 (2018).
578. Although, historically, players have been able to discharge their liability to an agent through the club. FIFA is reviewing this practice and under the new set of regulations, players might be required to pay their own costs – the player pays model.
579. For example, the EU Capital Requirements package, encompassing Regulation 575/2013 on prudential requirements for credit institutions and investment firms and Directive 2013/36 on access to the activity of credit institutions and the prudential supervision of credit institutions and investment firms, protects consumers from excessive risk-taking by bankers by determining the ratios between the fixed and variable components of the total remuneration so that a bankers' bonus cannot usually be greater than the fixed salary.

expertise and should be in a strong position vis-à-vis relations with agents. FIFA's proposals, as they stand at the time of writing, seek to impose a fee cap on agent fees when the agent is employed by both or either parties.

345. Another potential sporting justification relates to the suggestion that the prospect of agents receiving high fees encourages speculation and fosters contractual instability. This pulls against the principle of maintaining contractual stability which is one that underpins the FIFA RSTP.[580] This claim rests on the assumption that an agent exerts a powerful, and decisive, influence over the player and it fails to consider other sources of contractual instability, such as the conduct of the clubs.

346. The *Meca-Medina* method also highlights the importance of proportionality. Regarding the imposition of remuneration and representation restrictions on agents, less restrictive means of achieving the stated legitimate sporting objectives must be considered, as must the fee cap percentage, if that regulatory measure is adopted. Fees tend to be lower, the higher the value of the transaction, yet FIFA appears to be recommending a flat fixed cap and one that is not in line with current industry practice.[581]

§4. Nationality-Based Rules

347. Sport is structured on inherently discriminatory grounds. Athletes are separated according to a number of personal characteristics including sex, age, weight and nationality. The focus on separating participants according to nationality is somewhat of a 'European custom' and has developed due to the European model of sport promoting a national segmentation model in which sport is organised on a national basis with one governing body per sport, per country.[582] This approach places great importance on national competitions, national championships and competitions between national teams. National champions are celebrated, national records revered, and athletes have assumed an ambassadorial status for the countries they represent. Indeed, in order to reward such athletic achievement and to compensate athletes for their absence from the labour market due to their dedication to their sport, some States provide benefits to high-level sportspersons who have represented that country and achieved outstanding results.[583] Whereas the EU seeks ever closer union through the erosion of national borders and the abolition of

580. FIFA RSTP, 2019 Edition, Arts 13–18.

581. *See* Richard Parrish et al., *Promoting and Supporting Good Governance in the European Football Agents Industry*, European Commission Representation in Croatia 72–73 (2019), https://www.edgehill.ac.uk/law/files/2020/02/On-line-book-final.pdf October 2019 (accessed 2 Mar. 2020).

582. P. Delanney, cited in Stefaan Van den Bogaert, *Practical Regulation of the Mobility of Sportsmen in the EU Post Bosman* 339 (Kluwer Law International 2005).

583. In Case C-447/18 *UB v. Generálny riaditeľ Sociálnej poisťovne Bratislava* [2019] ECLI:EU:C:2019:1098, the Court found that a Member State which grants such a benefit to its national workers cannot refuse to grant it to workers who are nationals of other Member States without discriminating on the basis of nationality.

discrimination on grounds of nationality, the organisation of sport in Europe retains a pronounced national character. To preserve this national character, many sports bodies restrict access of non-nationals to national sporting events, a practice that potentially runs contrary to the general ethos underpinning European integration.

I. Nationality Discrimination in Team Sports

348. EU sports law can trace its roots to a preliminary reference made by a lowly District Court in Utrecht in 1973 concerning alleged nationality discrimination in motor-paced cycling. The UCI decided that from 1973, the two participants in the sport, the pacemaker and the stayer, had to be the same nationality on the grounds that world championships were intended to be competitions between national teams. Two Dutch professional pacemakers who routinely contracted with non-Dutch stayers objected to what they considered to be an infringement of EU laws on nationality discrimination.

349. The European Court's judgment – that the practice of sport is subject to EU law only in so far as it constitutes an economic activity – has been the cornerstone of EU sports law for many years.[584] For this mantra to work in practice, the Court needed to supplement it with a statement to the effect that the prohibition on nationality discrimination 'does not affect the composition of sport teams, in particular national teams, the formation of which is a matter of purely sporting interest and as such has nothing to do with economic activity'.[585] The Court then went on to explain that 'this restriction on the scope of the provisions in question must however remain limited to its proper objective'.[586] Had the Court not added these statements, national teams would have found themselves in the somewhat bizarre position of being unable to restrict selection to only nationals of that country. For the Advocate General in the case, it was 'common sense' for national teams to consist only of nationals of that country.[587] Less obvious was what actually amounts to a national team? Were the stayers the true national representatives or was it their connection with the pacer that created the bond? According to the Advocate General in *Walrave*, this 'makes all difference' as EU law was minded to favour treating national team sports as a special case where EU non-discrimination rules could not penetrate.[588]

350. Reference to 'the composition of sport teams, in particular national teams' suggests that while national team selection was at the forefront of the Court's thinking, other teams could avail themselves of this exception to exclude non-nationals.

584. Case 36/74 *Walrave & Koch v. Association Union cycliste internationale* [1974] ECR 1405, para. 4.
585. *Ibid.*, para. 8.
586. *Ibid.*, para. 9.
587. Case 36/74 *Walrave & Koch v. Association Union cycliste internationale* [1974] ECR 1405, Opinion of Advocate General Warner, para. 1426, first column.
588. Case 36/74 *Walrave & Koch v. Association Union cycliste internationale* [1974] ECR 1405, Opinion of Advocate General Warner, para.1427.

Soon after in *Donà*, the Court considered nationality restrictions in Italian club football.[589] Here, the Court found that rules limiting participation in football matches solely to the nationals of the State in question conflict with EU law unless such rules exclude foreign players from participation in certain matches for reasons which are not of an economic nature, which relate to the particular nature and context of such matches and are thus of sporting interest only.[590]

351. Nationality restrictions continued to be a feature of the sporting landscape in the years after *Walrave* and *Donà*. In the mid-1980s, the European Commission raised concerns as to the practice and discussions took place between the Commission and UEFA which resulted in UEFA adopting the 1991 3+2 rule, an agreement concluded with Martin Bangermann, the Vice President of the Commission.[591] From July 1992, national associations and UEFA could limit to three the number of foreign players whom a club may field in any first division match in their national championships and in UEFA competitions, plus two assimilated players who have played in the country in question for five years uninterruptedly, including three years in junior teams.

352. Litigation brought by footballer Jean-Marc Bosman ended the 3+2 rule.[592] The fact that the European Commission had sanctioned the practice in 1991 was insufficient to save it as the Court held that the Commission did not possess the power to authorise practices that are contrary to the Treaty.[593] However, the Court's assessment on the substantive merits of the 3+2 rule still merits attention.[594]

353. The Court established that while nationality quotas relate to the fielding of players and not to their employment by a club, a restriction on a worker's freedom of movement still exists as a restriction on participation also restricts the prospects of employment.[595] That could have ended the assessment as the 3+2 rule amounted to a form of direct discrimination that EU law orthodoxy asserts could only be saved by the Treaty-based derogations of public policy, public security and public health.[596] However, the Court proceeded to examine arguments, presented by UEFA, the Belgian Football Association URBSFA and some national governments,

589. Case 13/76 *Donà v. Mantero* [1976] ECR 1333.
590. *Ibid.*, para. 19.
591. Richard Parrish & Samuli Miettinen, *The Sporting Exception in European Union Law* 175 (T.M.C. Asser Press 2008).
592. Case C-415/93 *Union Royale Belge Sociétés de Football Association and others v. Bosman and others* [1995] ECR I-4921.
593. *Ibid.*, para. 136.
594. For monograph-length analysis *see* Stefaan Van den Bogaert, *Practical Regulation of the Mobility of Sportsmen in the EU Post Bosman* (Kluwer Law International 2005) and Roger Blanpain, *The Legal Status of Sportsmen and Sportswomen under International, European and Belgian and Regional Law* (Kluwer Law International 2003).
595. Case C-415/93 *Union Royale Belge Sociétés de Football Association and others v. Bosman and others* [1995] ECR I-4921, para. 120.
596. Article 45(3) TFEU.

seeking to justify nationality restrictions as per *Walrave* and *Donà* 'on non-economic grounds, concerning only the sport as such'.[597]

354. Three such justifications were presented, and each was demolished by the Court. First, it was argued that the 3+2 rule served to maintain the traditional link between each club and its country, a factor which was claimed to have great importance in enabling the public to identify with its favourite team and ensuring that clubs taking part in international competitions effectively represent their countries.[598] Dismissing this, the Court argued that a football club's link with the Member State in which it is established could not be regarded as any more inherent in its sporting activity than its links with its locality, town or region where no rules exist designed to maintain the connection. Furthermore, in international competitions, participation is limited to clubs which have achieved certain results in competition in their respective countries, without any particular significance being attached to the nationalities of their players.[599]

355. Second, on the justification relating to nationality restrictions being necessary to ensure a pool of players eligible to play for the national team, the Court countered that labour mobility enhances the prospects of players playing in other national associations and no rules exist limiting a national team's choice of players to one association.[600]

356. Third, the Court held that nationality restrictions are inadequate for maintaining a competitive balance between clubs because the richer teams can still recruit the best national players regardless.[601] This assessment did not, however, undermine the Court's wider view that rules designed to promote competitive balance in sport are, in principle, to be considered legitimate.[602]

357. Consequently, in answer to the question referred by the national court, the Court held that EU law 'precludes the application of rules laid down by sporting associations under which, in matches in competitions which they organise, football clubs may field only a limited number of professional players who are nationals of other Member States'.[603]

358. This statement struck an apparently devastating blow to those asserting that athletes playing for clubs should be representative of the country in which the club plays, in the same way that a national team should be composed of athletes representative of that country, as per *Walrave*. The national character of the European model of sport was, therefore, somewhat eroded by *Bosman*. The legacy of *Bosman*

597. Case C-415/93 *Union Royale Belge Sociétés de Football Association and others v. Bosman and others* [1995] ECR I-4921, para. 122.
598. *Ibid.*, para. 123.
599. *Ibid.*, paras 131–132.
600. *Ibid.*, paras 133–134.
601. *Ibid.*, para. 136.
602. *Ibid.*, para. 106.
603. *Ibid.*, para. 137.

has generated much academic attention.[604] A key consequence was that the European labour market for professional footballers became liberalised and clubs in national leagues became less representative of the country in which they play. For example, on Boxing Day in 1999, Chelsea FC fielded an entire starting eleven made up of non-British players. This was the first time in the history of British football that this had occurred.

359. This type of practice resulted in calls for a rethink and a re-regulation of the labour market so that national competitions retained a national character and national team sport was protected. Chief proponents of this were FIFA and UEFA who also observed the post-*Bosman* environment was characterised by a diminution of competitive balance across European football as the best players gravitate to the richest clubs, thus calling into question the unpredictability of match and championship outcomes. In response, at UEFA's Ordinary Congress in April 2005 in Estonia, UEFA introduced its locally trained player regulations, commonly referred to as the home-grown player rule.[605]

360. The rule requires every football team entering European club competitions to name eight 'home-grown' players in their 25-man squad. Four of these players must be 'club-trained', defined as a player who, irrespective of his nationality and age, has been registered with his current club for a period of three entire seasons or of 36 months while between the age of 15 and 21. Four of these players must be 'association-trained'; these fulfil the same criteria but with another club in the same national association. If a club fails to meet these quotas, the maximum number of players on the squad list for the competition is reduced accordingly.

361. FIFA also explored the idea of re-regulating the labour market for players by way of a '6+5 rule' requiring clubs to field six nationals in the starting eleven. This proposal was withdrawn in 2010, presumably on the grounds that the rule amounted to a type of direct nationality discrimination condemned in *Bosman*.[606] UEFA's approach was more nuanced in that location of training and not nationality was the criteria for eligibility. This subtle adjustment removed any scent of direct discrimination, thus enhancing UEFA's claim that its new quota is materially different from its 3+2 quota condemned in *Bosman*.

604. *See* for instance Antoine Duval & Ben Van Rompuy (eds), *The Legacy of Bosman. Revisiting the Relationship Between EU Law and Sport* (T.M.C. Asser Press 2016).

605. Incorporated by way of *Regulations of the UEFA Champions League 2006/07 Competition, Conditions for Registration: List A*, 22. Corresponding regulations were applied, and continue to apply, to UEFA's other club competitions.

606. For an assessment, *see* Felix Majani, *One Step Forward, Two Hops Backwards: Quotas – The Return. An Excavation into the Legal Deficiencies of the FIFA 6+5 Rule and the UEFA Home-Grown Players Rule in the Eyes of European Union Law*, 1–2 ISLJ 19 (2009). In fact, FIFA did initially seek to justify the 6+5 proposal by commissioning: INEA, *Expert Opinion on the Compatibility of the 6+5 Rule with European Community Law* (2008).

362. The mere fact that the home-grown player rule is silent on nationality as an eligibility criterion does not, however, remove it from the scope of EU law. Professional footballers could object to the rule on the grounds that it amounts to a provision which precludes or deters them from leaving their country of origin in order to exercise their freedom of movement. This is because a number of places in a club squad are reserved exclusively for locally trained players and this is likely to deter clubs from recruiting non-nationals. It can reasonably be assumed that more nationals are likely to meet the eligibility criteria than non-nationals and therefore the restriction on the player's freedom of movement can be considered to arise out of a case of indirect nationality discrimination.[607]

363. Restrictions arising out of indirect nationality discrimination are capable of justification with reference to the pursuit of legitimate sporting objectives. As established in *Bosman*, and confirmed in cases since, maintaining a balance between clubs by preserving a certain degree of equality and uncertainty as to results and encouraging the recruitment and training of young players are considered legitimate objectives.[608] Nevertheless, even if it is accepted that the restrictive effects of UEFA's rule can be justified, the suitability of the measure for securing the attainment of its objective must be assessed along with a consideration of whether the measure goes beyond what is necessary to attain it.

364. The proportionality of UEFA's rule has not yet been judicially confirmed although in 2014 the European Commission indicated favourable assessment. In 2014 in a 'reasoned opinion' under its infringement procedures, the Commission requested that Spain alter the rules on the composition of basketball teams as the quotas in place at the time for locally trained players led to indirect indiscrimination towards players from other Member States. The Commission accepted as legitimate the objectives put forward by Spain to justify these rules, which were to encourage the recruitment and training of young players and protecting the balance of competitions, but the Commission considered that Spain failed to demonstrated the appropriateness and proportionality of the quotas for each competition. In arriving at that position, the Commission used UEFA's quota as a reference point. It noted that whereas 32% of squad places in football are reserved for locally trained players, in Spanish Basketball the quota ranged between 40% and 88%.[609]

365. The requirements of EU law clearly constrain the ability of sports bodies to impose nationality-based rules within the territory of the EU. Brexit has freed the UK from such constraints and has resulted in a debate on the direction of travel for UK sport. Some governing bodies, such as the English Football Association (FA),

607. This was the conclusion of a study funded by the European Commission: Murray Dalziel et al., *Study on the Assessment of the Compatibility of UEFA's Home Grown Player Rule with Article 45 TFEU*, https://ec.europa.eu/assets/eac/sport/library/studies/final-rpt-april2013-homegrownplayer.pdf 30 Apr. 2013 (accessed 9 Apr. 2020).

608. Case C-415/93 *Union Royale Belge Sociétés de Football Association and others v. Bosman and others* [1995] ECR I-4921, para. 106.

609. European Commission, *Reasoned Opinion*, https://ec.europa.eu/commission/presscorner/detail/en/MEMO_14_293 16 Apr. 2014 (accessed 20 Mar. 2020).

see Brexit as an opportunity to restrict the participation of overseas players as a means of promoting the interests of the national team. This could be achieved through quota systems and imposing the same type of work permit requirements on EU nationals wanting to enter the UK as those experienced by non-EU nationals. Naturally, UK sportsmen and women wishing to enter the EU market could face similar restrictions. In contrast to the view of the FA, the English Premier League is generally resistant to the idea of limiting the number of overseas players from the EU as the league has developed a distinctly international character and this has, arguably, driven up standards and made the Premier League's broadcasting rights globally very marketable.

II. Discrimination Against Non-EU Nationals

366. Bosman concerned how nationality restrictions frustrated intra-EU migration, but the EU has entered into a number of international agreements with third States, with some containing provisions on the treatment of non-EU workers enshrining the principle of non-discrimination on the grounds of nationality. For example, prior to joining the EU, the Slovak Republic entered into one such agreement with the EU that, *inter alia*, provided that 'subject to the conditions and modalities applicable in each Member State: treatment accorded to workers of Slovak Republic nationality legally employed in the territory of a Member State shall be free from any discrimination based on nationality, as regards working conditions, remuneration or dismissal, as compared to its own nationals'.[610]

367. This provision was relied on by Maros Kolpak, a Slovak national, and a handball goalkeeper playing in the second division handball club TSV Ostringen in Germany. The national governing body of handball, the German Handball Federation (DHB), issued Kolpak with a player's licence indicating that he was to be treated as an overseas player (non-EU/EEA). This restricted his chances of participation in the team, as clubs were only permitted to field two such players.

368. On reference to the Court of Justice, the Court first established the horizontal effect of the provision, meaning that *Kolpak* could rely on it.[611] The Court proceeded to find that Article 38(1) of the EU/Slovak Republic Agreement precludes such discriminatory rules being applied to individuals who are already lawfully employed by a club established in a Member State.[612] In that regard, the Association Agreement did not regulate access to the host market, and as such, it did not extend a general right of free movement to Kolpak. His placement on the overseas list was captured by Article 38 as it pertained to working conditions in as much as it directly affected his participation in league and cup matches. He had less opportunity to play than nationals of EU/EEA Member States and this amounted to differential treatment on the grounds of his nationality.

610. Art. 38(1) of the EU/Slovak Republic Association Agreement, no longer in force.
611. Case C-438/00 *Deutscher Handballbund eV v. Maros Kolpak* [2003] ECR 1-4135, paras 24–30.
612. *Ibid.*, para. 58.

369. Attempts by the DHB to justify the rule on exclusively sporting grounds failed, namely its purpose was to safeguard training organised for the benefit of young players of German nationality and to promote the German national team.[613] The Court acknowledged the legitimacy of nationality discrimination within the context of national team selection, but repeated the approach taken in *Bosman* that this cannot be extended to club competitions. In any event, the argument regarding the protection of the national team was undermined as clubs in Germany were free to field an unlimited number of nationals from EU/EEA States.

370. The logic of *Kolpak* was repeated by the Court in *Simutenkov* in which a Russian footballer, legally employed in Spain, suffered the same fate as Kolpak and was put on the overseas list thus restricting his participation in the sporting competition. The differential treatment he suffered in relation to EU/EEA nationals ran contrary to the EU/Russia Agreement.[614] The same outcome was witnessed in *Kahveci* where a Turkish professional footballer playing in Spain suffered similar discrimination despite the existence of an EU/Turkey Association Agreement.[615]

371. It is worth repeating that these cases concern non-discrimination against third-country nationals who are already legally employed in a Member State of the EU. It does not extend a general right of free movement to such workers. The impact on sport should not, therefore, be overstated. However, neither should the impact be trivialised, particularly when set in the context of the *Bosman* judgment. In *Bosman*, the Court dismissed arguments that nationality quotas are necessary to protect national teams by maintaining a sufficient talent pool for national selectors to select from. The Court pointed out that national players, whose opportunities may be reduced by the presence of overseas players, can themselves benefit from the liberalised European labour market that *Bosman* helped create.[616] Since then, *Kolpak* has extended non-discrimination to some third-country nationals, and so the pool of players eligible for national team selection is further reduced.

372. The claim made by the Court in Bosman about the existence of a European labour market might hold for professional football, where all Member States have professional leagues, but not all sports, such as rugby and cricket, offer such rich and reciprocal employment opportunities. The England and Wales Cricket Board (ECB) has long expressed concerns about the impact of *Kolpak* on the pool of English qualified players and has informed the county sides (cricket clubs) that post-Brexit, *Kolpak* player registrations will be terminated and those players will effectively revert to being classified as overseas players.

613. *Ibid.*, para. 52.
614. Case C-265/03 *Simutenkov v. Ministerio de Educación y Cultura and Real Federación Española de Futbol* [2005] ECR I-2579.
615. Case C-152/08 *Real Sociedad de Fútbol SAD, Nihat Kahveci v. Consejo Superior de Deportes, Real Federación Española de Fútbol* [2008] ECR I-6291.
616. Case C-415/93 *Union Royale Belge Sociétés de Football Association and others v. Bosman and others* [1995] ECR I-4921, para. 134.

373. Some sports, such as cricket, are much more reliant on incomes generated by the national team than football, with the success of the national team being fundamental to the viability of some sports. This interdependency, with funds from the top generating talent from below, highlights the importance of measures designed to safeguard the national team. Although the football authorities have to a large extent lost this argument, it is conceivable that other sports with a greater existential investment in national teams could make a coherent case as to why nationality restrictions, perhaps couched as *sporting* nationality restrictions, should be retained or reintroduced.[617] Here the criteria do not relate directly to nationality, but eligibility to represent the country.

374. On the question of the benefits of a liberalised European labour market in sport, Weatherill considers the Court to be in error as it 'makes assumptions about the virtues of economic integration in the EU that fail to account of the specific nature of sport'.[618] The argument is that the sports market operates differently from more traditional markets which benefit from the type of market integration the Court favoured in *Bosman*. In other words, market integration does not create new jobs in sport; it merely facilitates the movement of a fixed number of athletes between a fixed number of clubs.

III. Nationality Discrimination in Individual Sports

375. The *Bosman* judgment gave great prominence to the issue of nationality discrimination in team sports, yet little attention was given to the picture in individual sports, such as triathlon, modern pentathlon, tennis, table tennis, badminton, rowing, weightlifting, wrestling and many others. A study for the European Commission published in 2010, in which one of the authors of this monograph participated, revealed the extent of discriminatory practices in these sports.[619] These practices included prohibiting access of non-nationals to national competitions, permitting access but restricting full participation (such as denying the possibility of becoming national champion or receiving medals and establishing national records) and imposing residency and club membership requirements as a condition of participation.

376. The range of justifications cited by sports bodies in defence of such practices included the desire of national sports bodies and sponsors to fund national athletes; the need to prepare for national representative events and to identify the best

617. For a discussion on the concept of sporting nationality and EU Law *see*: Jan Exner, *Sporting Nationality in the Context of European Union Law* (Springer 2019); Stefaan Van den Bogaert, *Practical Regulation of the Mobility of Sportsmen in the EU Post Bosman* 348–367 (Kluwer Law International 2005) and Stephen Weatherill, *Principles and Practice in EU Sports Law* 200–202 & 193–194 (Oxford Univ. Press 2017).

618. Stephen Weatherill, *Principles and Practice in EU Sports Law* 184 (Oxford Univ. Press 2017).

619. T.M.C. Asser Institute, Edge Hill University & Leiden University, *Study on the Equal Treatment of Non-Nationals in Individual Sports Competitions*, Study for the European Commission (2010).

national athletes; the need to nurture and give opportunities to young national athletes; the need to ensure integrity, fairness and competitive balance in sport; the need to preserve the national character of national championships; the desire of the public to identify with national athletes and stay engaged in the sport; the need to avoid a situation in which one nationality dominates many national championships and the need to retain media interest in the sport.[620]

377. The first scenario addressed in the Commission-funded study concerned access of athletes to national competitions such as a tennis tournament. The study recommended that such events should in principle be open access granting non-nationals participation on the same terms as nationals. However, limited exceptions to this principle were considered. For example, the structure and format of some competitions naturally require access limitations being imposed, such as restricting a Grand Slam Tennis tournament to 128 participants. The national sports body organising that competition might then want to reserve a number of places to nationals in order to promote the training and development of young players. Such limited and proportionate restrictions could be defended as a rule inherent in the organisation of a sporting event or the Court could break with its orthodoxy and accept justifications for such directly discriminatory practices.[621] This issue is returned to below in the discussion regarding the Court's judgment in *TopFit*.[622]

378. The second scenario concerned the question of who can take part in a national championship, events in which national titles are bestowed and athletes are selected for representative honours. In this regard, such events are imbued with a national character and the national purity of the event is often cherished by organisers, participants and the public. However, even here, the principle of open access for non-nationals can be maintained, subject to limited exceptions. For example, the exclusion of non-national athletes from national championships could be defended as an inherent rule in instances in which they exert too direct and substantial an influence on the outcome of the championship. This is especially the case in sports which involve direct eliminations, for instance the knockout system in boxing or judo. The corollary to this is that non-national athletes should be granted access to the championship when their influence is marginal and it is possible for the best national to be identified. Indeed, the Commission study identified sports with knockout systems to be more closed than those without.[623]

379. The related question of whether non-nationals can be awarded the title of national champion was the third issue considered in the 2010 study. For Weatherill,

620. *Ibid.*, at 219–225.

621. For other proposed exceptions to the general principle of open access *see* T.M.C. Asser Institute, Edge Hill University & Leiden University, *Study on the Equal Treatment of Non-Nationals in Individual Sports Competitions*, Study for the European Commission, 235–236 (2010).

622. Case C-22/18 *TopFit e.V. and Daniele Biffi v. Deutscher Leichtathletikverband e.V.* [2019] EU:C:2019:497.

623. T.M.C. Asser Institute, Edge Hill University & Leiden University, *Study on the Equal Treatment of Non-Nationals in Individual Sports Competitions*, Study for the European Commission, 239 (2010).

crowning a non-national as national champion would be a step too far as 'that would destroy the very nature of the contest' given that the object is to select the best national athlete in a specific discipline.[624] Nevertheless, in some sports, the title is open to non-nationals[625] and one could envisage a scenario in which non-nationals who have a sufficiently close connection with the country in question, such as through residency, could compete for the award of national title. Nevertheless, if challenged, the rule restricting the award to nationals could be defended as an inherent rule closely connected to the very purpose of the rule which is to identify the best national.

380. The final scenario relates the question of excluding non-nationals from winning national medals and setting national records. As the Commission study acknowledged, even though symbolic, such accolades can bring with them significant economic rewards such as sponsorship. Yet there is symbolism attached to the award of medals and records that transcends economic activity, the awarding of such being the essence of sport. This is not to say, as the General Court did in *Meca-Medina* that sport 'is essentially a gratuitous and not an economic act, even when the athlete performs it in the course of professional sport'.[626] This would be to conflate the act of participating in sport, which engages economic activity, with the symbolic recognition of excellence which is a purely sporting act. For that reason, the Commission study favours employing paragraph 8 of *Walrave*, rules of purely sporting interest, to remove such practices from the scope of the Treaty. For those uneasy about breathing new life into the *Walrave* formula, excluding non-nationals from receiving national medals and setting national records could be considered an inherent rule. The effects restrictive of free movement or competition could be considered inherent in the pursuit of the legitimate objective of crowning the best national.

IV. Nationality Discrimination in Amateur Sport

381. The Commission study referred to above was published shortly after the entry into force of Article 165 TFEU. The second paragraph of 165 refers to EU action in the field of sport being aimed at, *inter alia*, 'developing the European dimension in sport, by promoting fairness and openness in sporting competitions … ' The reference to 'openness' supports the study's general conclusion that open access to sporting events should be the starting principle from which limited exceptions could then apply. What was lacking was the judicial authority

624. Stephen Weatherill, *Principles and Practice in EU Sports Law* 202 (Oxford Univ. Press 2017).
625. In 2010, the Commission-funded study identified aquatics in Germany, biathlon in Cyprus, Estonia and Finland and gymnastics in France, Greece and Slovakia. *See* T.M.C. Asser Institute, Edge Hill University & Leiden University, *Study on the Equal Treatment of Non-Nationals in Individual Sports Competitions*, Study for the European Commission (2010).
626. Case T-313/02 *Meca-Medina and Majcen v. Commission* [2004] ECR II-3291, para. 45.

that Article 165 required the principle of open access to be taken more seriously by sports bodies – until, in 2019, the Court delivered its judgment in *TopFit*.[627]

382. *TopFit* has a clear connection with the issues discussed above, but its substance concerned discrimination in amateur sport. The case involved Daniele Biffi, an Italian national living in Germany. Biffi was a member of German athletics club TopFit, and he competed in the amateur senior German championships, organised by the German Athletics Association. In the senior category, he competed for the title of 'national champion', and he used his placings to advertise his business as an athletics coach and personal trainer.

383. In 2016, the German Athletics Association amended its rules to restrict the participation of non-nationals, who could now only compete 'without classification', meaning that participation was restricted to the first round of a running competition. Biffi objected to this on the grounds that, as a non-national, he could no longer compete in the German national championships on the same basis as those athletes with German nationality and this could result in him receiving less support from his athletics club. As a consequence of this, Biffi claimed he would be less able to integrate himself into German society and such treatment could also have a damaging effect on his business.

384. Biffi's claim in the German Court alleged infringement of EU law, but the German Court was undecided on whether the application of EU law to sport is always subject to the exercise of economic activity, particularly since the advent of EU citizenship rights and the entering into force of Article 165 TFEU, both provisions which are not dependent on the existence of economic activity. Consequently, the German Court made a reference to the Court of Justice regarding the interpretation of Articles 18, 21 and 165 TFEU.

385. The Advocate General declined the invitation to give EU citizenship rights, enshrined in Article 21 TFEU, horizontal effect and so connected Biffi's discrimination claim to his provision of services of an economic nature, this despite the referring court not requesting interpretation of Article 49 TFEU.[628] The Court departed from this Opinion.

386. Previously in *Commission v. France*, the Court established that every national of a Member State is assured freedom to enter another Member State in order to pursue an employed or self-employed activity and to reside there after having pursued such an activity. The rights granted to the individual extend to cover also access to social advantages such as leisure activities available in that Member State as a corollary to that freedom of movement.[629] In that regard, in *TopFit*, the

627. Case C-22/18 *TopFit e.V. and Daniele Biffi v. Deutscher Leichtathletikverband e.V.* [2019] EU:C:2019:497.

628. Case C-22/18 *TopFit e.V. and Daniele Biffi v. Deutscher Leichtathletikverband e.V.* [2019] EU:C:2019:497, Opinion of Advocate General Tanchev.

629. Case C-334/94 *Commission v. France* [1996] ECR I-01307, para. 21.

Court found that Articles 21 and 165 TFEU allow an EU citizen who is residing in another Member State to 'create bonds with the society of the State to which he has moved and in which he is residing or to consolidate them'[630] and that the rights of non-economically active individuals under Articles 18 and 21 apply to all private entities that exercise 'certain power over individuals' and are able 'to impose on them conditions'.[631] As such, Biffi's treatment constituted a restriction on the freedom of movement of EU citizens within the meaning of Article 21 TFEU.[632]

387. The Court's approach is significant in that it raises the prospect of sporting events becoming 'open-access'. Allowing non-nationals free access to sport would fundamentally alter the national character of the European model of sport. It would, as argued by the German Athletics Association, run counter to the perception that the public expects the national champion of a given State to be a national of that State[633] and it would challenge the basis on which national teams are selected. However, the Court's condemnation of the German rule was fact-specific and concerns as to the demise of the European model are premature.

388. The Court acknowledged that in sports with eliminatory heats, such as athletics, the presence of non-nationals is capable of preventing a national from winning the championship and hindering the designation of the best nationals.[634] In such circumstances, the Court accepted the legitimacy of limiting the participation of non-nationals as long as there is genuinely no mechanism allowing for their participation, such as participation in the early heats and/or without classification. Should such a mechanism be available, the total exclusion of that non-national would, according to the Court, fail proportionality control.[635] The Court's approach is therefore to assert that open access is the overarching principle from which sports bodies can derogate only if excluding non-nationals can be justified by objective considerations which are proportionate to the legitimate sporting objective pursued.

389. In this regard, *TopFit* has a significance in so far as the Court has explicitly accepted that directly discriminatory nationality measures can be justified beyond the Treaty-based derogations of public policy, public security and public health.[636] Far from representing a defeat for sports bodies and a judicial assault on the national character of the European model, the judgment offers opportunities for sports bodies to seek new means of justifying direct nationality discrimination, such as the need to preserve the national character, identity, purity, public confidence in and cultural significance of national sporting competitions. This clearly has a relevance for the analysis of discrimination in individual sports discussed above.

630. Case C-22/18 *TopFit e.V. and Daniele Biffi v. Deutscher Leichtathletikverband e.V.* [2019] EU:C:2019:497, para. 34.
631. *Ibid.*, paras 37–40.
632. *Ibid.*, para. 47.
633. *Ibid.*, para. 51.
634. *Ibid.*, para. 61.
635. *Ibid.*, para. 66.
636. Art 45(3) TFEU.

390. *TopFit* is also significant as it gives practical expression to, and judicially codifies, the much-cited reference in EU sports policy to the 'social significance' of sport and the need for 'openness in sporting competitions'.[637] Access to sport is now recognised as an activity facilitating social integration and amateur sport can no longer be regarded as an activity sitting outside the scope of the fundamental principles of free movement. *TopFit* also reveals a more explicit willingness on the part of the Court to read Article 165 horizontally into other Treaty provisions, in this instance Articles 18 and 21. Prior to that, reference in the sporting jurisprudence to Article 165 has been somewhat secondary.

§5. The Involvement of Stakeholders

391. According to one study, the transfer system approved by the Commission in 2001 and incorporated into the FIFA RSTP has not achieved its objectives.[638] The combination of the commercialisation of sport, the liberalisation of the market, rules imposing contractual stability and the lack of effectiveness of solidarity payments and training compensation have led to a diminution of competitive balance, where both national and international competitions are dominated by a small pool of clubs.[639] Similarly, the combination of rules and their enforcement, constituting a significant restriction on the freedom of the athletes, has also consolidated an imbalance between rights and obligations of the various stakeholders.[640] The power dynamic affecting the relationship between employers (clubs) and employees (players) is heavily affected by the operation of *lex sportiva*. Through the regulatory domain of governing bodies, the system of *lex sportiva* enshrines the imbalance of power in a number of employment-related aspects.

392. This is not to say that a system regulating the transfer of players in sport is not needed. Rather, these are arguments in favour of future reforms that may be more effective in guaranteeing the pursuit of legitimate objectives. The supranational nature of the sporting industry and its labour market, of which transnational mobility of players is a key feature, requires a supranational system of governance.

---

637. *See*, for example, Treaty of Amsterdam amending the Treaty on European Union, the Treaties establishing the European Communities and certain related acts – Declarations adopted by the Conference – Declaration on sport, OJ C 340, 10 Nov. 1997; European Council, Nice, 7–10 Dec. 2000, Conclusions of the Presidency. Annex IV, *Declaration on the specific characteristics of sport and its social function in Europe, of which account should be taken in implementing common policies* (2000); European Commission, *White Paper on Sport*, COM(2007) 391 final (2007), s. 2; European Commission, *Communication from the Commission to the European Parliament, the Council, the European Economic and Social Committee and the Committee of the Regions – Developing the European Dimension in Sport*, 11 COM(2011) 12 final (2011), s. 2. On 'openness', *see* Art. 165(2) TFEU.

638. KEA, *An update on change drivers and economic and legal implications of transfers of players*, European Commission (2018).

639. KEA/CDES, *Study on the Economic and Legal Aspects of Transfers of Players*, European Commission, 252 (2013).

640. Stefan Szymanski, *The economic arguments supporting a competition law challenge to the transfer system*, FIFPro [online] (2015).

Only a supranational system can overcome the difficulties of collating different national regulations, which may apply to stakeholders in a different manner depending on where they are located. Protecting the fairness and transparency of the competition, in a market that is inherently international and in which different rules and standards apply depending on where contracts are entered, is in itself a very powerful justification for any transfer system.[641]

393. An effective solution to one of the issues discussed would be to ensure greater engagement of the various stakeholders at all levels of the decision-making process. The legitimacy of any form of regulation depends on the acceptance of those individuals that are subject to them. Furthermore, the involvement of those affected by the decision would have a transformative effect on horizontal agreements between employers and their associations.[642]

394. Governing bodies have been traditionally reluctant to accept limitations in their regulatory functions and have jealously guarded the monopolistic powers that the European model endows on them. However, the commercialisation of sport has contributed to the rise of new stakeholders, such as organised player, club and league interests. These stakeholders have sought to challenge the perceived inequality enshrined in the organisational structure of the European model and push for greater democracy and representation of wider interests in the decision-making process.[643] In the absence of formal recognition of organised interests within sports governance, stakeholders have resorted to litigation, actual or threatened, as a means of affecting governance change. For example, Chapter 2 examined how litigation resulted in amendments being made to FIFA rules governing the mandatory release of players.

395. Litigation instigated by FIFPro in 2015 has also been influential in driving changes to FIFA regulations in the area of the RSTP and RWWI.[644] FIFPro's complaint focused on a number of aspects of the international transfer system, including the training compensation scheme and the provisions on contractual stability, and their proportionality.[645] FIFPro argued that the system reduced the ability of clubs to compete for players, and disincentivised recruitment, while also reducing players' opportunities to find employment and conditioned the terms under which the

641. Stephen Weatherill, *Principles and Practice in EU Sports Law* 240 (Oxford Univ. Press 2017).
642. *Ibid.*, at 278.
643. European Commission, *Commission staff working document. Impact assessment accompanying the White Paper on Sport*, SEC(2007) 935 final (2007), para. 4, and Borja García & Henk E. Meier, *Limits of Interest Empowerment in the European Union: The Case of Football*, 34(4) J. Eur. Integr. 359–378, 360 (2012).
644. FIFPro media release, *FIFPro legal action against FIFA transfer system*, https://www.fifproamerica.com/en/news/fifpro-action-against-transfer-system 18 Sep. 2015 (accessed 10 May 2020).
645. Antoine Duval, *Interview with Wil van Megen (Legal Director of FIFPro) on FIFPro's EU Competition Law complaint against the FIFA Transfer System*, Asser International Sports Law Blog, https://www.asser.nl/SportsLaw/Blog/post/interview-with-wil-van-megen-legal-director-of-fifpro-on-fifpro-s-eu-competition-law-complaint-against-the-fifa-transfer-system#_ftn1 29 Sep. 2015 (accessed 20 Apr. 2020).

employment is offered. The players' union also argued that the Commission failed to evaluate the impact of the transfer system, after the informal agreement struck in 2001.[646]

396. Implicitly, the complaint was a call for a regulatory approach that was more inclusive and representative of the various stakeholders.[647] Indeed, FIFPro withdrew the complaint when FIFA announced an agreement with the players' union, through which FIFPro itself was to be included in the newly created FIFA Football Stakeholders Committee. In it, FIFPro could work alongside the ECA, the European Leagues (EL) and other stakeholders to formulate reform proposals to be adopted by the FIFA Council.[648]

397. This case demonstrates how litigation, actual or threatened, can steer the conduct of governing bodies towards positions more in line with principles of good governance. However, legal challenges are expensive and time-consuming and they can disrupt relationships and result in heightened uncertainty for all parties.[649] To avoid seeing their regulatory autonomy progressively reduced under the pressure of litigation, governing bodies should consider adopting a more inclusive approach. Accepting a pooling of sovereignty with stakeholders with regards to decision-making could help maintain the self-regulation of the system.[650] The remainder of the section explores some options for a more inclusive form of sports governance.

I. From Collective Agreements to Social Dialogue

398. One method of addressing the imbalance of power in employment relationships is through collective bargaining. A system of collective bargaining is capable of ensuring a cooperative process of rule-setting and decision-making, reducing conflicts between sides. It also allows parties to take ownership of the setting and the implementation of the terms of the employment relationship.

399. However, collective bargaining agreements are effectively agreements between trade unions and trade associations (or employers' association). Effectively, these are associations of undertakings, and their agreements have the objective of protecting workers in relation to the terms and conditions of their employment. The nature of such agreements, and their ability to negatively affect

646. FIFPro, executive summary of the complaint, available at https://www.sportsintegrityinitiative.com/wp-content/uploads/2015/09/FIFPro-Complaint-Executive-Summary.pdf (accessed 21 Apr. 2020).
647. Nick De Marco & Alex Mills, *FIFPro challenge the football transfer system,* Blackstone Chambers Sports Law Bulletin, https://www.sportslawbulletin.org/fifpro-challenge-the-football-transfer-system/, 9 Feb. 16 (accessed 15 Mar. 2020).
648. FIFA, *FIFA and FIFPro sign landmark agreement and announce measures to enhance professional football,* https://www.fifa.com/who-we-are/news/fifa-and-fifpro-sign-landmark-agreement-and-announce-measures-to-enhan-2918747, 6 Nov. 2017 (accessed 9 Apr. 2020).
649. Richard Parrish, *Social Dialogue in European Professional Football,* 17(2) ELJ 213–229 (2011).
650. Andrea Cattaneo, *Social Dialogue and the Regulatory Power of Governing Bodies,* 17 (3–4) ISLJ 119–127 (2018).

third parties, renders them a classic example of conduct prohibited under Article 101 TFEU.[651] The case law of the Court of Justice has however clarified that, when these agreements seek to improve the working conditions of the employees, they pursue a social policy objective, and a strict application of competition law in this regard would undermine the very social policy objective pursued.[652] Where collective agreements in the sporting system would address matters related to the employment relationship, they would also consider those rules that express the regulatory power of sports bodies. Their inclusion in such agreements could effectively exempt them from the prohibitions of Article 101 TFEU.

400. One significant obstacle to the successful conclusion of collective agreements at the continental level is presented by the varying status of professional footballers under national laws of the Member States. Where players are classed as self-employed, they will also be prevented from entering a collective bargaining process.[653] This may explain the limited recourse to the system of collective agreements in Europe and the limited success of the Americanisation of industrial relations in European sports.

401. A possible alternative that could guarantee greater involvement of the European stakeholders and could address the traditional imbalance between players and clubs is the tool of Social Dialogue. Social Dialogue is an institutionalised forum created and supported by the EU institutions to establish a supranational governance in a range of policy fields.[654] The forum brings together representatives of both sides of the industry, the Social Partners, to discuss employment-related issues, with the aim to come to a resolution that could potentially inform a collective agreement. Social Dialogue is therefore an instrument that can be used to enhance stakeholders' participation in the governance of the system while protecting the value of self-regulation.[655]

402. In the sporting industry, an inherently international system in which private regulators establish rules to be enforced within the territories of Member States, the supranational character of Social Dialogue makes it particularly apt to guarantee wider involvement of the various stakeholders in the governance process. The system has therefore been promoted by the Commission, both in its White Paper on Sport and in its Communication on Developing a European Dimension of Sport.[656]

---

651. Stein Evju, *Collective Agreements and Competition Law. The Albany Puzzle, and Van der Woude*, 17 IJCLLIR 165 (2001).
652. Case C-67/96 *Albany International v. Stichting* [1999] ECR I-5751, para. 59, and C-115/97 *Brentjens' Handelsonderneming BV v. Stichting Bedrijfspensioenfonds voor de Handel in Bouwmaterialen* [1999] ECR I-06025, para. 56.
653. Antoine Duval & Oscar Van Maren, *The Labour Status of Professional Football Players in the European Union*, 8(3) Eur. Labour Law J. 258 (2017).
654. Michael Barry, James Skinner & Terry Engelberg (eds), *Research Handbook of Employment Relations in Sport* (Edward Elgar 2016).
655. European Commission, *White Paper on Sport*, COM(2007), 391 final (2007), s. 5.
656. *Ibid.*, s. 5.3, and European Commission, *Communication from the Commission to the European Parliament, the Council, the European Economic and Social Committee and the Committee of the Regions – Developing the European Dimension in Sport*, 11 COM(2011) 12 final (2011), s. 13.

By recommending the use of Social Dialogue, the Commission has attempted to instigate a shift towards a more institutionalised horizontal system of rule-setting in the sporting sector. Effectively, this fits perfectly with the prescription of Article 165 TFEU, which mandates the EU to promote cooperation between bodies responsible for sport.

403. In this regard, however, Social Dialogue reflects the limited competence that the EU has over particular areas of the employment relationship. Under Article 153 TFEU, the EU has competence to support and complement activities of Member States in this area, with some aspects such as regulation of salary, right of association, right to strike and to impose lockout expressly excluded from any possible harmonisation.[657] In the context of a limited competence, the EU institutions have chosen to provide funding and support for a forum in which independent parties may reach an agreement on matters of common interest.

404. The agreement is then assessed by the Commission, to ensure that it does not refer to matters outside the scope of the Committee, or that it legitimises unlawful restrictions imposed on employees.[658] Following the Commission's assessment, the Social Partners can choose to ask the Council to ratify the agreement and adopt it as an official act of the Union.[659] The Council could therefore adopt a Directive, imposing on the Member States an obligation to implement the substance of the agreement in their national legislation and within a set deadline. This implementation method would enshrine the agreement into EU law, with the consequence of sanctions being imposed in the event of non-compliance.

405. Despite the limits of EU competences and the need to rely on the institutions to formalise the arrangements, Social Dialogue still has the potential to be an effective means of regulation, if properly endorsed by relevant stakeholders and governing bodies. Indeed, rules agreed under the umbrella of Social Dialogue could escape the prohibitions set by Article 101 and Article 102 TFEU, as products of negotiation between representatives of both sides of the employment relationship. Matters discussed within the context of Social Dialogue need to be connected to improving the working conditions of labour. In sport, aspects discussed could range from the status and transfer of players; rules related to solidarity and contractual stability; rules prohibiting TPO of economic rights of players; rules regulating the forum and the procedures for dispute resolution; general contractual issues, including image rights; anti-doping rules; and match calendars, to name a few.[660]

---

657. However, the competence of the Union in the area is not strictly limited to a supporting role. According to Art. 5 TFEU, the EU can adopt measures to ensure the coordination of employment policies in the Member States. For a discussion of this aspect, *see* Paul Craig & Grainne De Búrca, *EU Law: Text, Cases, and Materials* 88 (Oxford Univ. Press 6th ed. 2015).
658. Parrish argued that an agreement of this sort would not be enforceable. *See* Richard Parrish, *Social Dialogue in European Professional Football*, 17(2) ELJ 213–229 (2011).
659. Art. 155 TFEU.
660. For a discussion of the range of topics that could be discussed in the context of Social Dialogue in Sport, *see* T.M.C. Asser Institute, Edge Hill University and the Katholieke Universiteit Leuven,

406. The issue of salary cap illustrates its possible application and also its complexity. Rules setting salary caps impose on clubs a maximum spending on players' salaries. They therefore affect the ability of clubs to acquire players on the market, as well as the ability of the players to enter into an employment relationship with the clubs.[661] In effect, these measures could be considered as decisions by an association of undertakings, the governing body, which fix the trading conditions and controls the investments on the market for players' services. However, while matters related to working conditions can be discussed and agreed upon by the Social Partners, the transposition of an agreement into EU secondary law may be prevented if it establishes a harmonised 'level of pay'.[662] So, in the event Social Partners would agree on a salary cap, they could only rely on its voluntary implementation, in light of the constitutional limits imposed by Article 153 TFEU.

407. In the U.S. Major Leagues, the salary cap is one of the elements agreed between the players' union and the association of the clubs as part of the collective bargaining process. This process legitimises the arrangement because insofar as the outcome of such a negotiation affects only those who are negotiating, collective bargaining agreements are shielded from competition law.[663]

408. In a similar fashion, Social Dialogue could be used within the EU to shield rules adopted by the governing bodies, provided that they are the product of an agreement which is deemed to improve the terms of the employment relationship. In the context of a collective agreement guaranteeing protection of players' rights in exchange for concessions, parties could be free to agree that the pursuit of objectives of common interest, such as the financial stability of the system, or the stability of employment relationships, may ultimately improve the working conditions of the players.

II. Social Dialogue in Professional Football

409. In the sports industry, the most successful example of use of Social Dialogue is the establishment of the EU Sectoral Social Dialogue Committee in the Professional Football Sector.[664] This committee was established in 2008, when the EU Commission accepted the joint request from FIFPro and the European Professional

---

Study into the Identification of Themes and Issues which can be Dealt with in a Social Dialogue in the European Professional Football Sector, Report for the European Commission (2008).

661. Aaron N. Wise & Bruce S. Meyer, *International Sports Law and Business*, 112 (Kluwer Law International 1997) and Wladimir Andreff & Stefan Szymansky, *Handbook on the Economics of Sport* 652 (Edward Elgar Publishing 2006).

662. Case C-268/06, *Impact v. Minister for Agriculture and Food and Others* [2008] ECR I-02483, paras 121–124.

663. *See* the U.S. Case *Mackey v. NFL*, 543 F.2d 606, 614–15 (8th Cir. 1976).

664. Another Sectoral Social Dialogue Committee has been set up on sport and active leisure industry, but has not been active since 2018.

Football Leagues (EPFL, now EL), thereby bringing to fruition a series of recommendations made to the stakeholders.[665] Alongside these two organisations, the ECA joined the Committee as third Social Partner.[666]

410. The Social Dialogue Committee in the Professional Football Sector signed an agreement on minimum requirements for players' contract in 2012.[667] The arrangement epitomises the benefits and the shortfalls of the Social Dialogue instrument. On the one hand, the Committee has concluded an agreement in a relatively short period of time since its creation. This contrasts with the operation of Social Dialogue in other industries, where Social Partners have strategically used Social Dialogue to lobby the EU institutions, rather than adopting binding measures.[668]

411. On the other hand, the football agreement has been criticised as being a mere repetition of standards already respected in many Member States. The minimum requirements are limited to identifying basic rights and obligations of clubs and players, and listing matters, such as health insurance and salary, that have to be necessarily included in contracts.[669] Furthermore, the Social Partners decided to avoid including the Council in the ratification process of the agreement, preferring to leave its implementation to the signatories and their affiliates. Social Partners themselves must therefore use their best endeavours to ensure that appropriate instruments are adopted at national level to implement the arrangement.[670] This type of implementation excluded Member States, and lacked any enforcement mechanism, thereby turning the agreement into a non-binding and voluntary arrangement which allowed significant discrepancies between national associations.

412. In fairness, this outcome is perfectly in line with the nature of the instrument used. The success or demise of Social Dialogue in specific sectors depends on the level of engagement of the relevant stakeholders, as well as on their perception of the social, political and economic context.[671] Social Dialogue is predicated on

---

665. *See* European Commission, *White Paper on Sport*, COM(2007) 391 final (2007), s. 5.3, and European Commission, *Communication from the Commission to the European Parliament, the Council, the European Economic and Social Committee and the Committee of the Regions – Developing the European Dimension in Sport*, 11 COM(2011) 12 final (2011), s. 13.
666. Michael Barry, James Skinner & Terry Engelberg (eds), *Research Handbook of Employment Relations in Sport* (Edward Elgar 2016) note that having two Partners – such as ECA and EL – representing the same side of the industrial relationship is quite a common circumstance in the context of Sectoral Social Dialogue.
667. Autonomous Agreement on Minimum Requirements Standard Players Contracts, https://ec.europa.eu/social/BlobServlet?docId=7678&langId=en 19 Apr. 2012 (accessed 9 Apr. 2020).
668. Berndt Keller & Sabrina Weller, *Sectoral Social Dialogue at EU Level: Problems and Prospects of Implementation*, 17(3) Eur. J. Ind. 227–243 (2011).
669. Richard Parrish, *The European Social Dialogue: A New Mode of Governance for European Football*, in *The Legacy of Bosman, Revisiting the Relationship Between EU law and Sport* 187–211, 200 (Antoine Duval & Ben Van Rompuy eds, T.M.C. Asser Press 2016).
670. Art. 18 of the Agreement.
671. Berndt Keller & Sabrina Weller, *Sectoral Social Dialogue at EU Level: Problems and Prospects of Implementation*, 17(3) Eur. J. Ind. 227–243 (2011).

discussing issues of common interest between the partners, as this encourages parties to engage. Conversely, as the system lacks powers of coercion over Social Partners in terms of matters discussed and implementation rules, it is not appropriate to deal with non-consensual issues. Soft policy measures are therefore more in line with the structure of Social Dialogue.

413. The inherent challenge to the operation of Social Dialogue in football is to ensure that the efforts put in place by the stakeholders produce effective results. While employment relationships are traditionally regulated through bilateral agreements between employer and employees, in sport this dynamic is constrained by the regulatory power of governing bodies. Here lies the major hindrance to the success of Social Dialogue. In order to guarantee that the outcome agreed by the Social Partners can be effectively implemented and enforced, some form of endorsement from the governing body is necessary. This would effectively require governing bodies to accept a form of regulation that would erode their regulatory power, but it would constitute a powerful incentive for stakeholders. Stakeholders would indeed perceive that their commitment to the Social Dialogue can lead to appreciable results. The difficult task is therefore to balance a significant level of participation by Social Partners, with the need to ensure the involvement of governing bodies.

414. In the case of the Social Dialogue in Professional Football, UEFA has an obvious interest in being involved and maintain some form of control over the operation of the Committee. However, UEFA cannot be considered a Social Partner, as it represents neither the clubs nor the players; Social Partners have therefore included UEFA as an Associate Party to the Committee. In this capacity, UEFA participates in the agenda setting of and the discussion of decision-making and implementation policies.[672] The level of control exercised by UEFA gains further prominence in consideration of the role of the Professional Football Strategy Council (PFSC), which approves in advance the topics for discussion of the Committee. The PFSC is a body established by UEFA in 2007 and comprises four UEFA vice presidents, representing the interests of the Member Associations and of UEFA, four members from the EL, four from ECA and four from FIFPro. Directly reporting to UEFA Executive Committee, the PFSC pursues a number of objectives, including identifying solutions for improving collaboration between the various stakeholders in European football and dealing with issues pertaining to the Social Dialogue in European professional football matters.[673]

415. The level of control exercised by UEFA, in its own capacity and through the operation of the PFSC, is consequently extensive. The perception of the stakeholders may therefore be that their interests will find protection only insofar as they align with UEFA's, alongside the other Social Partners. Deploying the necessary

672. Art. 4, Sectoral Social Dialogue Rules of Procedure and Michael Barry, James Skinner & Terry Engelberg (eds), *Research Handbook of Employment Relations in Sport* (Edward Elgar 2016).

673. UEFA, *Professional Football Strategy Council*, https://www.uefa.com/insideuefa/stakeholders/professional-football-strategy-council/index.html (accessed 9 Apr. 2020).

resources to reach an agreement under these constraints, with limited avenues available for enforcement, may then be seen as inefficient. This translates into results of limited significance, where Social Dialogue is mainly used as a tool to issue soft policy resolutions, such as the one adopted in relations to FIFA regulations on football agents.[674] Such soft agreements can heighten the appeal of the litigation route.

416. However, the litigation route is full of obstacles as well. While the threat of litigation has leveraged football stakeholders some success in the past, the EU Commission has consistently demonstrated a preference to establish a dialogue with governing bodies. In this regard, a veiled incentive for the stakeholders comes from the line drawn by the Commission in terms of the types of dispute it is willing to consider. In the press release of the *ISU* decision,[675] the Commission stated that disputes related to the governance of sport, including relations between different stakeholders, and disputes involving individual athletes are best dealt before at national level or before arbitral tribunals.[676] This should cause concerns, as national authorities may not be in a position to effectively address issues related to rules set by European or international governing bodies. In a system based on supranational private regulations, these rules have a cross-border effect that is not limited to the jurisdiction of national authorities and may significantly affect the activity of stakeholders based in various States across the EU. If the Commission was to follow its own recommendation, a number of issues relevant for European sportspersons could go unresolved.

417. Governing bodies wishing to avoid threats to their autonomy, on one side, and stakeholders prevented from having their complaints examined by the Commission, on the other, demonstrate the need for an alternative and more inclusive approach to sports governance. Renovated efforts are needed from all stakeholders and governing bodies to establish mutual trust that can lead to productive forms of cooperation.

§6. CONCLUSION

418. In Chapter 2 we considered how sports bodies adopted decisions that regulated the participation of 'third parties' wanting to gain access to the sports market. In it we argued that the legitimacy of sports governance is strengthened when decisions are untainted by conflicts of interest and legitimate sporting objectives are pursued in a proportionate manner.

674. *See* EU Sectoral Social Dialogue Committee for Professional Football: Resolution on Intermediaries/Agents, 17 Nov. 2017.
675. *See infra*, Chapter 2.
676. *See* European Commission, Press Release IP/16/3201, Antitrust: Commission sends Statement of Objections to International Skating Union on its eligibility rules, Brussels, 27 Sep. 2016.

419. This chapter has developed that theme, this time by looking at, although not exclusively, how sports bodies engage with stakeholders. The structure of the European model of sport places sports governing bodies in very powerful positions when it comes to determining who can participate in sport. This power extends mostly over stakeholders within the sporting 'family', but it also affects the choices of third parties, such agents, who want to access the sporting market. Furthermore, this power extends not only to the regulation of professional sport but also, in some cases, to the organisation of amateur sport. The commercialisation of sport, the rise of organised and litigious interests and the growing recognition of sport's importance to society is placing strain on this organisational model. Those who participate in sport are becoming less tolerant of the monopolistic regulatory power exercised by sports bodies.

420. Sports governing bodies need to decide how to respond. Weatherill has highlighted three strategies employed by sports bodies to safeguard their autonomy – the contractual, legislative and interpretative strategies.[677] Sports bodies will, no doubt, continue to pursue these strategies, but at the same time they need to reorientate their style of governance. The regulatory autonomy granted to sports governing bodies should be conditioned on the respect of EU law and the adoption of principles of good governance. This necessitates an opening up of their decision-making processes to a wider array of stakeholders. This represents the most effective way of securing the regulatory autonomy of sport. Some sports have recognised this and have taken steps at addressing stakeholder concerns. For example, FIFA and UEFA are more receptive than ever to the establishment of stakeholder bodies. Others have paid lip service, through, for example, the establishment of unrepresentative athlete commissions.

421. Stakeholder participation in sports governance does not undermine our belief that regulatory uniformity and strong central enforcement powers are desirable in sport. Neither should it result in decision-making paralysis. Ultimately, a sports governing body needs to take a decision and that decision cannot possibly satisfy all stakeholders. Our argument is that the EU should grant those sports who have, in good faith, considered the views of stakeholders, a wider margin appreciation under EU law than those who have not.[678] In this regard, democratising sports governance through stakeholder participation endows sport with a legitimacy it has often lacked in the past and this legitimacy can extend over the regulation of both stakeholders and third parties.[679]

422. The EU can claim some credit for these shifting governance styles. It has successfully managed to export its own approach to policymaking, which requires the consultation of affected parties and relevant stakeholders, to the sport system.

---

677. Stephen Weatherill, *Principles and Practice in EU Sports Law* 8–49 (Oxford Univ. Press 2017).
678. *Ibid.*, 165–169.
679. For a more systematic expansion of this idea *see* Lloyd Freeburn, *Regulating International Sport. Power, Authority and Legitimacy* 170–195 (Brill Nijhoff 2018).

From the promotion of good governance principles,[680] to the competence expressly granted to the EU to promote cooperation between bodies responsible for sport,[681] to the impact of the activity of the Commission and the judgment of the Court of Justice, the EU has progressively shifted the hierarchical nature of the sports governance system towards more horizontal and inclusive approach.[682] The sports pyramid is a different shape as a result.

680. European Commission, *White Paper on Sport*, COM(2007), 391 final (2007), s. 4.
681. Art. 165(3) TFEU.
682. Arnout Geeraert & Edith Drieskens, *Normative Market Europe: The EU as a Force for Good in International Sports Governance?*, 39(1) J. Eur. Intgr. 79, 87 (2017).

Chapter 4. Funding Sport

§1. INTRODUCTION

423. The commercialisation of sport and the liberalisation of the players' market that occurred following *Bosman* has pushed European clubs and governing bodies to explore a range of revenue streams and funding methods. The development of the economic dimension of the sporting industry and the aspirations of the various stakeholders to extract value from their activities shape the discussion of this chapter. Building on the aspects discussed in the previous chapters, this section will look at the impact EU law has had and continues having over the pursuit of commercial objectives by sports governing bodies and clubs. The focus of this section is on the interrelation between the conduct of sports stakeholders, the rules of the market and the impact of EU law over commercial rights and their exploitation in the sporting industry. In this context, it must be borne in mind that private investments in sports may have a significant impact on its organisation and rules.[683] While the discussion of rules related to sports funding is necessarily connected with other areas explored elsewhere in this monograph, such as rules on sanctioning events and rules protecting the integrity of competitions, this chapter analyses five specific areas: financial regulations; State aid rules; broadcasting rights; media rights and sponsorship.

424. The importance of media in sport has progressively increased, going hand in hand with the development of technology and favouring the commercialisation and commodification of sport. In football, the exploitation of broadcasting rights on traditional channels and, more recently, on over-the-top (OTT) platforms have become one of the most important sources of income for clubs and governing bodies.[684] Their relevance is connected with the progressively rising expenses that these stakeholders have to bear in relation to staging events and remunerating the participants. At the same time, developments in the area of advertising and ticketing are of great significance as well.

425. The European model of sport has developed characteristics that are intimately linked with the economic objectives of the industry. Some of these characteristics stakeholders have attempted to protect or challenge depending on their interest. The chapter will therefore discuss how the commercial aspirations of sports governing bodies and clubs have to be balanced with sporting objectives and with the rules of the EU's internal market. On the one hand, many European sporting

683. Sylvia Schenk, *Integrity of Sport*, in *Research Handbook on EU Sports Law and Policy* 431–447 (Jack Anderson, Richard Parrish & Borja García eds, Edward Elgar 2018).

684. *See* Deloitte, Football Money League 2020 Report, 5, https://www2.deloitte.com/content/dam/Deloitte/bg/Documents/finance/deloitte-uk-deloitte-football-money-league-2020%20(1).pdf (accessed 27 Apr. 2020).

entities tend to pursue a win-maximisation objective, rather than a profit maximisation agenda focussing on economic returns.[685] Financial success is of fundamental importance, but only insofar as it is instrumental to achieve success on the pitch.[686] On the other hand, rules are in place to guarantee that clubs and governing bodies do not benefit from unfair advantages against competitors, or do not restrict the market to a disproportionate extent.

§2. Financing Sport

426. The sporting industry is not exclusively guided by financial goals. The presence of an array of stakeholders, each with their own interests to protect, affects the logic directing the activity of clubs and governing bodies. The interests of fans and clubs may align, but are not necessarily the same. Fans do not support their clubs because of their financial significance, but because they attach a social and community value to them.[687] In turn, clubs take advantage of this narrative and emphasises their role as representatives of a community to attract fans.

427. The primary objective of sports clubs is to succeed in their sporting endeavours. In order to achieve such a goal, they require investments to cover different areas of their activity. These include the infrastructure and upkeep of facilities, investments on the labour market for players and staff, and investment on the marketing of their products.[688] The need to finance the activity of a sports club is common to both amateur and professional sports clubs, with differences related to the extent of the investments needed.

428. Traditionally, in Europe sport and physical activity is structured through the activity of voluntary sports clubs and individuals. Through this structure, clubs recruit their members, organise events and enter into local or regional competitions.[689] While household expenditure tends to be geared towards clubs' membership, and leisure and health-enhancing practice, public support, at local, regional or national level, is also available to finance sports participation.[690] The role of the State, in this regard, is to ensure that its citizens have the possibility to practise sport and it often translates into funding for public sports facilities or sports programmes.

---

685. Klaus Nielsen & Rasmus Storm, *Profit Maximization, Win Optimization and Soft Budget Constraints in Professional Team Sports*, in *When Sport Meets Business: Capabilities, Challenges, Critiques* 153–166 (Klaus Nielsen, Wagner Ulrich & Rasmus Storm eds, Sage Publications 2017).
686. Stefan Szymanski, *Sport Financing and Governance in Europe*, in *Contemporary Issues in Sports Economics* 65–80 (Wladimir Andreff ed., Edward Elgar 2011).
687. Stephen Morrow, *Football, Economics and Finance*, in *Routledge Handbook of Football Studies* 163–176 (John Hughson, Kevin Moore, Ramón Spaaij & Joseph Maguire eds, Routledge 2017).
688. Stefan Szymanski, *Sport Financing and Governance in Europe*, in *Contemporary Issues in Sports Economics* 65–80 (Wladimir Andreff ed., Edward Elgar 2011).
689. Bob Stewart, *Sport Funding and Finance* 6 (Routledge 2015).
690. Antti Laine & Hanna Vehmas, *Development, Current Situation and Future Prospects of the Private Sports Sector in Europe*, in *The Private Sport Sector in Europe: A Cross-National Comparative Perspective* 343–354 (Antti Laine & Hanna Vehmas eds, Springer 2017).

429. However, depending on whether sport is seen as a contributor to cultural aspects, well-being, or economics, it attracts different levels of funding from a varied range of actors. The financing methods may also depend on the function recognised to the sport, and the level of participation it attracts. Therefore, the approach to funding significantly varies between leisure and health sports practice, to amateur sports contest, to high-level professional sport. Different sources of funding tend to be directed towards specific categories, with private enterprises and governments tending to finance high-level sport, which can guarantee a significant level of media exposure.[691] This differentiation follows and reinforces the pyramidal structure of the European model, by guaranteeing that the highest level of funding is channelled towards the top echelon of the system. Conversely, systems that guarantee vertical solidarity can aim to counterbalance the hegemony of the top level in attracting funding.

430. The traditional model of funding for professional sports, and football in particular, was built around extracting value from three main sources: spectators, subsidies and sponsors.[692] Subsidies could come from private investors or from public entities. Public subsidies could be granted directly to governing bodies or clubs. Subsidies may also be deployed to build or renovate sports infrastructures or to fund programmes to develop athletes in preparation for international competitions.[693] In the past, it was common to see wealthy investors being the owners of clubs, Massimo Moratti for F.C. Inter and Roman Abramovich for Chelsea F.C. to name two. This is still the prevailing model for leagues at lower levels and grassroots sport. However, it has been argued that, at the elite level, the ownership structure has been subject to an internationalisation, with corporate style ownership and overseas shareholding.[694] The range of funding sources has also changed, replacing the previously mentioned ones with media, corporations, merchandising, and market for talents and capital.

431. The funding of sport cannot be considered as an area to study in isolation. Conduct pursuing financial objectives may have significant repercussions over other interests and objectives, such as the integrity of the system, the transparency of transactions, the stability of the competition, the competitive balance and the sustainability of sport at all levels. This explains the level of interest in this area that the EU institutions have demonstrated throughout the years.[695]

---

691. Wladimir Andreff, Jean Dutoya & Julien Montel, *A European Model of Sports Financing: Under Threat?*, 90 Rev. Jur. Eco. Sport 75–85 (2009).
692. Wladimir Andreff & Paul D. Staudohar, *European and Sports Business Models*, in *Transatlantic Sport: The Comparative Economics of North American and European Sports*, 23–49 (Carlos P. Barros, Ibrahimo Muradali & Stefan Szymanski eds, Edward Elgar 2002).
693. Bob Stewart, *Sport Funding and Finance* 7 (Routledge 2015).
694. Matt Andrews & Peter Harrington, *Off Pitch: Football's Financial Integrity Weaknesses, and How to Strengthen Them*, CID Working Paper No. 311, Harvard Kennedy School, 46 (2016) and Marc Rohde & Christoph Breuer, *The Market for Football Club Investors: A Review of Theory and Empirical Evidence from Professional European Football*, 17(3) ESMQ 265–289 (2017).
695. For an overview, *see* Sean O'Conaill, *Sustainable Financing in Football and the EU*, in *Research Handbook on EU Sports Law and Policy*, 246–260 (Jack Anderson, Richard Parrish & Borja García eds, Edward Elgar 2018).

432. In the Helsinki Report on Sport, the Commission mentioned how the increased commercialisation of sport in Europe could impair the solidarity between professional and amateur sport.[696] In the Nice Declaration, the Council also made reference to solidarity, stressing how the distribution of revenues between different levels of the sport system could be instrumental in preserving the principle.[697] In its White Paper on Sport, the Commission acknowledged the ability of sport to contributing to the pursuit of objectives of economic growth and job creation, and stressed its connection with tourism, urban regeneration and local and regional development.[698] The Commission also highlighted the need to maintain and develop sustainable financial models to support sports organisations. In this regard, the White Paper acknowledged that sport is partly funded through State resources.[699]

433. The 2011 Commission Communication 'Developing the European Dimension of Sport' included a section specifically dedicated to the economic dimension of sport.[700] The Commission recognised that the vast majority of sporting activities takes place in structures based on voluntary activity and that the sustainability of such structures can be a cause for concern. In this regard, the Commission reiterated the need to strengthen the financial solidarity between professional sport and grassroots.[701] The Commission stressed the economic impact of the commercialisation of intellectual property (IP) rights and broadcasting rights, as well as the contribution of public funding in financing sport. It is in the context of this framework, where private interests of governing bodies overlap with public interest, that the conduct employed to finance sport must be discussed.

§3. Financial Regulations

434. Sporting rules regulating the economic activity of clubs and governing bodies tend to pursue two fundamental objectives. The first is to guarantee a level playing field between those who take part in a competition. The notion of competitive balance has been discussed extensively in the literature and has been referred to numerous times to justify the exertion of control and the imposition of restrictions over the economic freedom of stakeholders.[702] Claims that measures are needed to protect or pursue competitive balance within leagues and competitions underlie

696. European Commission, *Report from the Commission to the European Council with a view to safeguarding current sports structures and maintaining the social function of sport within the Community framework – the Helsinki Report on Sport*, COM(1999) 644 (1999).
697. European Council, Nice, 7–10 Dec. 2000, Conclusions of the Presidency. Annex IV, *Declaration on the specific characteristics of sport and its social function in Europe, of which account should be taken in implementing common policies* (2000).
698. European Commission, *White Paper on Sport*, COM(2007), 391 final (2007), s. 3.
699. *Ibid.*, s. 3.2.
700. European Commission, *Communication from the Commission to the European Parliament, the Council, the European Economic and Social Committee and the Committee of the Regions – Developing the European Dimension in Sport*, 11 COM(2011) 12 final (2011).
701. *Ibid.*, s. 3.
702. Stefan Szymanski, *The Economic Design of Sporting Contests*, 41 JEL 1137–1187 (2003).

rules such as salary caps, the draft system in North American Sports, or in general systems of revenue sharing between clubs participating in events.

435. A second goal pursued through financial regulations is the economic viability of the system, with the intention of preventing clubs from disappearing under piles of debt. On paper, this is the main objective of rules such as FFP adopted by UEFA.[703] However, it could also be linked with rules preventing clubs from over-relying on investments of third parties, such as the banning of TPO of players, and stricter control on public spending and rules incentivising the pursuit of long-term profits.[704]

436. In a system regulated by economic objectives, competition law is applied to tackle the inefficiencies of the market, such as the financial instability of the system. Such inefficiency is the very product of the market regulation that imposed restrictions on freedom of clubs and players through the transfer system, and fostered imbalance between clubs.[705] Governing bodies have instead reacted to the inefficiency by imposing further restrictions on the ability of undertakings to compete with each other.

437. However, the pursuit of financial stability for the sporting system has been recognised by the Commission as a legitimate regulatory interest of sports governing bodies.[706] In this regard, it is relevant to notice that this type of objective stems from purely economic considerations. Indeed, the imposition of restrictions on the spending ability of clubs may prevent, or at least make considerably more difficult, the achievement of sporting objectives such as ensuring competitive balance within a league. These rules tend to sanction those teams which ordinarily would have to overspend to fill the gap with more powerful clubs, thereby creating or reinforcing a hegemony of elite clubs.[707]

438. In considering the characteristics of the European model of sport, the notion of competitive balance must be discussed. At a closer look, it is hard to consider that the pursuit of competitive balance may fall under this category. Measures that are traditionally employed to achieve and protect competitive balance are not common in the European system. For example, an effective means to pursue the

703. *See* Art. 2(2) C of the UEFA Clubs Licensing and Fair Play Regulations.

704. *See* European Commission, *Decision adopting the Arrangement for Cooperation between the European Commission and the Union of European Football Associations (UEFA),* COM(2014) 7378 final, s. 2.7, https://ec.europa.eu/assets/eac/sport/news/2014/docs/uefa2014_en.pdf (accessed 20 Apr. 2020). For a discussion on the legality of TPO restrictions, *see* Chapter 1.

705. KEA/CDES, *Study on the Economic and Legal Aspects of Transfers of Players,* 6–7 (European Commission, 2013). For a discussion of the impact of regulation on the market, *see* Geoff Pearson, *Sporting Justifications under EU Free Movement and Competition Law: The Case of the Football 'Transfer System'*, 21(2) ELJ 220–238 (2015).

706. European Commission, *Communication from the Commission to the European Parliament, the Council, the European Economic and Social Committee and the Committee of the Regions – Developing the European Dimension in Sport,* 11 COM(2011) 12 final (2011), s. 4.2.

707. Alexander Egger & Christine Stix-Hackl, *Sports and Competition Law: A Never-Ending Story?*, 23(2) ECLR 81–91 (2002).

competitive balance within a league would be the introduction of salary caps. A salary cap would limit the expenditure of clubs on players' wages, punish those who exceed in spending and redistribute funds to those clubs that comply with the rules.[708] Salary caps may take various forms. They can be hard caps, when the spending limit is a fixed amount for all the clubs; or the cap can be soft, with the limit calculated as a percentage of the revenues for each club. Finally, there can be a luxury tax connected with the salary cap, whereby clubs that exceed the cap pay a sum corresponding to their excess to the league, which then redistributes it to the virtuous teams.[709]

439. Although salary caps may pose antitrust concerns, as they effectively restrict clubs and players in their economic activity, they place all the competitors within the same spending limits. While salary caps are very common in the North American sports system, they are extremely rare in Europe, although employed in both Rugby codes (League and Union).[710] The salary cap adopted by the Premiership Rugby (Union) has been discussed in a case heard by Sports Resolution UK, an independent dispute resolution body for sport established in the UK. Tasked with assessing the legality of the salary cap under competition law, the panel held that the rules were not infringing competition law by object.[711] This is a valid position, considering that the objective of the salary cap is not to restrict the ability of clubs to operate on the market, but to ensure greater stability and competitive balance.[712] Questions remain as to whether the effects of the rules are restrictive beyond what is necessary to achieve the objective.

440. It is argued that several practical obstacles prevent the introduction of a successful form of salary cap in European football. In particular, the level of competition existing between clubs and leagues in the European market would require these rules to be implemented homogeneously throughout the continent. The rules would also have to be enforced strictly, to avoid attempts to evade their prescription by remunerating players in ways that run contrary to the regulations. The wealthiest clubs would most likely oppose the introduction of a salary cap, as its effect would be to redistribute a share of their market power towards smaller clubs. Furthermore, the European model of sport is built on the premise of open leagues, with promotion and relegation between levels. In effect, clubs complying with the salary cap of

708. This is the case with luxury taxes, which are common in the North American sports system. A luxury tax is a financial levy imposed on teams that spend beyond a set threshold. The proceeds of the tax are normally redistributed to the virtuous teams. *See* KEA/CDES, *Study on the Economic and Legal Aspects of Transfers of Players* 238 (European Commission, 2013).
709. Elizabeth Gustafson, *The Luxury Tax in Professional Sports*, in *Handbook on the Economics of Sport* 651–660 (Wladimir Andreff & Stefan Szymanski eds, Edward Elgar, 2006).
710. For example, in Rugby League, *see* Terry Robinson & Andrew Howarth, *The Impact of the Salary Cap in the European Rugby Super League*, 3(6) IJBM 3–7 (2008).
711. SR/Adhocsport/201/2019, *Premier Rugby Limited v. Saracens Limited.*
712. Benoit Keane, *Game-Changer: Why the Saracens Decision Will Transform the Governance of Sport*, CPI Antitrust Chronicle, April 2020, https://www.competitionpolicyinternational.com/game-changer-why-the-saracens-decision-will-transform-the-governance-of-sport/ (accessed 5 May 2020).

a top league that are relegated would have to terminate several contracts in order to avoid overspending in the lower league.[713]

441. An example of financial regulation in force in Europe comes from UEFA. Since 2009, the European governing body of football has implemented a series of rules aiming to increase the financial responsibility of European football clubs, with the objective of making the European football system stable and self-sufficient.[714] The FFP Regulations form part of the UEFA licensing scheme, imposing on clubs a series of requirements related to sporting structures, personnel and legal and financial aspects which must be satisfied in order for a club to be eligible to compete in UEFA club competitions. The UEFA CFCB can impose a range of penalties on clubs that fail to comply, ranging from economic sanctions to squad reduction, and even ineligibility to participate in European club competitions. Clubs that are found to have breached the Regulations can decide to settle the question with the CFCB through confidential agreements.[715] When a settlement is not possible, the matter will be referred to an Adjudicatory body, whose decision can be appealed before the CAS.[716]

442. The FFP regulations sanction those clubs that cannot reach a financial break-even between expenses paid and revenues collected during the monitored period. The rules adopted in 2010 established that a club would be punished if, within the three-year period previous to its application to obtain a licence, its expenses exceeded the relevant income by more than EUR 5 million.[717] During the first three years from the adoption of FFP, clubs were allowed to exceed the boundaries within certain limits.[718] Clubs were even permitted to fall outside the acceptable deviation, provided they could report a positive trend in their annual results, that would have demonstrated the possibility of reaching break-even in the near future.[719]

---

713. Harry Arne Solberg & Kjetil K. Haugen, *European Club Football: Why Enormous Revenues Are Not Enough?*, 13(2) Sport Soc. 329–343 (2010).
714. UEFA Club Licensing and Financial Fair Play Regulations. The latest edition published at the moment of writing is available at: https://www.uefa.com/MultimediaFiles/Download/Tech/uefaorg/General/02/56/20/15/2562015_DOWNLOAD.pdf (accessed 24 Apr. 2020).
715. Manchester City, Paris Saint German and Inter Milan were among the clubs sanctioned by UEFA. The Principles and process regulating voluntary agreements are found in Annex XII of the Regulations.
716. *See*, for example, CAS 2018/A/5808 – *AC Milan v. UEFA*.
717. Art. 57 of UEFA Club Licensing and Financial Fair Play Regulations, 2018 Edition. The acceptable deviation is a maximum of EUR 30 million, if the excess is entirely covered through equity injections from shareholders or related parties. *See* Art. 61 of UEFA Club Licensing and Financial Fair Play Regulations.
718. In the season 2013/2014 and 2014/2015, the acceptable losses were below EUR 45 million (phase 1), while in the following three seasons the limit was reduced to EUR 30 million (phase 2).
719. For an overview of the regulations, *see* Stefano Bastianon, *The Striani Challenge to UEFA Financial Fair-Play. A New Era after Bosman or Just a Washout?*, 11(1) CLR 7–39 (2015).

443. Importantly, the Regulations defined what could be considered relevant income for the purpose of the FFP assessment.[720] This includes gate receipts, broadcasting revenues, revenues from sponsorship and advertising, prize money and revenues from transfer market activity, and other operating income. However, the regulations place significant constraints over transactions with related parties. This was necessary in order to prevent owners and shareholders from circumventing the regulations by financing their clubs via overpaying sponsorships or injecting capital. Therefore, the rules establish that the terms and conditions of any transaction with related parties have to be equivalent to those prevailing in normal arm's-length transactions and, if they exceed this fair value standard, they will be adjusted accordingly.[721] Conversely, clubs are allowed to include as relevant income revenues derived from non-football activities, such as those derived from hospitality, provided that they have some connection with the activities of the clubs, their location or brand. This is consistent with one of the objectives of the rule, which is to encourage investments on facilities and activities profitable for the long-term benefit of the clubs.[722] Along the same lines, the Regulations exclude from the break-even calculation expenses that the club has incurred in investing on the youth and women's football development activities, community development activities and infrastructure. In essence, the relevant expenses are transactions on the player market and salaries.

444. In 2015, UEFA amended the rules and relaxed the application of the sanctions. Accordingly, clubs in financial difficulties may be allowed to seek a one-off 'voluntary settlement agreement' from the UEFA CFCB.[723] This allows clubs that have been subject to a significant change in ownership or control in the previous twelve months to operate beyond the limits of the break-even rule, provided that they have a solid plan to improve their situation. Moreover, the Regulations included exceptions for clubs from countries where the market is considered to have structural economic deficiencies.

445. In assessing the legality of FFP, the familiar approach examining the effects of the rules, the objectives, the inherency and proportionality should be followed. In a similar fashion to salary caps, one of the main effects of FFP has been to constrain clubs' ability to sign players on the market, as well as affecting the ability of players to earn and sign a contract with clubs. These effects are not unknown to the sporting system and to football in particular: for example, the transfer system in football has a comparable impact in restricting the freedom of clubs and players. However, the impact of such an effect should not be underestimated, as the trade of players is one of the funding streams for football clubs. This is particularly true for

720. UEFA Club Licensing and Financial Fair Play Regulations, Annex X.
721. *Ibid.*, Annex VI.
722. *Ibid.*, Annex X, C.
723. Art. 17, UEFA Club Licensing and Financial Fair Play Regulations (2018 Version). Annex II explains the criteria that must be satisfied in order to access the voluntary settlement agreement, which include: the club complied with the break-even requirement in the previous reporting period; there has been a change in ownership or control over the club; the club was not subject to a previous agreement or sanction for a breach of FFP rules.

smaller clubs which make up a considerable share of their revenues from selling their most talented players to richer clubs.[724] A system that restricts the ability of clubs to sell their players is also affecting their ability to draw revenues.

446. FFP aims to ensure the long-term financial viability of European football, and more specifically the integrity and continuity of international competitions for the entire season.[725] These objectives have been accepted by the CJEU and the Commission as legitimate in *ENIC*[726] and *Bosman*.[727] However, the rules must also be considered suitable and necessary to achieve their legitimate objectives and limited to the least restrictive means available to reach them. In this regard, it should be demonstrated that the financial stability of one team is necessary and directly linked with the existence of its competitors and the competition itself and that other measures, such as forms of salary caps, could not achieve the same results while being less restrictive.

447. The EU Commission has stated that it is in the interest of sports teams, clubs and athletes to protect the economic viability of other teams, athletes and clubs as competitors.[728]

448. In a recognition of the specificity of sport, this can be understood with reference to the interdependence existing between clubs. Clubs need the cooperation of their rivals to create joint products, whether that is the league or even just a game. Clubs make up a share of their revenues by selling their products, from hospitality to merchandise, to fans and customers of their rivals. If a club is unable to meet its obligations, the competitors would be financially damaged. It must therefore be accepted that clubs and players have a vested interest in ensuring the financial viability of the competitors.[729]

449. The Commission has also expressly stated that the objective of financial stability can be legitimately pursued through measures such as the FFP rules, which are considered to contribute to the sustainable development and healthy growth of

---

724. Harry Arne Solberg & Kjetil K. Haugen, *European Club Football: Why Enormous Revenues Are Not Enough?*, 13(2) Sport Soc. 329–343 (2010).

725. Furthermore, the rules aim also at protecting clubs' creditors and ensuring that clubs settle their liability with players, tax authorities and other clubs. *See* Art. 2(2) C of the UEFA Clubs Licensing and Fair Play Regulations.

726. *See* Case COMP/37 806: ENIC/ UEFA, para. 32 in relation to protecting the integrity of the competition.

727. Case C-415/93 *Union Royale Belge Sociétés de Football Association and others v. Bosman and others* [1995] ECR I-4921, paras 105–106 in relation to the need to maintain the financial viability of clubs.

728. *See* Joint Statement by Joaquín Almunia, Vice President, European Commission, and Michael Platini, President, UEFA (21 Mar. 2012), available at https://www.uefa.com/MultimediaFiles/Download/uefaorg/EuropeanUnion/01/77/21/58/1772158_DOWNLOAD.pdf (accessed 28 Apr. 2020).

729. Stephen Morrow, *Football, Economics and Finance*, in *Routledge Handbook of Football Studies* (John Hughson, Kevin Moore, Ramón Spaaij & Joseph Maguire eds, Routledge 2017).

sport in Europe.[730] However, this is just confirming the legitimacy of the objectives pursued, rather than providing a full assessment of the effects of the rules on the relevant market and consequently the proportionality of the restriction. In this relation, the Decisions of the Commission do not bind other institutions, and they do not prevent challenges from interested parties either.

450. Nevertheless, the political significance of these statements must be recognised. Indeed, it is highly unlikely that the Commission will take any action, as doing so might infringe the legitimate expectation that UEFA has developed in this regard.[731] In support of this consideration, in 2014 the Commission refused to examine a complaint against the FFP rules, as the matter was also the subject of a case before the national court in Brussels, which would have been fully capable of assessing the legality of the rules under EU competition law.[732] While not expressing any position on the merit of the complaint, the Commission held that, if necessary, the national court could have referred a preliminary question to the CJEU. This was effectively a political choice, as the Commission would have been best placed to assess the question, considering that FFP rules have effects on the entire EU market and not only on the Belgian territory.[733] The Belgian Tribunal de première instance, however, followed the suggestion of the Commission, and referred a question to the CJEU for a preliminary ruling on the compatibility of the FFP break-even rule with EU law, in particular competition law, freedom of movement of capital, freedom to invest and freedom of movement of workers and services.

451. Unfortunately, the Court of Justice rejected the opportunity to clarify the issue, holding that the question was manifestly inadmissible, as it considered itself incompetent to deal with it.[734] As UEFA is based in Switzerland, according to the Lugano Convention the CJEU would have been able to pronounce itself on the legality of FFP, and any recovery of damages suffered, only where the complainants

730. *See* European Commission, *Decision adopting the Arrangement for Cooperation between the European Commission and the Union of European Football Associations (UEFA),* COM(2014) 7378 final, s. 2.7, https://ec.europa.eu/assets/eac/sport/news/2014/docs/uefa2014_en.pdf (accessed 20 Apr. 2020) and European Commission, *Annex to the Commission Decision adopting the Arrangement for Cooperation between the European Commission and the Union of the European Football Associations (UEFA),* COM(2018) 876 final, s. 3.2.7, https://www.uefa.com/MultimediaFiles/Download/EuroExperience/uefaorg/EuropeanUnion/02/53/98/34/2539834_DOWNLOAD.pdf (accessed 8 Apr. 2020).
731. The protection of legitimate expectation is one of the general principles of EU law. *See* Damian Chalmers, Gareth Davies & Giorgio Monti, *European Union Law* 412 (Cambridge Univ. Press 2014).
732. Case AT.40105, UEFA Financial Fair Play Rules, Commission Decision rejecting the complaint, SG-Greffe (2014) 15691 COM(2014) 8028 final.
733. *See* Joint Statement of the Council and the Commission on the Functioning of the Network of Competition Authorities, para. 19.
734. Court of Justice of the European Union, Order of the Court – 16 Jul. 2015, Case C-299/15 *Striani and Others v. Union européenne des Sociétés de Football Association (UEFA) and Union Royale Belge des Sociétés de Football – Association (URBSFA)* [2015] ECLI:EU:C:2015:519.

would have demonstrated a direct interest to act.[735] Instead, the complainants were a football agent and a group of football fans, only indirectly affected by the restrictions imposed by the FFP.[736]

I. Assessing FFP

452. While the EU institutions have made recourse to procedural rules to avoid assessing the legality of FFP rules under EU law, the legitimacy of the Regulations and the sanctions they provide have been discussed by the CAS. Among the CAS jurisprudence on FFP, two decisions are worth discussing in this context.

453. The first concerns the appeal filed by Turkish football club Galatasaray against the proportionality of the sanction it received in 2015 for a breach of the break-even requirement. The club was sanctioned with exclusion from European competitions for the following two seasons in which the club would have qualified, and a limit on the overall cost of players for the next two reporting periods.[737] CAS had to review the legitimacy of the decision adopted by the Adjudicatory Chamber, and in doing so it considered the application of Articles 101 and 102 TFEU to the FFP regulations. In an interesting approach to this case, after having established that FFP does not restrict competition by object and effect, CAS applied a reasoning strikingly similar to the *Meca-Medina* test developed by the CJEU. CAS considered that, even if one would have considered the rules as a restriction, the FFP rules and the break-even principle were pursuing a legitimate objective and the restriction caused was inherent to such objective. The Court also held that the rules were having neither the object nor a demonstrable effect of restricting the market.[738]

454. The second case involved an appeal by AC Milan against a decision taken by the UEFA CFCB in 2018.[739] The club, after a change in ownership, was considered to be in breach of the break-even requirement for the reporting period 2015–2017. The CFCB Adjudicatory Chamber, in light of the size of the breach and considering it unrealistic for the club to comply with the FFP rules in the near future, refused to offer a settlement agreement. It thereby excluded AC Milan from participating in any European competition for the seasons 2018/2019 and 2019/2020. The club appealed the disciplinary sanction to CAS, arguing that the decision was disproportionate and the conditions to be eligible for a settlement agreement were not clear. In this context, it should be pointed out that such a system may be also considered to breach the principle of legal certainty and as such be relevant

735. Convention on jurisdiction and the recognition and enforcement of judgments in civil and commercial matters L339, 21 Dec. 2007, 3. As Switzerland is not a Member State of the EU, the Lugano II Convention on jurisdiction and the recognition and enforcement of judgments in civil and commercial matters regulates the matter.
736. Football Agent Daniel Striani, and groups of Manchester City and PSG fans.
737. CAS 2016/A/4492 – *Galatasaray v. UEFA*.
738. *Ibid.*, paras 62–79.
739. CAS 2018/A/5808 – *AC Milan v. UEFA*.

under EU law.[740] In any event, CAS agreed with the complainant, holding that UEFA CFCB failed to properly assess the changes in the factual situation, mainly in relation to the ownership of AC Milan, rendering the Decision disproportionate.[741]

455. The CAS, while considering the rules legitimate in principle, has therefore affirmed that the application of FFP may lead to disproportionate measures in individual cases. While the panel addressed the issue in order to assess the regularity of the procedure followed by UEFA, the question of transparency and proportionality of the sanctions may have effects on the application of EU law. In particular, the clarity of the criteria used within the sanctioning mechanism and the decision-making process is fundamental in ensuring the proportionality of the measures and therefore protecting the system against legal challenges.

456. In assessing the legitimacy of FFP rules, the economic nature of the regime needs noting, much like rules regulating the ownership of clubs discussed in *ENIC*. The objectives of these two sets of rules are however different, as FFP is not linked to protecting the integrity of the system per se but primarily its financial viability.[742] In light of the economic nature of the regulations, the application of Article 101(3) TFEU would require an analysis of the efficiency they create, the necessity of the restrictions and its proportionality. In this regard, efficiency should be interpreted as the ability of the system, or the undertakings active in it, to produce a product of a higher quality or at a lower cost.[743] UEFA has reported that the financial status of European clubs has significantly improved since the introduction of FFP, moving from a cumulative loss of EUR 1.7 billion in 2010 to EUR 615 million profit at the end of 2017.[744] This may demonstrate that the measure was necessary and effective in light of its objective – the improvement of the financial viability of European clubs – but does not necessarily discuss its efficiency and proportionality. Furthermore, losses do not equate to debts. Football clubs are still reliant on banks' credit, as well as private capital investors, lending sums that finance their operation on the transfers market.[745]

---

740. *See*, for example, Case C-110/03 *Belgium v. Commission* [2005] ECR I-2801, para. 30 and Case C-386/06 *R (International Association of Independent Tanker Owners (Intertanko)) v. Secretary of State for Transport* [2008] ECR I-4057, para. 69.
741. The matter was then referred back to UEFA CFCB to take a proportionate decision on the basis of the circumstances.
742. For a discussion on FFP rules and integrity objectives, *see* Mathias Schubert & Sean Hamil, *Financial Doping and Financial Fair Play in European Club Football Competitions*, in *The Palgrave Handbook on the Economics of Manipulation in Sport* 135–157 (Markus Breuer & David Forrest eds, Palgrave Macmillan 2018).
743. Christopher Townley, *Which Goals Count in Article 101 TFEU?: Public Policy and Its Discontents*, 32 ECLR 441–448 (2011).
744. UEFA, Club Licensing Benchmarking Report about European Football (2019), available at https://www.footballbenchmark.com/documents/files/UEFA%20Club%20Licensing%20Benchmarking%20report_2020_FY%202018.pdf (accessed 20 May 2020).
745. *See* Forbes, *The Lender Financing Soccer Clubs' Big-Money Transfers*, https://www.forbes.com/sites/robertkidd/2019/08/12/how-soccer-clubs-are-funding-big-money-transfers/#396c5d2025af, 12/8/2019 (accessed 20 Apr. 2020). For an analysis of the insolvency of football clubs, *see* Stefan Szymanski, *Entry into Exit: Insolvency in English Professional Football*, 64 Scott. J. Polit. Econ. 419–444 (2017).

457. In terms of the ability of FFP rules to improve the quality of the product offered, this discussion could be connected with an assessment of the effects of FFP on competitive balance. While FFP does not have as objective the improvement of competitive balance within European competitions, the Regulations are in fact likely to negatively affect it. The break-even requirement forces the clubs to focus on financial rather than sporting goals and this negatively affects their overall efficiency.[746] FFP rules reduce the possibility for lower-level clubs to compete with high earners, traditionally performing well on and off the pitch and with a solid fan base. The smaller clubs have fewer revenues at their disposal and tend to overinvest on the players' market to try and improve their performance on the field, and consequently on their financial books. As this conduct may lead to sanctions, including economic penalties, FFP is likely to further strengthen and protect the existing hegemony of European top-flight clubs.[747] This consideration is not affected by the redistribution of the sanctions paid from the clubs in breach, which UEFA has reported amounting to a total of EUR 4 million in the 2017/2018 season and EUR 4.7 million in the 2018/2019 season.[748]

458. The political support for FFP rules reflects the efforts of UEFA in instituting a dialogue with EU institutions. This approach has been effective in avoiding challenges to regulations and contributing to preserving the European model of sport.[749] Furthermore, the Regulations have been adopted with the agreement of the ECA, a powerful stakeholder in the football industry. It would be fair to assume that this may further prevent successful complaints coming from the clubs themselves. Indeed, it appears that this effort may have rendered the discussion of the legality of FFP rather doctrinal.

§4. State Aid

459. The pursuit of greater discipline and rationality in the economic management of sporting entities is fundamentally connected with the range of funding available to clubs and governing bodies. One of the consequences of the liberalisation of the players' market that occurred with *Bosman* has been the exponential growth in players' wages.[750] This increase has forced sports clubs to adopt more commercially driven strategies and to look for alternative sources of revenues. In

746. Ronan Gallagher & Barry Quinn, *Regulatory Own Goals: The Unintended Consequences of Economic Regulation in Professional Football*, 20(2) ESMQ 151–170 (2020).
747. Christopher Flanagan, *A Tricky European Fixture: An Assessment of UEFA's Financial Fair Play Regulations and Their Compatibility with EU Law*, 13 ISLJ 148–167 (2013).
748. Since its introduction, a total of EUR 77 million has been redistributed. *See* UEFA, *Report of the CFCB Investigatory Chamber*, 51, https://www.uefa.com/MultimediaFiles/Download/uefaorg/Clublicensing/02/63/75/26/2637526_DOWNLOAD.pdf (accessed 28 Apr. 2020).
749. Borja García & Stephen Weatherill, *Engaging with the EU in Order to Minimise Its Impact: Sport and the Negotiation of the Treaty of Lisbon*, 19(2) J. Eur. Public Policy 241 (2012).
750. According to Lago et al. the increase in spending on players is also a result of the increasing amount of income, especially coming from TV deals. *See* Umberto Lago, Rob Simmons & Stefan Szymanski, *The Financial Crisis in European Football: An Introduction*, 7(1) J. Sports Econ. 3–12 (2006).

times of economic hardship, in which clubs have to balance the obligations stemming from financial regulations with their win-maximisation strategy, seeking financial support from the State or other public authorities appears an attractive shortcut, if not the only feasible option.[751]

460. The intervention of the State on a private market is common practice in Europe and even praised as necessary.[752] However, in a market where rules operate to guarantee a level field of competition, EU law intervenes to ensure that this intervention does not disrupt that objective and distort the competition on the market to an excessive extent.

461. The connection between financial regulations in the sporting sector, such as the rules of FFP, and State aid provisions has been recognised by both the EU Commission and UEFA.[753] In a 2012 Statement, the two bodies acknowledged that the poor financial situation of some European clubs was tempting public authorities to step in and provide economic support. In this regard, the Statement argued that FFP and its objective of ensuring long-term investments in football were consistent with State aid provisions. This section will discuss how the European Union has approached public interventions on the private market in the sporting sector and what impact this may have on the European model of sport and the way it is funded.[754]

462. Under Article 107 TFEU, Member States are prohibited from granting any type of measure that may distort competition, by favouring certain undertakings or the production of certain goods. The provision covers any type of measure, regardless of its form or the authority issuing it. The Commission is tasked with assessing the legality of the specific measure adopted, on the basis of its effects on the relevant market.[755] Such a measure can then be approved if it pursues a common European objective, for which the intervention of the State is indispensable as the market does not offer alternatives. The principle of proportionality applies in the area as well, rendering illegal a measure that goes beyond the minimum necessary to

751. Klaus Nielsen & Rasmus Storm, *Profit Maximization, Win Optimization and Soft Budget Constraints in Professional Team Sports*, in *When Sport Meets Business: Capabilities, Challenges, Critiques* 153–166 (Klaus Nielsen, Wagner Ulrich & Rasmus Storm eds, Sage Publications 2017).
752. *See* the European Sport Charter issued by the Council of Europe. Art. 12 of the Charter states that 'Appropriate support and resources from public funds, that is, at national, regional and local levels, shall be made available for the fulfilment of the aims and purposes of this Charter.'
753. Joint Statement by Joaquín Almunia, Vice President, European Commission, and Michael Platini, President, UEFA 21 Mar. 2012, available at https://www.uefa.com/MultimediaFiles/Download/uefaorg/EuropeanUnion/01/77/21/58/1772158_DOWNLOAD.pdf (accessed 28 Apr. 2020).
754. For a more extensive discussion of the theme, *see* Andrea Cattaneo, *State Aid in Sport*, in *Research Handbook on EU Sports Law and Policy* 197–228 (Jack Anderson, Richard Parrish & Borja García eds, Edward Elgar 2018).
755. Case C-487/06P *British Aggregates v. Commission* [2008] ECR I-10515 and Case 248/84 *Germany v. Commission* [1987] ECR 4013 para. 17 and, for a comment, Luca Rubini, *The Elusive Frontier: 'Regulation' Under EC State Aid Law*, 8(3) EStAL 277–298 (2011).

achieve the objective and it is not administered transparently.[756] A measure granted to a private undertaking that provides an advantage without adequate remuneration, or beyond the conditions prevalent in the relevant market, will most likely be illegal following the scrutiny of the Commission.[757] An illegal aid will have to be recovered by the Member State, forcing the recipient to pay back any benefit received, plus any interest accrued.[758]

463. Sporting entities are undertakings under the scope of EU competition law, as they carry out a range of economic activities, such as selling tickets, entering into commercial agreements, or renting facilities. Any public funding granted to them must therefore comply with State aid rules. When a professional sports club receives financial support through public funding, it gains a competitive advantage over other clubs.[759] This may allow it to spend more on the transfer market and players' wages, thereby helping it to achieve success on the pitch, which in turn could translate into greater exposure and better commercial deals.[760] Furthermore, it must also be considered how modern professional clubs, especially in football, may be involved in a number of commercial activities only marginally related to their core business, such as hospitality, estates management, brand protection and entertainment. They will therefore be active in various markets and the granting of public funding may have indirect effects on most of them.[761]

464. The underlying assumption of this discussion is that an undertaking will not receive an unlawful advantage if the State operates as would any other private market operator. Generally, this means that funding would be granted as an investment that could be recouped in the future, in the prospect of long-term profitability rather than short-term gain.[762] However, this assessment requires consideration of the characteristics of the relevant market, including the commercial practices common

---

756. *See* European Commission: Notice on the notion of State aid as referred to in Art. 107(1) of the Treaty on the Functioning of the European Union C/2016/2946, OJ C 262 para. 140.
757. Adinda Sinnaeve, *Competition Policy, State Aid and State Enterprises*, in *Annual Proceedings of the Fordham Corporate Law Institute: International Antitrust Law and Policy* 67–91 (Barry Hawk ed., Juris Publishing 2001).
758. The Treaty does not mention the recovery of the aid, but it is a practice that can be inferred from the case law. *See* Case 70/72, *Commission v. Germany* [1973] ECR 813, para. 13.
759. Richard Craven, *State Aid and Sports Stadiums: EU Sports Policy or Deference to Professional Football*, 35(9) ECLR 453–460 (2014) and Tobias Traupel, *Football and State Aid: Really the Greatest Pastime in the World?*, 13(3) EStAL 414–425 (2014).
760. The range of effects that the Commission has connected with the granting of State aid measures is therefore wide. *See* Phedon Nicolaides, *A Critical Analysis of the Application of State Aid Rules to Sport*, 22(2) MJECL 209–223 (2015) and as an example *see* Decision of the Commission to open an investigation in the case State aid SA.33584 (2013/C) (ex 2011/NN), para. 40.
761. *See* the Decision of the Commission to open an investigation in *Real Madrid*, SA.33754. One of the effects of the measure under investigation was the granting of an area to FC Real Madrid that was going to be used by the club to build a hotel and a shopping mall.
762. *See* Case 234/84 *Commission v. Belgium* [1986] ECR 02263, para. 14, and Case C-305/89, *Italy v. Commission* [1991] EU:C:1991:142, para. 20. This approach was further confirmed in the Commission Decision SA.41612 – 2015/C (ex SA.33584 (2013/C) (ex 2011/NN)) implemented by the Netherlands in favour of the professional football club MVV in Maastricht, para. 35.

in that sector.[763] Transposing this principle into the sporting industry, the vast majority of sporting entities are not profitable, with a limited number of clubs owning the facilities they use.[764] Similarly, in assessing the adequacy of the return that must be sought by the awarding authority, one should consider the ability of clubs to benefit other economic sectors, by attracting tourism and publicity, for example. In this regard, a decision to provide financial support in this sense may be motivated by economic reasons, such as to guarantee tax flow, stimulate neighbouring markets and protect jobs.[765] Evidently, these are not objectives normally pursued by private market operators. However, factors that are not eminently economic may be considered in this assessment only if functional to obtain profits from the original investment.[766]

465. In relation to the sporting sector, it appears that the Commission has operated a distinction between the pursuit of public policies through sports funding, which grants benefits to the community, and the commercial objectives of private professional clubs. This discussion is therefore a further example of one of the principal characteristics of the European model of sport, namely the interplay between public policy objectives and private goals.

I. Public Interest and Sports Facilities

466. Under Article 107 TFEU, State aid rules provide the legal framework to strike a balance between the need for intervention of EU Member States on the market and the objective of protecting the fairness of the competition.[767] The underlying principle is that States and public authorities are entitled to intervene in the market, provided that a number of conditions are satisfied.

467. The application of this principle in the sporting sector is highly relevant in light of the cultural and societal importance of sport and the public objectives that may be pursued in this relation.[768] Sport not only is a leisure activity but also has a recognised significance in relation to the ability of local and national entities to boost integration and foster a sense of community. Similarly, providing financial

763. Gian Marco Galletti, *How Reasonable a Private Investor Can Be Assumed to Be? Corsica Ferries France*, 52(4) CML Rev. 1095–1110 (2015).
764. *See* the Decision of the Commission to open an investigation on the case Aide d'Etat SA 35501 (2013/N) – France Financement de la construction et de la rénovation des stades pour l'EURO, 2016 COM(2013) 9103 final, para. 275, and the Decision of the Commission to open an investigation in the case State aid SA.33584 (2013/C) (ex 2011/NN).
765. *See* European Commission, *Communication from the Commission Europe 2020: A Strategy for Smart, Sustainable and Inclusive Growth*, COM(2010) 2020 final.
766. Case C-303/88 *Italy v. Commission* [1991] ECR I-1433, para. 21: '[S]uch decisions may be motivated not solely by the likelihood of an indirect material profit but also by other considerations, such as a desire to protect the group's image or to redirect its activities.'
767. Art. 107(2) TFEU establishes that aid with social character or to make good the damage caused by exceptional circumstances have to be allowed by the European Commission.
768. For an historical analysis of the involvement of public authorities in sport, *see* Barry Houlihan, *The Government and Politics of Sport* (Routledge 1991).

support to sporting entities active at a local, regional or national level may fulfil a range of public policies: the developing of local sports facilities may enhance grass-roots participation in sport and have positive effects on health and education, as well as employment.[769] Benefits from public intervention are not limited to the grass-roots level; there may be a public policy rationale behind the provision of public funding to professional sporting entities. Public authorities may consider the importance of clubs for the community, not only as a cultural factor but also as a marketing tool for the development of the region.[770]

468. The EU institutions have recognised that the intervention of the State to fund sporting entities may be necessary in some circumstances and particular regard has been paid to the financing of sports infrastructures, which has been considered to fall under the responsibilities of Member States.[771] The favourable approach of the EU institutions towards funding for sports infrastructures is consistent with the wording of Article 165 TFEU and its stated goal to promote European sporting issues, a system based on voluntary activity and the social and educational function of sport. These are, once again, public policy objectives whose pursuit should not be demanded to private investors. As such, they may represent a type of common European interest, insofar as the facilities are open to the general public and private operators are reluctant to invest. Such a rationale has been promoted by the Court of Justice as well when it approved the aid granted to non-profit organisations in *Hamr Sport*[772] and *Magic Mountain Kletterhallen.*[773]

469. The recognition of the existing public policy objectives in the funding of sporting facilities underlined also the approach taken by the Commission in adopting the General Block Exempting Regulation No 651/2014 (GBER II).[774] GBER II specifically addresses aid granted in the sports sector, establishing that, under certain conditions, they do not have an appreciable effect on the market. In particular, public investment in sports infrastructures will be exempt from the prohibition if the facility will be used for more than one purpose, it will be open to the public, and if assigned to third parties, a fair and transparent tender process has been followed.

769. Tobias Traupel, *Football and State Aid: Really the Greatest Pastime in the World?*, 13(3) EStAL 414–425 (2014).

770. *See* Richard Craven, *Football and State Aid: Too Important to Fail?*, 14(3–4) ISLJ 205–217 (2014) and Christopher Durand & Emmanuel Bayle, *Public Assistance in Spectator Sport: A Comparison Between Europe and the United States*, 2(2) EJSS 1–19 (2002).

771. *See* European Commission, *Commission staff working document. Impact assessment accompanying the White Paper on Sport*, SEC(2007) 935 final (2007), para. 3.2.2, and the Decision of the Commission in Case C4/2008 Investment of the municipality of Rotterdam in the Ahoy Complex, point 67.

772. Case T-693/14 *Hamr – Sport a.s. v. European Commission* [2016] ECLI:EU:T:2016:292.

773. Case T-162/13 *Magic Mountain Kletterhallen GmbH and Others v. European Commission* [2016] ECLI:EU:T:2016:341.

774. Under Art. 109 TFEU, the Council can delegate to the Commission powers to adopt legislative measures exempting some specific types of aid from the obligation under Art. 107 TFEU, when they create enough benefit to outweigh any market distortion caused.

The measure has therefore recognised the concept of multifunctional arenas, comprising any type of recreational facility that offers cultural and recreational services, with the exception of leisure parks and hotel facilities.[775]

470. The impact of the Regulation on the financing of professional sport clubs is reduced by establishing that the facilities may not be used by a single professional club, and that they have to be available to other sporting entities for at least 20% of the year. Finally, the exemption applies only to funding below EUR 15 million, or where the cost of the entire project is lower than EUR 50 million. It is therefore clear that this measure applies to funding with a relatively limited economic relevance, that tend to have an impact at local level.

471. The Commission was able to adopt the GBER II in light of the experience gained in assessing a number of measures in the years preceding the Regulation.[776] In this regard, it referred to public policy objectives in its Decision to exempt the tax benefit scheme for undertakings investing in sports infrastructure implemented by the Hungarian Government.[777] In light of the unfavourable market conditions for private investors, the intervention of the State was considered necessary to pursue the objective of increasing sports participation by providing well-equipped sporting facilities. While the direct beneficiaries of the scheme were sports associations and clubs, the measure was held to provide benefits to the wider community.[778]

472. Similarly, in 2013 the Commission approved a number of State aid granted for the construction or renovation of multifunctional arenas, respectively in *Erfurt*,[779] *Jena*,[780] *Uppsala*,[781] and *Brussels*.[782] The cases presented some common features, in that the need for such investments was not met by the market, and the facilities funded were open to the wider public and capable of hosting a range of different events. The measures were providing a competitive advantage to individual sporting entities that were using the facilities, including a professional football club participating in UEFA competitions.[783] However, the Commission gave precedence to the public policy argument and exempted the measures as necessary

775. GBER II, Art. 55(3).
776. Benoit Keane, *The Application of Competition Law in the Entertainment and Sport Sectors*, 5 JECLP 592–601 (2014).
777. Decision of the Commission in the Case SA.31722 – Hungary, Supporting the Hungarian sport sector via tax benefit scheme, COM(2011) 7287 final.
778. The Decision makes explicit reference to the five most popular sports in Hungary, i.e., football, basketball, ice hockey, water polo, and handball. *See ibid.*, para. 28.
779. Commission Decision of 20.03.2013 on State aid SA.35135 (2012/N) – Germany Multifunktionsarena der Stadt Erfurt, hereinafter 'Erfurt'.
780. Commission Decision of 20.03.2013 on State aid SA.35440 (2012/N) – Germany Multifunktionsarena der Stadt Jena, hereinafter 'Jena'.
781. Commission Decision of 02.05.2013 on State aid SA.33618 (2012/C) which Sweden is planning to implement for Uppsala arena, hereinafter 'Uppsala'.
782. Commission Decision of 20.11.2013 on State aid SA.37109 (2013/N) – Belgium Football stadiums in Flanders, hereinafter 'Brussels'.
783. *See Brussels*, para. 3.

and proportionate. In the context of these Decisions, the Commission drew a connection with Article 165 TFEU and its goal to enhance the social, educational and health dimension of sport. It further reiterated that it considered a responsibility of the State to guarantee the construction of facilities for sporting and cultural events, even when this also directly benefits professional sporting entities.[784]

473. This approach was later confirmed in the Decision allowing a series of measures funding the renovation of French football stadiums in preparation to host the EURO 2016.[785] While the facilities were to be used by professional football clubs, which were renting them from the municipalities at market price, they were available to the municipalities for a whole range of events of a different nature. Once again, the Commission upheld the societal and cultural value of sport and sought to protect the right of the public to access facilities.[786] In this regard, it considered the investment complying with objectives of common European interest, and fulfilling the State's responsibility.[787] The proportionality of the measure was achieved by the imposition of a control system and appropriate fees paid by the users, which counteracted the anticompetitive effects caused.

II. State Aid to Professional Football Clubs

474. While financing sports infrastructures may be an activity comprised within the range of responsibilities of the State towards its citizens, more caution must be used when subsidies are granted to professional sports clubs. The decision-making activity of the EU Commission in this field has seen a dramatic increase in the period between 2010 and 2017, after relative silence interrupted only by two cases assessed in the 1990s – *Public Grants to Professional Clubs*,[788] and *Salva Calcio*.[789] Starting from 2010, the Commission has opened a number of investigations after complaints filed by private citizens and undertakings, who were reluctant to see public funding being distributed to professional sports clubs in time of financial hardship. These investigations concerned the use of a range of rescue measures to bail out football clubs in crisis. This is not uncommon and may take the form of

784. *See* Decision of the Commission in Case C4/2008 Investment of the Municipality of Rotterdam in the Ahoy Complex, point 67, and *Erfurt* paras 13 and 14, *Jena* paras 15 and 16, and *Uppsala* paras 26 and 48.
785. Decision of the Commission on Aide d'Etat SA 35501 (2013/N) – France Financement de la construction et de la rénovation des stades pour l'EURO, 2016 COM(2013) 9103 final.
786. Jacob Kornbeck, *State Aid and Access to Sport – Lessons for VAT Law*, 18(2) EStAL 138–156 (2019).
787. *See* SA 35501, para. 273.
788. SG (2001) D/288165 French Subsidies for Youth Training N118/00, Press Release IP/01/599 of 25 Apr. 2001. In this case, France introduced a funding scheme for professional football clubs that were equipped or were committing to build a State-approved youth training centre. The aid was exempted in light of its underlying objective of promoting the education and training of young French athletes.
789. *See* Press Release IP/04/854, Commission asks Italy to change its rules on accounting by professional sports clubs ('Salva calcio'). In this case, the Commission required Italy to amend the law regulating the financial accounting of professional football clubs, which was allowing them to submit accounts underestimating true costs and losses.

administrative practice, under which clubs are allowed to use a municipal stadium under favourable conditions, credit loaned by State-controlled financial institutions and even different taxation regimes.

475. The first group of measures assessed by the Commission were granted by Dutch municipalities to local football clubs, namely Vitesse, NEC, Willem II, MVV Maastricht, Den Bosh and PSV Eindhoven.[790] Through these measures, the municipalities were allowing the clubs to overcome financial difficulties, either by partially waiving their debts,[791] significantly lowering the rent for sporting facilities[792] or granting more favourable conditions on it,[793] or finally by entering into commercial agreements highly favourable to the club.[794] In these instances, the Commission considered that the public authorities behaved as private market operators: in the event of a bankruptcy, the clubs would not have been able to repay the debts and the municipalities would have been prevented from recovering any fund whatsoever. It was therefore preferable to extend the loan, waive part of it, or in any event guarantee the viability of the club. However, in few instances, the conduct of the public authority significantly differed from that of private creditors, which in the same situation refused to waive their claims.[795] In any event, the Commission decided that the measures were granted under market conditions, or as part of a restructuring plan for the clubs.[796]

476. Following these Decisions, the Commission assessed the conduct of Spanish public financing institutions which granted Valencia FC, Hercules FC and Elche CF counter-guarantees for loans they contracted, in return for pledges on the shares of the clubs and counter-guarantees from the shareholders.[797] In this instance, the Commission considered that the guarantee was rendered necessary by the fact that private operators were not willing to invest, wary of the risk of insolvency of the clubs. As it was held that there was no restructuring plan in place, these measures were considered illegal.[798] However, in the appeal lodged by Hercules FC against the Decision, the General Court sided in favour of the club, annulling the Decision by holding that the Commission failed to give reasons as to how it analysed the

790. *See* Decision of the Commission to open an investigation in the case State aid SA.33584 (2013/C) (ex 2011/NN). The Commission decided to open one cumulative investigation on the different measures, despite them being granted by a number of local authorities.
791. SA.33584, Vitesse Football Club, paras 43 and 44, and Commission Decision SA.41612 – 2015/C (ex SA.33584 (2013/C) (ex 2011/NN)) implemented by the Netherlands in favour of the professional football club MVV in Maastricht, para. 16, and SA.33584, Den Bosch, paras 35 and 36.
792. SA.33584 Willem II, paras 29 and 30.
793. SA.33584 NEC, paras 24–28 and 47. The Commission found that the Dutch Authority based its decision solely on one of two discording legal opinions, without giving reasons as to why it chose one and disregarded the other.
794. SA.33584, PSV Eindhoven, paras 33 and 34.
795. SA.33584, MVV para. 55, and SA.33584, Den Bosch, paras 35 and 36.
796. Commission Decision on the Measure SA.41613 – 2015/C (ex SA.33584 – 2013/C (ex 2011/NN)), paras 57–58.
797. SA.36387 Aid to Valencia football clubs, paras 9–12.
798. European Commission, Press Release IP/16/2401, State aid: Commission decides Spanish professional football clubs have to pay back incompatible aid, Brussels, 4 Jul. 2016.

value of the counter-guarantee offered by the club and its shareholder.[799] Similarly, the Decisions against Valencia FC and Helche CF were also annulled by the General Court. In both instances, the Court stressed that the Commission failed to demonstrate that the clubs did receive an unlawful advantage, by obtaining guarantees not available on the market. In essence, the Commission failed to take account of the various circumstances affecting the position of the clubs on the market and could therefore not substantiate the claim that a private market operator would have acted differently from the public financial institutions.[800]

477. In another group of cases decided by the Commission, the measures involved respectively a form of tax exemption granted by Spain to a selected number of football clubs,[801] and a land transfer agreement between Real Madrid FC and the city of Madrid.[802] In the first case, Spanish legislation granted non-profit status to Real Madrid CF, Athletic Club Bilbao, Club Atlético Osasuna and FC Barcelona.[803] The status qualified them for a reduced tax rate on their commercial income that was not available to other clubs.[804] While the Commission considered that the measure provided an illegal advantage to selected undertakings by using State resources, the EU General Court took a different view. The Court held that the Commission erred in considering only the tax rate applied, without considering the difference in terms of deductions that were available on the basis of the different status.[805] An appropriate assessment would have given an account of both elements, before coming to a decision as to the existence of an advantage and its extent.

478. In the second investigation, the agreements related to the transfer of land properties between the city of Madrid and Real Madrid CF were considered to depart from a fair evaluation of the land, therefore providing an illegal advantage to the club.[806] Again, the General Court annulled the Decision of the Commission, holding that the institution merely considered the value of one of the land property transferred, ignoring the other properties involved in the arrangement and thereby failing to consider all the necessary elements of the transaction. As such, the Commission did not demonstrate that the measure was granting an illegal advantage to the club.[807]

---

799. Case T-766/16 *Hércules Club de Fútbol v. Commission* [2019] ECLI:EU:T:2019:173.
800. Case T-732/16 *Valencia Club de Fútbol v. Commission* [2020] ECLI:EU:T:2020:98 and T-901/16 *Elche Club de Fútbol v. Commission* [2020] ECLI:EU:T:2020:97.
801. Decision of the Commission to open an investigation in the case State aid SA.29769 (2013/C) (ex 2013/NN) – Spain State aid to certain Spanish professional sport clubs.
802. Decision of the Commission to open an investigation in the case State aid SA.33754 (2013/C) (ex 2013/NN) – Spain Real Madrid CF.
803. Ley 10/1990, de 15 de octubre, del Deporte, BOE de 17 de Octubre de 1990.
804. *See* SA.29769, para. 7.
805. Case T-865/16 *Fútbol Club Barcelona v. Commission* [2019] ECLI:EU:T:2019:113, para. 38.
806. Commission Decision on State aid, SA.33754 (2013/C) (ex 2013/NN) implemented by Spain for Real Madrid CF.
807. Case T-791/16 *Real Madrid Club de Fútbol v. Commission* [2019] ECLI:EU:T:2019:346, para. 122.

479. The successful appeals filed by the clubs in the cases heard before the General Court must be ascribed to the failure of the Commission in assessing the economic impact of the various elements of the transactions assessed. As opposed to the Decisions on funding granted for sporting facilities, where the societal and cultural value of sport was stressed, the measures granted directly to professional football clubs were still assessed by making exclusive reference to economic factors. However, in an area where the Commission should have adopted a strict economic approach to assess the legality of the aid, it has been defeated by the sporting entities. This demonstrates how sporting entities have embraced the application of EU law to their activity, and have not attempted to rely on outdated claims of immunity. Instead, the specificity of the sports market must be considered as an element of the assessment, in the application of economic criteria.

480. The set of investigations discussed demonstrates that the Commission is willing to accommodate the specific needs of the sport system, where they can be justified under public policy objectives. Instead, a more orthodox approach has been adopted when the measures were aimed at bailing out clubs from their debts without a restructuring plan, or where an advantage was granted to highly successful professional clubs. This reminds us of the continuous interplay between the pursuit of public policy, delegated to sporting bodies, and the commercial interests they are required to pursue as private actors. It is in this context that the connection between the enforcement of State aid rules and the objectives of the sport system, such as protecting the competitive balance and ensuring financial stability, may be observed.

481. The objective underlining EU State aid rules, that of ensuring a level field of competition in the market, has also underlined the EU strategy in the Brexit negotiations. As we are writing before the negotiations on the future relationship between the UK and the EU have been finalised, we cannot establish the nature of the arrangement in relation to the State aid provisions. However, insofar as the UK will be a member of the World Trade Organisation, general provisions on public subsidies will continue to apply. Nevertheless, it is likely that the UK will have greater freedom to invest in grassroots sports, as such a conduct does not present a significant threat to European counterparts. Instead, it is possible that public investments at elite level could be met with criticism, both at national level and by European competitors.

§5. Sports Broadcasting Rights

482. The ability of sporting entities, clubs, leagues and governing bodies to strike lucrative commercial agreements has become progressively more important in parallel with the commercialisation of sport. The effects of the liberalisation of the players' market, combined with the development of pay TV channels in Europe, has created a connection between media and live sport that appears indissoluble.[808]

808. For a discussion on this theme, *see* Katrien Lefever, *New Media and Sport: International Legal Aspects* (T.M.C. Asser Press 2012).

483. As opposed to other areas discussed elsewhere in this monograph, in the context of the exploitation of broadcasting and media rights, sports governing bodies and sporting entities adopt conduct that is almost exclusively motivated by economic objectives, namely the maximisation of profits. It would therefore be correct to assume that in this area the protection of competition within the internal market takes precedence over sporting objectives. Instead, the protection of public policy objectives seems to be left to NCAs and legislative instruments. While the restrictive conduct put in place in the area may affect consumers, in their ability to access the rights, the objectives of public policy related to the cultural, societal and even political importance of sport are relegated to a limited role.[809]

484. The inherent characteristics of the European model of sport, and in particular the interdependence and solidarity between participants and competitors, may be considered in this discussion.[810] The protection of such characteristics has been used by governing bodies, sporting entities, and broadcasters in an attempt to justify conduct that restricts the market, such as collective selling of broadcasting rights and territorial exclusivity.[811] The next section will therefore assess how the EU institutions have approached the range of conduct that is so fundamentally linked to the European model of sport and its financing. It will also assess if a balance has been struck among the different interests involved in the area.

485. A number of reasons may explain the economic and legal relevance of sports broadcasting rights. On the one hand, media operators have progressively realised that live sports events are premium content, capable of captivating the most lucrative share of the audience for broadcasters and advertisers. This is due to the nature of the product, a unique event that cannot be replicated: viewers have to tune in during the course of the event and once this is terminated, there is limited value in any further reproduction.

486. On the other hand, the rights owners, namely sports governing bodies, leagues and clubs, have also progressively realised that by managing their rights effectively, they could become an important player in the market, being the supplier of the product themselves.[812] Today, in Europe the commercialisation of sports rights is conducted at central/collective level by the league or the association organising the competition, with limited exceptions related to rights exploited on some specific platforms.

---

809. Accessing sports contents may constitute a means to catalyse the national identity and build social cohesion, but also a way to promote physical activity and enhance the health and well-being of citizens. *See* Claude Jeanrenaud, & Stefan Késenne, *The Economics of Sport and the Media* (Edward Elgar 2006).
810. Stefan Szymanski, *The Economic Design of Sporting Contests*, 41 JEL 1137–1187 (2003).
811. *See* José Luis Arnaut, *Independent European Sport Review*, A report by José Luis Arnaut (2006), paras 3.76 et seq.
812. According a report produced by SportBusiness Consulting, the global value of sports media rights in 2019 was USD 51 billion, with a forecast of USD 55 billion by 2022. *See* SportBusiness Consulting, *Global Media Report 2019*, https://www.sportbusiness.com/consulting/sportbusiness-consulting-global-media-report-2019/ (accessed 28 Apr. 2020).

487. To face the ever-increasing costs of acquiring media rights and producing content, broadcasters seek to purchase the rights to broadcast events from the league – or the national association, rather than individually from each club. The collective selling, or acquisition, of rights is indeed more favourable to media operators as it reduces transaction costs.[813] Further to this, broadcasters will also seek to obtain the exclusivity on the rights, which guarantees that a share of the audience will necessarily have to subscribe or tune in to their channel to watch the event, thereby allowing them to recoup the investment borne.

488. The collective selling of broadcasting rights raises a number of antitrust concerns, since it clearly implies a restriction of the competition on the market. These arrangements prevent individual clubs from operating freely in the market and impose on broadcasters an obligation to negotiate with an entity that has monopoly, or quasi-monopoly power. They may also affect the final consumers, by reducing their choice over products, the type of subscription and price and could ultimately entail a constraint of their right to access information. The restrictions caused by collective selling are often counterbalanced with some positive and pro-competitive effects, usually defined in terms of economic efficiencies, such as the reduction of transaction costs mentioned above. The exclusivity itself may create efficiency as the licensee has full control of the conditions of distribution of the product and may be able to guarantee access to the broadcast to a substantial portion of the population.

489. Finally, sporting bodies have claimed that collective selling, and the sharing of the revenues thereby obtained, may be necessary to pursue the competitive balance of the competitions they organise.[814] This would ultimately lead to a more profitable product when placed on the market and a more effective promotion of clubs in smaller markets. However, these effects are not an immediate consequence of the collective selling, but they are rather a possible outcome of a mechanism implementing revenue redistribution.[815]

I. The Market for Sports Broadcasting Rights

490. When analysing the effects of a restrictive conduct such as collective selling, the relevant market must be established. Different markets may be identified on the basis of specific criteria, such as how attractive is the event for the viewers and the advertisers, whether there are substitutes for this event, the characteristics of the event itself and national preferences.[816] In the upstream market, where broadcasters

813. Decision COMP/C.2-37.398 – Joint selling of the commercial rights of the UEFA Champions League, para. 148.
814. *See* Stefan Szymanski, *The Economic Design of Sporting Contests*, 41 JEL 1137–1187 (2003) for a study on the relation between collective selling of broadcasting rights and competitive balance.
815. Furthermore, collective selling is not the only possible way to share revenues between teams taking part in the competition. *See* Decision COMP/C.2-37.398 – Joint selling of the commercial rights of the UEFA Champions League, para. 131.
816. *Ibid.*, s. 4.1.3.

purchase the rights from the rights owners, horizontal agreements between clubs prevent individual clubs from competing for the sale of those rights. Setting the price for all the rights may also be construed as a form of price-fixing, a type of conduct explicitly prohibited under Article 101 TFEU. Finally, there may be an output restriction if the range of rights on offer is reduced.[817]

491. In the downstream market, broadcasters compete for audience and advertising revenues. Collective selling on the upstream market creates barriers to entry in the downstream market as well, especially where there are dominant broadcasters capable of foreclosing access to new operators. This downstream market has traditionally been seen as national, due to varying preferences of the public, language barriers and differences in legislation.[818] Whether the development of the market has affected the relevance of this consideration, and to what extent, is open to debate.[819]

492. A league that sells its rights collectively behaves as an association of undertakings, whose decisions restrict the competition on the market under Article 101 TFEU. The conduct will therefore be prohibited, unless the conditions provided for in Article 101(3) TFEU are cumulatively satisfied. These conditions require the examining authority to assess the overall effects of the agreement and to consider whether it creates efficiencies capable of outweighing the restriction caused.[820]

493. The EU Commission has analysed this theme in a number of cases. In *Champions League*,[821] UEFA distributed the rights for the group stage and the final phase of the Champions League on behalf of the participating teams. UEFA sold the free-to-air and pay TV rights on an exclusive basis to one broadcaster per territory, in a multi-year package.[822] The system raised a number of concerns. UEFA had a monopoly over the supply of the product, and the awarded broadcaster was granted control of all the rights for its territory with no differentiation as to the platform or the form in which they were exploited. Furthermore, the arrangement prevented

---

817. Philip Kienapfel & Andreas Stein, *The Application of Articles 81 and 82 EC in the Sport Sector*, 3 Competition Policy Newsletter 6–14 (2007).
818. Decision of the Commission in Case 37398, Joint selling of the commercial rights of the UEFA Champions League, OJ 2003 L 291/25, para. 90, Case COMP/38.173, Collective selling of FA Premier League's broadcasting rights, para. 23, and finally Case COMP/C-2/37.214, Joint selling of the media rights to the German Bundesliga para. 19.
819. In Joined Cases C-403/08 and C-429/08 *FA Premier League and others v. QC Leisure and others, Karen Murphy v. Media Protection Services Ltd* [2011] ECR I-9083, at para. 140, the FAPL submitted that in the context of the licensing of broadcasting rights on a territorial basis '[t]he broadcaster selling the cheapest decoder cards has the potential to become, in practice, the broadcaster at European level, which would result in broadcast rights in the European Union having to be granted at European level'.
820. Case T-112/99 *Métropole télévision (M6) and others* [2001] ECR II-2459, para. 74, and Case T-328/03 *O2 (Germany) GmbH & Co. OHG v. Commission of the European Communities* [2006] ECR II-1231, paras 69 et seq. For a discussion in relation to the application of this principle in sport, *see* Oliver Budzinski, *The Institutional Framework for Doing Sports Business: Principles of EU Competition Policy in Sports Markets*, Ilmenau Economics Discussion Papers 70 (2011).
821. Commission Decision COMP/C.2-37.398, Joint selling of the commercial rights of the UEFA Champions League.
822. *Ibid.*, para. 3.2.

clubs from exploiting the rights individually and could foreclose the market due to the duration of the exclusivity. Finally, the bundling of the rights could result in output restrictions on the downstream market, leaving a number of rights unexploited.[823]

494. In analysing the conduct, the Commission found that the collective system was reducing transaction costs, by creating a single point of sale and a more efficient system of exploitation of rights. It was also benefitting broadcasters by allowing them to programme the entire season in advance, which would in turn guarantee coverage for the entire tournament. Finally, the arrangement allowed the creation of a brand, managed and protected at a collective level.[824]

495. The Commission, however, required UEFA to amend its selling arrangement to curb the restriction caused. The rights had to be sold through a competitive and transparent bidding process; the exclusivity had to be limited to a three-season period to prevent the creation of dominant positions on the market; the rights had to be divided into packages, each conferring the right to broadcast specific content on different platforms; and finally, clubs were allowed to individually sell those rights left unsold by UEFA, and to jointly exploit less valuable rights, such as deferred highlights and new media rights.[825]

496. The remedies identified by the Commission, although specific to the circumstances of the case and the relevant market analysed, constituted a model for future Decisions, respectively considering the selling for Premier League and Bundesliga rights.[826] While in relation to the selling of rights for the German Bundesliga the decision adopted the same conditions seen in *Champions League*, in *Premier League* the Commission imposed a further requirement. In order to curb the dominant position of the incumbent broadcaster, the institution imposed the no-single buyer rule and a prohibition of unconditional bids.[827]

497. This set of Decisions considered the selling arrangements under an orthodox antitrust approach, only mentioning in passing the theme of the specificity of

823. *Ibid*. For a discussion on the restrictive effects of joint selling on the market *see* T.M.C. Asser Institute, *Study on Sports Organisers' Rights in the European Union* 77 (T.M.C. Asser Institute 2014).
824. Decision COMP/C.2-37.398, Joint selling of the commercial rights of the UEFA Champions League, paras 148–149, 154–157 and 179.
825. *Ibid*., paras 3.4.1.2 and 3.4.1.3. For a discussion on the subdivision of the right in packages *see* Stephen Weatherill, *The Sale of Rights to Broadcast Sporting Events under EC Law*, in *European Sports Law* 311–377 (Stephen Weatherill ed., T.M.C. Asser Press 2014).
826. Case COMP/38.173, Collective selling of FA Premier League's broadcasting rights, and Case COMP/C-2/37.214, Joint selling of the media rights to the German Bundesliga.
827. Case COMP/38.173, Collective selling of FA Premier League's broadcasting rights, para. 36(e).

sport, and the solidarity goal that would have been achieved through collective selling.[828] The focus was rather on the use of sports rights as a market tool, through which broadcasters were capable of establishing their presence. In turn, the approach of UEFA and other governing bodies was more successful in justifying the reliance of the system on the selling of rights as source of income, rather than the protection of the solidarity among competitors as an inherent characteristic of the European model of sport.

II. Consumers, Citizens and Territorial Exclusivity

498. Among the conditions that must be cumulatively satisfied in order to exempt restrictive agreements under Article 101(3) TFEU, it is prescribed that consumers receive a fair share of the benefits created by the arrangement, balancing out the negative effects suffered.[829] In the cases mentioned, however, the analysis of the Commission neglected to give this aspect proper consideration.[830] Consumers were held to benefit from a restrictive arrangement when it would produce efficiency on the upstream market, under the assumption that this would be passed on to consumers. Indeed, the Commission considered that broadcasters benefitting from collective selling would have in turn offered their consumers a higher quality product.[831] However, the additional exclusivity clauses prevent the public from exercising a choice between different platform operators. Furthermore, as the broadcasters had to pay a premium price for the exclusivity, the cost will certainly be passed on to the consumers.[832] The exclusivity in a commercial agreement is a legitimate conduct, but its use should be assessed carefully.[833]

499. As the analysis of the Commission paid little attention to the interest of consumers, NCAs intervened. Under Regulation 1/2003,[834] NCAs are mandated to apply both national competition law and EU competition law to conduct affecting their territory. National legislation has been adopted in the Member States to transpose Articles 101 and 102 TFEU at national level, and cover conduct that affects

---

828. Decision COMP/C.2-37.398, Joint selling of the commercial rights of the UEFA Champions League, para. 131. This was confirmed also by Kienapfel and Stein, according to whom the financial solidarity argument had no impact on the Assessment under Art. 101(3). *See* Philip Kienapfel & Andreas Stein, *The Application of Articles 81 and 82 EC in the Sport Sector*, 3 Competition Policy Newsletter 6–14, 12 (2007).

829. Communication from the Commission – Guidelines on the application of Art. 81(3) of the Treaty, 2004/C 101/08, OJ C 101, paras 95 et seq. and 102.

830. For a discussion on this aspect, *see* Ben Van Rompuy, *Economic Efficiency: The Sole Concern of Modern Antitrust Policy?: Non-Efficiency Considerations under Article 101 TFEU* (Kluwer Law International 2012).

831. Decision COMP/C.2-37.398, para. 171.

832. Financial Times, *Sky Raises Prices after Premier League Auction: Pay-TV Channel Paid £300 Million More than Expected for Rights* 18 Mar. 2015, https://www.ft.com/content/54473a9c-cda2-11e4-8760-00144feab7de (accessed 29 Apr. 2020).

833. Case 262/81 *Coditel SA et al v. Ciné-Vog Films SA et al (Coditel II)* [1982] ECR 3381, para. 15.

834. Council Regulation (EC) No 1/2003 of 16 Dec. 2002 on the implementation of the rules on competition laid down in Arts 81 and 82 of the Treaty OJ L 1, Arts 1–25.

exclusively the national market.[835] The decisions of NCAs over conduct restrictive of competition may therefore vary, as they refer to their own national markets. In any event, their decision practice is relevant for the purpose of our analysis, as NCAs are part of the enforcement system of EU law from Regulation 1/2003.

500. In an attempt to counterbalance the restriction caused on consumers and guarantee broader access to the rights, a number of European NCAs analysed collective selling arrangements. The German *Bundeskartellamt* held that the share of the benefit granted to consumers was inadequate and suggested alternative ways to allow fans to access the rights, or at least some of them, without having to subscribe to the incumbent pay TV.[836] Similarly, in the UK in 2008 the Office of Communications (Ofcom) abandoned the idea of imposing a 'no single buyer rule' to the selling of Premier League rights on the national market, as this would have required consumers to subscribe to various broadcasters in order to acquire the entire content.[837] The rule was later reintroduced following a new investigation concluded in 2016, in which Ofcom attempted to strike a balance between the interest of the fans watching Premier League games in TV and those attending the games.[838] In other instances, the duration of the exclusivity was limited to a three-year maximum in Spain, and in France.[839]

501. The right of consumers and citizens to access sporting events cannot be seen only in an economic perspective, but it is fundamentally connected with their cultural significance. Fearing a migration of all the rights to pay TV, the EU has recognised the cultural role of major events and their importance for its citizens.[840] The Audiovisual Media Services Directive grants Member States discretion to draw up a list of events which, in light of their societal importance for a Member State, must be freely accessible to its citizens. The scheme protects the rights of citizens to

835. In the UK, the Competition Act 1998 mirrors the provisions of EU competition law to cover conduct that has an effect limited to the national market of the United Kingdom. As this is national legislation, Brexit will not have an immediate effect on it.
836. Bundeskartellamt, *Joint selling of media rights for the games of the 1st and 2nd German football leagues (Bundesliga) from the 2013/2014 season onwards*, available at http://www.bundeskartellamt.de/SharedDocs/Entscheidung/EN/Fallberichte/Kartellverbot/2012/B6-114-10.pdf?__blob=publicationFile&v=2 (accessed 29 Apr. 2020).
837. Ofcom *Pay TV second consultation: Access to premium content* (London 2008).
838. *See* Ofcom, *Competition Act investigation into the sale of live UK audio-visual media rights to Premier League matches,* 8 Aug. 2016 https://www.ofcom.org.uk/about-ofcom/latest/bulletins/competition-bulletins/all-closed-cases/cw_01138 (accessed 30 Apr. 2020).
839. In relation to Spain, *see* SNC/0029/13 *Mediapro y Clubs de Futblol II*. In relation to France, Decision de l'Autorite' de Concurrence 14-MC-01, *Mesure conservatoire du 30 juillet 2014 relative à la demande de mesures conservatoires présentée par la société beIN Sports France dans le secteur de la télévision payante*, 30 Jul. 2014.
840. Council Directive 89/552/EEC of 3 Oct. 1989 on the coordination of certain provisions laid down by Law, Regulation or Administrative Action in Member States concerning the pursuit of television broadcasting activities, OJ L 298, also known as 'Television Without Frontiers' now included in Directive 2010/13/EU of the European Parliament and of the Council of 10 Mar. 2010 on the coordination of certain provisions laid down by law, regulation or administrative action in Member States concerning the provision of audiovisual media services (Audiovisual Media Services Directive), OJ L 95.

access broadcasting of events of cultural relevance for the nation. However, in doing this, it has a significant impact on the market, as it restricts the range of rights available, reserving some for free-to-air broadcasting. The measure effectively partitions the market for the related rights along national lines, in itself disrupting the idea of a single market for broadcasting rights in sport. Furthermore, the nature of the legislative instruments chosen for the scheme, a Directive which must be implemented in national legislation, leaves a significant degree of discretion to Member States.

502. The regime introduced by the Directive has been challenged on a number of cases.[841] The Directive does not prohibit the acquisition of rights by pay TV operators, but it limits their ability to exercise exclusivity over the rights acquired.[842] Furthermore, free-to-air operators, which traditionally have less bidding power than pay TV operators, were receiving a competitive advantage.

503. FIFA and UEFA have therefore disputed the selection submitted by Belgium and the UK, which included in their list of protected events the entire final phases of the Football World Cup and European Championships.[843] In its response, the Court noted that the selection of those events had little impact on the market as they were staged only every four years and as such were unlikely to drive up subscriptions. The Court also confirmed the degree of discretion retained by Member States in defining the events that had to be protected.[844] Finally, the Court recognised that any restrictive effect of the selection was offset by the social objectives pursued by the system.[845]

504. A fundamental element connected to the collective selling of broadcasting rights is the territorial exclusivity often included in the licensing agreement. The set of decisions mentioned above, while accepting the legality of collective selling, also had the effect of legitimising the territorial exclusivity.

505. The legality of territorial exclusivity was finally assessed by the Court of Justice. In its selling practice, the Premier League was imposing on the broadcaster to which it awarded the rights a contractual obligation to encrypt their signal to any viewer outside the territory for which the broadcaster was licensed. Although not

---

841. *See*, for example, Case T-33/01 *Infront WM AG v. Commission* [2005] ECR II-05897. For an overview, *see* Tom Evens, Paul Smith & Petros Iosifidis, *The Political Economy of Television Sports Rights* 107 (Palgrave Macmillan 2013).
842. Pay TV operators may still exercise their exclusive broadcasting rights when they have offered those rights to free-to-air broadcasters at a market rate, and no free-to-air operator has acquire them.
843. *See* Case T-385/07 *Fédération internationale de football association (FIFA) v. European Commission* [2011] ECR II-00205 and T-68/08 *Fédération internationale de football association (FIFA) v. European Commission* [2011] ECR II-00349, and Case T-55/08 *Union des associations européennes de football (UEFA) v. European Commission* [2011] ECR II-00271.
844. Case T-55/08 *Union des associations européennes de football (UEFA) v. European Commission* [2011] ECR II-00271, para. 17.
845. The Decision of the General Court was later confirmed by the CJEU. Judgment in Case C-201/11 P, C-204/11 P and C-205/11 P, *UEFA and FIFA v. Commission* [2013] ECR 00000.

illegal per se under EU law, exclusivity clauses have a restrictive effect on the market, due to their ability to divide it alongside national lines.[846] This selling model was therefore assessed by the Court of Justice in *Murphy*.[847] In the case, the Premier League brought an action against a pub owner who subscribed to a Greek pay TV operator in order to broadcast the Premier League matches in her commercial premises. The Court of Justice was therefore asked to consider whether the selling practice was compatible with European Union law. The CJEU held that the practice of granting licences including absolute territorial exclusivity restricted the cross-border provision of services under Article 56 TFEU and breached Article 101 TFEU as well, as by portioning the market it was eliminating the competition between European broadcasters.[848]

506. The attack on territorial exclusive licences marked a significant departure from the approach taken by the Commission in *Champions League* and *Premier League*, where the market for sports rights was held to be national.[849] That approach was supported by the Audiovisual Media Services Directive, which, by allowing discretion to the Member States to protect events of cultural importance for their population, demonstrated an appreciation of the differences in cultural and linguistic preferences among Member States. As opposed to this, in *Murphy* the Court signalled a move towards a European market for sports rights.[850]

507. While the relevant market in individual cases may differ on the basis of the product discussed, it is clear that European consumers have developed a preference for international events and a number of broadcasters are active on multiple European National Markets.[851] The existence of a European market for sports broadcasting rights was also inferred by the Commission in *Eurovision*. In the case, a system of collective purchasing of rights, capable of reducing the competition among participants and leading to output restriction, was held to facilitate the cross-border activity of broadcasters and develop a single European broadcasting market.[852]

508. This section has highlighted the range of different interests that may be involved in the area of sports broadcasting rights. First and foremost, governing

846. Joined Cases C-403/08 and C-429/08 *FA Premier League and others v. QC Leisure and others, Karen Murphy v. Media Protection Services Ltd* [2011] ECR I-9083, paras 137–138, citing Case 262/81 *Coditel SA et al v. Ciné-Vog Films SA et al (Coditel II)* [1982] ECR 3381, para. 15.

847. Joined Cases C-403/08 and C-429/08 *FA Premier League and others v. QC Leisure and others, Karen Murphy v. Media Protection Services Ltd* [2011] ECR I-9083.

848. *Ibid.*, paras 140–145. Furthermore, the restriction was neither necessary nor proportionate. For an analysis of the case, *see* Johan Lindholm & Anastasios Kaburakis, *Cases C-403/08 and C-429/08 FA Premier League Ltd and Others v QC Leisure and Others; and Karen Murphy v Media Protection Services Ltd, 4 Oct 2011*, in *Leading Cases in Sports Law* 271–286 (Jack Anderson ed., T.M.C. Asser Press 2013).

849. Decision COMP/C.2-37.398, para. 90, and Case No IV/37.214 – DFB, para. 19, and Case COMP/38.173, para. 5.1.

850. Sara Moya Izquierdo & Miguel Troncoso Ferrer, *Football Broadcasting Business in the EU: Towards Fairer Competition?*, 5(6) JECLP 353–363 (2014).

851. *BskyB* in the UK, *Sky Deutschland* in Germany and *Sky Italia* in Italy are all controlled by News Corp.

852. Decision 93/403/EEC – IV/32.150 – *EBU/Eurovision System*, paras 58–61.

bodies have successfully sensitised the EU institutions on the importance of broadcasting rights and their reliance on this source as a funding stream for their own viability. However, considerations related to the cultural and societal importance of sport must be combined with an appreciation of legitimate commercial objectives of broadcasters, governing bodies and clubs. While the institutions have in this sector adopted an approach paying little regard to the theme of specificity of sport, the application of Article 165 TFEU could effectively support a system devoted to openness and fairness for consumers, as well as for participants.

§6. Media Rights

509. In the market for sports rights, a significant evolution has started. Alongside traditional broadcasters, such as free-to-air and pay televisions, other services are seizing the opportunities offered on the digital landscape and are progressively eroding the market power of established operators. The entry into the market of social media platforms, on-demand channels and over-the-top players is a reflection of the change in consumption habits of sports fans. The interest demonstrated by these operators confirms the attractiveness that sporting events are still capable of raising. The level of exposition and interaction that media coverage offers to professional sport is a phenomenal driver for other revenue streams, from sponsorship to stadium attendance. This phenomenon has to be considered in discussing the exploitation and the protection of media and IP rights and its effect on the European model of sport.

510. The relevance of sports contents on media outlets has increased in parallel with the demise of traditional public service channels, which are now mostly relegated to broadcast major events. In a reflection of the general development in the broad communication system, the vast majority of premium sports events have progressively shifted to subscription channels, and progressively attracted a range of media operators.[853] In this context, a number of decisions taken by antitrust authorities have favoured the emergence in the market for sports rights of non-traditional media outlets. Antitrust authorities have intervened to ensure wider access of consumers to the rights. Instead, governing bodies are starting to take advantage of the situation to increase revenues by exploring new markets. Whether deploying new commercial strategies was a consequence of the decisions of antitrust authorities, or the latter merely recognised a development in the market, this connection cannot be ignored.

511. In a decision over the legality of the collective selling of rights of the German Bundesliga, the *Bundeskartellamt* held that, in order to guarantee consumers a fair share of the benefit, the system should have guaranteed the possibility to access

853. Phil Carling, *Addressing the Football Rights Plateau*, https://www.sportcal.com/Insight/Opinion/126697, 4 Jul. 2019 (accessed 30 Apr. 2020).

highlights through transmission channels other than the incumbent operator, including traditional free-to-air TV, but also Internet and mobile TV.[854] Similarly, already in 2009, Ofcom suggested that the restrictive effects caused by the exclusivity of selling arrangements could be curbed by making some matches available on multiple platforms, thereby enhancing the benefits received by consumers.[855]

512. As an example of the approach of governing bodies, since the 2009–2012 cycle, UEFA distributes the rights for the competitions it organises on a neutral platform basis. Under this selling model, successful bidders benefit from exclusivity throughout the entire matches across all media platforms, including television, Internet and mobile.[856] The neutral platform system raises some doubts in relation to its efficiency since it grants operators discretion as to the choice of the platform used for the exploitation of the rights. This leaves open the possibility that some rights will be excluded from specific platforms and markets and allows the incumbent broadcasters to prevent the development of competitors on other platforms.[857] The system, therefore, may not be per se convincing in satisfying consumers' interests, and it might also pose questions in relation to the protection of competition on the market. Furthermore, the evolution of the market for sports rights has seen traditional telecommunications companies entering the race alongside established operators. The former can offer services on a number of neighbouring markets and bundle together pay TV and broadband services.[858] The neutral platform approach has favoured the emergence of these operators in the sports media market. However, questions related to the use of their dominant position to influence neighbouring markets may be raised.

513. While the decisions of the antitrust authorities and the introduction of the neutral platform system of rights may have set in motion a migration of rights to media platforms, the value of such rights has not been significantly affected in the short term. Up until 2019, the fees paid by major pay TV broadcaster to acquire exclusive rights on sporting events were still higher than those paid by new media operators, which have still a relatively limited role in the market.[859] The relatively

854. Bundeskartellamt, *Joint selling of media rights for the games of the 1st and 2nd German football leagues (Bundesliga) from the 2013/2014 season onwards*, available at http://www.bundeskartellamt.de/SharedDocs/Entscheidung/EN/Fallberichte/Kartellverbot/2012/B6-114-10.pdf?__blob=publicationFile&v=2 (accessed 30 Apr. 2020).

855. Ofcom (2009) *Pay TV: Phase Three Document: Proposed Remedies*. For a discussion on the emergence of the market for media rights, *see* Petros Iosifidis & Paul Smith, *The European Television Sports Rights Market: Balancing Culture and Commerce*, Paper presented at the Private Television in Europe (2011).

856. This model has been subsequently implemented by a number of national governing bodies including the English Football Premier League and the Italian Serie A.

857. Katrien Lefever, *New Media and Sport: International Legal Aspects* 150 (T.M.C. Asser Press 2012).

858. Paul Smith, Tom Evens & Petros Iosifidis, *The Next Big Match: Convergence, Competition and Sports Media Rights*, 31(5) Eur. J. Commun. 536–550 (2016).

859. To give an example, in the Premier League 2019–2022 media rights cycle, Amazon reportedly paid GBP 90 million for one of seven packages, allowing it to broadcast only ten matches from one Bank Holiday and all ten from the Boxing Day fixture programme. *See* Richard Conway, *Premier League*

slow take-up from new media operators may be explained by the fact that the system forced them to compete with established broadcasters, usually vertically integrated, for media contents that they could not easily afford.[860]

514. It must, however, be acknowledged that the European market for sports rights has seen a rise in interest by social media operators, video-on-demand players and OTT operators.[861] This follows the example of the United States, where media platforms such as Amazon, Twitter and Facebook have started to offer live broadcasts of some sporting events. Similarly, Amazon has for the first time been awarded a package of rights for the English Premier League for the period 2019–2022. In other European countries, OTT platforms have secured rights packages awarding the rights for a limited number of matches or for matches of foreign leagues.[862] The entering into the market of these players reflects a development in the way sport and entertainment products are consumed, whereby customers are now more likely to access sports contents through Smart TVs, tablets and smartphones and the services offered by the various platforms are perceived as interchangeable.[863] Social media platforms can guarantee a very significant market penetration rate and a level of interaction that was unknown to traditional broadcasters.[864] These developments may be considered a factor to explain a decrease in the number of pay TV subscriptions that can be observed in some national markets, while the effect on the value of the rights is still not clear.[865]

I. Online Distribution

515. The shift from the traditional broadcasting distribution system to online transmission poses significant challenges for right owners, licensees and authorities. Effective protection of the various interests at stake requires a European strategy that clarifies the notions applicable and guarantees cover throughout the internal market. First, it must be discussed whether sporting events can be subject to any form of copyright protection, how the author of a work in this area can be identified and within this context what is the role of the organiser and that of the broadcaster.

---

rights: What Does Amazon Deal Mean for Rivals, the League and Fans?, https://www.bbc.co.uk/sport/football/44400005 8 Jun. 2018 (accessed 30 Apr. 2020).

860. T.M.C. Asser Institute, *Study on sports organisers' rights in the European Union,* Study commissioned by the European Commission, 78 & 102 (2014).

861. Over-the-top platforms, also known as OTT, are providers who transmit content via online streaming as a stand-alone product. *See* European Parliament, Directorate General for Internal Policies, *Over-the-Top players (OTTs),* available at http://www.europarl.europa.eu/RegData/etudes/STUD/2015/569979/IPOL_STU(2015)569979_EN.pdf (accessed 30 Apr. 2020).

862. *See* SportBusiness Consulting, *Global Media Report 2019*, https://www.sportbusiness.com/consulting/sportbusiness-consulting-global-media-report-2019/ (accessed 28 Apr. 2020).

863. Johan Lindholm, *The Netflix-ication of Sports Broadcasting*, 18 ISLJ 99–101 (2019).

864. Ofcom *Communications Market Report*, 2018 available at https://www.ofcom.org.uk/__data/assets/pdf_file/0022/117256/CMR-2018-narrative-report.pdf (accessed 30 Apr. 2020).

865. After the record GBP 5.1 billion paid for the 2016–2019 cycle, inflated by the competition between Sky and BT, the Premier League was able to get GBP4.46 Billion for the 2019–2022 cycle. *See* Richard Conway, *Premier League Rights: What Does Amazon Deal Mean for Rivals, the League and Fans?*, https://www.bbc.co.uk/sport/football/44400005, 8 Jun. 2018 (accessed 30 Apr. 2020).

516. The CJEU has shown itself receptive to the desire of rights' owners to protect the investment made in producing the sporting events they organise. This aspiration finds support in Article 165 TFEU: its prescription to take into account the specific features of sport may justify a push for greater protection of sporting events.[866] In *Murphy*, the Court accepted that Member States could be allowed to grant protection to a sporting event and its organiser, but not to the point of creating a new set of rights and only insofar as the measure adopted is proportionate and necessary to the purpose of achieving goals of public interest.[867]

517. This could have been interpreted as an incentive for a greater use of copyright protection in this area. Along this line, Article 12 of the Draft Directive on Copyright in the Digital Single Market granted sporting event organisers the right of reproduction and communication to the public of the footage of the event. This would have allowed rights owners to prevent unauthorised exploitation of footage, whether made by broadcasters, media operators or individuals attending the match.[868] However, in *Murphy* the Court also found that sporting events cannot be subject to copyright. What can be protected is the set of elements resulting from labour and skills that can be reproduced on a physical format, such as the commentary, the music anthem and the logos of the teams and the competition.[869] However, if these elements are not separated from the content itself, then the protection granted will indirectly extend over the event and its footage.

518. Once established that some form of protection can be granted, the challenge is to frame the extent of such protection within the rules of the EU internal market. In an ever-developing Digital Single Market, contents can circulate freely, disrupting one of the core funding streams of elite professional sports: the territorial nature of licensing of sports media rights.[870]

519. A number of principles enshrined in EU copyright law could facilitate this process. According to the Cable and Satellite Directive, the transmission of content is subject to the rules established in the Member States in which the signal originates.[871] This would mean that media players that have legally purchased the rights to specific contents in their Member State could offer copyright-protected content to viewers in another Member State. As opposed to this, the common practice is for

866. *See* Joined Cases C-403/08 and C-429/08 *FA Premier League and others v. QC Leisure and others, Karen Murphy v. Media Protection Services Ltd* [2011] ECR I-9083, para. 100.
867. *Ibid.*, para. 96. *See* also Richard Parrish, *Lex Sportiva and EU Sports Law*, 37 EL Rev. 716–733 (2012).
868. European Commission. COM/2016/0593 final-2016/0280 (COD) [2016] Proposal for a Draft Directive on Copyright in the Digital Single Market. This provision was later deleted from the version of the Directive adopted by the EU.
869. *See* Joined Cases C-403/08 and C-429/08 *FA Premier League and others v. QC Leisure and others, Karen Murphy v. Media Protection Services Ltd* [2011] ECR I-9083, paras 96 et seq.
870. Raymond Boyle, *Battle for Control? Copyright, Football and European Media Rights*, 37(3) Media Cult. Soc. 359–375 (2015).
871. Art. 1(2) (b), Council Directive 93/83/EEC of 27 Sep. 1993 on the coordination of certain rules concerning copyright and rights related to copyright applicable to satellite broadcasting and cable retransmission, OJ L 248.

right holders to include in their licensing arrangement an obligation on the broadcasters to encrypt the signal to customers outside the territory of the Member State for which they have received the rights. As mentioned above, this conduct protects the exclusive licence of the rights' holders in a territory, and its effect is to restrict the development of the market towards an internal European market, by dividing it along national boundaries.[872]

520. It does not help that at EU level there is no complete harmonisation of the Copyright discipline either. Copyright arises and is protected under national law. The EU has adopted rules related to its enforcement, and national courts have developed a common approach to the use of blocking injunctions to prevent access to websites and servers allowing infringement of copyrights.[873] However, the existence of different regulatory frameworks at national level prevents the emergence of a competition between providers in different Member States.[874]

521. Another principle to be mentioned comes from the Information Society Directive.[875] According to Article 3, once authors have consented to have tangible copies of their work released on the market, they cannot control subsequent distributions of those copies. After the first copy, the right of the author is exhausted. However, exceptions are made in relation to broadcasting rights and media rights, whereby the communication of the work to the public is not exhausted if the work is distributed in cinemas or via television.[876]

522. The two principles demonstrate how the task of the European institutions in this area is not a simple one. Effectively, the institutions have to strike a balance between a range of interests that often seem conflicting. The protection and exploitation of media rights raise concerns related to the need to promote the use of media and technological platforms as an incentive for market growth, the effective protection of the rights' holders and the fundamental rights of end users, such as freedom of expression and freedom of information.[877]

---

872. Joined Cases C-403/08 and C-429/08 *FA Premier League and others v. QC Leisure and others, Karen Murphy v. Media Protection Services Ltd* [2011] ECR I-9083, paras 140–145.
873. Petteri Gunther, *The Plan for a Digital Single Market in Europe and Reforming EU Copyright Rules to Develop a Market-Oriented Approach to Reduce Infringement on the Internet*, 38(1) EIPR 43–55 (2015).
874. Pablo Ibáñez Colomo, *Copyright Licensing and the EU Digital Single Market Strategy*, in *Cambridge Handbook of Antitrust, Intellectual Property and High Technology*, 339–357 (Roger D. Blair & Daniel Sokol eds, Cambridge Univ. Press 2016).
875. Directive 2001/29/EC of the European Parliament and of the Council of 22 May 2001 on the harmonisation of certain aspects of copyright and related rights in the information society (Information Society Directive), OJ L 167.
876. Art. 3, Information Society Directive.
877. Charter of Fundamental Rights of the European Union, Art. 11 of the on freedom of expression and information.

II. Digital Single Market

523. Starting from 2014, the EU Commission has developed and pursued the objective of regulating the Digital Single Market. A number of provisions have been adopted with the aim of harmonising the rules in the sector and seeking to improve legal security for the content producers, the service providers and the customers. The measures, which include the reformed Copyright Directive,[878] the Cross-border Portability Regulation,[879] and the Geo-blocking Regulation[880] may all have a significant impact on the sporting sector.

524. The Copyright Directive seeks to strengthen the protection of rights' holders against online platforms that profit from unauthorised use of their work. Critics of the legislation have argued that the way chosen to pursue this objective may run contrary to the protection of fundamental freedoms on the Internet.[881] The most relevant provisions of the Directive are respectively Article 15 and Article 17. The first provision, named by critics the 'link tax', aims at simplifying the licensing of content online and requires press publishers to pay a fair compensation to the authors of works they reproduce. This may be ranging from articles to videos or other contents which are commonly used by aggregation services to attract a greater audience. The rules should apply exclusively to publishers and news agencies, to the exclusion of academic and scientific journals and any other medium that does not have editorial responsibilities. Article 17 requires that online platforms work with rights' owners to prevent the unauthorised upload and use of copyrighted content. Liability is imposed on those profit-making providers that allow the infringement. Whether the technology used for this purpose is a form of filtering, or a different recognition system, it is for the rights owners and content sharing platform to decide. This latter provision, however, effectively shifts the task of controlling and preventing infringements from the right holders to the media platform.

525. In relation to sports event organisers, a provision granting a statutory right to sporting event organisers that was included in the draft version of the Directive was dropped in the measure finally approved.[882] However, it is worth noting that the EU Parliament debate preceding the adoption of the draft version drew a connection between these provisions and Article 165(1) TFEU. The reference to the contribution to European sporting issues was interpreted as including the protection

878. Directive (EU) 2019/790 of the European Parliament and of the Council of 17 Apr. 2019 on copyright and related rights in the Digital Single Market and amending Directives 96/9/EC and 2001/29/EC OJ L 130.

879. Regulation (EU) 2017/1128 of the European Parliament and of the Council of 14 Jun. 2017 on cross-border portability of online content services in the internal market, OJ L 168/1.

880. Regulation (EU) 2018/302 of the European Parliament and of the Council of 28 February 2018 on addressing unjustified geo-blocking and other forms of discrimination based on customers' nationality, place of residence or place of establishment within the internal market, OJ L 60I.

881. Sallie Spilsbury, *Rewriting the Rule Book? The Latest on the Draft Copyright Directive*, 17(1) ESLJ 1 (2019).

882. Art. 12, Proposal for a Draft Directive on Copyright in the Digital Single Market. European Commission. COM/2016/0593 final-2016/0280 (COD) [2016].

of intellectual property of sports events' organisers.[883] While the attempt has been short-lived, this further demonstrates the attention that EU institutions have placed on the importance of the exploitation of media rights as a funding stream for elite sport in Europe.

526. The Regulations on Geo-blocking and Cross-border Portability appear to provide a way to address the disproportionate effect that territorial exclusivity may have on legitimate subscribers, consumers and on the internal market in general.[884] These measures have to be considered in the context of the approach progressively developed by the Commission on territorial exclusivity. In 2014, the Commission opened a set of investigations into licensing agreements between major film studios and pay TV broadcasters.[885] The investigations, however, expressly excluded sports rights, under the justification that rights holders in this area had already adjusted their contracts to exclude absolute territorial protection.[886] Ignoring its own decisional practice, the Commission did not entertain the idea of imposing an obligation on the studios to market the rights on a pan-European basis.[887] However, it still found that restrictions on the selling of content in response to unsolicited requests from customers located in a Member State different from the one where the signal is produced were in breach of Article 101(1) TFEU.[888]

527. In a similar fashion, in instances of geo-blocking, consumers are denied access to websites in certain Member States or redirected to other websites operating in their own Member States. Such a strategy allows the commercial operator to impose different conditions on the consumers depending on where they are based, thereby disrupting the notion of a single market. To prevent this type of conduct, Regulation 2018/302 prohibits geo-blocking measures that partition the market and discriminate against consumers on the basis of their location, unless they can be objectively justified by express reference to reasons of public policy such as protection of consumers, environmental causes, taxation, etc.[889]

---

883. *See* EU Parliament, Report of Committee on Legal Affairs on the proposal for a directive of the European Parliament and of the Council on copyright in the Digital Single Market (COM(2016)0593 – C8-0383/2016 – 2016/0280(COD)).
884. Pablo Ibáñez Colomo, *Copyright Licensing and the EU Digital Single Market Strategy*, in *Cambridge Handbook of Antitrust, Intellectual Property and High Technology*, 339–357 (Roger D. Blair & Daniel Sokol eds, Cambridge Univ. Press 2016).
885. Press Release: Antitrust: Commission investigates restrictions affecting cross border provision of pay-TV services. European Commission – IP/14/15, 13 Jan. 2014.
886. Benoit Keane, *The Application of Competition Law in the Entertainment and Sport Sectors*, 5 JECLP 592–601 (2014).
887. In the *Eurovision* Decision, the Commission accepted a system of joint acquisition of rights as it was considered to contribute to the development of a single European broadcasting market. Decision of the Commission in the case IV/32.150 – *Eurovision*.
888. Press Release IP/15/5432, Antitrust: Commission sends Statement of Objections on cross-border provision of pay-TV services available in UK and Ireland, 23 Jul. 2015.
889. Regulation (EU) 2018/302 of the European Parliament and of the Council of 28 February 2018 on addressing unjustified geo-blocking and other forms of discrimination based on customers' nationality, place of residence or place of establishment within the internal market, OJ L 60I, 2 Mar. 2018.

528. Clearly, this conduct may affect consumers of sports contents or sports products. However, an express exception exists regarding the audiovisual sector and in particular in relation to services for the provision of access to broadcasts of sports events which are provided on the basis of exclusive territorial licences.[890] The EU has thereby recognised that the financing of the sector is highly dependent on the use of territorial exclusivity clauses in its activity on the sports media rights market.

529. To justify this position, on one side it is argued that a pan-European market would reduce the diversity of content available to consumers. It is assumed that in a European-wide market with a significant expansion on the number of competitors, broadcasters would focus on mass-appeal products. In turn, this would have a consequent knock-on effect on funding available for competitions with fewer followers. On the other side, pan-European licences would naturally be more expensive than licences limited to a national territory. Imposing such licences would squeeze the market in favour of the larger broadcasting companies that have subsidiaries established throughout Europe and can afford an investment of this magnitude. Finally, a complete ban on geo-blocking would also conflict with the scheme provided by the Audiovisual Media Services Directive, which effectively partitions the market along national lines in relation to broadcasting rights for event of cultural importance. As such geo-blocking measures in relation to the sporting media sector would be justified.[891]

530. To mitigate the impact of the Geo-blocking Regulation, Regulation 2017/1128 guarantees consumers the portability across borders of online contents that they have legitimately acquired.[892] This allows consumers who have subscribed to a content licensed in the territory of one Member State to access that content when they are temporarily in another Member State. Through this reform, the EU has targeted a form of territorial restriction, and in some relation a limit of the EU copyright regime. Effectively, the Regulation excludes any breach of copyright for the user and the broadcaster that reproduces the content in a Member State that is different from the one of residence.[893] In other words, the content will be subject to copyright in the State in which it is first broadcasted or transmitted, and nowhere else.

531. While this may be perceived as substantially weakening of the position of the rights' holders, the model is consistent with the country of origin principle established in the Cable and Satellite Directive. Furthermore, the need to respect the current licensing model and financing mechanism in sport is still prominent. By imposing a temporary limit in the Portability Regulation, as well as excluding the audiovisual sector from the Geo-blocking Regulation, the EU institutions have demonstrated once again a particular attention to the characteristics of the sector and the

890. *See* Recital 8 of the Regulation.
891. Report of the Sports Rights Owners' Coalition, *The impact of potential changes to geo-blocking regulation on sport*, 7 (2020).
892. Regulation (EU) 2017/1128 of the European Parliament and of the Council of 14 Jun. 2017 on cross-border portability of online content services in the internal market, OJ L 168.
893. *See* Recital 24 of the Regulation.

importance of its funding model for the European model of sport. The approach taken by the EU institutions in the area of online distribution of sporting content and related copyright protection is a clear attempt to pay respect to those characteristics that are considered to be fundamental to the European model of sport. These include the characteristics of the market for sports rights, which despite a clear evolution is still thought as divided along national lines. In this context, rules that seek to harmonise the conditions on the market and work towards a digital single market tend to provide exceptions for the sporting sector.

532. A greater push towards the creation of a pan-European market may be in line with other industries where harmonisation has been taken further. It may also seem appealing for customers who would be able to afford a cheaper subscription and a greater range of contents. However, the cost to acquire a pan-European licence for broadcasters or media operators would be such to drive smaller operators outside the market, or further strengthen the dominance of a few broadcasters that are already active in various markets. The objectives of protecting the competition on the market and the financing of the European model of sport, still fundamentally anchored to the selling of national sports rights on the domestic market, go hand in hand in the approach taken by the EU institutions.

533. The area of sports broadcasting and media rights is one that will be most affected by Brexit. The conduct of UK governing bodies and media operators will still be subject to the application of EU law, in relation to their activity on the territory of the EU. In this regard, the selling of Premier League rights in the EU will have to comply with EU law. Similarly, while the UK will not transpose the measures that are part of the Digital Single Market and Data Protection packages, these provisions will continue to apply whenever governing bodies, clubs and operators conduct activities within the EU internal market. At national level, however, EU law provisions will cease to apply. Where national instruments have transposed them at national level, as the Competition Act 1998 does in relation to EU competition law, and the Broadcasting Act 1996 in relation to the Audiovisual Media Services Directive, the UK authorities will be free to decide to amend such provisions. In relation to the latter in particular, governing bodies will have to be consulted as rights owners are affected. The choice will be between eliminating the protection to listed events or protecting the ability of UK residents to maintain access to them. The range of interests highlighted in this connection – cultural and societal goals, the promotion of well-being and increasing participation, brand exposure and commercial objectives – will have to be given appropriate consideration.

§7. Advertising and Ticketing

534. One of the most relevant sources of income for the sports system comes from private investments, in the form of sponsorship and advertising. The ability of attracting and protecting investments is of fundamental importance for the commercial viability of the system. This area attracts a broad range of interests, from consumers' protection, integrity of sport and rights of participants. In this regard, this topic overlaps with the analysis of the authority exercised by SGBs in sanctioning events and the rules related to the ability of individual athletes to sign endorsement contracts. The following section will assess the way EU institutions have addressed the area of sponsorship and marketing under the perspective of governing bodies, athletes and national authorities.

535. Sports governing bodies must pursue a range of objectives. These may be sporting objectives, such as recruiting and training young sportspersons but necessarily, a governing body will have to pursue economic objectives as well, in order to finance the sporting side of its activity. Within the European model of sport, a sporting association has the monopoly over the organisation of a specific sport. This allows the association to adopt rules establishing who is entitled to organise events and participate in them. Governing bodies may also negotiate exclusive arrangements with their commercial partners in an attempt to block the entry of competitors on the market, a very effective strategy when combined with restrictions on participants.[894] While the organisation of sport has been addressed in Chapter 2, this section will discuss some of the issues mentioned in reference to the commercial conduct of governing bodies and athletes.

536. In this regard, it must be remembered that, while the regulatory authority of a governing body can be justified to pursue objectives such as ensuring the regularity of competitions, or guaranteeing the safety of spectators and participants, the exercise of such power is subject to review.[895] The CJEU has long established that, where a governing body holds a position of dominance on the market for the organisation of sporting events, it cannot abuse such power in order to foster its own commercial objectives on another market, namely the one for the marketing of sports events.[896] Short of imposing an outright separation between the regulatory and commercial functions pursued by a governing body, *MOTOE* required transparency and fairness in carrying out these functions.[897]

537. A similar stance had already been taken by the Commission, which in *FIA* imposed amendments to the distribution of regulatory and commercial powers. In the case, the Commission required FIA to drop the tight leash used to impose loyalty to track owners, teams, drivers and commercial partners like broadcasters, and conversely to restrict the access of competitors.[898] Similar to *MOTOE*, in *FIA* and

894. Katarina Pijetlovic, *European Model of Sport: Alternative Structures*, in *Research Handbook on EU Sports Law and Policy* 326–360 (Jack Anderson, Richard Parrish & Borja García eds, Edward Elgar 2018).

895. Arnout Geeraert, *Limits to the Autonomy of Sport: EU Law*, in *Action for good governance in international sports organisations* 151–184 (J. Alm ed., Play the Game/Danish Institute for Sports Studies 2013) and Samuli Miettinen, *Policing the Boundaries Between Regulation and Commercial Exploitation: Lessons from the MOTOE Case*, 3(4) ISLJ 13 (2008).

896. Case C-49/07, *Motosykletistiki Omospondia Ellados NPID (MOTOE) v. Elliniko Dimosio* [2008] ECR I-04863, para. 53.

897. *Ibid.*, Opinion of Advocate General Kokott, para. 95 and Stephen Weatherill, *Article 82 EC and Sporting 'Conflict of Interest': The Judgment in MOTOE*, 1–2 ISLJ 3–7 (2009).

898. Press Release IP/99/434, Commission opens formal proceedings into Formula One and other international motor racing series European Commission, 30 Jun. 1999.

ISU the Commission recognised the need for a governing body to exercise regulatory powers on its sector, but not to the extent of preventing the organisation or exploitation of other events, unless this could have been justified for safety reasons, or to protect fair and orderly conduct in sport.

538. Governing bodies are therefore entitled to regulate their own sport and those who participate in it, as well as being allowed to extract revenues from the related commercial and marketing activities. However, their conduct must be transparent, fair and proportionate in order to avoid undue restraints on participants, event organisers, commercial operators and consumers.

I. Advertising

539. When sport associates itself with commercial entities, possible threats to the integrity of sport, its image and its economic interests can arise. On the one hand, this requires governing bodies, clubs and athletes to be mindful of entering into agreements with companies or industries that may have a reputation conflicting with the objectives of ensuring health and well-being, social inclusion and good governance principles. On the other hand, an efficient form of protection against free riders must be in place, to guarantee that private investments made by advertisers are protected and incentivised.

540. When discussing the area of sports advertising in the context of EU law, three main interests have to be considered: the protection of the EU internal market, the protection of consumers, and the private economic interests of the sports governing bodies or events' organisers. Public authorities can intervene to guarantee that the interests at stake are fully considered and a balance is struck. One concern in this regard is therefore related to the fragmentation of the EU internal market for sports advertising and its effect on the funding of sport and the regularity of the competitions. Where differing regulatory systems exist between Member States, sports teams established in a State that prohibits a form of advertising, or the advertising of a specific product, may have to compete with teams from a State where that advertising is allowed. Teams from this State can therefore access a stream of revenues not available in other States, in turn affecting the conditions of the competition.[899] Similar issues arise for organisers of sporting events. Events may have to be relocated to avoid advertising restrictions, with significant repercussions for the competition and the undertakings associated with it.[900] Considerations related to the functioning of the internal market may therefore justify harmonising measures in the area.

541. The balance between the protection of consumers and the regulation of the internal market, and its limits, were considered in *Tobacco Advertising*.[901] This case

899. Case C-376/98 *Germany v. Parliament and Council* [2000] ECR I-8419, para. 64.
900. *Ibid.*, para. 110.
901. Case C-376/98 *Germany v. Parliament and Council* [2000] ECR I-8419.

arose when the EU decided to restrict tobacco advertising in a move that had severe effects on the funding available to the sport system.[902] Indeed, the tobacco industry was traditionally active in sports advertising, as it considered it an effective instrument to counteract the association of tobacco products with bad health.[903] In an attempt to extend the scope of its legislative competence beyond the limits set by the Treaties, the EU adopted Directive 2003/33[904] prohibiting tobacco advertising in the press, in radio broadcasting, in information society services and through tobacco-related sponsorship.[905]

542. This alongside the provision banning tobacco advertising on television effectively put an end to tobacco advertising and sponsorship in sport.[906] However, in the absence of an exclusive legislative competence to harmonise legislation in the area of public health, the Directive was justified under the need to ensure the functioning of the internal market.[907]

543. Member States retain the ability to intervene on the national market for advertising and pursue legitimate objectives, such as the protection of consumers, although within the limits imposed by the principle of proportionality.[908] Restrictions on alcohol-related sponsorship are in place in States such as France, Austria, and Ireland among others. States are free to impose similar rules on betting advertising, insofar as they do not restrict the freedom to provide services in the EU to an excessive extent.[909]

544. The application of internal market law on the sporting market is likely to incentivise the emergence of secondary markets. Through greater flexibility in offer and distribution, third parties may attract consumers and erode the commercial power of governing bodies and rights owners. In turn, governing bodies and rights owners may pressure public authorities to intervene and protect their economic interests. This is often the case for the area of ambush marketing. This is the unauthorised association with an event, a team or an individual and its sponsor with a

---

902. Borja García & Henk E. Meier, *Global Sport Power Europe? The Efficacy of the European Union in Global Sport Regulation*, 55(4) JCMS 850–870 (2017).
903. Case C-376/98 *Germany v. Parliament and Council* [2000] ECR I-8419, para. 64.
904. Directive 2003/33/EC of the European Parliament and of the Council of 26 May 2003 on the approximation of the laws, regulations and administrative provisions of the Member States relating to the advertising and sponsorship of tobacco products, OJ L 152.
905. Stephen Weatherill, *The Limits of Legislative Harmonisation Ten Years after Tobacco Advertising: How the Court's Case Law Has Become a 'Drafting Guide.'*, 12 German L.J. 827 (2011).
906. Council Directive 89/552/EEC of 3 Oct. 1989 on the coordination of certain provisions laid down by Law, Regulation or Administrative Action in Member States concerning the pursuit of television broadcasting activities, OJ L 298. The Directive has now been amended and included into the Audiovisual Media Services Directive.
907. Public health falls under the shared competence area under Art. 4 TFEU.
908. *See* Recital 10, Directive (EU) 2018/1808 of the European Parliament and of the Council of 14 Nov. 2018 amending Directive 2010/13/EU on the coordination of certain provisions laid down by law, regulation or administrative action in Member States concerning the provision of audiovisual media services (Audiovisual Media Services Directive) in view of changing market realities, OJ L 303.
909. Case C-262/02, *Commission of the European Communities v. France* [2004] EU:C:2004:431.

view to exploiting their goodwill for commercial purposes.[910] This type of conduct corrodes the value of exclusive sponsoring rights by claiming an association without having permission to do it.

545. Ambush marketing is not immediately regulated by EU law, and it was only briefly mentioned in the Staff Working Document accompanying the White Paper on Sport as an area of growing concern, but where no common definition and rules have been adopted.[911] Other existing EU provisions may be applicable as this type of conduct normally falls under private law. The instances may therefore be regulated under contractual provisions, or rules on intellectual property, or protection against misleading advertisements. However, the strategy adopted by ambushers is particularly effective against these forms of protection, which can only cover parties to a contract or the unauthorised use of a registered mark.[912] As such, the commercial imperative pursued by governing bodies requires greater protection and legislation specifically targeting ambush marketing at sporting events.[913]

II. Athletes' Endorsement

546. Governing bodies exercise a level of control over various stakeholders, including athletes. This control may be necessary to ensure the safety and integrity of competitions, but it also extends over conduct of a commercial nature. When governing bodies impose restrictions that affect the commercial aspirations of athletes, they may be subject to challenge. The CJEU addressed this issue in *Deliège.*[914] As mentioned in Chapter 1, in the case the Court held that selection rules for competing at international championships were capable of restricting athletes' freedom to provide services, although they were ultimately deemed to be inherent and necessary to the organisation of sport.[915]

---

910. Mark James & Guy Osborn *Tickets, Policy and Social Inclusion: Can the European White Paper on Sport Deliver?*, 1–2 ISLJ 61 (2009).

911. European Commission, *Commission staff working document. Impact assessment accompanying the White Paper on Sport*, SEC(2007) 935 final (2007), s. 3.2.4.

912. Ambushers tend to imply an association while staying clear from registered IP rights. *See* Nick Shi Qiang Sim, *Ambush Marketing in Major Sports Events: War Minus the Shooting?*, 10(7) JIPLP 536–550 (2015).

913. Stephen Weatherill, *Principles and Practice in EU Sports Law* 40 (Oxford Univ. Press 2017).

914. Joined Cases C-51/96 and C-191/97 *Deliège v. Ligue francophone de Judo et disciplines Associeés Asb* [2000] ECR I-2549. The issue was also incidentally addressed in *Donà* and *Bosman*. *See* Case 13/76 *Donà v. Mantero* [1976] ECR 1333, para. 12, and Case C-415/93 *Union Royale Belge Sociétés de Football Association and others v. Bosman and others* [1995] ECR I-4921, para. 73.

915. Regardless of its status and the economic value attached to its performance. *See* Joined Cases C-51/96 and C-191/97 *Deliège v. Ligue francophone de Judo et disciplines Associeés Asb* [2000] ECR I-2549, para. 64.

547. In a system based on solidarity and mutuality of contribution, rules imposing limits on the commercial aspirations of individuals may be acceptable if necessary and proportionate to ensure its functioning.[916] In this connection, governing bodies must avoid conflicts of interest and act transparently in their relation with athletes and third-party organisers. While direct restrictions on the athletes' freedom to enter into sponsorship contracts have not been assessed by the EU institutions, two decisions – one from the European Free Trade Association (EFTA) Court of Justice[917] and the other from the German *Bundeskartellamt* – signal a path that could be followed in future challenges.

548. In *Kristoffersen*, the EFTA Court assessed the authorisation system employed by the Norwegian Ski Federation (NSF) for the athletes wishing to enter into individual sponsorship contracts.[918] In this instance, Kristoffersen wanted to enter into a sponsorship deal with Red Bull, to include its logo on the helmet and headgear during NSF sanctioned races. However, NSF had already concluded a similar contract covering all the athletes entering the competitions and did not authorise the individual sponsorship agreement.

549. Clearly, such a system constitutes a restriction of the athletes' freedom to provide services and as such, to be acceptable, it must be proportionate to the legitimate objectives pursued.[919] In this regard, it must be noted that the NSF is a non-profit entity, mainly funded by its own commercial activities.[920] The governing body did not share the revenues it collected but used them to cover the expenses of its members while on tour, the training and development of both professional athlete and younger athletes, as well as the recruitment and education of children and funding of activities at recreational level. Drawing from the case law of the CJEU, the EFTA Court found that the restriction discussed was justified by the need to ensure that revenues were distributed to the various levels of the system, in order to protect the recruitment and development of young athletes.[921] However, the proportionality of such a restriction could only be guaranteed if a substantial part of the income was effectively used to pursue the legitimate objectives and athletes were receiving a share of the sponsorship contracts' revenues. Furthermore, the Court stressed the mutual interdependence between governing bodies and athletes and in this light the need to ensure a fair balance between the interest of the governing body and that of its members.[922]

---

916. Dirk Brinckman & Erik Vollergbregt, *The Marketing of Sport and Its Relation to E.C. Competition Law*, 5 ECLR 281–288 (1998).
917. The EFTA Court has authority over the interpretation of the Agreement on the EEA for the members of the EFTA.
918. EFTA Court 16 Nov. 2018, Case E-8/17, *Kristoffersen/NSF*.
919. Art. 33 of the EEA Agreement reproduces Art. 56 TFEU.
920. In 2015 NSF gained 71% of its income from marketing activities. Case E-8/17, *Kristoffersen/NSF*, paras 9–10.
921. Case C-325/08 *Olympique Lyonnais SASP v. Olivier Bernard and Newcastle UFC* [2010] ECR I-02177, para. 39.
922. EFTA Court 16 Nov. 2018, Case E-8/17, *Kristoffersen/NSF*, para. 124.

550. While the EFTA Court assessed a restriction under freedom of movement, the German *Bundeskartellamt* examined the legitimacy of Rule 40(3) of the Olympic Charter and its application by the German Olympic Committee (DOSB) under the lens of competition law. Rule 40(3) essentially establishes that, except when permitted by the IOC, no competitor, coach or official participating in the Olympics may use their person, name, picture or sports performance for advertising purposes during the Games.[923] The claimed objectives of the Rule are to protect the Games from over-commercialisation, keep the focus on the athletes' performance, and most importantly preserve the revenue collecting strategy of the IOC. More pragmatically, the goal is to avoid advertisements by brands unaffiliated with the organisers, thereby protecting the value of the IOC's own sponsorship deals.[924] While the IOC asserts that 90% of the funding collected is redistributed to the wider sporting movement, the fundamental objective behind Rule 40 is clearly a commercial one.

551. The Association of German Athletes filed a complaint with the *Bundeskartellamt* against the DOSB, which enforces Rule 40 on its members. The complaint argued that such a rule constituted a restriction on the freedom of athletes to self-market themselves, and in particular an abuse of the dominant position held by the Olympic Committee in the market for the organisation and marketing of Olympic Games.

552. Similar to the findings of the EFTA Court in *Kristoffersen*, the *Bundeskartellamt* considered that athletes participating in the Olympics could not benefit from a share of the advertising revenues collected by the organiser, despite being the key features of the event, and the event itself representing the height of their sporting career. As such, restricting their ability to self-marketing had a significant impact on their revenues. In this light, despite recognising as legitimate the objective of preventing illegal advertising during the Olympics, the restriction was held to be disproportionate. This led to commitments made by the DOSB and the IOC to enhance advertising opportunities for German athletes during the Olympics, including the use of images and terminology previously prohibited.[925]

553. While these decisions do not form part of the case law or decision practice of the EU institutions, their impact may be relevant for the future development of the European model of sport. Indeed, they confirm how challenges to the regulatory

923. International Olympic Committee (IOC) ((n.d.)). Use of a Participant's image for advertising purposes during the Rio 2016 Olympic Games, available at https://stillmed.olympic.org/media/Document%20Library/OlympicOrg/IOC/What-We-Do/Protecting-Clean-Athletes/Athletes-Space/Rule-40-Rio-2016-QA-for-Athletes.pdf (accessed 30 Apr. 2020).

924. John Grady, *Analyzing Rule 40's Restrictions on Using Athletes in Olympic Sponsorship at Rio 2016*, 15(1) ESLJ (2017).

925. Bundeskartellamt, Press Release: German Athletes and their sponsors obtain further advertising opportunities during the Olympic Games following Bundeskartellamt action – IOC and DOSB undertake to change the advertising guidelines, available at https://www.bundeskartellamt.de/SharedDocs/Publikation/EN/Pressemitteilungen/2019/27_02_2019_DOSB_IOC.pdf?__blob=publicationFile&v=2 (accessed 30 Apr. 2020).

power exercised by private entities like governing bodies over individuals' commercial abilities are possible both under the rules of the internal market and under competition law. The economic objectives pursued by the NSF and the DOSB were considered legitimate. However, it appears that their restrictive effect on the ability of athletes to market themselves and their performance will be subject to a strong proportionality test, ensuring that the commercialisation of sport guarantees a fair share of opportunities to its participants.

III. Tickets Sales Arrangement

554. Notwithstanding the relevance of media rights in the sports industry, sports clubs and event organisers are heavily reliant on the selling of admission tickets as a funding source. Governing bodies, clubs and events' organisers have therefore significant incentives to effectively control tickets sale arrangements and distribution channels. When restrictions on sale arrangements are placed, they may be justified by the need to ensure the safety of spectators at sporting competitions. However, if the restriction is pursuing an economic objective, its legitimacy may be less clear.

555. As another form of secondary market, the control tendency of sports governing bodies has reached this area as well. As such, it has also attracted the interest of the EU institutions on a number of occasions. The Commission examined the exclusive rights granted by the 1990 FIFA World Cup organisers to an Italian travel agency to offer and distribute package tours including tickets to the matches.[926] The granting of a worldwide exclusivity over the distribution of the tour-tickets bundle package restricted the competition between tour operators on the market and the consumers' access to tickets, thereby breaching what is now Article 101 TFEU. As the same service could have been provided by a number of operators, without risks for the safety of the spectators, the Commission held that the restriction was neither justified nor proportionate.[927] The decision to bundle together two products was only a strategy adopted by the dominant undertaking to extract further value and force customers to acquire a product that they did not necessarily want.

556. The objective of ensuring consumers reasonable access to tickets guided the Commission in two further cases. In the first one, the organising committee of France '98 restricted access to tickets to customers that could provide a postal address in France.[928] This conduct constituted an indirect discrimination on the ground of nationality, as the requirement could be satisfied more easily by French

---

926. Commission Decision 92/521/EEC Distribution of package tours during the 1990 World Cup (1992) OJ L326/31. For further discussion, *see* Chris Watson & Christine Graham, *European Regulation of Media Rights*, in *Handbook on International Sports Law* 398–429 (James Nafziger & Stephen Ross eds, Edward Elgar 2011).

927. Commission Decision 92/521/EEC, para. 116. The decision was also discussed in European Commission, *Commission staff working document. Impact assessment accompanying the White Paper on Sport*, SEC(2007) 935 final (2007), s. 3.2.3.1.

928. Commission Decision relating to a proceeding under Art. 82 of the EC Treaty, Case IV/36.888 – 1998 Football World Cup, O.K. 2000 L5/55.

nationals. Furthermore, it was also considered an abuse of dominant position by the event organiser, effectively limiting the production to the prejudice of consumers.[929] However, the need to segment the sale territory along national lines in order to avoid clashes between fans and ensure safety of spectators could be a justification outweighing the restrictive effect. Nevertheless, the Commission considered the restriction disproportionate, holding that fans purchasing tickets before knowing the teams taking part in the competition could not represent a sufficient threat to the safety of others.[930]

557. In a second group of cases, the Commission assessed the exclusivity granted by the organising committees of the 2004 Athens Olympics and the 2006 FIFA World Cup, to VISA and MasterCard respectively.[931] Customers purchasing tickets from the online pages of the organising committees could only pay with VISA for the Olympics and MasterCard for the World Cup. The Commission required that reasonable alternatives were provided to the customers, through either other sales channels or payment methods, in order to exclude infringements of competition law.[932] In this regard, it must be noted that the Commission, in its attempt to ensure reasonable access to tickets, focused on the economic dimension of this activity, with no reference to the societal value of sport. Instead, the role of sport as a tool for social inclusion and the importance of accessing sports events, which appear in other provisions such as the Audiovisual Media Services Directive, was highlighted in the White Paper on Sport.[933]

558. Ticketing policies may also restrict the ability of consumers to resell legitimately purchased tickets. Technological advancements have a significant impact on the way consumers access tickets. Online anonymity had made it easier for individuals to engage with secondary markets, thereby also favouring certain activities such as ticket touting. Traditionally, access to these markets is regulated by private law, whereby the seller imposes contractual conditions on the buyer not to resell the ticket without authorisation.[934] However, the shortfall of private law instruments has also been translated into a push for greater public regulation.[935]

---

929. Chris Watson & Christine Graham, *European Regulation of Media Rights*, in *Handbook on International Sports Law* 401 (James Nafziger & Stephen Ross eds, Edward Elgar 2011).
930. 2000/12/EC: Commission Decision– 1998 Football World Cup (1999) OJ L5/55.
931. Press Release IP/03/738, Commission clears ticketing arrangements for the Athens Olympic Games, 23 May 2003 and Press Release IP/05/519, Competition: Commission welcomes improved access to tickets for the 2006 World Cup, 2 May 2005.
932. The cases were discussed in European Commission, *Commission staff working document. Impact assessment accompanying the White Paper on Sport*, SEC(2007) 935 final (2007), s. 3.2.3.3.
933. *See* European Commission, *White Paper on Sport*, COM(2007), 391 final (2007), s. 2.5 and Mark James & Guy Osborn *Tickets, Policy and Social Inclusion: Can the European White Paper on Sport Deliver?*, 1–2 ISLJ 61 (2009).
934. Mark James & Guy Osborn, *The Olympics, Transnational Law and Legal Transplants: The International Olympic Committee, Ambush Marketing and Ticket Touting*, 36(1) Leg. Stud. 93–110 (2016).
935. Stephen Weatherill, *Principles and Practice in EU Sports Law* 39 (Oxford Univ. Press 2017).

559. In this regard, possible reasons for consumers' protection, public order and the protection of the economic interests of right holders may prove a sufficient incentive for the intervention of national public authorities. Restrictions on the resale of tickets can be justified by the need to maintain segregation between fans in order to reduce instances of antisocial behaviours and prevent crowd disorder.[936] However, the measure will be proportionate only if the specific event presents risks for the safety of the spectators. As opposed to this, James & Osborn have noted that the legislative approach in the area is rather giving priority to protecting the governing bodies' commercial imperative.[937]

560. At European level, the measures dealing with ticketing and secondary markets are focused on the protection of consumers. In this relation, a number of Directives target unfair commercial practices, contract terms and consumers rights.[938] As part of this strategy, the EU has adopted Directive 2019/2161 to collect, amend and modernise the protection granted to consumers in the European market.[939] The measure seeks to enhance enforcement measures and increase transparency in the market, while leaving discretion to Member States to adopt more stringent rules. Of particular relevance for sporting events, the Directive imposes on resellers the obligation to declare whether they are professional traders and it includes a ban on the resale of tickets acquired through automated software.[940]

§8. CONCLUSION

561. This chapter has sought to analyse the approach taken by the EU institutions towards themes related to the use of funding in sport. The chapter has focused on four main areas, namely the regulations on the use of funding by professional sports clubs, the rules related to the use of public funding in sport and the rules surrounding the exploitation of one of the most relevant source of funding in sport, broadcasting and media rights.

562. The analysis of these areas has highlighted that the EU institutions have been sensitive to the objectives and needs of governing bodies and sporting actors.

936. Taylor LJ *Final Report into the Hillsborough Stadium Disaster*, Cmnd 962 (London: HMSO, 1990). This was also the rationale behind the adoption of the Criminal Justice and Public Order Act 1994, part of the legislative package passed in the UK in the aftermath of the Hillsborough disaster.
937. Mark James & Guy Osborn, *The Olympics, Transnational Law and Legal Transplants: The International Olympic Committee, Ambush Marketing and Ticket Touting*, 36(1) Leg. Stud. 93–110 (2016).
938. *See* Unfair Commercial Practices Directive (2005/29/EC), Unfair Contract Terms Directive (1993/13/EC), Consumer Rights Directive (2011/83/EC).
939. Directive 2019/2161of the European Parliament and of the Council amending Council Directive 93/13/EEC of 5 Apr. 1993, Directive 98/6/EC of the European Parliament and of the Council, Directive 2005/29/EC of the European Parliament and of the Council and Directive 2011/83/EU of the European Parliament and of the Council as regards better enforcement and modernisation of EU consumer protection rules, OJ L 328/7.
940. Recital 50 of Directive 2019/2161.

Objectives of public interests that were highlighted in other chapters have appeared in this discussion as well. For example, in relation to State Aid, it has been highlighted how the social and cultural importance of sport justifies the intervention of the State in support of greater participation.

563. But in these areas, two other fundamental objectives have been developed. Within the European sport system, stakeholders must accept restrictions to safeguard the sustainability of the system. Furthermore, governing bodies are entitled to protect the financing sources on which they rely. Therefore, the EU institutions have framed their intervention in the area of sports funding to ensure that the objective of sustainability and funding of the system are legitimately pursued. In this regard, when the commercial activity of sporting entities is inspired by recognised objectives of public interest, such as the training of players, the distribution of resources and the functioning of the system, the EU institutions will accept proportionate restrictions. Alternatively, when clubs and governing bodies appear to pursue merely private objectives, such as in the selling of broadcasting rights, or in relation to the granting of public funding to professional clubs, the EU will assess the conduct under an economic perspective.

564. The discussion in this area has highlighted the need for a fair balance between the interests at stake. The intervention of public authorities should offer greater transparency to the system, where the protection of legitimate objectives of a public nature is sometimes conflated with the private economic aspirations of governing bodies. In this regard, the role of the EU is to guarantee that the rules that come under its scrutiny respect the principles of good governance and do not disproportionately prejudice the legitimate interests of all the industry stakeholders.

Conclusions: The EU, the European Model and the Pandemic

565. The European model of sport has demonstrated its resilience. It has survived two World Wars, the political division of Europe, the challenges of embracing professionalism, the growth of commercialisation, technological change, governance scandals, global financial shocks and, most recently, it is facing up to the consequences of a pandemic that effectively closed down global sport.

566. Adjusting to the establishment and maturation of the EU has been, and continues to be, another such challenge. Sport is organised along national lines; the style of governance tends to promote the monopoly power of governing bodies and the jurisdiction of ordinary courts is largely ousted by the extensive use of arbitration clauses. In this light, it is not hard to see how this pulls against the organisational instincts of the EU in which a single market is favoured, nationality-based discrimination is resisted, monopoly power is controlled, and the market is governed by the rule of law.

567. Throughout this monograph we have explored whether the organisational model of sport and that of the EU can coexist and find mutually acceptable common ground. Our claim is that sport has a special character that distinguishes it from what might be termed 'normal' industries. For example, competition in the sports sector is characterised, not by cut-throat competition but by mutual interdependence and solidarity. Sports bodies need some space to devise rules that promote the regularity and proper functioning of competitions including rules that promote fairness, solidarity, integrity, safety, competitive balance and the development of young athletes. Our starting principle is that sports bodies should have autonomy to devise such rules free from undue economic, political and legal EU influence.

568. This autonomy is not, however, absolute. We claim that sporting autonomy should be conditioned on substantive and procedural grounds. Substantively, we find merit in the methodological approach adopted by the Court in *Meca-Medina*, and we see further merit in this approach being applied within the context of both competition and free movement laws. This approach asserts that, first, a contextual assessment of the sporting rule and an examination of whether the rule pursues legitimate sporting objectives must be undertaken. Second, it must be established whether the restrictive effects of that rule are inherent in the pursuit of the objectives and, third, the rule must remain proportionate to those objectives. A positive assessment in each leaves the sporting rule untouched by EU law. We acknowledge that the EU's jurisprudential journey of discovery in relation to sporting rules has not always been applied consistently and alternative approaches have been applied to sporting disputes. Setting aside the now-defunct 'purely sporting rules' approach developed in *Walrave*, more orthodox approaches have been applied. A traditional restriction – justification – proportionality analysis has been favoured by the Court in some free movement cases, notably in *Bosman*, *Lehtonen* and *Bernard*. In the context of competition cases, the Commission has been known to resort to a traditional economic assessment under Articles 101 and 102 TFEU, most notably in relation to collective selling of media rights cases.

569. In the monograph we have highlighted how the EU's approach has gradually entered into the sports system. Arbitral tribunals are increasingly basing their analysis of contested sporting rules under these parameters.

570. The procedural grounds for sporting autonomy have been incrementally developed through the jurisprudence of the Court, the decisional practice of the Commission and the emerging sports policy of the EU. The central message in this regard is that sporting rules must be devised in a way that respects good governance. They should be untainted by conflicts of interest and should be devised allowing for the adequate involvement of stakeholders. Throughout this monograph, we have revealed that a recurring source of challenge to the European model of sport has come from increasingly organised and assertive stakeholders who feel disempowered within the prevailing governance structures of sport. Stakeholders must be part of the system of sports governance and acquire rights within it, but equally they must accept proportionate restrictions on their commercial freedoms and they must contribute to the achievement of legitimate sporting objectives to the benefit of the system.

571. In this regard, the EU has not only helped identify the problem but also offered potential solutions through the provision of social dialogue and its structured dialogue with the sports movement. Ultimately, however, it is a matter for the sports movement how it addresses the issue of stakeholders' representation, but it is clear that the pyramid is changing shape. Once passive recipients of regulation sitting at the base of pyramid, stakeholders are now a more prominent feature at higher levels of the hierarchy, fattening its middle, although the pace of change is more pronounced in some sports than others.

572. We have explored the theme of conditional sporting autonomy through the lens of three key features of sporting activity: *organising sport*, *playing sport* and *funding sport*.

573. Organising sport: Our claim here is that the European model of sport is organisationally both efficient and deficient. The sporting landscape is populated by organisationally efficient rules designed to pursue a range of legitimate sporting objectives. Sport could not operate without them, and the sports movement is entitled to regulatory space to devise, implement and enforce rules that are essentially in the public interest. However, public authorities should not be absent from the discussion of what amounts to public interest. Furthermore, the hierarchical governance structure of the European model equips sports bodies with a powerful array of regulatory weapons and creates overwhelming incentives for sports bodies to use their monopolistic regulatory power to advance their own commercial interests. The restrictive effects of these conflicts of interest are capable of being reinforced by questionable dispute resolution practices that see aggrieved parties unable to have their EU-derived rights sufficiently aired. In this context, the EU's role is to supervise the system chosen by the sports movement and not to substitute these preferences for its own. This is best illustrated by the EU's approach to authorisation rules. The Court and the Commission have resisted the temptation to insist on a separation of the regulatory and commercial functions of a sports governing body, instead focussing the conflict of interest remedy on governance solutions. In this context, EU oversight is not a threat to the governance of the European model, but a source of improvement.

574. Playing sport: The regulatory power of sports governing bodies is such that they can exercise a decisive influence over who can participate, and on what terms, in regulated organised sport at both professional and amateur levels. The development of transfer systems and nationality-based eligibility rules in sport adds a new layer of labour regulation to that already provided for by law, and in some instances, conflicts arise between the private and public regulatory regimes. The operation of transfer systems has also created a market, often quite lucrative, that third parties such as agents wish to access. Sports bodies have therefore extended their powers to regulate not only the immediate sporting stakeholders but also economically active third parties. The exercise of this private regulatory power over other private economic actors has drawn the attention of public bodies such as the EU. If this were not the case, the objectives of the EU could be defeated by private parties. As EU law has evolved, the necessity of Treaty-based rights having to be dependent on the exercise of economic activity has loosened and with that, the organisation of amateur sport has also entered the EU's regulatory space. EU scrutiny has revealed that while nationality-based discrimination may have a legitimate role in sport, the grounds for such discrimination are often historically rooted, wholly unjustified and counterproductive to sport. Above all, EU scrutiny of rules regulating the practice of sport has empowered stakeholders. Our claim is that this stakeholder empowerment endows the exercise of private regulatory power in sport with a legitimacy it has often lacked.

575. Funding sport: Funding is required for sport to be properly organised and practised. However, sport often favours funding practices, such as media rights sales, that are designed to segment markets along national lines so that profits can be maximised. These practices potentially conflict with the EU's single market approach and this is compounded when damaging conflicts of interest taint sports governance. Allowing sport unconditional autonomy to devise practices that fund its activity is not a serious consideration. The sports system does not operate in a void. Just as a transfer market attracts third parties who want to benefit from the economic activity being conducted within it, so the practice of sport attracts the interest of connected economic sectors. Sponsors, broadcasters and investors see the commercial opportunities of sport, consumers (fans) wish to purchase sport to satisfy their entertainment requirements and the State sees investment in sport as an investment in a public good. This activity generates important revenues for sport, allowing it to fulfil one of its core functions, that of solidarity, which is a particular feature of the European model. Our claim is that given the connection between sport and related economic sectors, the EU has had to patrol the borders of this activity in order to ensure that the pursuit of apparently legitimate sporting objectives does not, in fact, act as a mask for private commercial gain. Such activity risks imposing damaging impacts not only on sport but also on the growth, technological development, vibrancy and plurality of other markets. Despite this bigger picture, our assessment of EU scrutiny in this area reveals a distinct sensitivity to the needs of sport. For example, the collective selling of broadcasting rights and the national sales model have not been fatally undermined by the application of EU law despite the obvious tensions with the anti-cartel and single market ethos of the EU. The effect of the coronavirus pandemic on sport will, no doubt, require this sensitivity to be extended for many years to come.

§1. The Coronavirus Pandemic and the European Model of Sport

576. In the first half of 2020, the World Health Organisation (WHO) declared the coronavirus (COVID-19) outbreak a pandemic. The highly contagious and deadly nature of the disease and the absence of vaccines or treatments resulted in many governments throughout the world taking unprecedented 'lockdown' and social-distancing measures. These measures effectively closed down much economic and social activity, including sport. The impact on the organisation, playing and funding of sport has been immense, and the effects are likely to be felt for years to come. Our reflections on the impact of the pandemic on sport have not benefitted from a healthy passage of time. Indeed, they are written during a period of lockdown in the UK. Nevertheless, in the coming months and years, it is worth considering how the European model of sport will be affected by the pandemic and what role public authorities, such as the EU, will play in the post-pandemic sports world. Sport might not be able to recover entirely on its own and this raises fundamental questions about the autonomy of sport: to what extent does the sports movement need to reconsider its relationship with public authorities and third-party event organisers?

577. In response to the pandemic, sports leagues and tournaments throughout the world were suspended or cancelled. The French football league was cancelled without the season having been completed, with the league placings at the time of abandonment being used to determine the league winners, European qualifiers and relegated clubs. In the Netherlands, the premature curtailment of the *Eredivise* in April 2020 resulted in no title winners and no teams being relegated, a decision at odds with the promotion and relegation principle that has underpinned the European model of sport for decades. Major international sporting events quickly fell victim to the outbreak: the Formula One season suspended, Grand Slam Tennis tournaments postponed, the EURO 2020 football tournament postponed until 2021, the World Snooker Championship postponed, world cricket halted, the finals of the UEFA Champions League and Europa League postponed, the 2020 Tokyo Olympic and Paralympic Games postponed to 2021. Many other sporting events suffered the same fate.

578. The effects on sport are significant and potentially devastating. Of significant inconvenience is the disruption to the rhythm of sport, but many of the issues caused by this can be addressed without likely EU intervention. For example, temporary dispensations can be made to sporting regulations such as extensions to contract end dates and variations to registration periods.[941] Arbitration, national laws or collective agreements, where in force, are most likely to be the arenas for dispute resolution in these areas. Of far greater significance is the financial crisis the sector is facing. The shutdown, even on a temporary basis, risks undermining important revenues derived from match-day income, broadcasting, sponsorship and player trading. In this environment, sports governing bodies face significant challenges in fulfilling their solidarity functions, and ultimately the impending financial crisis could threaten the survival of some sports bodies including clubs, leagues, tournaments or sports governing bodies. Sport will need to assess how to adjust to this new financial climate, but its freedom of action remains bounded by a number of considerations, including the availability of revenue streams from sectors that have suffered themselves and the limitations stemming from the requirements of national and EU law.

579. In team sports, the most significant running cost for clubs is player salaries. The coronavirus outbreak is, therefore, likely to result in demands for cost control measures to be extended. In the immediate aftermath of the outbreak, the sports movement adopted some short-term emergency measures. Pay deductions and deferrals between players and clubs were negotiated across a number of sports, and some football leagues and federations instituted emergency solidarity funds for members.[942] At government level, a number of States across Europe put in place more formal, although temporary, job retention and employment benefit schemes designed to encourage employers to retain employees who were not working as normal. The UK 'furlough' scheme allowed employers affected by the UK lockdown to have up to 80% of their usual monthly wage covered by the government, up to a maximum of GBP 2,500. Some English Premier League football clubs initially took up this offer, only to change their minds following negative publicity. Lower down the league structure, the furlough scheme was more widely adopted by sports clubs.

580. In the longer term, one would anticipate more sports wanting to introduce salary control measures, such as salary caps, and strengthened financial licensing rules, such as FFP. It can also be envisaged that due to the shutdown, many clubs will report losses under current FFP regulations and so may face sanctioning in the unlikely event the regulations are applied without consideration to the unprecedented context of such losses being posted. This could give rise to legal disputes, where the compatibility of such measures with EU law might be raised.[943] Should

---

941. *See*, for example, FIFA, COVID-19. Football Regulatory Issues, version 1, https://img.fifa.com/image/upload/zyqtt4bxgupp6pshcrtg.pdf April 2020 (accessed 7 May 2020).
942. *See* Michele Colucci, Sean Cottrell & Rustam Sethna, *Coronavirus and Its Impact on Football*, http://www.sportslawandpolicycentre.com/SLPC%20LIS%20Survey%20-%20Final%20-%205%20May%202020.pdf 5 May 2020 (accessed 7 May 2020).
943. In June 2020, UEFA announced a relaxation of the FFP rules to account for the adverse financial effects that COVID-19 had on clubs. *See* UEFA, Temporary Emergency Measures for Financial Fair Play, https://www.uefa.com/insideuefa/news/newsid=2642261.html (accessed 22 Jun. 2020).

strengthened cost control measures be introduced, they will need to pass EU scrutiny. The goals of securing financial rationality and the viability of the sector have often been claimed as legitimate sporting objectives necessitating a softening of the application of EU law: UEFA defends its FFP rules on these grounds. In light of the crisis, and assuming the system does not experience a rapid post-virus recovery, one could envisage the veracity of these claims to be strengthened. Yet, for cost control measures to be introduced or extended in sport requires adherence to the principles underpinning the concept of conditional autonomy developed throughout this work, including the involvement of stakeholders. If a new cost control regulatory landscape is to take hold, and for litigation to be avoided, a new era of bargaining between management and labour needs to emerge. As discussed in Chapter 3, the EU can assist this dialogue through the provision of the social dialogue passages in the Treaty.

581. Even though cost control measures are likely to be defended on the grounds of promoting the financial viability of sport, the coronavirus outbreak also raised concerns regarding competitive balance in sport. More commercially profitable leagues and clubs are better placed to weather the financial fallout from the pandemic, yet they still face financial pressures and their reaction to the crisis could damage competitive balance within sports. For example, wealthier leagues and clubs could seek to exploit new commercial opportunities, such as the individual selling of broadcasting rights, as opposed to the current widespread use of collective selling. As detailed in Chapter 4, the Commission has yet to establish whether collective selling is indispensable for the achievement of competitive balance in sport, instead focussing its analysis on the economic efficiency arguments under Article 101(3) TFEU. The coronavirus crisis might encourage proponents of solidarity in sport to be bolder in connecting sporting regulations to competitive balance arguments.

582. Financial viability and competitive balance arguments could also extend to labour market-related regulations. If sport experiences a financial recession post coronavirus, one might anticipate clubs in those sports that operate transfer systems to readjust their approach to player recruitment and development. Some might abandon expensive youth training programmes, whereas others might want to invest in them so as to cut the expensive reliance on the transfer market to recruit players. Under both scenarios, governing bodies will want to incentivise the development of young players, an objective considered to be of legitimate sporting concern by the EU. However, the proportionality of training compensation schemes is subject to scrutiny by the EU, as confirmed by the Court in *Bernard*. Attempts by sports bodies to expand training compensation sums to levels that pay little regard to the actual investment made in developing the players are unlikely to pass proportionality control. Sports bodies should resist the temptation to use the crisis to reintroduce a transfer system dressed in training compensation clothes.

583. Even before the crisis, clubs were always looking for new financial investments or a reduction of costs. At the time of writing, FIFA is looking to introduce a new set of football agent regulations that includes provision for a fee cap on agent commissions. The coronavirus outbreak and resulting financial uncertainty might be cited in support of claims that club costs connected to the payment of agent fees need reducing, although in line with our reasoning expressed in Chapter 2, we consider other sporting justifications to have stronger merit in this regard. Elsewhere, clubs might argue that regulatory restrictions on inward investment into clubs require reassessment. For example, club ownership requirements, including limitations on multiple club ownership, operates in European football and since 2015, FIFA has enacted a worldwide prohibition on TPIs in football clubs, a once valuable source of income for some clubs. Incentives for clubs to circumvent such prohibitions may be increased in times of financial crisis. If clubs feel that their survival is threatened by the restrictive nature of such regulations, they could resort to litigation or look to explore alternative structures such as the development of cross-border or breakaway leagues, the formation of which is strongly discouraged under the European model of sport.

584. Athletes have also experienced hardship during the global closure of sport. Many self-employed athletes were unable to benefit from emergency government employment schemes which were directed at employees, including Croatian footballers who are not classified as such by the national association. As discussed in Chapter 2, many athletes in pre-coronavirus times felt undervalued and under-rewarded by their respective governing bodies. The temptation to engage with financially prosperous third-party event organisers might be irresistible for athletes, and, equally, governing bodies might not be able to resist working alongside such third parties.

585. As discussed above, many countries across Europe have adopted interventionist schemes to soften the financial blow of lockdown on the economy. At the time of writing, none have adopted sports-specific schemes, although, in France, a State-guaranteed loan of approximately EUR 224 million was made available in case of a shortfall in the broadcasting rights caused by an ending of the agreement between the league and the broadcasters.[944] Should a coronavirus inspired financial crisis sweep sport, further such State aid measures including debt cancellations and infrastructure investments can be anticipated and as discussed in Chapter 4, this potentially engages Article 107 TFEU.

586. For those subject to lockdown measures, one of the most challenging aspects was the inability to access sport, as a source of physical activity and mental well-being or for pure entertainment. Many individuals have also suffered considerable financial loss and so their capacity to access sport has been diminished post lockdown and as a consequence, revenue streams for sport have been seriously disrupted. This poses a significant challenge for the sports movement, and it necessitates a rethink about some of the principles that have endured throughout the life of the European model. One such consideration concerns the relationship between sport and public authorities. The pandemic confirms an evolving trend – that sport does not operate in a vacuum and it cannot solve all the issues it faces alone. Public

944. *See ibid.*

authorities, such as the EU, should be part of this conversation and with a sensitivity to the needs of the sector, it can be part of the solution.

Selected Bibliography

Anderson, J., *The Legality of Boxing. A Punch Drunk Love?* (Routledge Cavendish 2007).

Anderson, J., *Modern Sports Law* (Hart 2010).

Anderson, J., *Leading Cases in Sports Law* (T.M.C. Asser Press 2013).

Anderson, J., *The EU's Role on Doping in Sport*, in Anderson, J., Parrish, R. & García, B. (eds), *Research Handbook on EU Sports Law and Policy*, 79–97 Edward Elgar (2018).

Andreff, W., Dutoya, J., & Montel, J., *A European Model of Sports Financing: Under Threat?,* 90 Rev. Jur. Eco. Sport 75–85 (2009).

Andreff, W. & Staudohar, P., *European and Sports Business Models*, in Barros, C., Muradali I. & Szymanski, S. (eds). *Transatlantic Sport: The Comparative Economics of North American and European Sports*, 23–49 (Edward Elgar 2002).

Andrews, M. & Harrington, P., *Off Pitch: Football's Financial Integrity Weaknesses, and How to Strengthen Them*, CID Working Paper No. 311, Harvard Kennedy School, 46 (2016).

Arnaut, J., *Independent European Sport Review*, A report by José Luis Arnaut (2006).

Baquero Cruz, J., *Between Competition and Free Movement: The Economic Constitutional Law of the European Community* (Hart 2002).

Barry, M., Skinner, J. & Engelberg, T. (eds), *Research Handbook of Employment Relations in Sport* (Edward Elgar 2016).

Bastianon, S., *The Striani Challenge to UEFA Financial Fair-Play. A New Era after Bosman or Just a Washout?*, 11(1) CLR 7–39 (2015).

Beloff, M. et al., *Sports Law* (Hart 2012).

Berry, A., *Challenging Football Transfer Windows: A Disproportionate Response to a Legitimate Aim*, 20 Sport & Law Journal 1 (2012).

Blanpain, R., *The Legal Status of Sportsmen and Sportswomen under International, European and Belgian and Regional Law* (Kluwer Law International 2003).

Borchardt, K., *The ABC of European Union Law*, 10 Publication Office of European Union (2010).

Boyle, R., *Battle for Control? Copyright, Football and European Media Rights*, 37(3) Media Cult. Soc. 359–375 (2015).

Braun, J., *Article 87 EC*, in Castendyk, O. et al. (eds), *European Media Law*, 207–244 (Kluwer Law International 2008).

Brinckman, D. & Vollergbregt, E., *The Marketing of Sport and Its Relation to E.C. Competition Law*, 5 ECLR 281–288 (1998).

Selected Bibliography

Budzinski, O., *The Institutional Framework for Doing Sports Business: Principles of EU Competition Policy in Sports Markets*. Ilmenau Economics Discussion Papers 70 (2011).

Bulmer, S., *The Governance of the European Union: A New Institutionalist Approach*, 13 JPP 351–380 (1993).

Cattaneo, A., *Social Dialogue and the Regulatory Power of Governing Bodies*, 17 (3–4) ISLJ 119–127 (2018).

Cattaneo, A., *State Aid in Sport*, in Anderson, J., Parrish, R. & García, B. (eds), *Research Handbook on EU Sports Law and Policy*, 197–228 (Edward Elgar 2018).

Chaker, A., *Study of National Sports Legislations in Europe* (Council of Europe 1999).

Chalmers, D., Davies, G. & Monti, G., *European Union Law*, (Cambridge Univ. Press 2014).

Cherpillod, I., *'CAS 98/200 AEK Athens and Slavia Prague v UEFA'*, in Wild, A. (ed.), *CAS and Football: Landmark Cases*, 11 (T.M.C. Asser Press 2011).

Colucci, M. & Bellia, O. (eds.), *Transfers of Football Players, A Practical Approach to Implementing FIFA Rules* (Sports Law and Policy Centre 2020).

Colucci, M., Cottrell, S. & Sethna, R., *Coronavirus and Its Impact on Football*, http://www.sportslawandpolicycentre.com/SLPC%20LIS%20Survey%20-%20Final%20-%205%20May%202020.pdf, 5 May 2020 (accessed 7 May 2020).

Craig, P. & De Búrca, G., *EU Law: Text, Cases, and Materials* (6th ed., Oxford Univ. Press 2015).

Craven, R., *State Aid and Sports Stadiums: EU Sports Policy or Deference to Professional Football*, 35(9) ECLR 453–460 (2014).

Craven, R., *Football and State Aid: Too Important to Fail?*, 14(3–4) ISLJ 205–217 (2014)

Dalziel, M., Downward, P., Parrish, R., Pearson, G. & Semens, A., *Study on the Assessment of the Compatibility of UEFA's Home Grown Player Rule with Article 45 TFEU*, https://ec.europa.eu/assets/eac/sport/library/studies/final-rpt-april2013-homegrownplayer.pdf, 30 April 2013 (accessed 20 May 2020).

de Dios Crespo Pérez, J. et al., *Contractual Stability: Breach of Contract*, in Wild, A. (ed.), *CAS and Football: Landmark Cases*, 37–105 (T.M.C. Asser Press 2012).

Deloitte, *World in Motion: Annual Review of Football Finance 2019* (2019).

Deloitte, *Football Money League 2020 Report*, https://www2.deloitte.com/content/dam/Deloitte/bg/Documents/finance/deloitte-uk-deloitte-football-money-league-2020%20(1).pdf (accessed 27 April 2020).

De Marco, N., *Compelled Consent – Pechstein & the Dichotomy and Future of Sports Arbitration*, Blackstone Chambers Sports Law Bulletin, https://www.blackstonechambers.com/news/analysis-compelled_consent_/, 4 July 2016 (accessed 25 March 2020).

De Marco, N., *Football and the Law* (Bloomsbury Professional 2018).

De Marco, N., Reck, A. & Fida, P., *Third Party Investment*, in De Marco, N. QC (ed.), *Football and the Law*, 183–212 (Bloomsbury 2018).

De Marco, N., *The Right to a Fair Hearing in Sports' Cases: Lessons from the ECtHR's Decision in Mutu & Pechstein*, LawInSport, https://

www.lawinsport.com/topics/item/the-right-to-a-fair-hearing-in-sports-cases-lessons-from-the-ecthr-s-decision-in-mutu-pechstein, 15 October 2018 (accessed 18 January 2020).

De Marco, N., *TPO in Football: What It Is, How It Is Developing, and What It Should Be*, Blackstone Chambers Sports Law Bulletin, https://www.sportslawbulletin.org/tpo-football-what-it-how-it-developing-and-what-it-should-be/, 6 January 2020 (accessed 14 January 2020).

De Weger, F., *The Jurisprudence of the FIFA Dispute Resolution Chamber* (T.M.C. Asser Press 2016).

Drywood, E., *'When We Buy a Young Boy ... ': Migrant Footballers, Children's Rights and the Case for EU Intervention*, in Iusmen, I., & Helen Stalford, H. (eds.) *The EU as a Children's Rights Actor*, 191–221 (Barbara Budrich 2016).

Duff, A., *Scottish Update: A Brief Synopsis of Newsworthy Matters Concerning Football, Rugby & Others from 1997 to Date*, 6(3) Sport & Law Journal (1997).

Durand, C. & Bayle, E., *Public Assistance in Spectator Sport: A Comparison Between Europe and the United States* 2(2) EJSS 1–19 (2002).

Duval, A., *Lex Sportiva: A Playground for Transnational Law*, 19 ELJ 822–842 (2013).

Duval, A., *The Court of Arbitration for Sport and EU Law: Chronicle of an Encounter*, 22(2) MJECL (2015).

Duval, A., & Van Rompuy, B., *The Compatibility of Forced CAS Arbitration with EU Competition Law: Pechstein Reloaded*, available at SSRN: http://ssrn.com/abstract=2621983 (2015)

Duval, A., *The FIFA Regulations on the Status and Transfer of Players: Transnational Law-Making in the Shadow of Bosman*, in Duval, A. & Van Rompuy, B. (eds), *The Legacy of Bosman, Revisiting the Relationship Between EU Law and Sport*, 81–116 (T.M.C. Asser Press 2016).

Duval, A., *Not in My Name! Claudia Pechstein and the Post-Consensual Foundations of the Court of Arbitration for Sport*, Max Planck Institute for Comparative Public Law & International Research, Research Paper No. 2017-01.

Duval, A., & Van Maren, O., *The Labour Status of Professional Football Players in the European Union*, 8(3) Eur. Labour Law J. 258 (2017).

Duval, A., *RFC Seraing at the Court of Arbitration for Sport: How FIFA's TPO Ban Survived (Again) EU Law Scrutiny*, Asser International Sports Law Blog, https://www.asser.nl/SportsLaw/Blog/post/rfc-seraing-at-the-court-of-arbitration-for-sport-how-fifa-s-tpo-ban-survived-again-eu-law-scrutiny, 26 April 2017 (accessed 13 January 2020).

Duval, A., *Seraing v FIFA: Why Rumours of CAS's Death Have Been Greatly Exaggerated*, Asser International Sports Law Blog, https://www.asser.nl/SportsLaw/Blog/post/seraing-vs-fifa-why-the-rumours-of-cas-s-death-have-been-greatly-exaggerated, 10 September 2018 (accessed 14 January 2020).

Duval, A., *The 'Victory' of the Court of Arbitration for Sport at the European Court of Human Rights: the End of the Beginning for the CAS*, Asser International Sports Law Blog, https://www.asser.nl/SportsLaw/Blog/post/the-victory-of-the-court-of-arbitration-for-sport-at-the-european-court-of-human-rights-the-end-of-the-beginning-for-the-cas, 10 October 2018 (accessed 17 January 2020).

Selected Bibliography

Engelhard, A. & Milanovic, L., *An Overview of the Dispute Between FIBA & EuroLeague – Is There and End in Sight*, LawInSport https://www.lawinsport.com/topics/item/an-overview-of-the-dispute-between-fiba-euroleague-is-there-an-end-in-sight, 25 February 2018 (accessed 12 July 2019).

European Commission, *The Impact of European Union Activities on Sport*, Study by Coopers and Lybrand for DG X of the European Commission (1995).

European Commission, *Study on Doping Prevention: A Map of Legal, Regulatory and Prevention Practice Provisions in EU 28* (2015).

Evens, T., Smith, P. & Iosifidis, P., *The Political Economy of Television Sports Rights* (Palgrave Macmillan 2013).

Evju, S., *Collective Agreements and Competition Law. The Albany Puzzle, and van der Woude,* 17 IJCLLIR 165 (2001).

Exner, J., *Sporting Nationality in the Context of European Union Law* (Springer 2019)

Feintuck, M., *'The Public Interest' in Regulation* (Oxford Univ. Press 2004).

Foster, K., *Developments in Sporting Law*, in Allison, L. (ed.), *The Changing Politics of Sport* (Manchester Univ. Press 1993).

Foster, K., *Can Sport Be Regulated by Europe?: An Analysis of Alternative Models*, in Caiger, A. & Gardiner, S. (eds), *Professional Sport in the EU: Regulation and Re-regulation*, 57–60 (T.M.C. Asser Press 2000).

Foster, K., *Lex Sportiva and Lex Ludica: The Court of Arbitration for sport's jurisprudence*, in Blackshaw, I. et al. (eds), *The Court of Arbitration for Sport 1984–2004* (T.M.C. Asser Press 2006).

Foster, K., *Is There a Global Sports Law*, in Siekmann, R. & Soek, J. (eds), *Lex Sportiva: What Is Sports Law*? (T.M.C. Asser Press 2012).

Flanagan, C., *A Tricky European Fixture: An Assessment of UEFA's Financial Fair Play Regulations and Their Compatibility with EU Law*, 13 ISLJ 148–167 (2013).

Freeburn, L., *A Breakaway League in Professional Cycling: Issues for the Governance and Organisation of the Sport*, 13(3/4) ISLJ 193 (2013).

Freeburn, L., *Regulating International Sport: Power, Authority and Legitimacy* (Brill Nijhoff 2018).

Gallagher, R. & Quinn, B., *Regulatory Own Goals: The Unintended Consequences of Economic Regulation in Professional Football*, 20(2) ESMQ 151–170 (2020).

Galletti, G., *How Reasonable a Private Investor Can Be Assumed to Be? Corsica Ferries France,* 52(4) CML Rev. 1095–1110 (2015).

García, B., *The Independent European Sport Review: Half Full or Half Empty?*, 4(3) ESLJ (2007).

García, B., *UEFA and the European Union: From Confrontation to Co-operation*, 3(3) JCER 202 (2007).

García, B., *The 2001 Informal Agreement on the International Transfer System*, I-2011 European Sports Law and Policy Bulletin 17–29 (2011).

García, B., & Weatherill, S., *Engaging with the EU in Order to Minimise Its Impact: Sport and the Negotiation of the Treaty of Lisbon*, 19(2) J. Eur. Public Policy 241 (2012).

García, B., & Meier, H., *Limits of Interest Empowerment in the European Union: The Case of Football*, 34(4) J. Eur. Integr. 359–378 (2012).

García, B., & Meier, H., *Global Sport Power Europe? The Efficacy of the European Union in Global Sport Regulation*, 55(4) JCMS, 850–870 (2017).

García, B., & De Wolf, M., *European Law and the Governance of Sport*, in Anderson, J., Parrish, R. & García, B. (eds), *Research Handbook on EU Sports Law and Policy*, 79–97 (Edward Elgar 2018).

Gardiner, S. & Welch, R., *The Contractual Dynamics of Team Stability Versus Player Mobility: Who Rules 'The Beautiful Game'?*, 5(1) ESLJ 1–14 (2007).

Gardiner, S., *Sports Law* (Routledge 2012).

Gauthier, R., *The International Olympic Committee, Law, and Accountability* (Routledge 2017).

Geeraert, A., *Limits to the Autonomy of Sport: EU Law*, in Alm, J. (ed.), *Action for Good Governance in International Sports Organisations*, 151–184 (Play the Game/Danish Institute for Sports Studies 2013).

Geeraert, A., *The Role of the EU in Better Governance in International Sports Organisations*, in Alm, J. (ed.), *Action for Good Governance in International Sports Organisations*, 25–37 (Play the Game/Danish Institute for Sports Studies 2013).

Geeraert, A., *The EU in International Sports Governance: A Principal Agent Perspective on EU Control of FIFA and UEFA* (Palgrave Macmillan 2016).

Geeraert, A., & Drieskens, E., *Normative Market Europe: the EU as a Force for Good in International Sports Governance?,* 39(1) J. Eur. Integr. 79–94 (2017).

Geeraert, A., *Sports Governance Observer 2018. An Assessment of Good Governance in Five International Sports Federations* (Play the Game/Danish Institute for Sports Studies 2018).

Geey, D., *Multiple Football Club Ownership: Disparities Between Rules*, https://www.danielgeey.com/post/multiple-football-club-ownership-disparities-between-rules/ (accessed 10 January 2020).

GHK, *Volunteering in the European Union*, Study for the Directorate General for Education and Culture (2010) https://ec.europa.eu/citizenship/pdf/doc1018_en.pdf (accessed 27 March 2020).

Grady, J., *Analyzing Rule 40's Restrictions on Using Athletes in Olympic Sponsorship at Rio 2016*, 15(1) ESLJ (2017).

Grayson, E., *Sport and the Law* (Butterworths 1998).

Greenfield, S. & Osborn, G., *Law and Sport in Contemporary Society* (Frank Cass 2000).

Grell, T., *Multi-Club Ownership in European Football – Part 1: General Introduction and the ENIC Saga*, Asser International Sports Law Blog, https://www.asser.nl/SportsLaw/Blog/post/multi-club-ownership-in-european-football-part-i-general-introduction-and-the-enic-saga-by-tomas-grell, 24 October 2017 (accessed 9 January 2020).

Grell, T., *Multi-Club Ownership in European Football – Part II: The Concept of Decisive Influence in the Red Bull Case,* Asser International Sports Law Blog, https://www.asser.nl/SportsLaw/Blog/post/multi-club-ownership-in-european-football-part-ii-the-concept-of-decisive-influence-in-the-red-bull-case-by-tomas-grell, 25 October 2017 (accessed 9 January 2020).

Gunther, P., *The Plan for a Digital Single Market in Europe and Reforming EU Copyright Rules to Develop a Market-Oriented Approach to Reduce Infringement on the Internet*, 38(1) EIPR 43–55 (2015).

Gustafson, E., *The Luxury Tax in Professional Sports*, in Andreff, W. & Szymanski, S. (eds), *Handbook on the Economics of Sport*, 651–660 (Edward Elgar (2006).

Haffner, A., *Why the International Skating Union Was Found in Breach of EU Competition Law*, LawInSport, https://www.lawinsport.com/topics/item/why-the-international-skating-union-was-found-in-breach-of-eu-competition-law, 17 January 2018 (accessed 12 July 2019).

Halgreen, L., *European Sports Law – A Comparative Analysis of the European and American Models of Sport* (Forlaget Thompson 2004).

Harbo, T., *The Function of the Proportionality Principle in EU Law*, 16(2) ELJ 158–185 (2010).

Harding, J., *Behind the Glory: 100 Years of the PFA* (Breedon Books 2009).

Henry, I., *European Models of Sport: Governance, Organisational Change and Sports Policy in the EU*, 50(1) Hitotsubashi J. Arts Sci. 41 (2009).

Hock, B. & Gomtsian, S., *Private Order Building: The State in the Role of the Civil Society and the Case of FIFA*, 17 ISLJ 197 (2018).

Houlihan, B., *The Government and Politics of Sport* (Routledge 1991).

House of Lords, European Union Committee, 16th Report of Session 2010-11, *Grassroots Sport and the European Union*, The Stationary Office Limited, HL Paper 130 (2011).

Ibáñez Colomo, P., *Copyright Licensing and the EU Digital Single Market Strategy*, in Blair, R. & Sokol, D. (eds), *Cambridge Handbook of Antitrust, Intellectual Property and High Technology*, 339–357 (Cambridge Univ. Press 2016).

INEA, *Expert Opinion on the Compatibility of the 6+5 Rule with European Community Law* (2008).

Infantino, G., *Meca-Medina: A Step Backwards for the European Sports Model and Specificity of Sport*, https://www.uefa.com/MultimediaFiles/Download/uefa/KeyTopics/480401_DOWNLOAD.pdf, 2 October 2006 (accessed 16 July 2019).

Iosifidis, P. & Smith, P., *The European Television Sports Rights Market: Balancing Culture and Commerce*, Paper presented at the Private Television in Europe (2011).

James, M. & Osborn, G., *Tickets, Policy and Social Inclusion: Can the European White Paper on Sport Deliver?*, 1–2 ISLJ 61 (2009).

James, M. & Osborn, G., *The Olympics, Transnational Law and Legal Transplants: The International Olympic Committee, Ambush Marketing and Ticket Touting*, 36(1) Leg. Stud. 93–110 (2016).

James, M., *Sports Law* (Palgrave 2017).

Jeanrenaud, C. & Késenne, S., *The Economics of Sport and the Media* (Edward Elgar 2006).

Kaburakis, K., *The US and EU Systems of Sport Governance: Commercialized v Socio-Cultural Model – Competition and Labor Law*, 3–4 ISLJ 108–127 (2008).

Keane, B., *The Application of Competition Law in the Entertainment and Sport Sectors*, 5 JECLP 592–601 (2014).

Keane, B., *Game-Changer: Why the Saracens Decision Will Transform the Governance of Sport*, CPI Antitrust Chronicle, April 2020, https://

www.competitionpolicyinternational.com/game-changer-why-the-saracens-decision-will-transform-the-governance-of-sport/ (accessed 5 May 2020).

Kedzior, M., *Effects of the EU Anti-Doping Laws and Politics for the International and Domestic Sports Law in Member States*, 7(1/2) ISLJ 111–114 (2007).

Keller, B. & Weller, S., *Sectoral Social Dialogue at EU Level: Problems and Prospects of Implementation*, 17(3) Eur. J. Ind. 227–243 (2011).

Késenne, S., *The Bosman Case and European Football*, in Wladimir Andreff, W. & Szymanski, S. (eds), *Handbook on the Economics of Sport*, 632–641 (Edward Elgar 2006).

Késenne, S., *The Peculiar International Economics of Professional Football in Europe*, 54(3) Scott. J. Political. Econ. 388–399 (2007).

Kienapfel, P. & Stein, A., *The Application of Articles 81 and 82 EC in the Sport Sector*, 3 Competition Policy Newsletter 6–14 (2007).

Komninos, A., *Eco Swiss China Time Ltd v Benetton International NV (C126/97)*, 37(2) CML Rev. 459 (2000).

Koops, J. & Gjovalin Macaj, G. (eds), *The European Union as a Diplomatic Actor* (Palgrave Macmillan 2015).

Kornbeck, J., *State Aid and Access to Sport – Lessons for VAT Law*, 18(2) EStAL 138–156 (2019).

KEA, CDES, EOSE, *Study on Sports Agents in the European Union*, a Study commissioned by the European Commission (2009).

KEA/CDES, *Study on the Economic and Legal Aspects of Transfers of Players* (European Commission, 2013).

KEA European Affairs and ECORYS, *An Update on Change Drivers and Economic and Legal Implications of Transfers of Players: Final Report to the DG Education, Youth, Culture and Sport of the European Commission*, (2018).

KMPG, *Project TPO*, https://www.ecaeurope.com/media/1682/tpo-report.pdf, 8 August 2013 (accessed 12 January 2020).

Lago, U., Simmons, R. & Szymanski, S., *The Financial Crisis in European Football: An Introduction*, 7(1) J. Sports Econ. 3–12 (2006).

Laine, A. & Vehmas, H., *Development, Current Situation and Future Prospects of the Private Sports Sector in Europe*, in Laine, A. & Vehmas, H. (eds), *The Private Sport Sector in Europe: A Cross-National Comparative Perspective*, 343–354 (Springer 2017).

Laskowski, J., *Solidarity Compensation Framework in Football Revisited*, 18 ISLJ 150–184 (2019).

Lanfranchi, P. & Taylor, M., *Moving with the Ball: The Migration of Professional Footballers* (Berg 2001).

Lefever, K., *New Media and Sport: International Legal Aspects* (T.M.C. Asser Press 2012).

Lewis, A. & Taylor, J., *Sport: Law and Practice* (Bloomsbury 2014).

Lindholm, J. & Kaburakis, A., *Cases C-403/08 and C-429/08 FA Premier League Ltd and Others v QC Leisure and Others; and Karen Murphy v Media Protection Services Ltd, 4 Oct 2011*, in Anderson, J. (ed.), *Leading Cases in Sports Law*, 271–286 (T.M.C. Asser Press 2013).

Lindholm, J., *Can I Please Have a Slice of Ronaldo? The Legality of FIFA's Ban on Third Party Ownership under European Union Law*, 15 ISLJ 137–148 (2016).

Selected Bibliography

Lindholm, J., *The Netflix-ication of Sports Broadcasting*, 18 ISLJ 99–101 (2019).

Linstrom-Rossi, L., De Waele, S. & Vaigauskaite, D., *Application of EC Antitrust Rules in the Sport Sector: An Update*, Competition Policy Newsletter 3 (2005).

Majani, F., *One Step Forward, Two Hops Backwards: Quotas – The Return. An Excavation into the Legal Deficiencies of the FIFA 6+5 Rule and the UEFA Home-Grown Players Rule in the Eyes of European Union Law* 1–2 ISLJ 19 (2009).

Marzal, T., *From Hercules to Pareto: Of Bathos, Proportionality, and EU Law*, 15(3) ICON 621–648 (2017).

Mataija, M., *Private Regulation and the Internal Market: Sports, Legal Services, and Standard Setting in EU Economic Law* (Oxford Univ. Press 2016).

Mavromati, D., *The Validity of FIFA's Arbitration Clause and the Independence of the CAS: A Detailed Review of the RFC Seraing Cases*, LawInSport https://www.lawinsport.com/topics/item/the-validity-of-fifa-s-arbitration-clause-and-the-independence-of-the-cas-a-detailed-review-of-the-rfc-seraing-cases, 4 October 2018 (accessed 13 January 2020).

Mavromati, D., *Riza v Turkey: European Court of Human Rights Gives Further Guidance on Establishing Independent Arbitral Tribunals*, LawInSport, https://www.lawinsport.com/topics/item/riza-v-turkey-european-court-of-human-rights-gives-further-guidance-on-establishing-independent-arbitral-tribunals#_ftn1 5 February 2020 (accessed 12 April 2020).

McArdle, D., *Dispute Resolution in Sport. Athletes, Law and Arbitration* (Routledge 2015).

Mekenkamp, K., *FIFA's Provision on the Protection of Minors – Part 3: The Compatibility of Article 19 with EU Law*, Asser International Sports Law Blog, https://www.asser.nl/SportsLaw/Blog/post/fifa-s-provision-on-the-protection-of-minors-part-3-the-compatibility-of-article-19-with-eu-law-by-kester-mekenkamp, 03 June 2017 (accessed 30 April 2020).

Mestre, A., *The Law of the Olympic Games* (T.M.C. Asser Press 2009).

Miettinen, S., *The 'Independent European Sport Review': A Critical Overview*, 3(4) ISLJ 57–62 (2006).

Miettinen, S., *Policing the Boundaries Between Regulation and Commercial Exploitation: Lessons from the MOTOE Case*, 3(4) ISLJ 11–18 (2008).

Morrow, S., *Football, Economics and Finance*, in Hughson, J. Moore, K., Spaaij, R. & Maguire, J. (eds), *Routledge Handbook of Football Studies*, 163–176 (Routledge 2017).

Mortelmans, K., *Towards Convergence in the Application of the Rules on Free Movement and on Competition*, 38 CML Rev. 613–649 (2001).

Moya Izquierdo, S. & Troncoso Ferrer, M., *Football Broadcasting Business in the EU: Towards Fairer Competition?*, 5(6) JECLP 353–363 (2014) .

Murray, S., *Sports Diplomacy: Origins, Theory and Practice* (Routledge 2018).

Nicolaides, P., *A Critical Analysis of the Application of State Aid Rules to Sport*, 22(2) MJECL 209–223 (2015).

Nielsen, K. & Storm, R., *Profit Maximization, Win Optimization and Soft Budget Constraints in Professional Team Sports*, in Nielsen, K., Wagner, U. & Storm, R. (eds), *When Sport Meets Business: Capabilities, Challenges, Critiques*, 153–166 (Sage Publications 2017).

O'Conaill, S., *Sustainable Financing in Football and the EU*, in Anderson, J., Parrish, R. & García, B. (eds), *Research Handbook on EU Sports Law and Policy*, 246–260 (Edward Elgar 2018).

O'Leary, L., *Employment and Labour Relations Law in the Premier League, NBA and International Rugby Union* (T.M.C. Asser Press 2017).

Parrish, R., *Sports Law and Policy in the European Union* (Manchester Univ. Press 2003).

Parrish, R. & Miettinen, S., *The Sporting Exception in European Union Law* (T.M.C. Asser Press 2008).

Parrish, R. et al., *The Lisbon Treaty and EU Sports Policy*, Report for the European Parliament Committee on Culture and Education, European Parliament (2010).

Parrish, R., *Social Dialogue in European Professional Football*, 17(2) ELJ 213–229 (2011).

Parrish, R., *Lex Sportiva and EU Sports Law*, 37 EL Rev. 716–733 (2012).

Parrish, R., *Case C-36/74 Walrave and Koch [1974] ECR 1405*, in Anderson, J. (ed.) *Leading Cases in Sports Law*, 45–64 (T.M.C. Asser Press 2013).

Parrish, R., *Article 17 of the FIFA Regulations on the Status and Transfer of Players: Compatibility with EU Law*, 22(2) MJECL 256–282 (2015).

Parrish, R., *The European Social Dialogue: A New Mode of Governance for European Football*, in Duval, A. & Van Rompuy, B. (eds), *The Legacy of Bosman, Revisiting the Relationship between EU law and Sport*, 187–211 (T.M.C. Asser Press 2016).

Pearson, G., *Sporting Justifications under EU Free Movement and Competition Law: The Case of the Football 'Transfer System'*, 21(2) ELJ 220–238 (2015).

Peiffer, C., *RFC Seraing & Doyen Sports v FIFA: Changing the Rules of the Game in International Sports Arbitration?*, N. Y. Univ. J. Int. Law Politics, 1359, http://nyujilp.org/wp-content/uploads/2019/09/NYI410.pdf, 29/07/19 (accessed 14 January 2020).

Pijetlovic, K., *EU Sports Law and Breakaway Leagues in Football* (T.M.C. Asser Press 2015).

Pijetlovic, K., *FINA's Decision to Allow Market Access to Rival Competitions – A Turn of the Tide in Professional Swimming*, LawInSport www.LawinSport.com, 26 March.2019 (accessed 12 July 2019).

Poli, R., Ravenel, L. & Besson, R., *Transfer Values and Probabilities: The CIES Football Observatory Approach* (CIES Football Observatory 2016).

Reeb, M., *The Role and Functions of the Court of Arbitration for Sport*, in Blackshaw, I. et al. (eds), *The Court of Arbitration for Sport 1984–2004* (T.M.C. Asser Press 2006).

Richardson, J., *European Union: Power and Policy-Making* (3rd ed., Routledge 2006).

Robinson, T. & Howarth, A., *The Impact of the Salary Cap in the European Rugby Super League*, 3(6) IJBM 3–7 (2008).

Rofe, S. (ed.), *Sport and Diplomacy: Games Within Games* (Manchester Univ. Press 2018).

Rohde, M. & Breuer, C., *The Market for Football Club Investors: A Review of Theory and Empirical Evidence from Professional European Football*, 17(3) ESMQ 265–289 (2017).

Rossi, G. et al., *Sports Agents and Labour Markets* (Routledge 2016).
Rubini, L., *The Elusive Frontier: 'Regulation' under EC State Aid Law*, 8(3) EStAL, 277– 298 (2011).
Schenk, S., *Integrity of Sport*, in Anderson, J., Parrish, R. & García, B. (eds), *Research Handbook on EU Sports Law and Policy*, 431–447 (Edward Elgar 2018).
Schubert, M. & Hamil, S., *Financial Doping and Financial Fair Play in European Club Football Competitions*, in Breuer, M. & Forrest, D. (eds), *The Palgrave Handbook on the Economics of Manipulation in Sport*, 135–157 (Palgrave Macmillan 2018).
Shi Qiang Sim, N., *Ambush Marketing in Major Sports Events: War Minus the Shooting?*, 10(7) JIPLP 536–550 (2015).
Shuibhne, N., *Exceptions to the Free Movement Rules*, in Barnard, C. & Peers, S. (eds), *European Union Law* (Oxford Univ. Press 2017).
Siekmann, R., *Is Sport "Special" in EU Law and Policy?*, in Blanpain, R. (ed.), *The Future of Sports law in the European Union – Beyond the EU Reform Treaty and the White Paper*, 37–49 (Kluwer Law International 2008).
Siekmann, R. & Soek, J., *The European Union and Sport: Legal and Policy Documents* (T.M.C. Asser Press 2005).
Siekmann, R. & Soek, J., *Models of Sport Governance in the European Union: The Relationship between State and Sport Authorities*, 3–4 ISLJ 93–102 (2010).
Sinnaeve, A., *Competition Policy, State Aid and State Enterprises*, in Hawk, B. (ed.), *Annual Proceedings of the Fordham Corporate Law Institute: International Antitrust Law and Policy*, 67–91 (Juris Publishing 2001).
Smith, A. & Stewart, B., *The Special Features of Sport: A Critical Revisit*, 13(1) Sport Mgt Rev. 1–13 (2010).
Soek, J., *Sport in National Sports Acts and Constitutions: Definition, Ratio Legis and Objectives*, 3–4 ISLJ 28–36 (2006).
Smith, P., Evens, T. & Iosifidis, P., *The Next Big Match: Convergence, Competition and Sports Media Rights*, 31(5) Eur. J. Commun. 536–550 (2016).
Solberg, H. & Haugen, K., *European Club Football: Why Enormous Revenues Are Not Enough?*, 13(2) Sport Soc. 329–343 (2010).
Spilsbury, S., *Rewriting the Rule Book? The Latest on the Draft Copyright Directive*, 17(1) ESLJ 1 (2019).
SportBusiness Consulting, *Global Media Report 2019*, https://www.sportbusiness.com/consulting/sportbusiness-consulting-global-media-report-2019/ (accessed 28 April 2020).
Sports Law and Policy Centre, *The Bernard Case. Sports and Training Compensation*, I-2010 European Sports Law and Policy Bulletin (2010).
Sports Rights Owners' Coalition, *The Impact of Potential Changes to Geo-Blocking Regulation on Sport* (2020).
Stewart, B., *Sport Funding and Finance* (Routledge 2015).
Stix-Hackl, C. & Egger, A., *Sports and Competition Law: A Never-Ending Story?*, 23(2) ECLR 81–91 (2002).
Szymanski, S., *The Economic Design of Sporting Contests*, 41 JEL 1137–1187 (2003).
Szymanski, S., *The Comparative Economics of Sport* (Palgrave Macmillan 2010).

Szymanski, S., *Sport Financing and Governance in Europe*, in Andreff, W. (ed.), *Contemporary Issues in Sports Economics*, 65–80 (Edward Elgar 2011).

Szymanski, S., *The Economic Arguments Supporting a Competition Law Challenge to the Transfer System*, FIFPro [online] (2015).

Szymanski, S., *Entry into Exit: Insolvency in English Professional Football*, 64 Scott. J. Polit. Econ. 419–444 (2017).

Terraz, T., *Can a Closed League in e-Sports Survive EU Competition Law Scrutiny?*, Asser International Sports Law Blog, https://www.asser.nl/SportsLaw/Blog/?tag=/EU-Law, 08 August 2019 (accessed 17 January 2020).

Thomas, D., *The Retain and Transfer System*, in Andreff, W. & Szymanski, S. (eds), *Handbook on the Economics of Sport*, 630 (Edward Elgar 2006).

T.M.C. Asser Institute, Edge Hill University and the Katholieke Universiteit Leuven, *Study into the Identification of Themes and Issues Which Can Be Dealt with in a Social Dialogue in the European Professional Football Sector* (Report for the European Commission 2008).

T.M.C. Asser Institute, Edge Hill University & Leiden University, *Study on the Equal Treatment of Non-Nationals in Individual Sports Competitions* (Study for the European Commission 2010).

T.M.C. Asser Institute, *Study on Sports Organisers' Rights in the European Union* (Study commissioned by the European Commission; T.M.C. Asser Institute 2014).

Tokarski, W. et al., *Two Players One Goal? Sport in the European Union* (Meyer and Meyer 2004).

Townley, C., *Which Goals Count in Article 101 TFEU?: Public Policy and Its Discontents*, 32 ECLR 441–448 (2011).

Traupel, T., *Football and State Aid: Really the Greatest Pastime in the World?*, 13(3) EStAL 414–425 (2014).

Van den Bogaert, S., *Practical Regulation of the Mobility of Sportsmen in the EU Post Bosman* (Kluwer Law International 2005).

Van den Bogaert, S. & Vermeersch, A., *Sport and the EC Treaty: A Tale of Uneasy Bedfellows?*, 31 EL Rev. 821 (2006).

Van der Vijver, T., *Article 102 TFEU: How to Claim the Application of Objective Justifications in the Case of Prima Facie Dominance Abuses?*, 129 JECLP (2012).

Van Maren, O. et al., *Debating FIFA's TPO Ban*, Asser International Sports Law Blog Symposium, 3–4 ISLJ 233 (2015).

Van Rompuy, B., *Economic Efficiency: The Sole Concern of Modern Antitrust Policy?: Non-efficiency Considerations under Article 101 TFEU* (Kluwer Law International 2012).

Van Rompuy, B., *EU Commission Adopts First-Ever Antitrust Prohibition Decision on Regulatory Aspects of Sport*, Regulating for Globalisation, http://regulatingforglobalization.com/2018/02/12/eu-commission-adopts-first-ever-antitrust-prohibition-decision-regulatory-aspects-sport/?print=pdf, 12 Dec. 2018 (accessed 9 April 2020).

Vermeersch, A., *The European Union and the Fight Against Doping in Sport: On the Field or on the Sidelines?*, 4(1) ESLJ (2006).

Verdonk, T., *Rivalry among Sports Associations: The Compatibility of Sports Associations' Exclusivity Clauses with EU Competition Law*, 38(2) ECLR 86 (2017).

Watson, C. & Graham, C., *European Regulation of Media Rights*, in Nafziger, J. & Ross, S. (eds), *Handbook on International Sports Law*, 398–429 (Edward Elgar 2011).

Weatherill, S., *Resisting the Pressures of Americanization: The Influence of European Community Law on the European Sport Model*, in Greenfield, S. & Osborn, G. (eds), *Law and Sport in Contemporary Society*, 157–181 (Frank Cass 2000).

Weatherill, S., *Anti-doping Revisited – The Demise of the Rule of Purely Sporting Interest*, 27 ECLR 645–657 (2006).

Weatherill, S., *Article 82 EC and Sporting 'Conflict of Interest': The Judgment in MOTOE*, 1–2 ISLJ 3–7 (2009).

Weatherill, S., *Fairness, Openness and the Specific Nature of Sport: Does the Lisbon Treaty Change EU Sports Law*, 3– 4 ISLJ 11–17 (2010).

Weatherill, S., *EU Sports Law: The Effect of the Lisbon Treaty*, Oxford Legal Studies Research Paper No. 3/2011 (2011).

Weatherill, S., *The Limits of Legislative Harmonisation Ten Years after Tobacco Advertising: How the Court's Case Law Has Become a 'Drafting Guide.'*, 12 German L.J. 827 (2011).

Weatherill, S., *Is There Such Thing as EU Sports Law*, in Siekmann, R. & Soek, J. (eds), *Lex Sportiva: What Is Sports Law?* (T.M.C. Asser Press 2012).

Weatherill, S., *Case C-519/04 P Meca-Medina [2006] ECR I-6991*, in Anderson, J. (ed.), *Leading Cases in Sports Law*, 137–151 (T.M.C. Asser Press 2013).

Weatherill, S., *The Sale of Rights to Broadcast Sporting Events under EC Law*, in Weatherill, S. (ed.), *European Sports Law*, 311–377 (T.M.C. Asser Press 2014).

Weatherill, S., *Principles and Practice in EU Sports Law* (Oxford Univ. Press 2017).

Wild, A., *CAS and Football: Landmark Cases* (T.M.C. Asser Press 2011).

Yilmaz, S., Esson, J., Darby, P., Drywood, E. & Mason, C., *Children's Rights and the Regulations on the Transfer of Young Players in Football*, 55(1) Int. Rev. Sociol. Sport 115–124 (2018).

Table of Cases

European Union

Case 26/62 *NV Algemene Transport- en Expeditie Onderneming van Gend en Loos v. Nederlandse Administratie der Belastingen* [1963] ECR 1
Case 70/72 *Commission v. Germany* [1973] ECR 813
Case 36/74 *Walrave v. Union Cycliste Internationale* [1974] ECR 1405
Case 43/75 *Gabrielle Defrenne v. Société anonyme belge de navigation aérienne Sabena,* [1976] ECR 455
Case 13/76 *Donà v. Mantero* [1976] ECR 1333
Case 27/76 *United Brands v. Commission* [1978] ECR 207
Case 85/76 *Hoffmann-La Roche & Co. AG v. Commission* [1979] ECR 00461
Case 15/81 *Gaston Schul Douane Expediteur BV v. Inspecteur der Invoerrechten en Accijnzen, Roosendaal* [1982] ECR I-1409
Case 262/81 *Coditel SA et al v. Ciné-Vog Films SA et al (Coditel II)* [1982] ECR 3381
Case 322/81 *Nederlandshce Banden – Industrie Michelin* NV *v. Commission* [1983] ECR 3461
Case 234/84 *Commission v. Belgium* [1986] ECR 02263
Case 66/85 *Lawrie Blum v. Land Baden-Württemberg* [1986] ECR 2135
Case 248/84 *Germany v. Commission* [1987] ECR 4013
Case 222/86 *UNECTEF v. Heylens* [1987] ECR 4097
Case C-303/88 *Italy v. Commission* [1991] ECR I-1433
Case C-305/89 *Italy v. Commission* [1991] EU:C:1991:142
Case C–55/94 *Gebhard v. Consiglio dell'Ordine degli Avvocati e Procuratori di Milano* [1995] ECR I–4165
Case C-415/93 *Union Royale Belge Sociétés de Football Association and others v. Bosman and others* [1995] ECR I-4921
Case C-334/94 *Commission v. France* [1996] ECR I-01307
Case C-106/96 *United Kingdom v. Commission* [1998] ECR I-2729
Case C-67/96 *Albany International v. Stichting* [1999] ECR I-5751
C-115/97 *Brentjens' Handelsonderneming BV v. Stichting Bedrijfspensioenfonds voor de Handel in Bouwmaterialen* [1999] ECR I-06025
Case C-126/97 *Eco Swiss China Time Ltd v. Benetton International NV* [1999] ECR I-03055
Case C-176/96 *Lehtonen and Castors Canada Dry Namur-Braine ASBL v. Fédération royale belge des sociétés de basket-ball (FRBSB)* [2000] ECR I-02681

Table of Cases

Cases C-51/96 and C-191/97 *Deliège v. Ligue francophone de Judo et disciplines Associeés Asb* [2000] ECR I-2549
Case C-281/98 *Roman Angonese v. Cassa di Risparmio di Bolzano SpA.* [2000] ECR I-4139
Case C-376/98 *Germany v. Parliament and Council* [2000] ECR I-8419
Case T-112/99 *Métropole télévision (M6) and others* [2001] ECR II-2459
Case C-309/99 *J.C.J. Wouters, J.W. Savelbergh, Price Waterhouse Belastingadviseurs BV v. Algemene Raad van de Nederlandse Orde van Advocaten* [2002] ECR I-1577
Case C-438/00 *Deutscher Handballbund v. Kolpak* [2003] ECR I-4135
Case C-262/02 *Commission of the European Communities v. France* [2004] EU:C:2004:431
Case T-313/02 *Meca-Medina and Majcen v. Commission*, [2004] ECR II-3291
Case T-33/01 *Infront WM AG v. Commission* [2005] ECR II-05897
Case T-193/02 *Laurent Piau v. Commission of the European Communities* [2005] ECR II-209
Case C-110/03 *Belgium v. Commission* [2005] ECR I-2801
Case C-265/03 *Simutenkov v. Ministerio de Educación y Cultura and Real Federación Española de Futbol* [2005] ECR I-2579
Case T-328/03 *O2 (Germany) GmbH & Co. OHG v. Commission of the European Communities* [2006] ECR II-1231
Case C-519/04 P *David Meca-Medina and Igor Majcen v. Commission of the European Communities* [2006] ECR I-6991
Case C-95/04 P *British Airways v. Commission* [2007] ECR I-2331
Case T-201/04 *Microsoft Corp. v. Commission of the European Communities* [2007] ECR II-03601
Case C-341/05 *Laval un Partneri* [2007] ECR I-11767
Case C-243/06 *SA Sporting du Pays de Charleroi, G-14 Groupment des Clubs de Football Européens v. Fédération Internationale de Football Association (FIFA)* [2008] ECLI:EU:C:2008:649
Case C-244/06 *Dynamic Medien Vertriebs GmbH v. Avides Media AG* [2008] ECR I-505
Case C-268/06, *Impact v. Minister for Agriculture and Food and Others* [2008] ECR I-02483
Case C-386/06 *R (International Association of Independent Tanker Owners (Intertanko)) v. Secretary of State for Transport* [2008] ECR I-4057
Case C-487/06P *British Aggregates v. Commission* [2008] ECR I-10515
Case C-49/07 *Motosykletistiki Omospondia Ellados NPID (MOTOE) v. Elliniko Dimosio* [2008] ECR I-4863
Case C-152/08 *Real Sociedad de Fútbol SAD, Nihat Kahveci v. Consejo Superior de Deportes, Real Federación Española de Fútbol* [2008] ECR I-6291
Case C-325/08 *Olympique Lyonnais v. Olivier Bernard and Newcastle UFC* [2010] I-2177
Case T-385/07 *Fédération internationale de football association (FIFA) v. European Commission*[2011] ECR II-00205
Case T-55/08 *Union des associations européennes de football (UEFA) v. European Commission* [2011] ECR II-00271

Case T-68/08 *Fédération internationale de football association (FIFA) v. European Commission* [2011] ECR II-00349
Joined Cases C-403/08 and C-429/08 *FA Premier League and others v. QC Leisure and others, Karen Murphy v. Media Protection Services Ltd* [2011] ECR I-9083
Case C-209/10 *Post Danmark v. Konkurrencerådet* [2012] 4 CMLR 23
Case C-1/12 *Ordem dos Técnicos Oficiais de Contas (OTOC) v. Autoridade da Concorrência* [2013] EU:C:2013:127
Case C-201/11 P, C-204/11 P and C-205/11 P *UEFA and FIFA v. Commission* [2013] ECR I-00000
Case C-299/15 *Daniele Striani and Others v. Union européenne des Sociétés de Football Association (UEFA) and Union Royale Belge des Sociétés de Football – Association (URBSFA)* [2015] EU:C:2015:519
Case T-693/14 *Hamr – Sport a.s. v. European Commission* [2016] ECLI-:EU:T:2016:292
Case T-162/13 *Magic Mountain Kletterhallen GmbH and Others v. European Commission* [2016] ECLI:EU:T:2016:341
Case C-90/16 *The English Bridge Union Limited v. Commissioners for Her Majesty's Revenue & Customs* [2017] ECLI:EU:C:2017:814
Case T-766/16 *Hércules Club de Fútbol v. Commission* [2019] ECLI-:EU:T:2019:173
Case T-865/16 *Fútbol Club Barcelona v. Commission* [2019] ECLI:EU:T:2019:113
Case T-791/16 *Real Madrid Club de Fútbol v. Commission* [2019] ECLI-:EU:T:2019:346
Case C-447/18 *UB v. Generálny riaditel' Sociálnej poist'ovne Bratislava* [2019] ECLI:EU:C:2019:1098
Case C-22/18 *TopFit e.V. and Daniele Biffi v. Deutscher Leichtathletikverband e.V.* [2019] EU:C:2019:497
Case T-732/16 *Valencia Club de Fútbol v. Commission* [2020] ECLI:EU:T:2020:98
Case T-901/16 *Elche Club de Fútbol v. Commission* [2020] ECLI:EU:T:2020:97

Decisions of the Commission

92/521/EEC: Commission Decision – Distribution of package tours during the 1990 World Cup (1992) OJ L326/31
93/403/EEC: Commission Decision – EBU/Eurovision System (1993) OJ L 179/23
Case No. IV/37.400 – Project Gandalf, OJ C 70, 13 March 1999
2000/12/EC: Commission Decision– 1998 Football World Cup (1999) OJ L5/55
Unpublish Commission decision of 9 December 1999, Case 36851, C.U. de Lille/ UEFA (Mouscron)
Case N118/00: French Subsidies for Youth Training, 25 April 2001
Cases COMP 35.163: Notification of FIA Regulations, COMP 36.638: Notification by FIA/FOA of agreements relating to the FIA Formula One World Championships, COMP 36.776: GTR/FIA, Notice published 13 June 2001 OJ C 169
Case COMP/37 806: ENIC/UEFA, 25 June 2002
Case COMP 38.158: Meca-Medina and Majcen, 1 August 2002
Case COMP/C.2-37.398 – Joint selling of the commercial rights of the UEFA Champions League, 23 July 2003
Case COMP/37792: Microsoft, 24 March 2004

Table of Cases

Case COMP/C-2/37.214 – Joint selling of the media rights to the German Bundesliga, 19 January 2005
Case COMP/38.173, Collective selling of FA Premier League's broadcasting rights, 22 March 2006
Case C4/2008 Investment of the municipality of Rotterdam in the Ahoy Complex, 22 September 2009
Case SA.31722 – Sport infrastructure development scheme (Hungary), 9 November 2011
Case SA.33584 (2013/C) (ex 2011/NN): State aid to Dutch football clubs, 6 March 2013
Case SA.33618 (2012/C) which Sweden is planning to implement for Uppsala arena, 2 May 2013
Case SA.37109 (2013/N) – Belgium Football stadiums in Flanders, 20 November 2013
Case SA.35135 (2012/N) – Germany Multifunktionsarena der Stadt Erfurt, 20 March 2013
Case SA.35440 (2012/N) – Germany Multifunktionsarena der Stadt Jena, 20 March 2013
Case SA 35501 (2013/N) – France Financement de la construction et de la rénovation des stades pour l'EURO, 18 December 2013
Case AT.40105: UEFA Financial Fair Play Rules, 24 October 2014
Case SA.41612 – 2015/C (ex SA.33584 (2013/C) (ex 2011/NN)) implemented by the Netherlands in favour of the professional football club MVV in Maastricht, 4 July 2016
Case SA.41613 – 2015/C (ex SA.33584 – 2013/C (ex 2011/NN)) Aid to Dutch Football Club PSV, 4 July 2016
Case SA.33754: Aid to Real Madrid-ES, 4 July 2016
Case SA.29769: Aid to certain football clubs – ES, 4 July 2016
Case SA.36387 Aid to Valencia football clubs, 4 July 2016
Case AT.40208: International Skating Union's Eligibility Rules, 8 December 2017

Other Jurisdictions

Belgium

Regional Court of Brussels, Judgment of 24 July 2015
Brussels Court of Appeal, Judgment of 18 August 2018

UK

Walker v. Crystal Palace Football Club [1910] 1 KB 87
Kingaby v. Aston Villa FC, The Times 27 and 28 March 1912
Eastham v. Newcastle United Football Club Ltd and others [1964] Ch. 413, 430
Hendry v. WPBSA [2001] All ER (D) 71
The Queen (on the application of) English Bridge Union Limited v. The English Sports Council v. The Scottish Sports Council, The Sports Council for Wales, The Sports Council for Northern Ireland, The United Kingdom Sports Council, The Secretary of State for Culture, Media and Sport [2015] EWHC 2875

Switzerland

Swiss Federal Tribunal, Judgment of 27 May 2003, *Lazutina & Danilova v. Comité International Olympique (IOC) & Fédération Internationale de Ski (FIS)* 4P_172/2006, 22 March 2007 (*Guillermo Cañas v. ATP Tour*)
4A_558/2011, 27 March 2012 (*Matuzalem*)
4A_260/2017 20 February 2018 (*Seraing*)

US

Case 3:18-cv-07393 *Shields and others v. FINA*, 12/07/2018, Class Action Complaint for Violations of the Sherman Act and the Common Law
Mackey v. NFL, 543 F.2d 606, 614–15 (8th Cir. 1976)

European Court of Human Rights

Mutu & Pechstein v. Switzerland, nos 40575/10 et 67474/10, 2 October 2018
Ali Riza and Others v. Turkey, 30226/10, 28/01/20

EFTA Court

EFTA Court 16 November 2018, Case E-8/17, *Kristoffersen/NSF*

CAS Awards

Case CAS 98/200 – *AEK Athens and Slavia Prague v. UEFA*
Case CAS 2007/A/1298/1299/1300 – *Heart of Midlothian v/ Webster & Wigan Athletic FC*
CAS 2008/A/159 – *FC Shakhtar Donetsk (Ukraine) v/ Mr. Matuzalem Francelino da Silva (Brazil) & Real Zaragoza SAD (Spain) & FIFA*
CAS 2008/A/1485, *Midtjylland v. FIFA*
CAS 2010/A/2145-2147 – *Udinese Calcio S.p.a. v. Morgan De Sanctis & Sevilla FC Sad*
CAS 2012/A/2862 *FC Girondins de Bordeaux*
CAS 2013/3365 – *Juventus Football Club S.p.A. v. Chelsea Football Club Ltd*
CAS 2014/A/3813 – *Real Federación Española de Fútbol (RFEF) v. Fédération Internationale de Football Association (FIFA)*
CAS 2014/A/3792 – *Futbol Club Barcelona v. FIFA*
CAS 2014/O/3781 & 3782, *Sporting Clube de Portugal Futebol SAD v. Doyen Sports Investment Limited*
CAS 2016/A/4490 – *RFC Seraing v. FIFA*
CAS 2016/A/4492 – *Galatasaray v. UEFA*
CAS 2018/A/5808 – *AC Milan v. UEFA*

National Arbitration

FAPL v. West Ham United, FAPL Disciplinary Committee, 27 April 2007
Sheffield United FC v. West Ham United FC, FA Rule K Arbitration, 2009
SR/Adhocsport/201/2019, *Premier Rugby Limited v. Saracens Limited*

Table of Cases

UEFA

UEFA Club Financial Control Body, Adjudicatory Chamber
Case AC-01/2017, *Rasenballsport Leipzig GMBH & FC Red Bull Salzburg GMBH*, 16/06/2017

Table of Legislation

EU Primary Legislation

Treaty Establishing the European Economic Community [1957] 298 U.N.T.S. 11
Article 2
Single European Act [1987] OJ L 169/1
Treaty of Amsterdam amending the Treaty on European Union, the Treaties establishing the European Communities and certain related acts [1997] OJ C 340
Treaty on European Union (Consolidated Version), Treaty of Maastricht [1992], OJ C 325/5
Charter of Fundamental Rights of the European Union OJ C 326
Article 11
Treaty of Lisbon amending the Treaty on European Union and the Treaty establishing the European Community [2007] OJ C306/01

Consolidated version of the Treaty of the European Union, OJ C 326

Article 3
Article 4
Article 5

Consolidated version of the Treaty on the Functioning of the European Union, OJ C 326

Article 2
Article 3
Article 4
Article 5
Article 6
Article 18
Article 21
Article 26
Article 45
Article 56
Article 52
Article 62
Article 63
Article 101
Article 102

Article 107
Article 109
Article 114
Article 152 (ex 129)
Article 155
Article 165

EU Secondary Legislation

Regulation (EEC) No 2821/71 of the Council of 20 December 1971 on application of Article 85 (3) of the Treaty to categories of agreements, decisions and concerted practices, OJ L 285
Council Directive 77/388/EEC of 17 May 1977 on the harmonization of the laws of the Member States relating to turnover taxes – Common system of value added tax: uniform basis of assessment, OJ L 145
Council Directive 89/552/EEC of 3 October 1989 on the coordination of certain provisions laid down by Law, Regulation or Administrative Action in Member States concerning the pursuit of television broadcasting activities, OJ L 298
Council Directive 93/83/EEC of 27 September 1993 on the coordination of certain rules concerning copyright and rights related to copyright applicable to satellite broadcasting and cable retransmission, OJ L 248
Council Directive 94/33/EC of 22 June 1994 on the Protection of Young People at Work, OJ L 216
Article 1
Article 5
Directive 2001/29/EC of the European Parliament and of the Council of 22 May 2001 on the harmonisation of certain aspects of copyright and related rights in the information society (Information Society Directive), OJ L 167
Council Regulation (EC) No 1/2003 of 16 December 2002 on the implementation of the rules on competition laid down in Articles 81 and 82 of the Treaty OJ L 1
Article 10
Directive 2003/33/EC of the European Parliament and of the Council of 26 May 2003 on the approximation of the laws, regulations and administrative provisions of the Member States relating to the advertising and sponsorship of tobacco products, OJ L 152.
Decision No 291/2003/EC of the European Parliament and of the Council of 6 February 2003 establishing the European Year of Education through Sport 2004, OJ L043.
Directive 2004/38/EC of the European Parliament and of the Council of 29 April 2004 on the right of citizens of the Union and their family members to move and reside freely within the territory of the Member States amending Regulation (EEC) No 1612/68 and repealing Directives 64/221/EEC, 68/360/EEC, 72/194/EEC, 73/148/EEC, 75/34/EEC, 75/35/EEC, 90/364/EEC, 90/365/EEC and 93/96/EEC, OJ L 158.
Articles 27–33
Directive 2010/13/EU of the European Parliament and of the Council of 10 March 2010 on the coordination of certain provisions laid down by law, regulation or

administrative action in Member States concerning the provision of audiovisual media services (Audiovisual Media Services Directive), OJ L 95

Regulation (EU) No 575/2013 of the European Parliament and of the Council of 26 June 2013 on prudential requirements for credit institutions and investment firms and amending Regulation (EU) No 648/2012, OJ L 176

Directive 2013/36/EU of the European Parliament and of the Council of 26 June 2013 on access to the activity of credit institutions and the prudential supervision of credit institutions and investment firms, amending Directive 2002/87/EC and repealing Directives 2006/48/EC and 2006/49/EC, OJ L 176

Regulation (EU) No 1288/2013 of the European Parliament and of the Council of 11 December 2013 establishing 'Erasmus+': the Union programme for education, training, youth and sport and repealing Decisions No 1719/2006/EC, No 1720/2006/EC and No 1298/2008/EC, OJ L 347

Regulation (EU) 2016/679 of the European Parliament and of the Council of 27 April 2016 on the protection of natural persons with regard to the processing of personal data and on the free movement of such data, and repealing Directive 95/46/EC (General Data Protection Regulation), OJ L 119

Regulation (EU) 2017/1128 of the European Parliament and of the Council of 14 June 2017 on cross-border portability of online content services in the internal market, OJ L 168

Regulation (EU) 2018/302 of the European Parliament and of the Council of 28 February 2018 on addressing unjustified geo-blocking and other forms of discrimination based on customers' nationality, place of residence or place of establishment within the internal market, OJ L 60I

Directive (EU) 2018/1808 of the European Parliament and of the Council of 14 November 2018 amending Directive 2010/13/EU on the coordination of certain provisions laid down by law, regulation or administrative action in Member States concerning the provision of audiovisual media services (Audiovisual Media Services Directive) in view of changing market realities, OJ L 303

Directive (EU) 2019/790 of the European Parliament and of the Council of 17 April 2019 on copyright and related rights in the Digital Single Market and amending Directives 96/9/EC and 2001/29/EC, OJ L 130

Directive 2019/2161 of the European Parliament and of the Council amending Council Directive 93/13/EEC of 5 April 1993, Directive 98/6/EC of the European Parliament and of the Council, Directive 2005/29/EC of the European Parliament and of the Council and Directive 2011/83/EU of the European Parliament and of the Council as regards better enforcement and modernisation of EU consumer protection rules, OJ L 328/7

Notice, Guidelines, Policy Measures

European Commission, A People's Europe, Reports from the ad hoc Committee, COM (1984) 446 Final

Resolution of the Council and of the representatives of the Governments of the Member States, meeting within the Council of 3 December 1990 concerning an action programme on nutrition and health, 3 December 1990, OJ C 329

European Commission, *The European Community and Sport*, SEC (91) 1438, 31/07/91 (1991)

Table of Legislation

Resolution of the Council and of the representatives of the Governments of the Member States, meeting within the Council on a code of conduct against doping in sport, 8 February 1992, OJ C 44

Treaty of Amsterdam amending the Treaty on European Union, the Treaties establishing the European Communities and certain related acts – Declarations adopted by the Conference – Declaration on sport, OJ C 340, 10/11/1997

European Commission, *The European Model of Sport*, Consultation Document of DGX, s.14 (1998).

European Commission, *The Development and Prospects for Community Action in the Field of Sport, Commission Staff Working Paper* (1998)

European Commission, *Communication from the Commission to the Council, European Parliament, the Economic and Social Committee and the Committee of the Regions – Community support plan to combat doping in sport*, COM/99/0643 (1999)

European Commission, *Report from the Commission to the European Council with a view to safeguarding current sports structures and maintaining the social function of sport within the Community framework – the Helsinki Report on Sport*, COM(1999) 644 (1999)

Conclusions of the Council and the Representatives of the Governments of the Member States, meeting within the Council of 4 December 2000 on combatting doping, 2000/C 356/01, 12/012/2000

European Council, Nice, 7–10 December 2000, Conclusions of the Presidency. Annex IV, *Declaration on the specific characteristics of sport and its social function in Europe, of which account should be taken in implementing common policies* (2000)

Communication from the Commission – Guidelines on the application of Article 81(3) of the Treaty, 2004/C 101/08, OJ C 101

European Commission, *White Paper on Sport*, COM(2007) 391 final (2007)

European Commission, *Commission staff working document. Impact assessment accompanying the White Paper on Sport*, SEC(2007) 935 final (2007)

European Parliament Resolution of 8 May 2008 on the White Paper on Sport (2007/2261(INI))

European Commission, *Communication from the Commission: Europe 2020: A Strategy for Smart, Sustainable and Inclusive Growth*, COM(2010) 2020 final

European Commission, *Communication from the Commission to the European Parliament, the Council, the European Economic and Social Committee and the Committee of the Regions – Developing the European Dimension in Sport*, 11 COM(2011) 12 final (2011)

European Commission, *Commission staff working document 'Sport and Free Movement' Accompanying document to the Communication from the Commission to the European Parliament, the Council, the European Economic and Social Committee and the Committee of the Regions – Developing the European Dimension in Sport* SEC (2011) 66 final (2011)

European Parliament Report on the European Dimension in Sport, 21 November 2011, 2011/2087 (INI)

Council of the European Union, *EU contribution to the revision of the World Anti-Doping Code*, 6846/12, https://register.consilium.europa.eu/doc/srv?l=EN&f=ST%206846%202012%20INIT 23 Feb. 2012 (accessed 17 July 2019)

Proposal for a Council Recommendation on promoting health-enhancing physical activity across sectors, COM/2013/0603 final – 2013/0291 (NLE)

European Commission, *Decision adopting the Arrangement for Cooperation between the European Commission and the Union of European Football Associations (UEFA),* C(2014) 7378 final, https://ec.europa.eu/assets/eac/sport/news/2014/docs/uefa2014_en.pdf (accessed 20 April 2020)

Conclusions of the Council of the European Union, Sport Diplomacy (Council of Europe, Doc. 14279/16)

European Commission, *High Level Group on Sport Diplomacy*, http://ec.europa.eu/assets/eac/sport/policy/cooperation/documents/290616-hlg-sd-final-report_en.pdf June 2016 (accessed 8 April 2020)

European Commission, *High Level Group on Grassroots Sport*, http://ec.europa.eu/assets/eac/sport/policy/cooperation/documents/290616-hlg-gs-final-report_en.pdf June 2016 (accessed 8 April 2020)

Council of the European Union, *Council Conclusions on Sport Diplomacy*, 14279/16, http://data.consilium.europa.eu/doc/document/ST-14279-2016-INIT/en/pdf 23 Nov. 2016 (accessed 8 April 2020)

European Commission: Notice on the notion of State aid as referred to in Article 107(1) of the Treaty on the Functioning of the European Union C/2016/2946, OJ C 262

Resolution of the Council and of the representatives of the Governments of the Member States, meeting within the Council, on further developing the EU Structured Dialogue on sport (2017)

Council of the European Union, *Work Plan for Sport (1 July 2017–31 December 2020)*, 9639/17, http://data.consilium.europa.eu/doc/document/ST-9639-2017-INIT/en/pdf 24 May 2017 (accessed 8 April 2020)

European Commission, *Annex to the Commission Decision adopting the Arrangement for Cooperation between the European Commission and the Union of the European Football Associations (UEFA)*, C(2018) 876 final, https://www.uefa.com/MultimediaFiles/Download/EuroExperience/uefaorg/EuropeanUnion/02/53/98/34/2539834_DOWNLOAD.pdf (accessed 8 April 2020)

Resolution of the Council and of the Representatives of the Governments of the Member States, meeting within the Council, on a European Union Work Plan for Sport for 2011-2014, 2011/C 162/01; 2014-2017, 2014/C 183/03 & 2017-2020, 9639/17

Council of Europe

Council of Europe, Committee of Ministers: Appendix to Recommendation No. R(92)13 rev, European Sports Charter (adopted by the Committee of Ministers on 24 September 1992 at the 480th meeting of the Ministers' Deputies and revised at their 752nd meeting on 16 May 2001)

Council of Europe Convention No.135, *Anti-Doping Convention*, Strasbourg, 16,XI,1989

Table of Legislation

International Conventions

Convention on jurisdiction and the recognition and enforcement of judgments in civil and commercial matters L339, 21 Dec. 2007 (Lugano II Convention)
UN Resolution 58/5, 17 November 2003, Sport as a means to promote education, health, development and peace

National Legislation

Greece

Greek Road Traffic Code, Law No. 2696/1999
S49

Spain

Ley 10/1990, de 15 de octubre, del Deporte, BOE de 17 de Octubre de 1990

Switzerland

Swiss Federal Act on Private International Law (PILA)
Articles 190–191

United Kingdom

Broadcasting Act 1996
Competition Act 1998

Sport

International Olympic Movement, *Olympic Charter*
Fundamental Principles of Olympism no.3
Fundamental Principles of Olympism no.5
International Olympic Committee, *Common position of the Olympic and Sports Movement on the implementation of the new Treaty on the Functioning of the European Union (TFEU) on sport (Lisbon Treaty)*, 2 January 2010, https://www.idrettsforbundet.no/contentassets/ed8107d55ad049dfa26b610dbbaac62c/common_position_of_the_olympic_and_sports_movement.pdf (accessed 29 March 2020)

FIFA

FIFA Statutes (2018 Edition)

Article 11

FIFA Regulations on the Status and Transfer of Players (2019 Edition)

Definitions
Article 5
Article 6
Article 12
Article 12 bis
Article 13

Article 14 bis
Article 15
Article 17
Article 18 bis
Article 18 ter
Article 19
Article 20
Article 21
Article 22
Article 23
Article 24
Annex 1
Article 2
Article 3
Article 4

UEFA

UEFA Statutes (2018 Edition)

Article 49

Regulations of the UEFA Champions League (2018-21 Cycle)

Article 5
Article 43.06

UEFA Clubs Licensing and Fair Play Regulations (2018 Edition)

Article 2
Article 17
Article 57
Article 61
Annex II
Annex VI
Annex X

FINA

FINA General Rules (2014 Edition)

General Rule 4.1
General Rule 4.5

FIH

FIH Regulations on Sanctioned & Unsanctioned Events (2013 Edition)

Article 2.1
Article 2.2

UCI

Table of Legislation

UCI Regulations (2019 Edition)

s3, 1.2.019
S3, 1.2.022

ISU

Constitution and General Regulations (2016 Edition)

Rule 102

Miscellaneous

EU Sectoral Social Dialogue Committee for Professional Football

Resolution on Intermediaries/Agents, 17/11/17
Autonomous Agreement on Minimum Requirements Standard Players Contracts

Index

The numbers here refer to paragraph numbers

Adonnino Committee, 93
Advertising, 133, 148, 305, 424, 443, 491, 539–545, 550, 552
Agents, 114, 125, 186, 254, 257, 321–323, 327, 330, 334, 337, 339, 343, 419, 574
Alternative dispute resolution (ADR), 14, 21. 22
Amateur sport, 95, 102, 238, 253, 254, 381–390, 419, 429, 432, 574
Abuse of a dominant position, 201
Ambush Marketing, 544, 545
Amsterdam Declaration on Sport, 230
Anticompetitive practices, 140, 155
Arbitration in sport, 165
Arnaut Report, 120, 121
Article 165 TFEU, 84, 91–98, 125, 126, 198, 214, 235, 248, 276, 320, 381, 384, 402, 468, 472, 508, 516
Athletes, 1, 11, 13, 15–17, 22, 32, 33, 71, 72, 78, 79, 85, 101, 105, 106, 125, 130, 134, 135, 137, 138, 152, 153, 156, 158, 164, 236, 237, 241, 244, 245, 249, 252, 254, 262, 264, 280, 301, 347, 358, 374, 383, 391, 416, 430, 447, 534, 539, 546–553, 567, 584
Authorisation or eligibility rules, 92, 149–154, 574
Autonomy of sport, 82, 125, 245, 254, 263, 318, 420, 576

Bach, Thomas, 158
Barcelona, 477
Basketball, 155, 283, 323, 364
Bernard, 76, 100, 277, 279, 290, 314, 318, 568, 582
Bosman, 8, 19, 56, 57, 59, 66, 68, 94, 117, 118, 157, 206, 265, 266, 270, 272, 290, 292, 293, 300, 358, 361, 363, 366, 369, 371, 372, 374, 375, 423, 446, 459, 568
Boxing, 32, 132, 358, 378
Brexit, 60, 309, 365, 372, 481, 533
Bridge, 30
Breakaway leagues, 583
Broadcasting, 168, 188, 365, 423, 424, 433, 443, 482–489, 501, 504, 507, 508, 515, 521, 529, 533, 541, 561, 563, 575, 581, 585
Bundesliga, 208, 496, 511
Bundeskartellamt, 500, 511, 547, 550–552

Champions League, 170, 183, 184, 212, 221, 493, 496, 506, 577
Charleroi, 221–223, 227
Court of Arbitration for Sport (CAS), 10, 22
Clearing house, 281, 322, 338
Club location, 125, 127, 206–217
Collective agreements or bargaining, 398–408, 578
Communication on Sport, 9, 101, 102, 124, 214, 236, 238, 239
Competition law, 51, 52, 57, 73, 77–83, 99, 115, 119, 122, 138, 144, 147, 148, 165, 166, 174, 199, 201, 211, 214, 225, 240, 262, 264, 284, 287, 325, 399, 407, 436, 439, 450, 463, 499, 533, 550, 553, 557
Competitive balance in sport, 356, 376, 581
Conditional autonomy, 125, 129, 248, 580
Consumer protection, 534, 559
Contract stability, 190, 271
Copyright law, 519
Council of Europe, 29–31, 98, 109, 229, 234, 235, 238
Council of the European Union, 98, 109
Court of Justice, 6, 28, 30, 36, 39, 42, 55,

58, 61, 63, 66, 70, 77, 80, 85, 117, 125, 142, 165, 179, 196, 199, 201, 202, 206, 221, 223, 240, 244, 265, 283, 314, 318, 330, 340, 368, 384, 399, 422, 451, 468, 505, 547
COVID-19, 576
Cross-border leagues, 125, 127, 206–217
Cricket, 218, 372, 373, 577
Cycling, 93, 228, 348

Data protection, 59, 237, 533
De Sanctis, 296
Deliège, 70. 73, 77, 96, 546
Direct effect, 56, 463
Discrimination, 44, 92, 102, 125, 265, 325, 348–390, 556, 566, 574
Donà v. Mantero, 65, 265
Doping, 22, 78, 106, 133, 166, 228–239
Dual representation, 339

Eastham, 256, 257
Economic activity, 17, 26, 28, 57, 62–69, 89, 118, 160, 176, 253, 327, 341, 349, 380, 384, 434, 439, 574, 575
Employment contracts, 260, 333
English National Investment Company (ENIC), 165, 170, 171, 172, 174–176, 180, 182, 185, 250, 251, 446, 456
English Premier League, 188, 194, 208, 365, 514, 579
Environmental protection, 115, 119, 139, 359, 527, 578
Equal treatment, 306
Erasmus, 110, 112
European Club Association (ECA), 226, 334, 396, 409, 414, 458
European Commission, 7, 36, 58, 78, 105, 110, 120, 126, 128, 140, 149, 155, 174, 181, 201, 205, 211, 231, 249, 268, 282, 326, 336, 340, 351, 364
European Football Agents Association (EFAA), 340
European Free Trade Association (EFTA), 547–550, 552
European Model of Sport, 1–125, 158, 170, 182, 210, 227, 231, 247, 248, 252–254, 260, 273, 347, 358, 387, 419, 425, 440, 458, 461, 465, 484, 509, 531, 532, 553, 565, 570, 576–586
European Leagues (EL), 210, 212, 396
European Parliament, 98, 112, 116, 122, 230
European Union (EU), 1–125, 196, 231
EU sports law, 22, 25–26, 41, 77, 91, 125, 165, 202, 227, 243, 348, 349
EU sports policy, 91–98, 115, 234, 390
Exemption criteria and decisions, 176

FIA (Fédération Internationale de l'Automobile), 140, 141
FIFA
 Player Agent Regulations (PAR), 324, 327, 331
 Regulations on the Status and Transfer of Players (RSTP), 190, 192–194, 203, 257, 271, 278, 279, 293, 299, 302, 304, 309, 345, 391, 395
 Regulations on Working with Intermediaries (RWWI), 331–335, 395
FIFPro (Fédération Internationale des Associations de Footballeurs), 205, 269, 303, 334, 336, 396, 409, 414
Financial Fair Play (FFP), 61
Football, 65, 100, 127, 157, 168, 173, 186, 191, 203, 209, 214, 225, 255, 257, 270, 282, 292, 315, 321, 324, 337, 350, 360, 373, 409–417, 445
Formula One (F1), 140, 141, 577
Freedom of movement, 43, 50, 51, 63, 67, 76, 265, 283, 284, 314, 315, 353, 362, 386, 450, 550
 Free movement of goods, 2, 44, 56, 314
 Free movement of services, 56, 200
 Free movement of workers, 37, 200, 265, 304
 Freedom of establishment, 43, 56
Funding sport, 3, 6, 109, 125, 423–564

G14, 221, 222, 226
Globalisation of sport, 35, 565
Governance of sport, 125, 416
Grassroots sport, 101, 104, 112, 430, 481

Handball, 367
Harmonisation of laws, 98, 110
Helsinki Report on Sport, 96, 119, 232, 432
High-Level Group on Sport Diplomacy, 108

Image rights, 405
Inherent rules, 74, 77

Insolvency, 476
Intellectual property rights, 211
Internal market, 2, 37, 40, 42, 52, 93, 114, 425, 483, 515, 518, 540–542, 544, 553
International Olympic Committee (IOC), 1
International Skating Union (ISU), 12

Judo, 70
Justifications, 44, 49–54, 69, 75, 131, 137, 152, 275, 343, 354, 377

Kolpak, 310, 367, 368, 370–372
Kristoffersen, 548, 552

Legitimate sporting objectives, 4, 91, 121, 125, 129, 163, 180, 200, 201, 216, 248, 341, 343, 346, 363, 418, 568, 570, 573, 575, 580
Lehtonen, 74, 96, 283, 290, 568
Lex sportiva, 32–36, 164, 197, 198, 260, 391
Licensing, 322, 325, 331, 338, 441, 524
Listing of major events, 501, 510
Lugano II Convention, 61

Manchester City, 169
Match-fixing, 14, 88, 175, 181, 249
Matuzalem, 295, 296
Meca-Medina, 52, 77, 78, 85, 121, 122, 128, 163, 165, 185, 201, 202, 224, 226, 229, 240–251, 341, 343, 380, 453, 568
Media Rights, 14, 115, 125, 174, 211, 423, 483, 487, 495, 509–514, 518, 521, 522, 525, 528, 533, 554, 568, 575
Minors in sport, 271, 304–318, 335
Monopolies, 15, 16, 22, 175, 255, 488, 493, 535, 566, 573
MOTOE (Motosykletistiki Omospondia Ellados NPID), 89, 130–139, 142–148, 159, 162, 536, 537
Motorcycling, 89, 143–145, 148
Mouscron, 213, 215
Multifunctional arenas, 469, 472
Multiple club ownership, 127, 168–185, 583
Murphy, 100, 290, 505, 506, 516, 517

Nationality-based sports rules, 125, 254, 347, 365, 566, 574
Navracsics, 108
New York Convention, 165, 196
Nice Declaration on Sport, 97, 233, 432

Olympic Games, 15, 23, 130, 151, 551
Olympic movement, 1, 127, 157
Organisation of sport, 9, 72, 78, 125, 253, 347, 535, 536, 546
Oulmers, 221
Over-the-Top, 424, 509
Ownership of clubs, 176, 456

Pandemic, 565–586
Pay TV, 482, 493, 500–502, 505, 512–514, 526
Pechstein, 166
Piau, 89, 324–330, 338, 340, 341
Player release, 125, 218–227
Premier League, 194, 208, 365, 496, 500, 505, 506, 533
Price fixing, 490
Principle of conferral, 38
Project Gandalf, 211
Proportionality, 39, 44, 51, 69, 73, 74, 83, 91, 122, 137, 181, 202, 205, 226, 245, 266, 275, 276, 281, 284, 288–291, 305, 316, 318, 320, 346, 364, 388, 395, 445, 449, 453, 455, 456, 462, 473, 543, 549, 553, 568, 582
Protected or listed events, 533
Protected period, 299, 300, 319
Pubs, 505
Public health, 44, 50, 102, 353, 389, 542
Public policy, 44, 45, 138, 165, 204, 353, 389, 465, 467–469, 471, 472, 480, 483, 527
Public security, 44, 50, 353, 389
Purely sporting rules, 91, 92, 121, 568
Pyramid structure, 126, 214

Quotas, 353, 360, 364, 371

Real Madrid, 477, 478
Red Bull, 169, 183–185, 548
Registration of players, 265
Relocation of clubs, 213
Restrictive practices, 21
Right to a fair trial, 166, 237
Rugby, 209, 323, 372, 439

Salary Cap, 406, 407, 434, 438–440, 445, 446, 580
Sanctions, 152, 163, 216, 244, 246, 260, 266, 270, 299, 300, 302, 312, 325, 329,

333–335, 404, 441, 455, 457
Seraing, 195–202, 204, 205, 250
Selection rules, 72, 546
Self-regulation, 21, 124, 397, 401
Short news reports, 231
Simutenkov, 370
Social dialogue, 105, 125, 236, 334, 336, 398–417, 580
Solidarity in sport, 581
Solidarity payments, 138, 278, 280, 281, 343, 391
Specificity of sport, 4, 8, 24, 122, 131, 245, 263, 294, 296, 323, 448, 508
Sport and society, 32
Sporting autonomy, 8, 84, 104, 131, 568, 570, 572
Sports governing bodies, 1, 20, 28, 33, 36, 53, 59, 90, 125, 126, 131, 137, 160, 218, 228, 247, 252, 263, 266, 419, 420, 423, 425, 437, 483, 486, 535, 540, 555, 574, 578
Sport diplomacy, 108–110, 116
Sports law, 22, 25–26, 32–36, 41, 77, 91, 125, 227, 349
Stakeholders, 4, 11, 17, 69, 105, 124, 125, 137, 219, 227, 248, 249, 254, 269, 285, 303, 322, 323, 336, 337, 391–397, 401, 402, 413, 415, 416, 419–425, 546, 563, 570, 571, 574, 580
State aid, 45, 50, 423, 459–466, 472, 474–481, 562, 585
Subsidiarity, 39
Supremacy of EU law, 56, 125, 145, 160, 167, 199, 216, 237, 249, 307, 365, 423, 479, 533, 574
Swimming, 156
Swiss Federal Tribunal (SFT), 164

Third-country nationals, 371
Third party ownership (TPO), 125, 186–205
Ticketing, 424, 534–538, 558, 560
TopFit, 96, 100, 102, 217, 377, 381, 382, 389, 390
Trademarks, 399, 547
Training compensation, 100, 270, 272–281, 321, 322, 343, 391, 395, 582
Transfer system, 59, 67, 191, 255–271, 391, 395, 574, 582
Transfer windows, 260, 282–291, 321
Treaties
  Constitutional Treaty, 94, 406
  Lisbon Treaty, 98, 107
  Maastricht Treaty, 37, 94, 107
  Nice Treaty, 97
  Single European Act, 37
  Treaty of Amsterdam, 28, 95
  Treaty of Rome, 37
  Treaty on European Union, 38, 64, 120
  Treaty on the Functioning of the European Union, 41
  UCI (Union Cycliste International), 12

UEFA (Union européenne des Sociétés de Football Association), 451
  UEFA Champions League, 183, 184, 577
  UEFA Clubs Licensing and Fair Play Regulations, 435, 446
Unilateral termination of employment contracts, 268, 295, 300
US model of sport, 156, 169, 208

Vertical agreements, 21, 56, 513
Violence in sport, 34, 150, 156, 164, 165, 204
Volunteering, 21, 22, 101, 102

Walrave, 55, 56, 63, 64, 68, 69, 92, 121, 199, 242, 349, 351, 353, 358, 380, 568
Webster, 295, 296
White Paper on Sport, 114, 122, 214, 234, 432, 545, 557
Workers, 32, 37, 50, 57, 63, 67, 74, 105, 137, 200, 252, 265, 304, 366, 399
World Anti-Doping Agency (WADA), 10, 228
World Cup, 23, 149, 153, 218, 557
Wouters, 79, 85, 179, 180, 185, 201

Youth players and training, 39, 272, 273, 280, 473

www.ingramcontent.com/pod-product-compliance
Lightning Source LLC
Chambersburg PA
CBHW072244240926
51846CB00012B/260
* 9 7 8 9 4 0 3 5 2 6 1 3 3 *